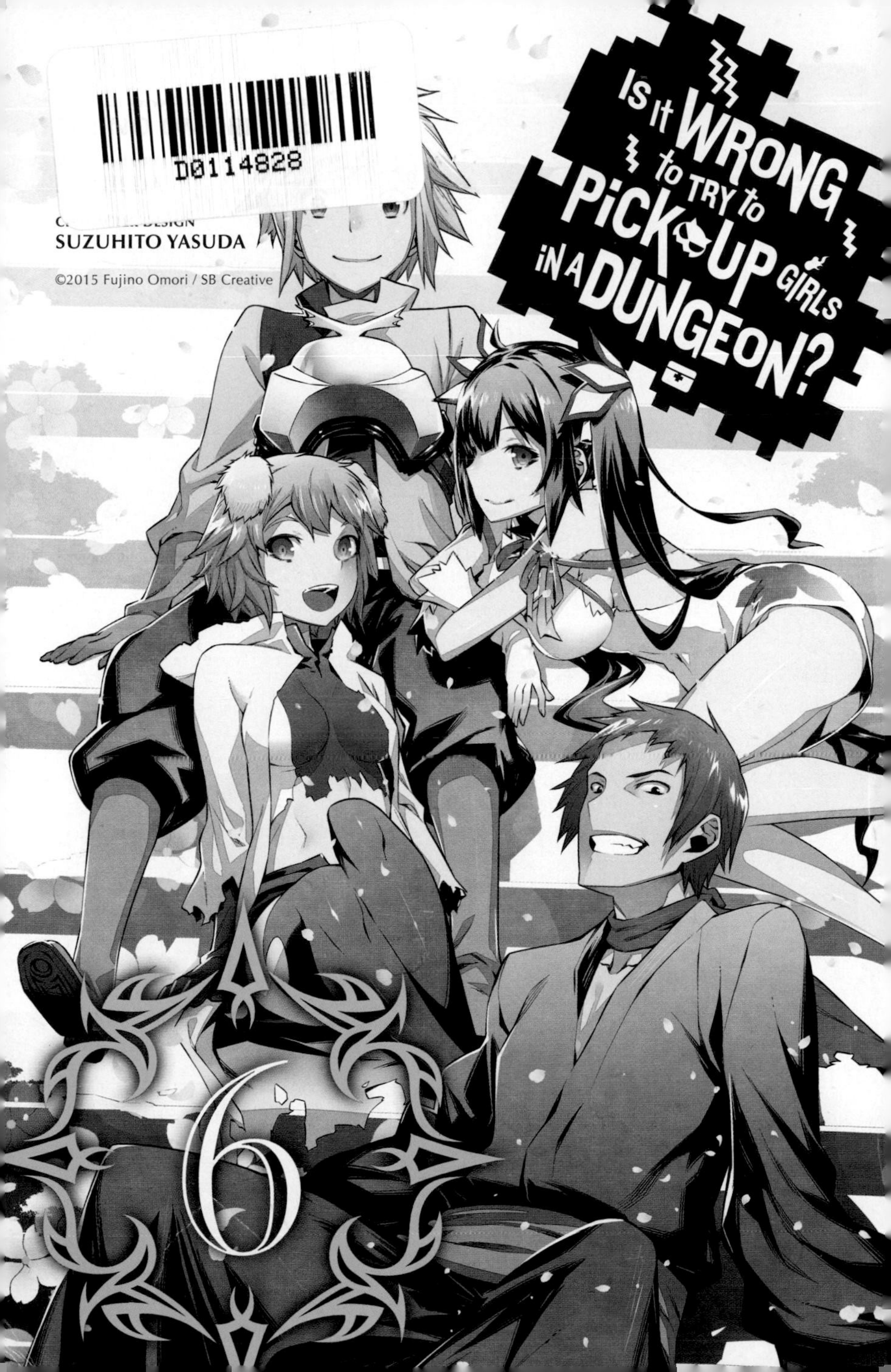

Is it WRONG to TRY to PiCK UP GiRLS iN A DUNGEON?
6
DESIGN
SUZUHITO YASUDA
©2015 Fujino Omori / SB Creative

contents 6

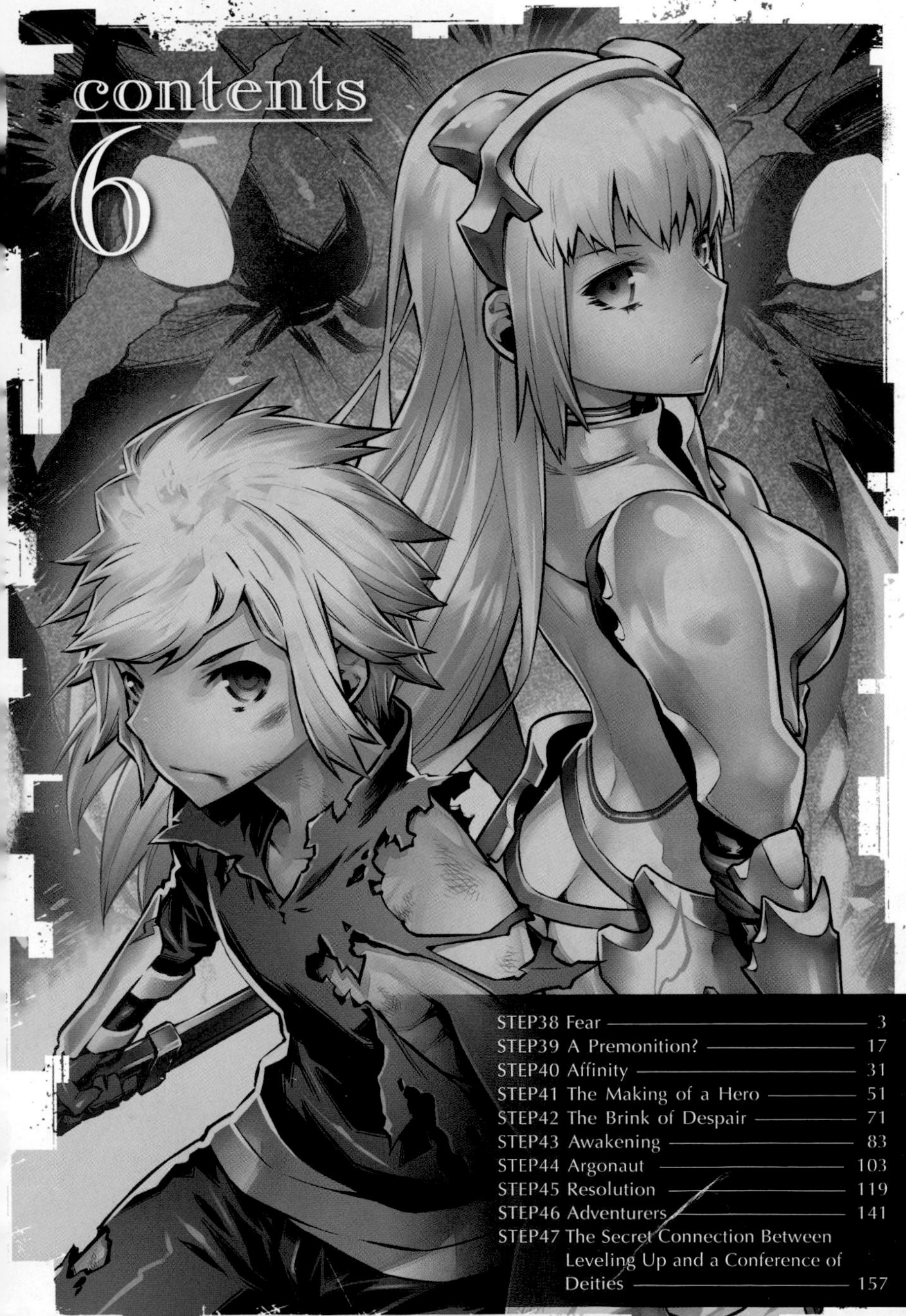

STEP 38 ▸▸ FEAR

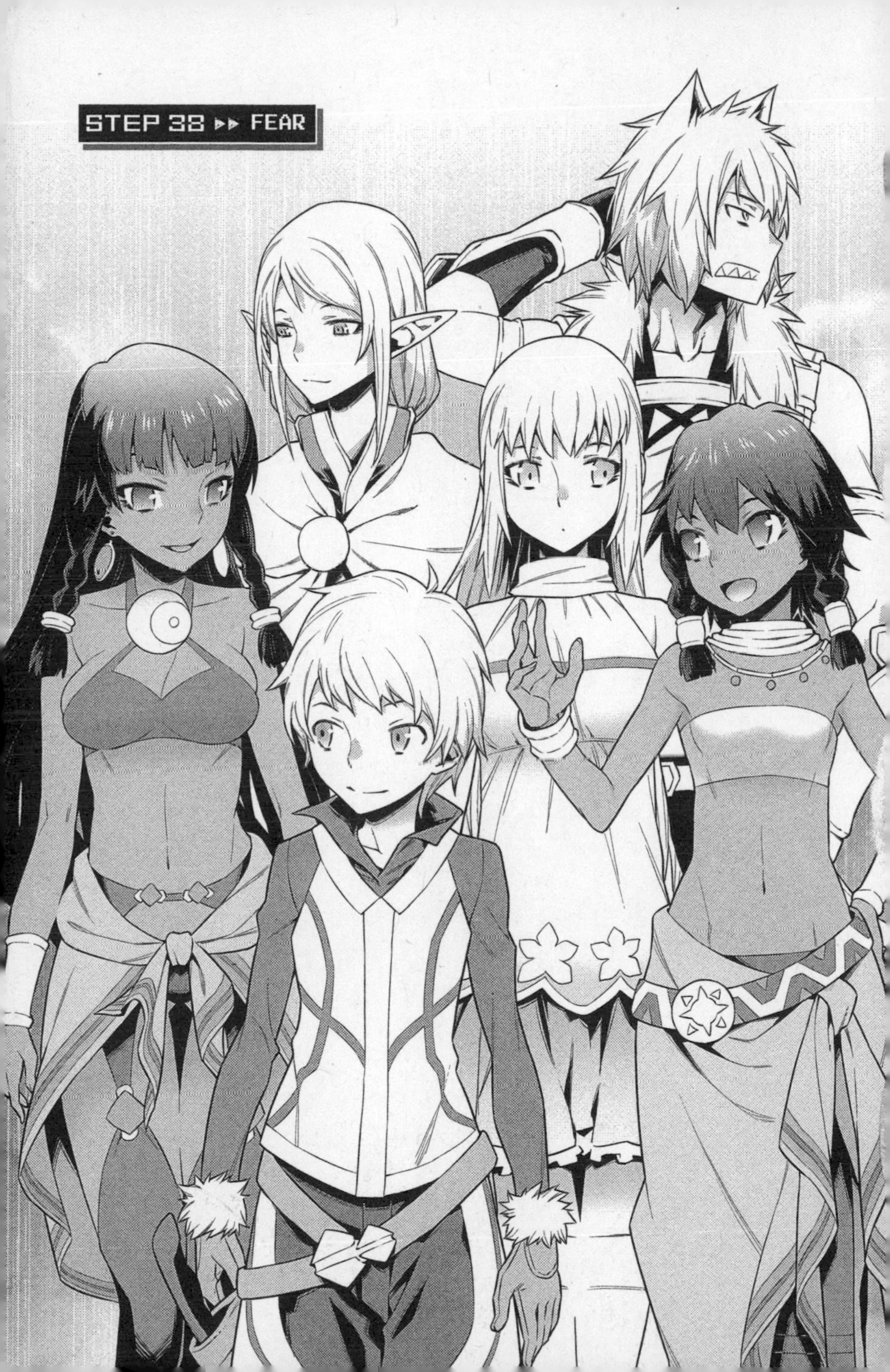

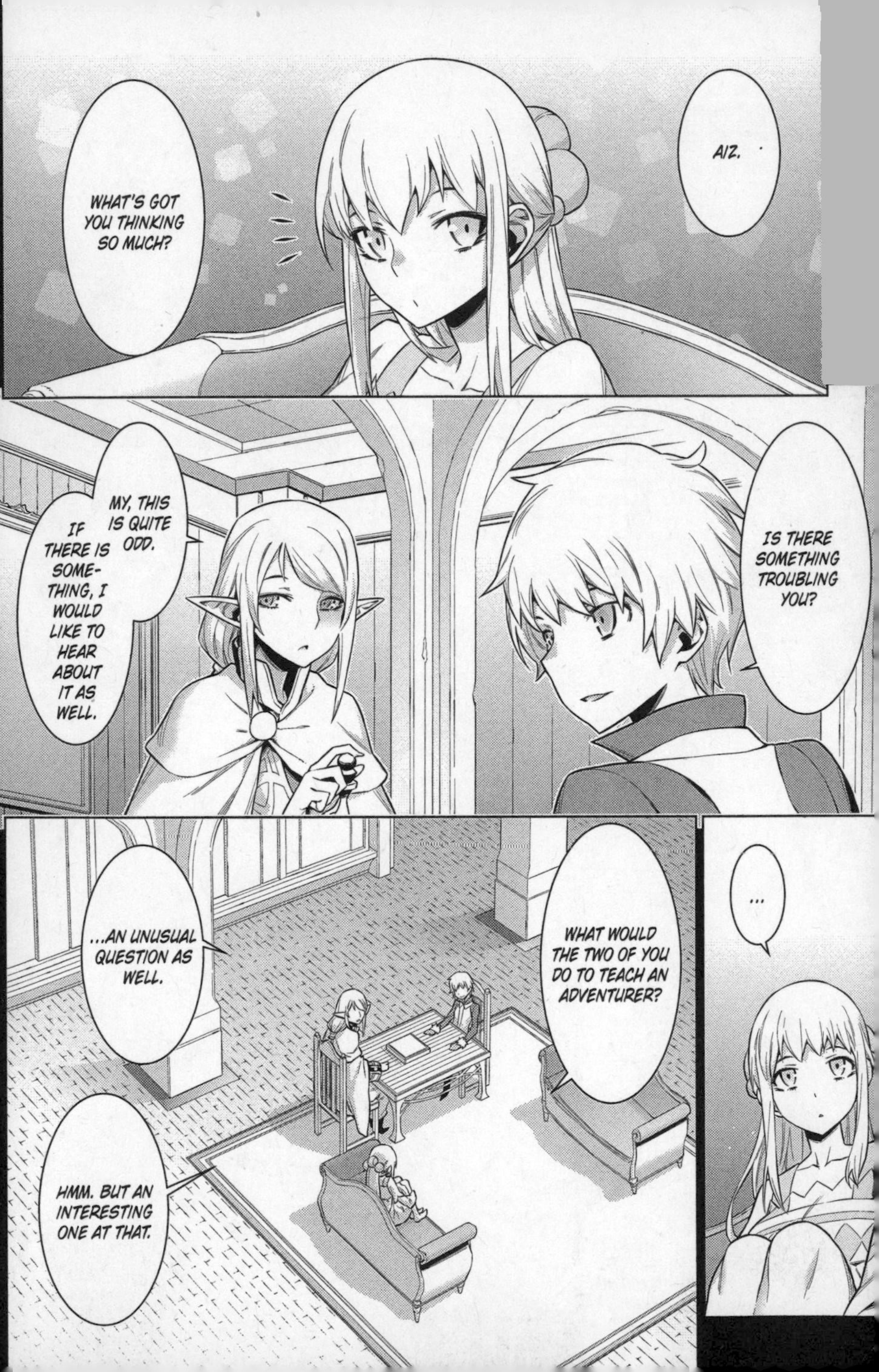
AIZ.
WHAT'S GOT YOU THINKING SO MUCH?
IS THERE SOMETHING TROUBLING YOU?
MY, THIS IS QUITE ODD.
IF THERE IS SOME-THING, I WOULD LIKE TO HEAR ABOUT IT AS WELL.
...
WHAT WOULD THE TWO OF YOU DO TO TEACH AN ADVENTURER?
...AN UNUSUAL QUESTION AS WELL.
HMM. BUT AN INTERESTING ONE AT THAT.

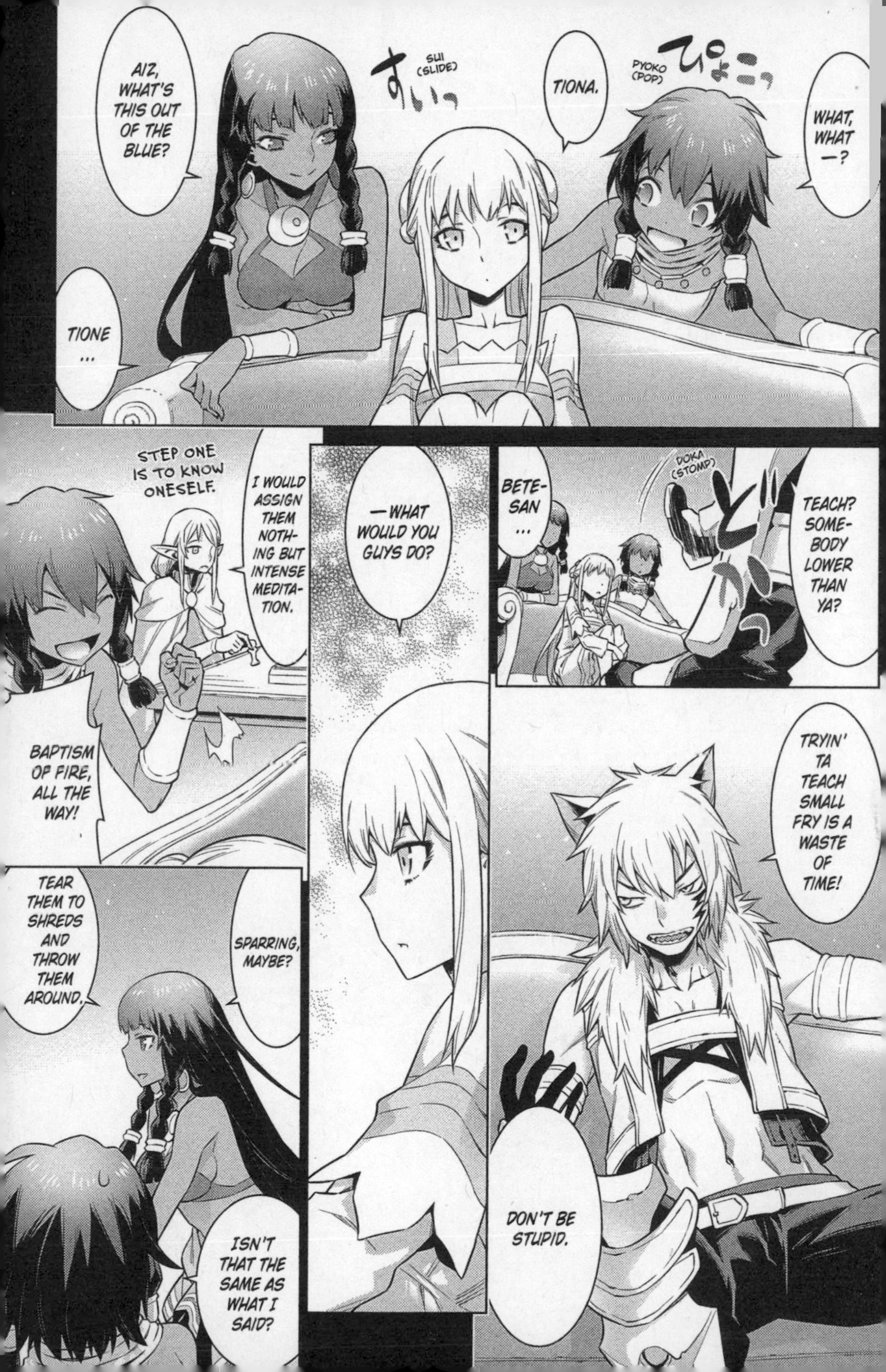
WHAT, WHAT—?
PYOKO (POP)
ぴょこっ
TIONA.
SUI (SLIDE)
すいっ
AIZ, WHAT'S THIS OUT OF THE BLUE?
TIONE...
TEACH? SOMEBODY LOWER THAN YA?
DOKA (STOMP)
どかっ
BETE-SAN...
TRYIN' TA TEACH SMALL FRY IS A WASTE OF TIME!
DON'T BE STUPID.
—WHAT WOULD YOU GUYS DO?
I WOULD ASSIGN THEM NOTHING BUT INTENSE MEDITATION.
STEP ONE IS TO KNOW ONESELF.
BAPTISM OF FIRE, ALL THE WAY!
SPARRING, MAYBE?
TEAR THEM TO SHREDS AND THROW THEM AROUND.
ISN'T THAT THE SAME AS WHAT I SAID?

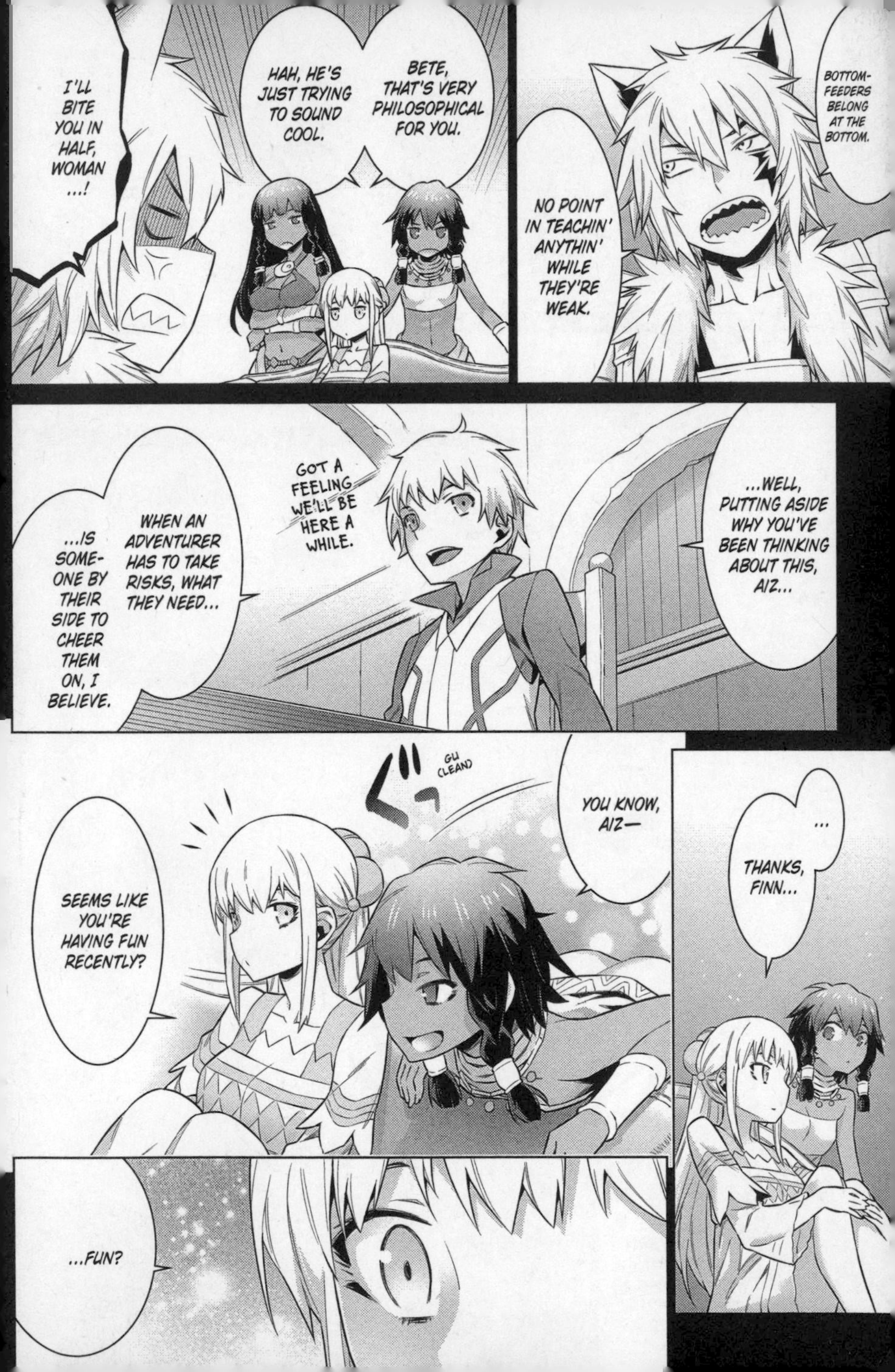
BOTTOM-FEEDERS BELONG AT THE BOTTOM.
NO POINT IN TEACHIN' ANYTHIN' WHILE THEY'RE WEAK.
BETE, THAT'S VERY PHILOSOPHICAL FOR YOU.
HAH, HE'S JUST TRYING TO SOUND COOL.
I'LL BITE YOU IN HALF, WOMAN...!
...WELL, PUTTING ASIDE WHY YOU'VE BEEN THINKING ABOUT THIS, AIZ...
GOT A FEELING WE'LL BE HERE A WHILE.
WHEN AN ADVENTURER HAS TO TAKE RISKS, WHAT THEY NEED...
...IS SOMEONE BY THEIR SIDE TO CHEER THEM ON, I BELIEVE.
...
THANKS, FINN...
ぐっ
GU (LEAN)
YOU KNOW, AIZ—
SEEMS LIKE YOU'RE HAVING FUN RECENTLY?
...FUN?

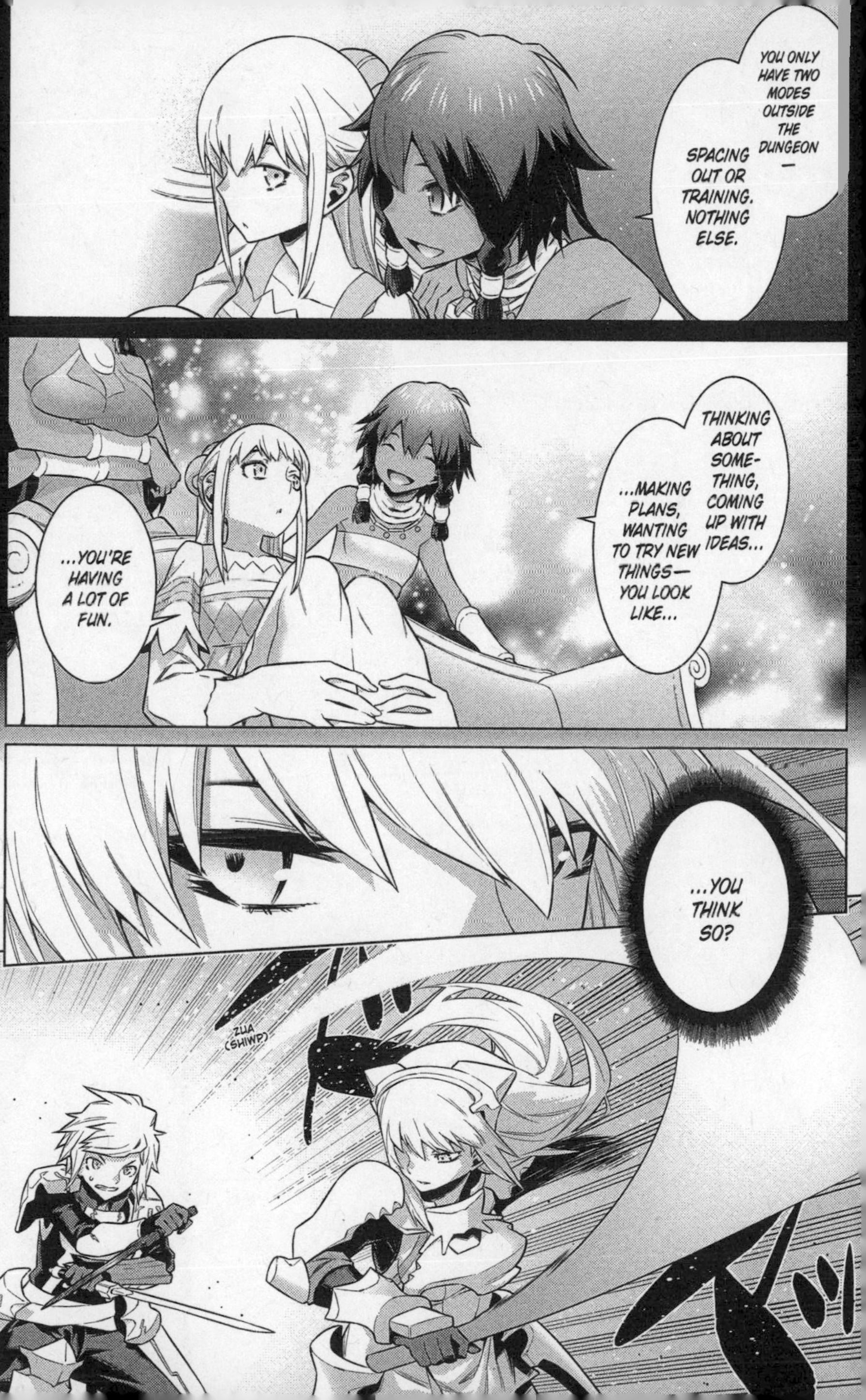

YOU ONLY HAVE TWO MODES OUTSIDE THE DUNGEON—
SPACING OUT OR TRAINING. NOTHING ELSE.
THINKING ABOUT SOME-THING, COMING UP WITH IDEAS...
...MAKING PLANS, WANTING TO TRY NEW THINGS— YOU LOOK LIKE...
...YOU'RE HAVING A LOT OF FUN.
...YOU THINK SO?
ZUA (SHIWP)

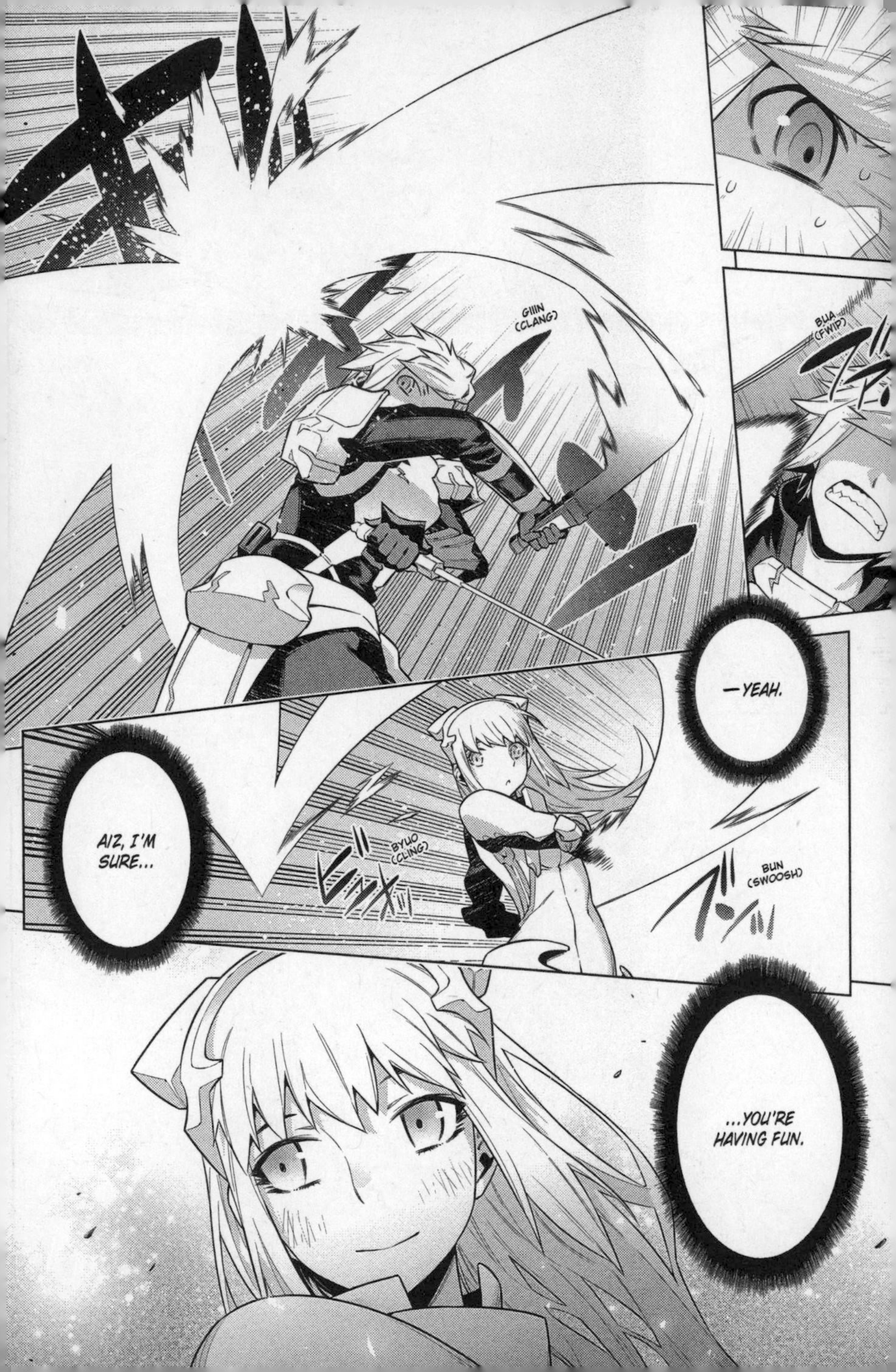
BUA (FWIP)
GIIN (CLANG)
—YEAH.
BUN (SWOOSH)
BYUO (CLING)
AIZ, I'M SURE...
...YOU'RE HAVING FUN.

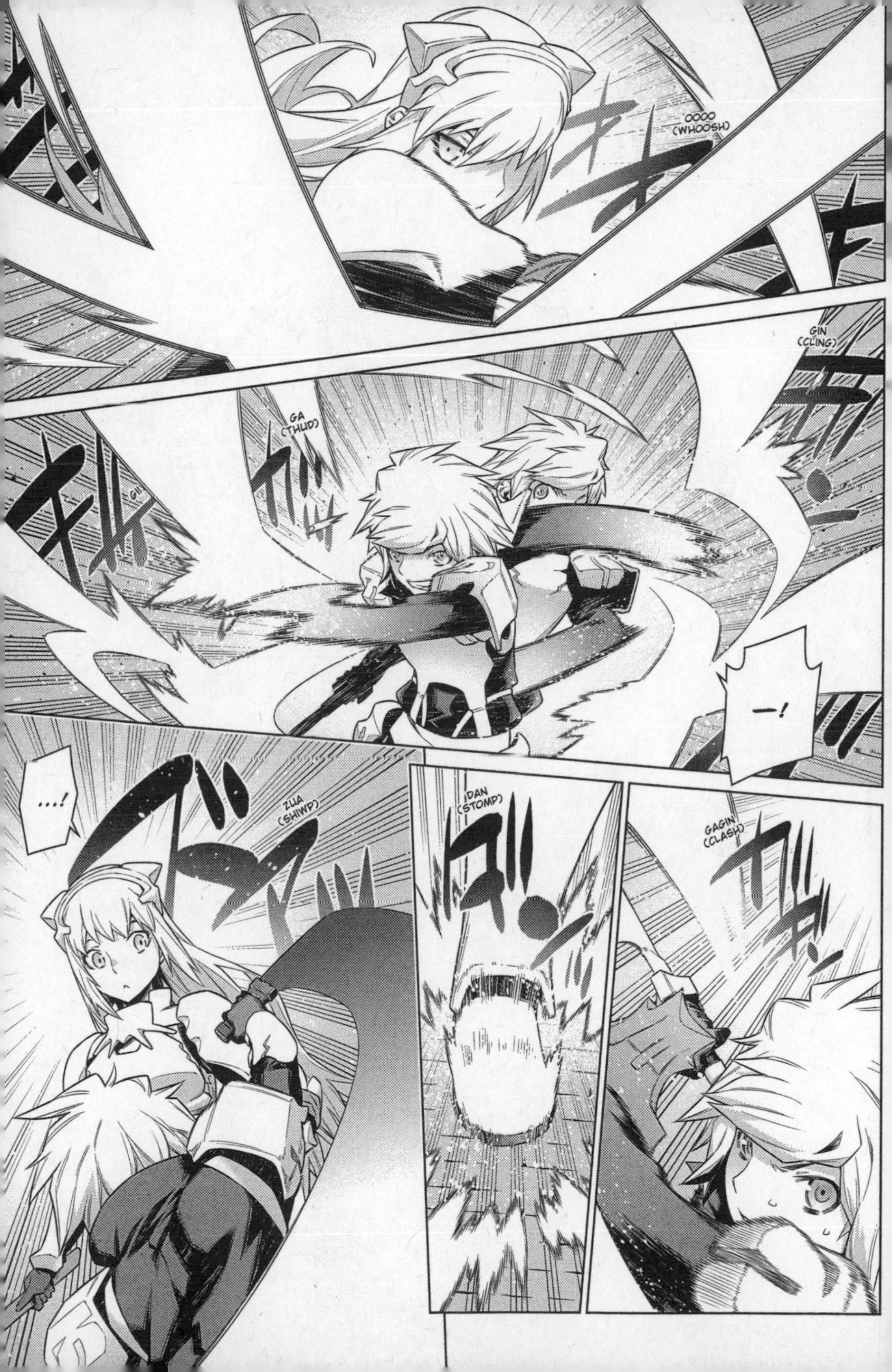

OOOO (WHOOSH)
GIN (CLING)
GA (THUD)
—!
GAGIN (CLASH)
DAN (STOMP)
ZUA (SHWIP)
...!

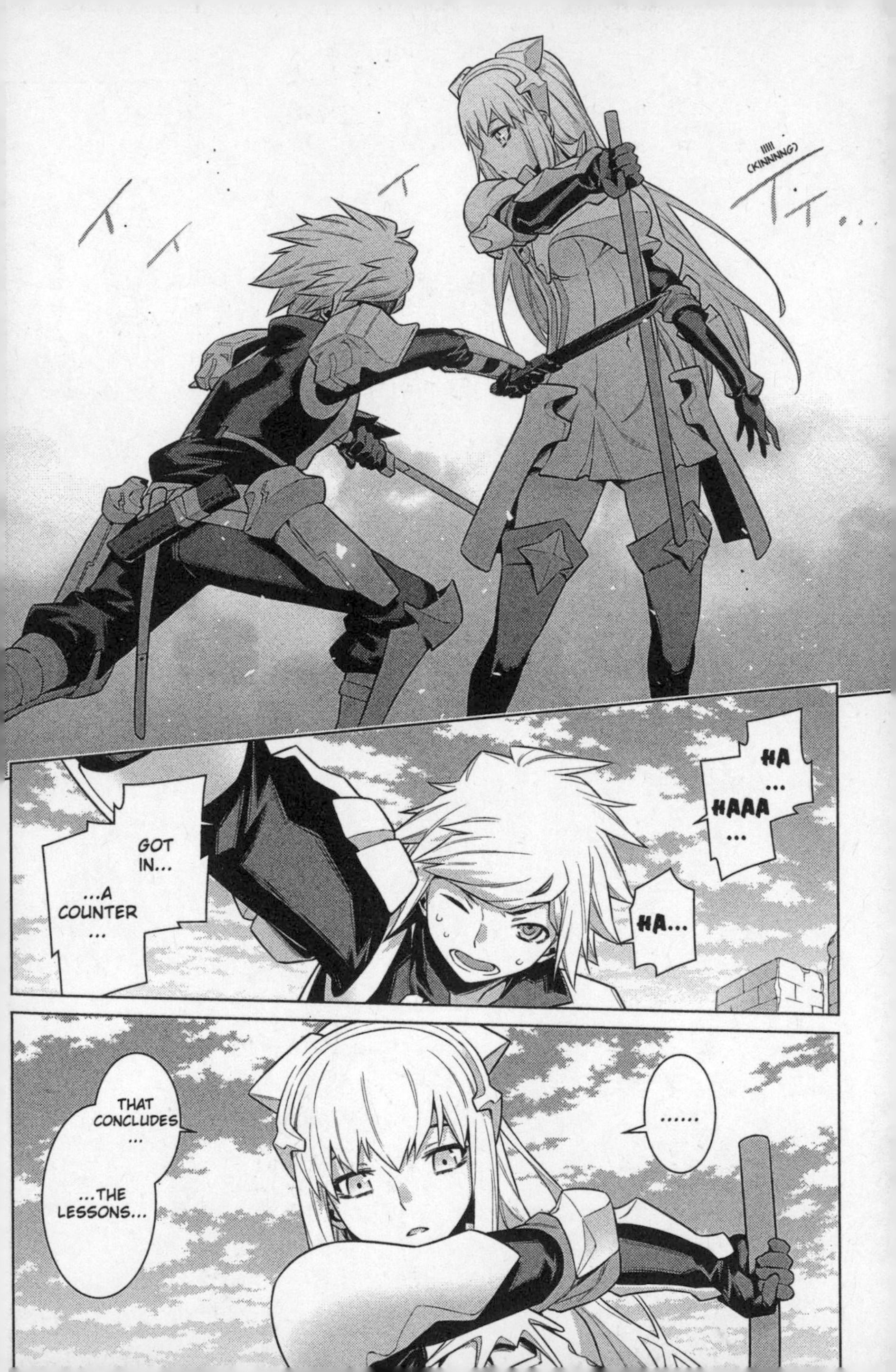
IIIII
(KINNNNG)
HA
...
HAAA
...
HA...
GOT
IN...
...A
COUNTER
...
......
THAT
CONCLUDES
...
...THE
LESSONS...

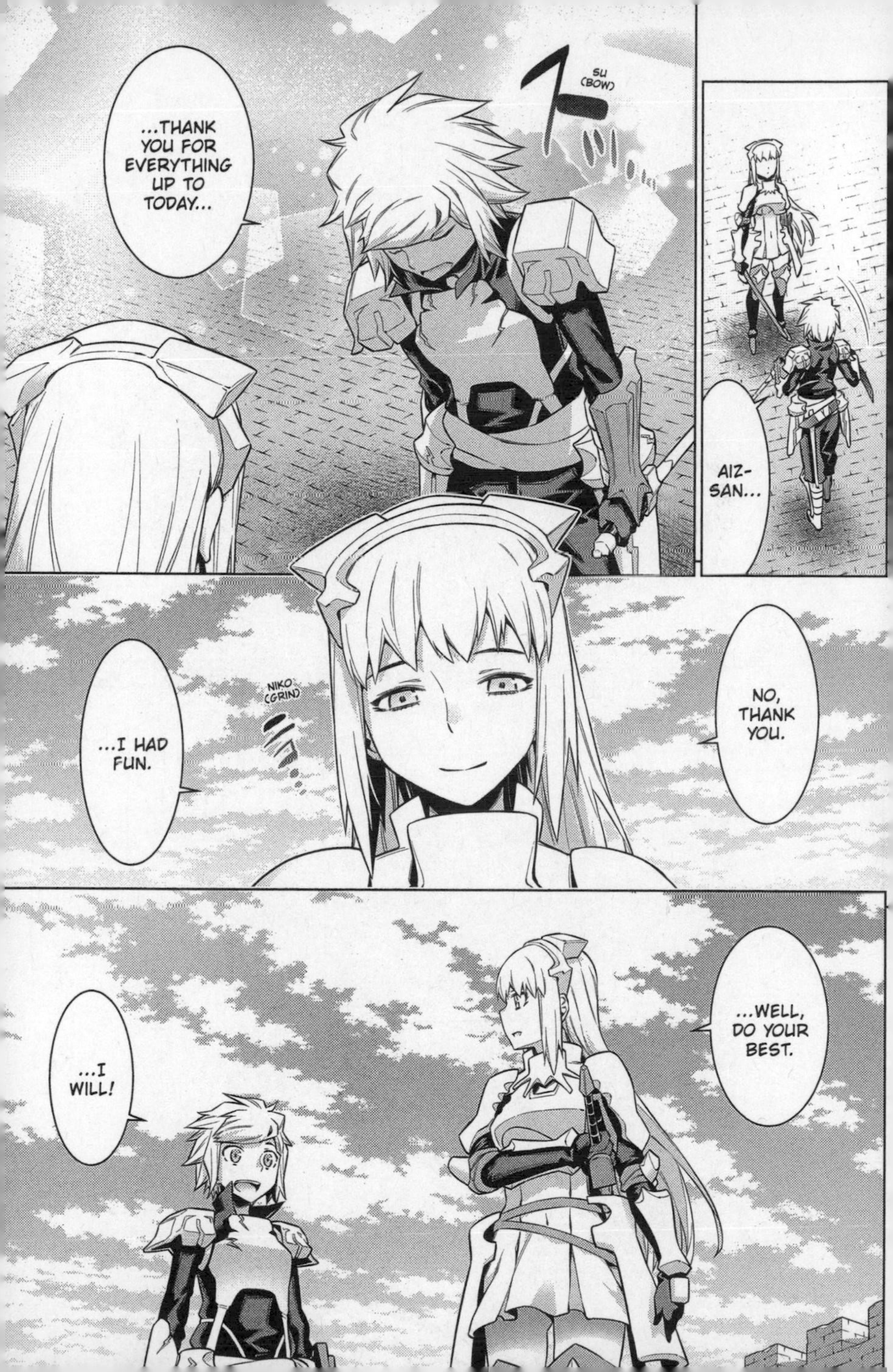
AIZ-SAN...
SU (BOW)
...THANK YOU FOR EVERYTHING UP TO TODAY...
NO, THANK YOU.
NIKO (GRIN)
...I HAD FUN.
...WELL, DO YOUR BEST.
...I WILL!

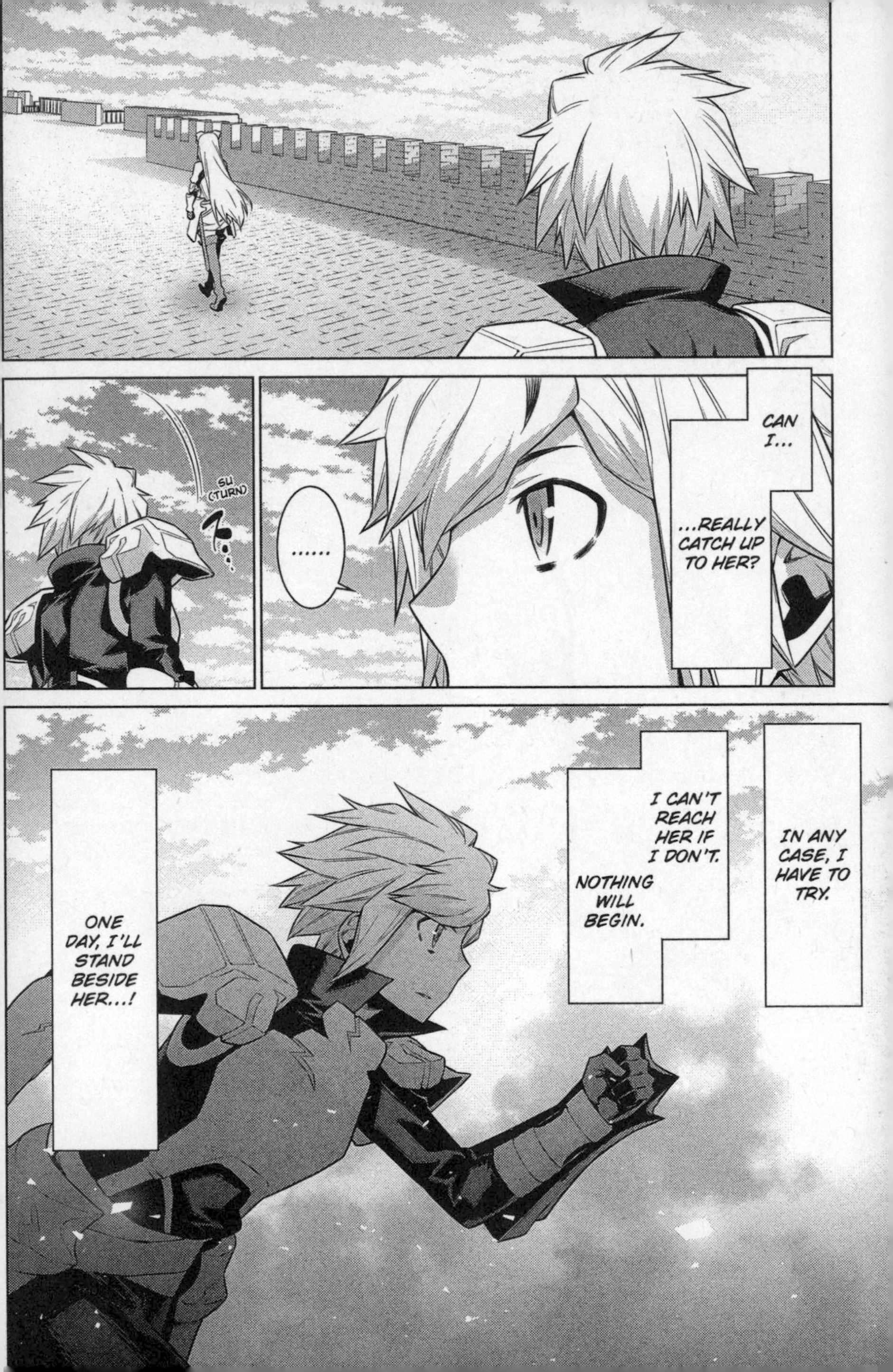
CAN I...
...REALLY CATCH UP TO HER?
......
SU (TURN)
IN ANY CASE, I HAVE TO TRY.
I CAN'T REACH HER IF I DON'T.
NOTHING WILL BEGIN.
ONE DAY, I'LL STAND BESIDE HER...!

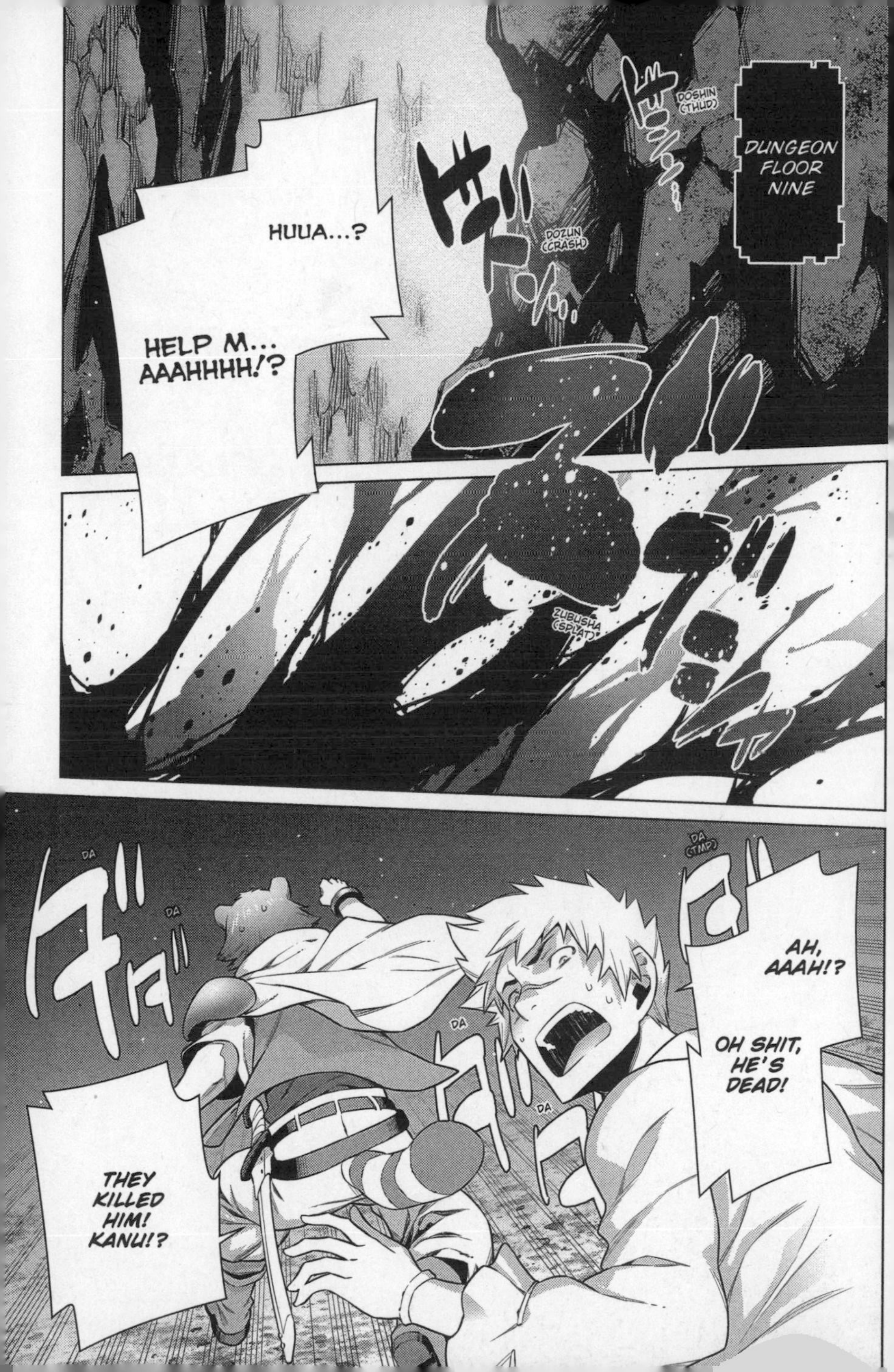
DUNGEON FLOOR NINE
DOSHIN (THUD)
DOZUN (CRASH)
HUUA...?
HELP M... AAAHHHH!?
ZUBUSHA (SPLAT)
DA (TMP)
AH, AAAH!?
OH SHIT, HE'S DEAD!
DA
DA
DA
DA
THEY KILLED HIM! KANU!?

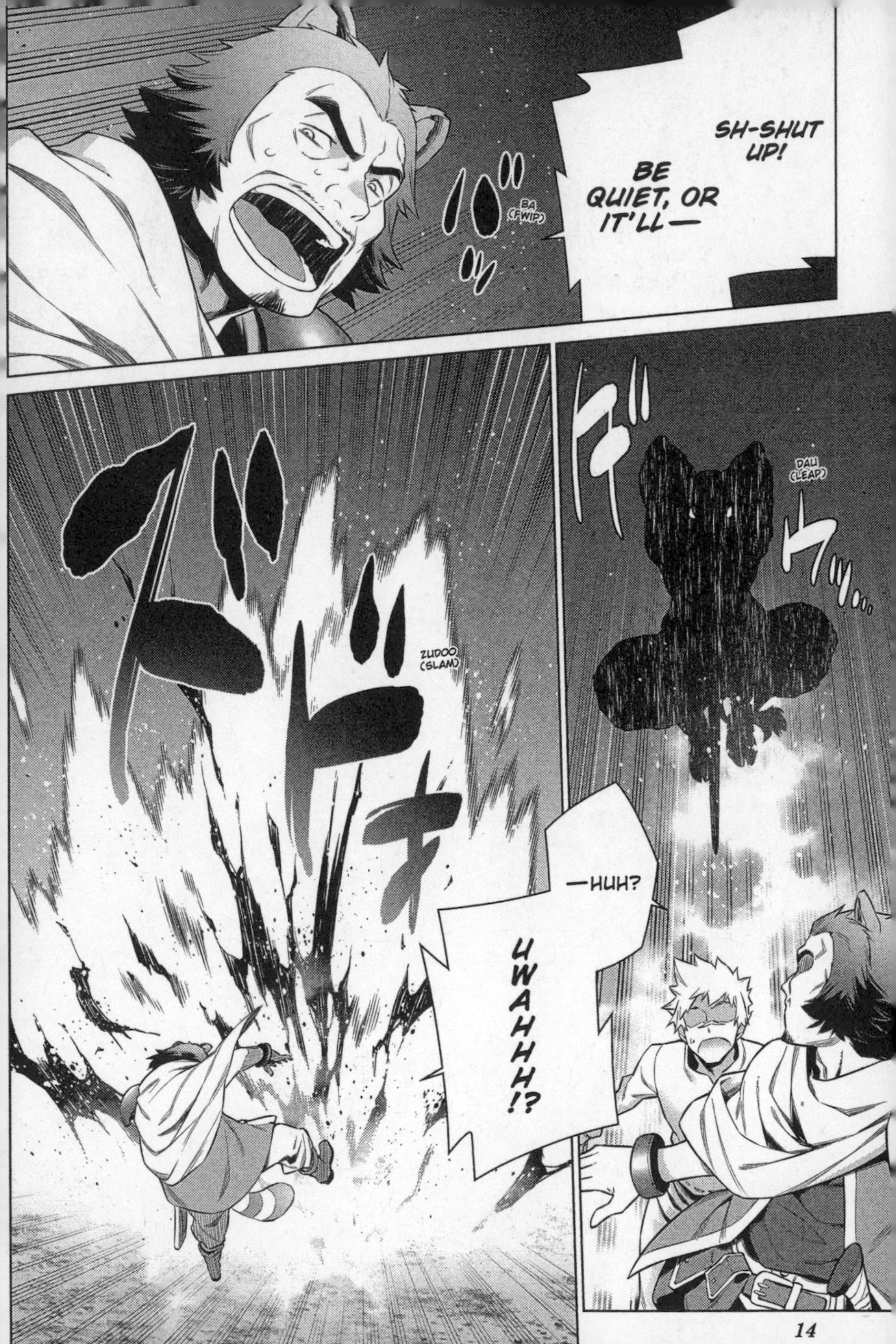

SH-SHUT UP!
BE QUIET, OR IT'LL—
BA (FWIP)
DAU (LEAP)
—HUH?
UWAHHH!?
ZUDOO (SLAM)

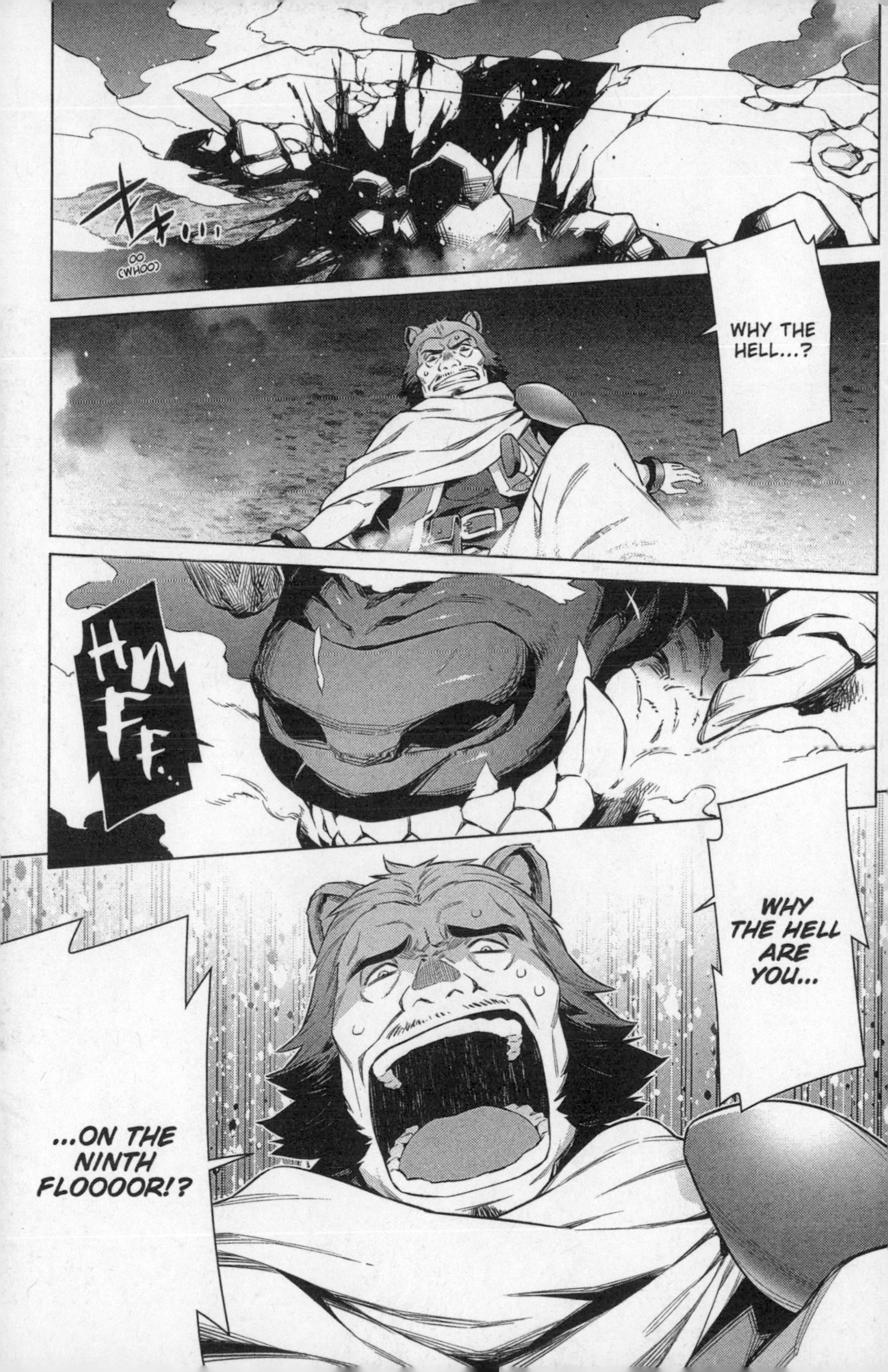
OO
(WHOO)
WHY THE HELL...?
HnFF.
WHY THE HELL ARE YOU...
...ON THE NINTH FLOOOOR!?

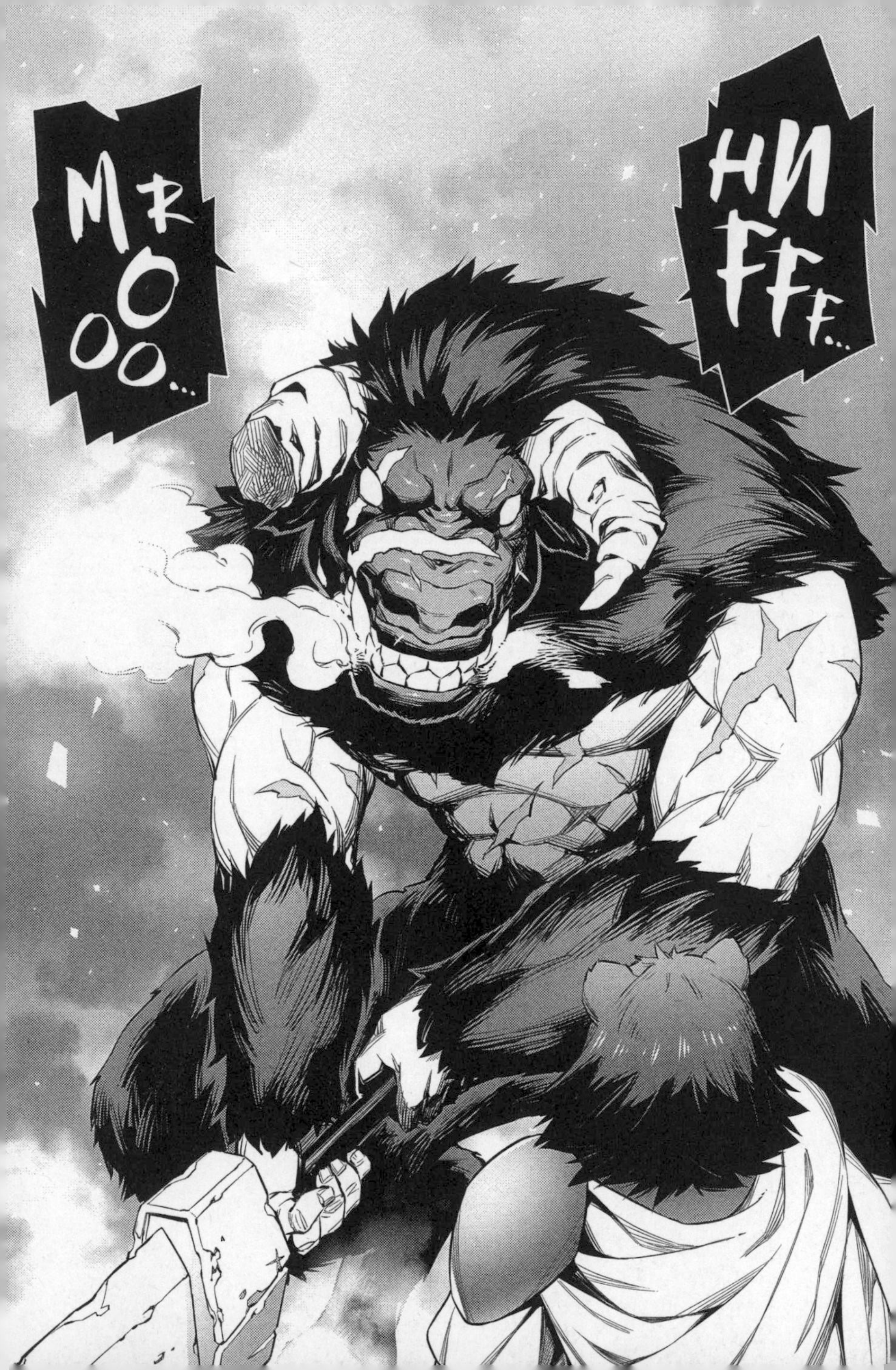
HUFFF...
MROOO...

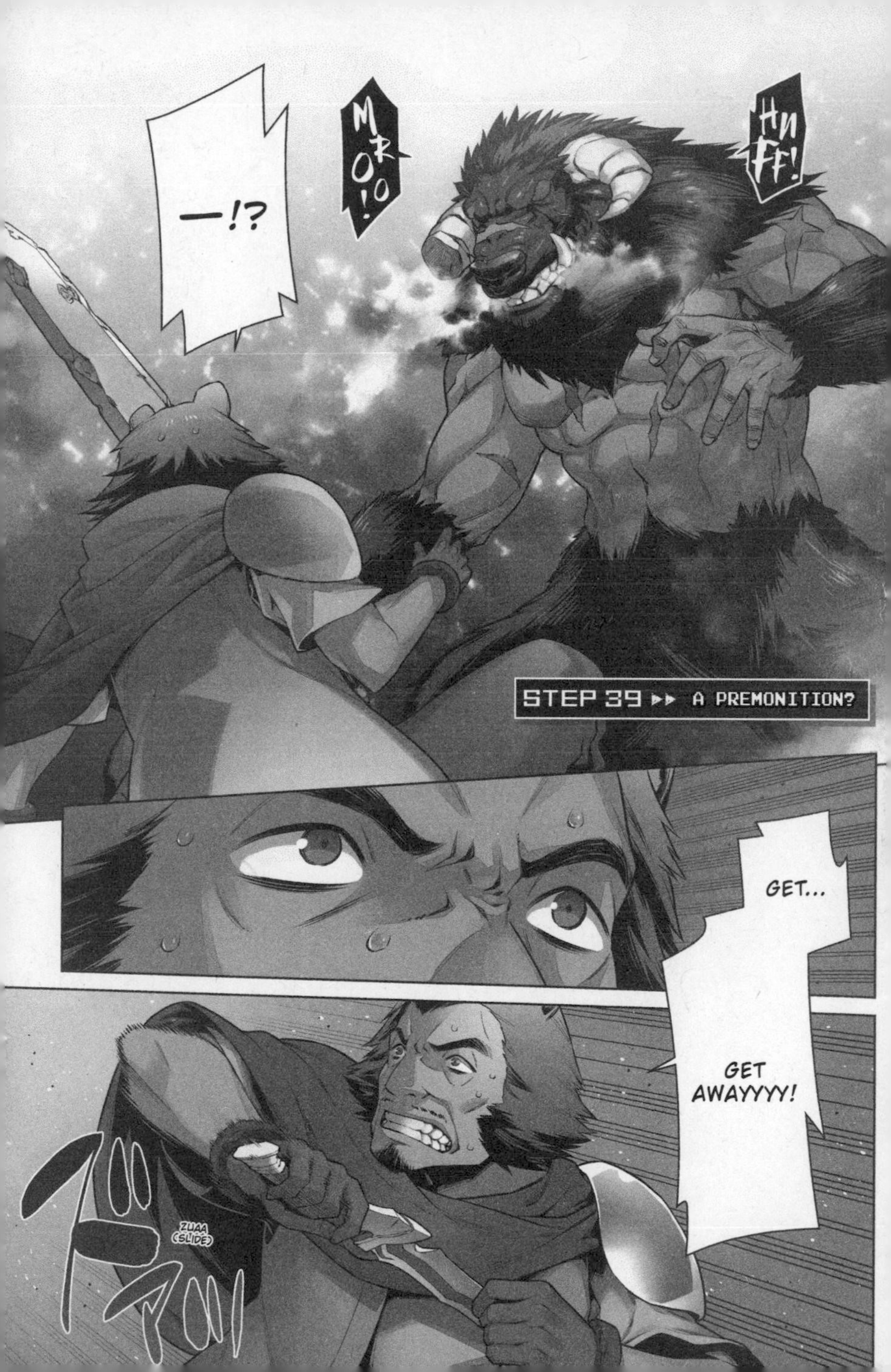
HUFF!
MROO!
—!?
STEP 39 ▸▸ A PREMONITION?
GET...
GET AWAYYYY!
ZUAA (SLIDE)

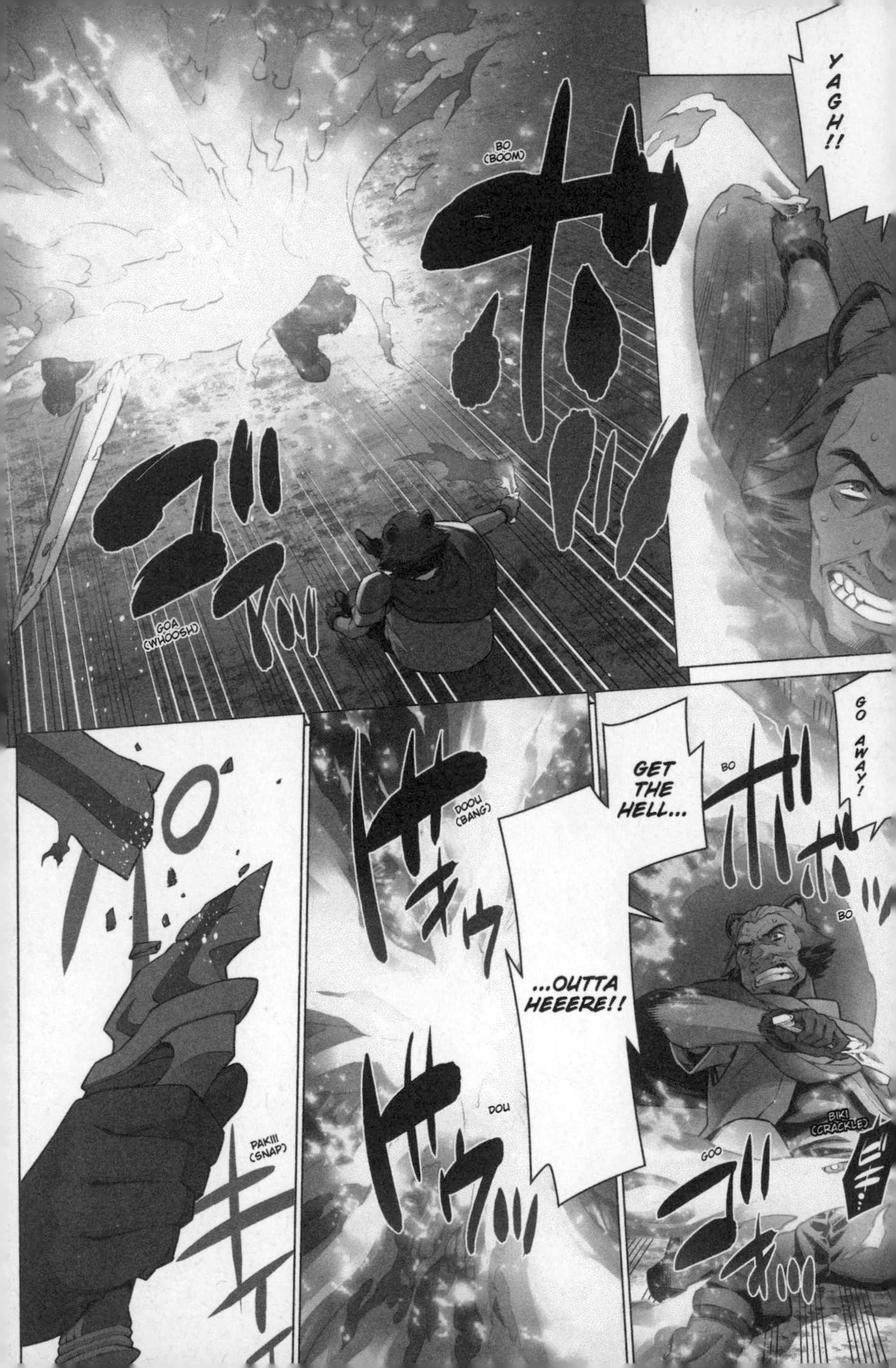
YAGH!!
BO (BOOM)
GOA (WHOOSH)
GO AWAY!
GET THE HELL...
BO
BO
...OUTTA HEEERE!!
BIKI (CRACKLE)
GOO
DOOU (BANG)
DOU
PAKIII (SNAP)

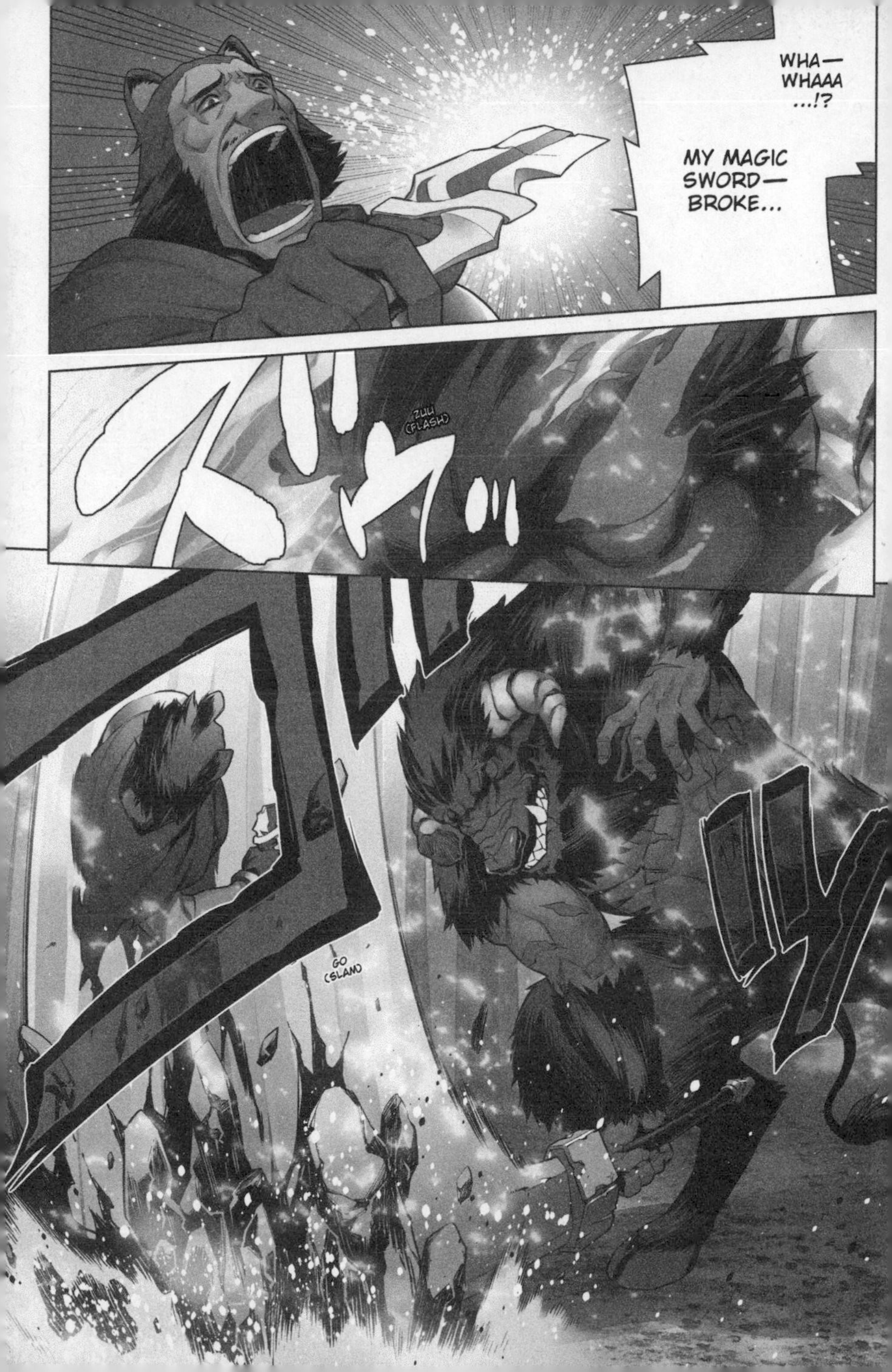
WHA—
WHAAA
...!?
MY MAGIC
SWORD—
BROKE...
ZUU
(FLASH)
GO
(SLAM)

Is it WRONG to try to PICK UP GIRLS in a DUNGEON?

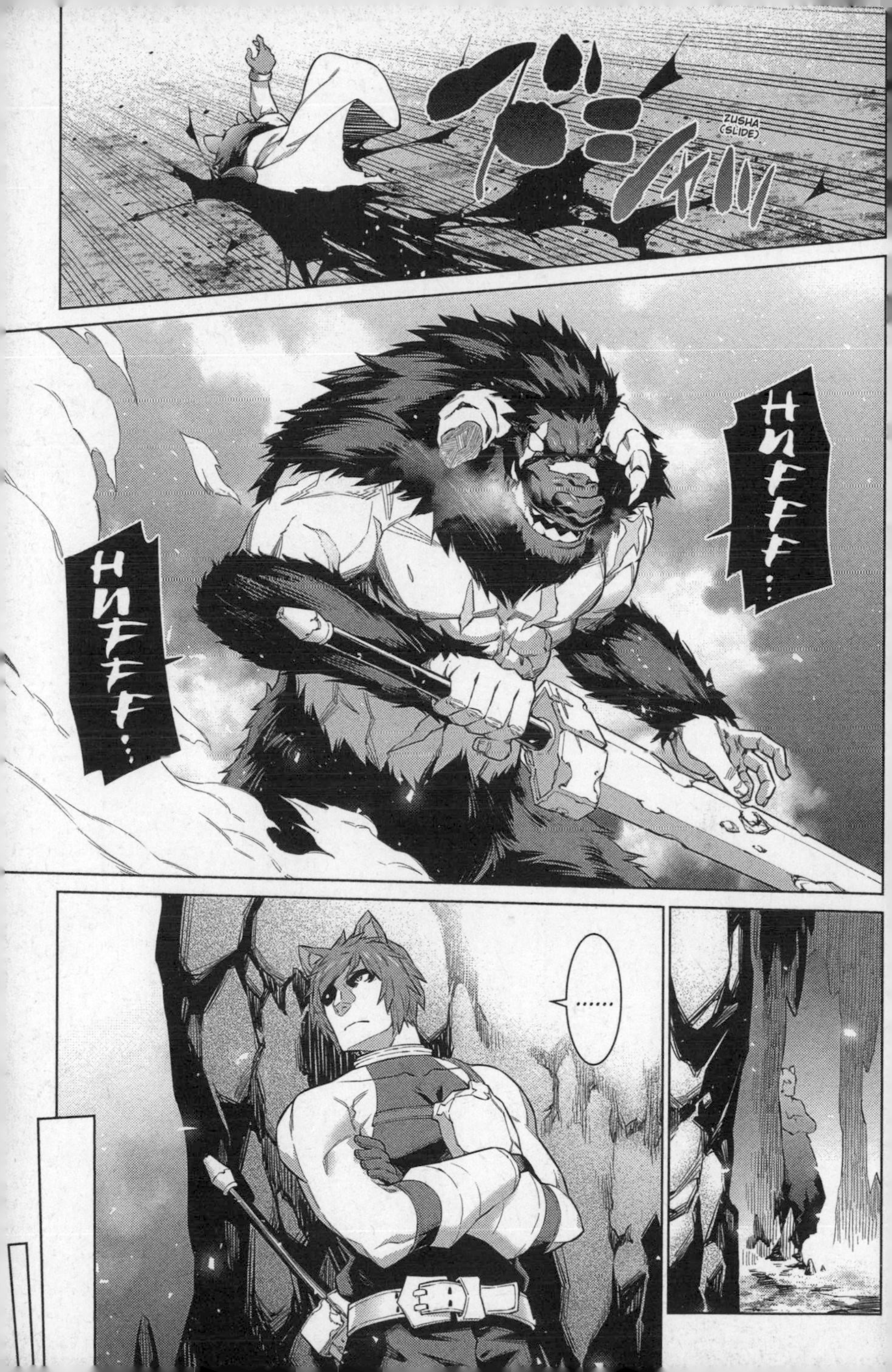
ZUSHA (SLIDE)
HUFFFF...
HUFFFF...
......

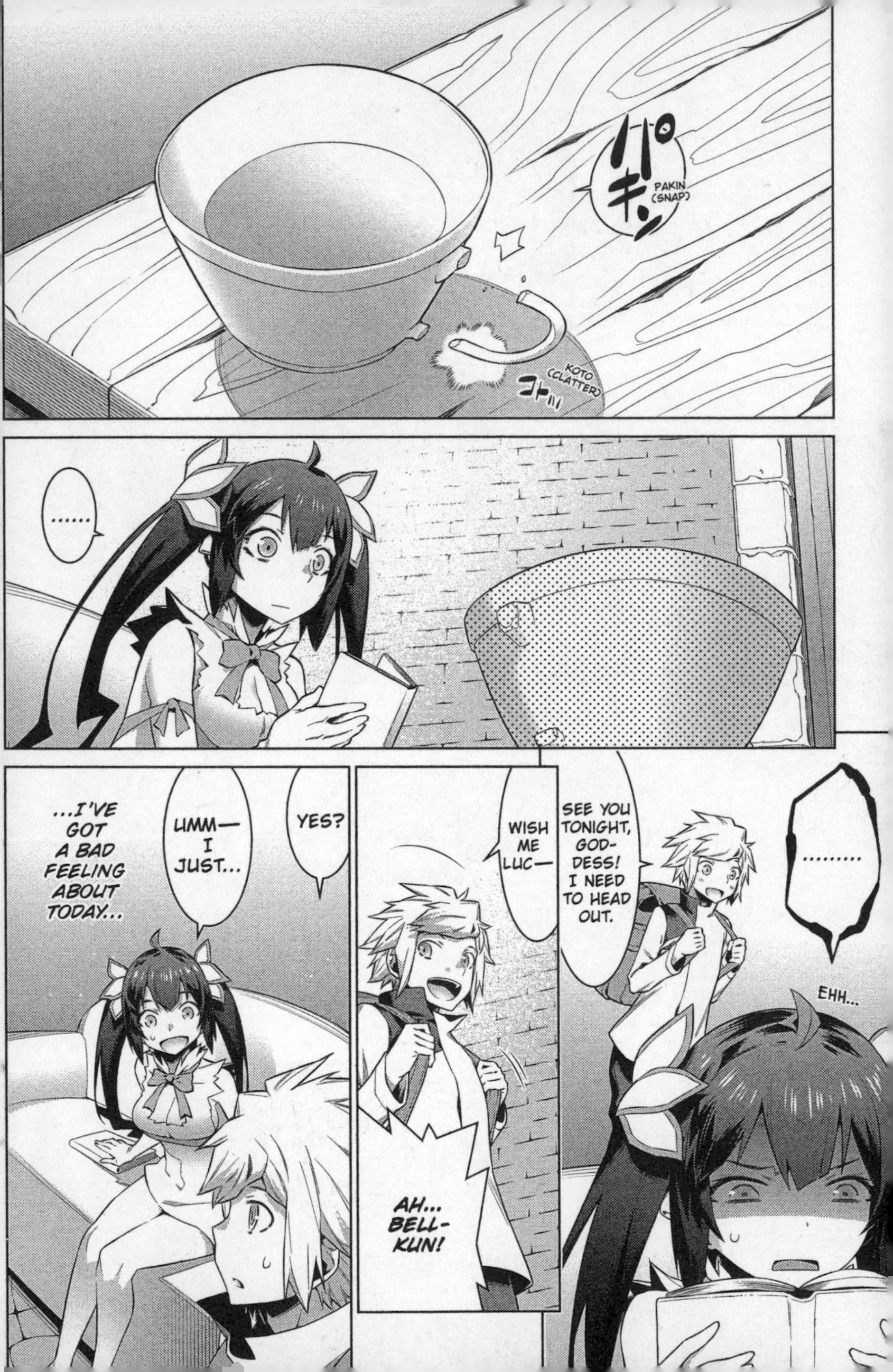
パキン
PAKIN (SNAP)
コトッ
KOTO (CLATTER)
......
....
SEE YOU TONIGHT, GOD-DESS! I NEED TO HEAD OUT.
EHH...
WISH ME LUC—
AH... BELL-KUN!
YES?
UMM— I JUST...
...I'VE GOT A BAD FEELING ABOUT TODAY...

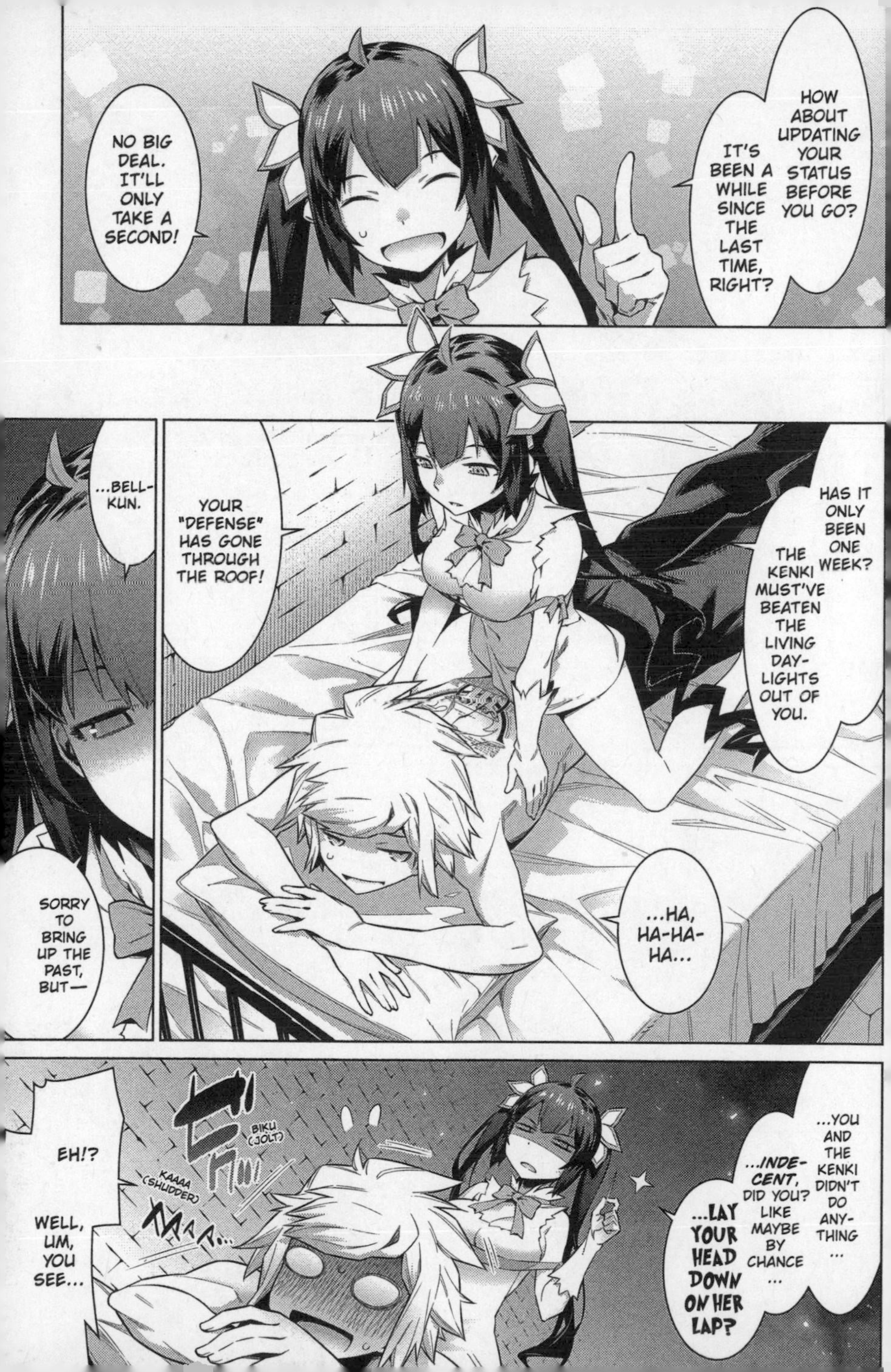
HOW ABOUT UPDATING YOUR STATUS BEFORE YOU GO?
IT'S BEEN A WHILE SINCE THE LAST TIME, RIGHT?
NO BIG DEAL. IT'LL ONLY TAKE A SECOND!
HAS IT ONLY BEEN ONE WEEK?
THE KENKI MUST'VE BEATEN THE LIVING DAY-LIGHTS OUT OF YOU.
...HA, HA-HA-HA...
YOUR "DEFENSE" HAS GONE THROUGH THE ROOF!
...BELL-KUN.
SORRY TO BRING UP THE PAST, BUT—
...YOU AND THE KENKI DIDN'T DO ANY-THING ...
...INDE-CENT, DID YOU? LIKE MAYBE BY CHANCE ...
...LAY YOUR HEAD DOWN ON HER LAP?
BIKU (JOLT)
KAAAA (SHUDDER)
EH!?
WELL, UM, YOU SEE...

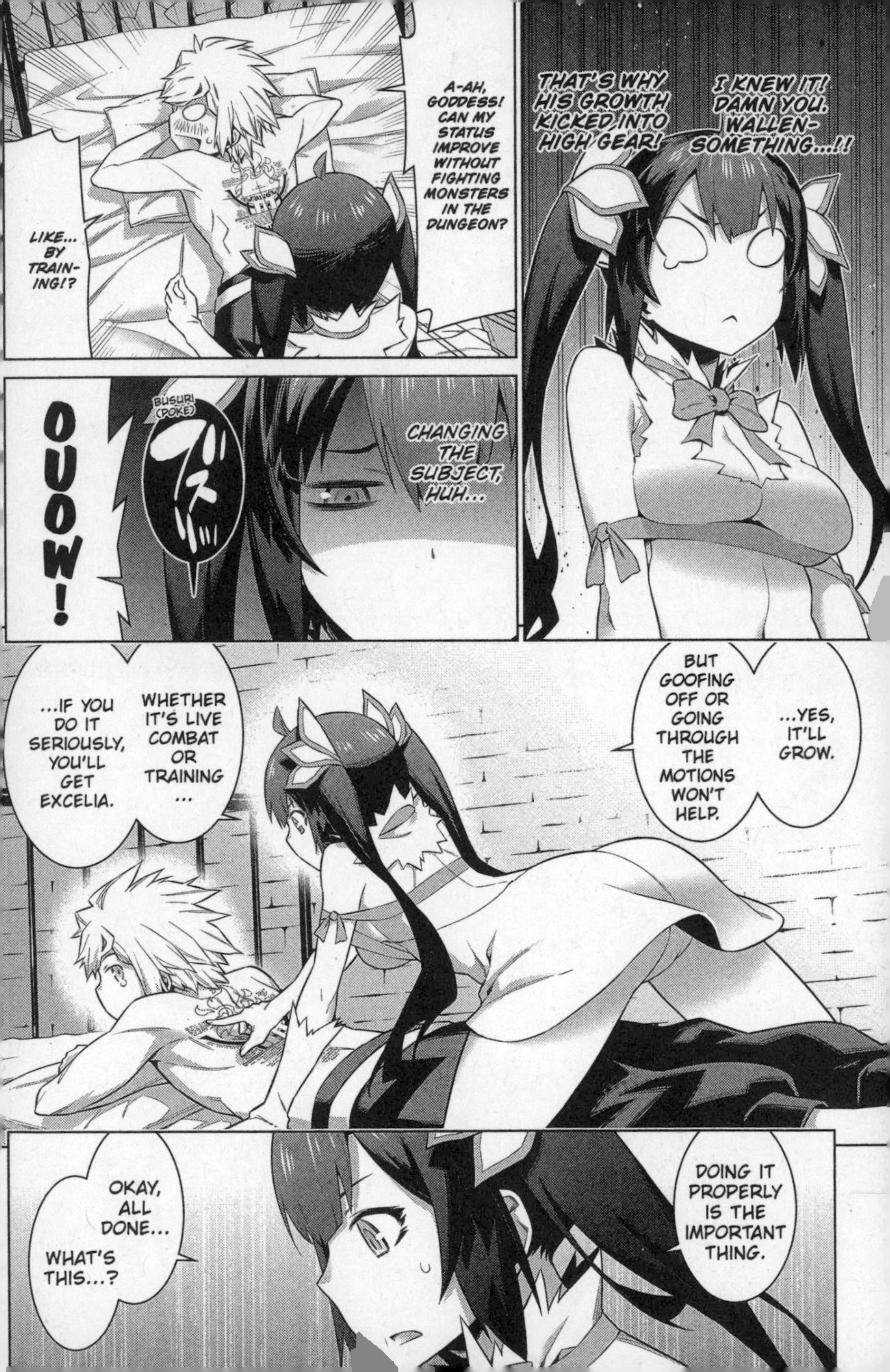
I KNEW IT! DAMN YOU. WALLEN-SOMETHING...!!
THAT'S WHY HIS GROWTH KICKED INTO HIGH GEAR!
A-AH, GODDESS! CAN MY STATUS IMPROVE WITHOUT FIGHTING MONSTERS IN THE DUNGEON?
LIKE... BY TRAINING!?
CHANGING THE SUBJECT, HUH...
BUSURI (POKE)
OUOW!
...YES, IT'LL GROW.
BUT GOOFING OFF OR GOING THROUGH THE MOTIONS WON'T HELP.
WHETHER IT'S LIVE COMBAT OR TRAINING...
...IF YOU DO IT SERIOUSLY, YOU'LL GET EXCELIA.
DOING IT PROPERLY IS THE IMPORTANT THING.
OKAY, ALL DONE...
WHAT'S THIS...?

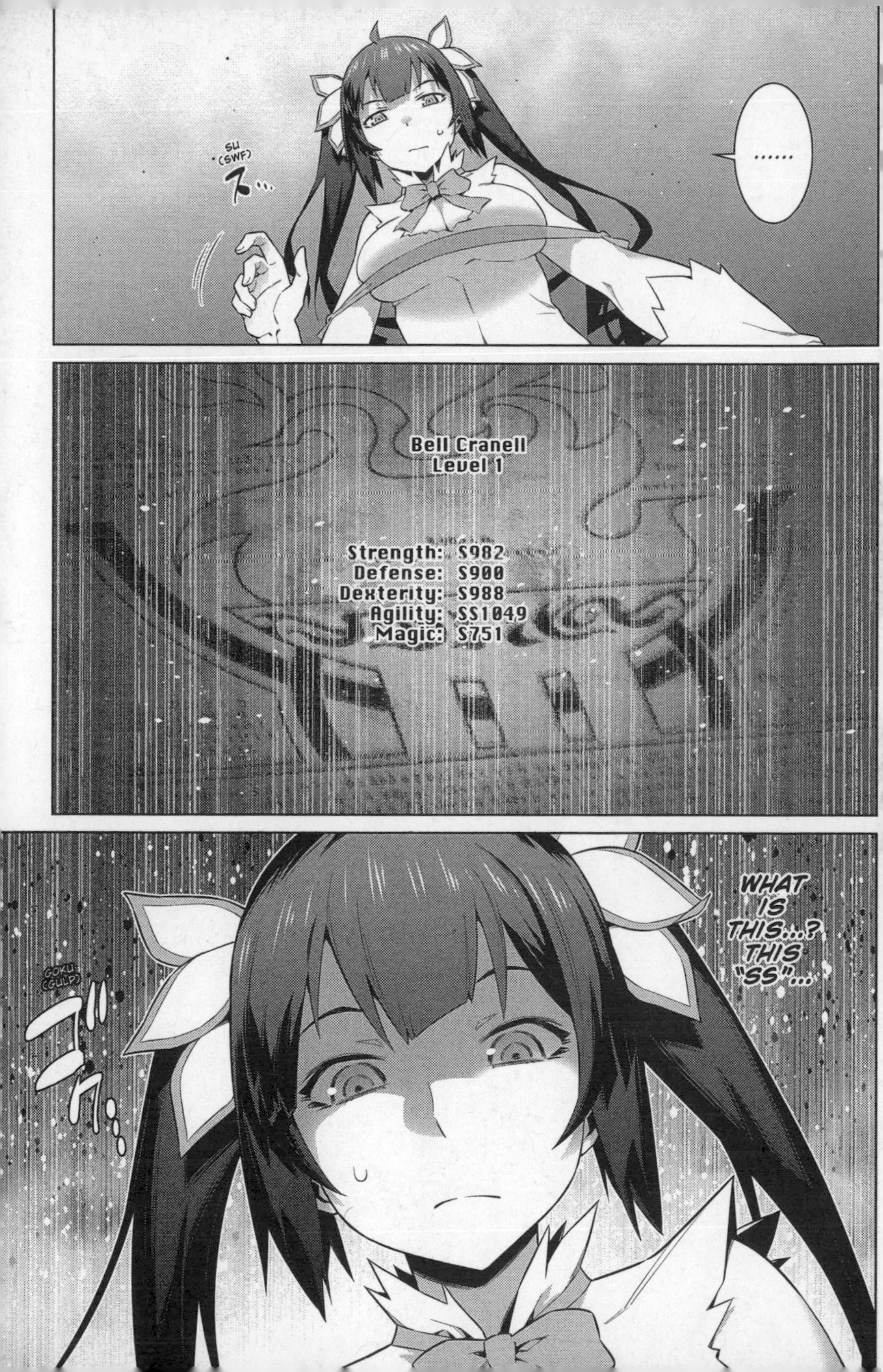
......
SU (SWF)
ス...
Bell Cranell
Level 1
Strength: S982
Defense: S900
Dexterity: S988
Agility: SS1049
Magic: S751
WHAT IS THIS...? THIS "SS"...
GOKU (GULP)
ゴク...

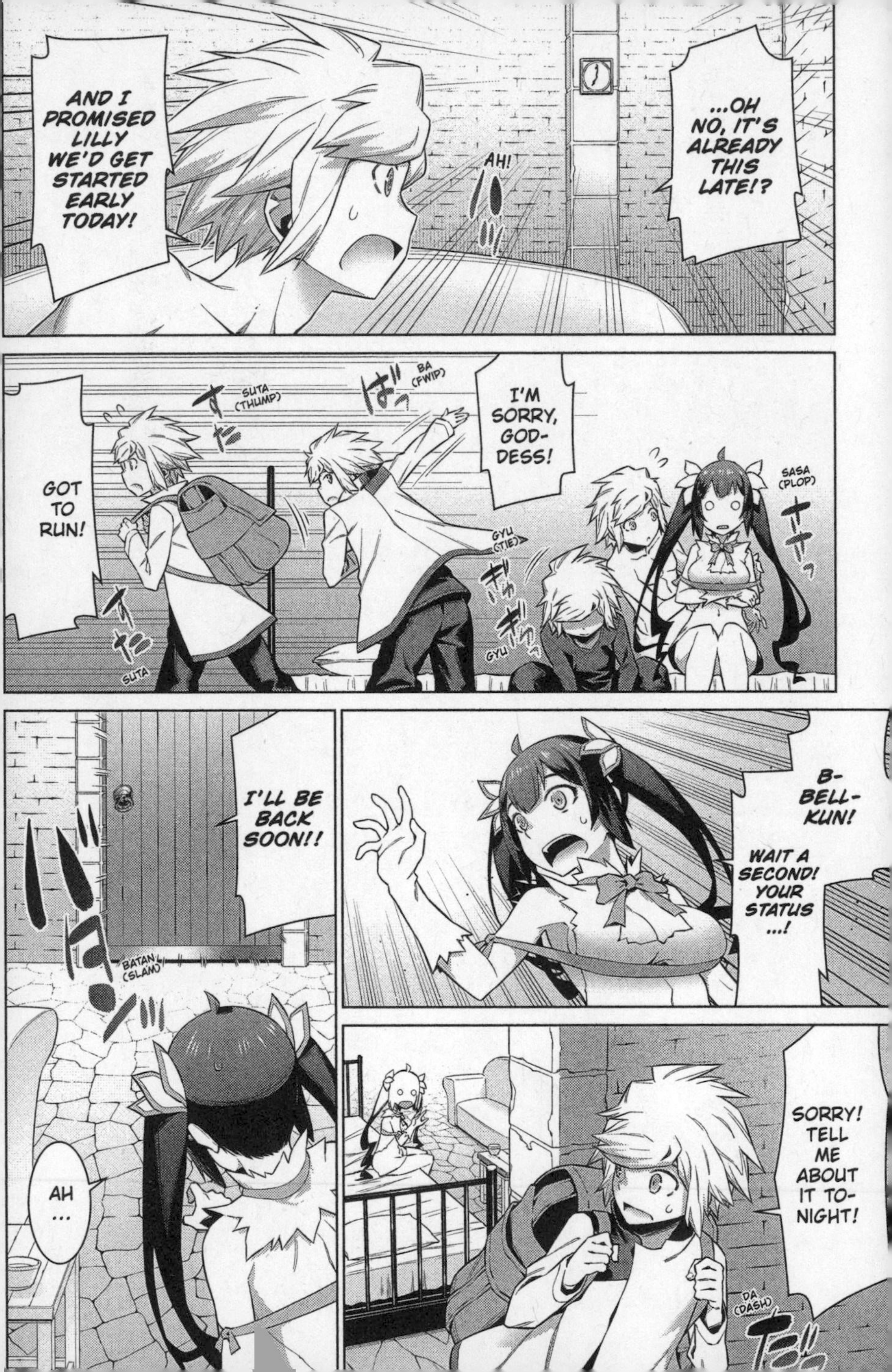
...OH NO, IT'S ALREADY THIS LATE!?
AH!
AND I PROMISED LILLY WE'D GET STARTED EARLY TODAY!
SASA (PLOP)
I'M SORRY, GOD-DESS!
GYU (TIE)
GYU
BA (FWIP)
SUTA (THUMP)
GOT TO RUN!
SUTA
B-BELL-KUN!
WAIT A SECOND! YOUR STATUS ...!
I'LL BE BACK SOON!!
BATAN (SLAM)
SORRY! TELL ME ABOUT IT TO-NIGHT!
DA (DASH)
AH ...

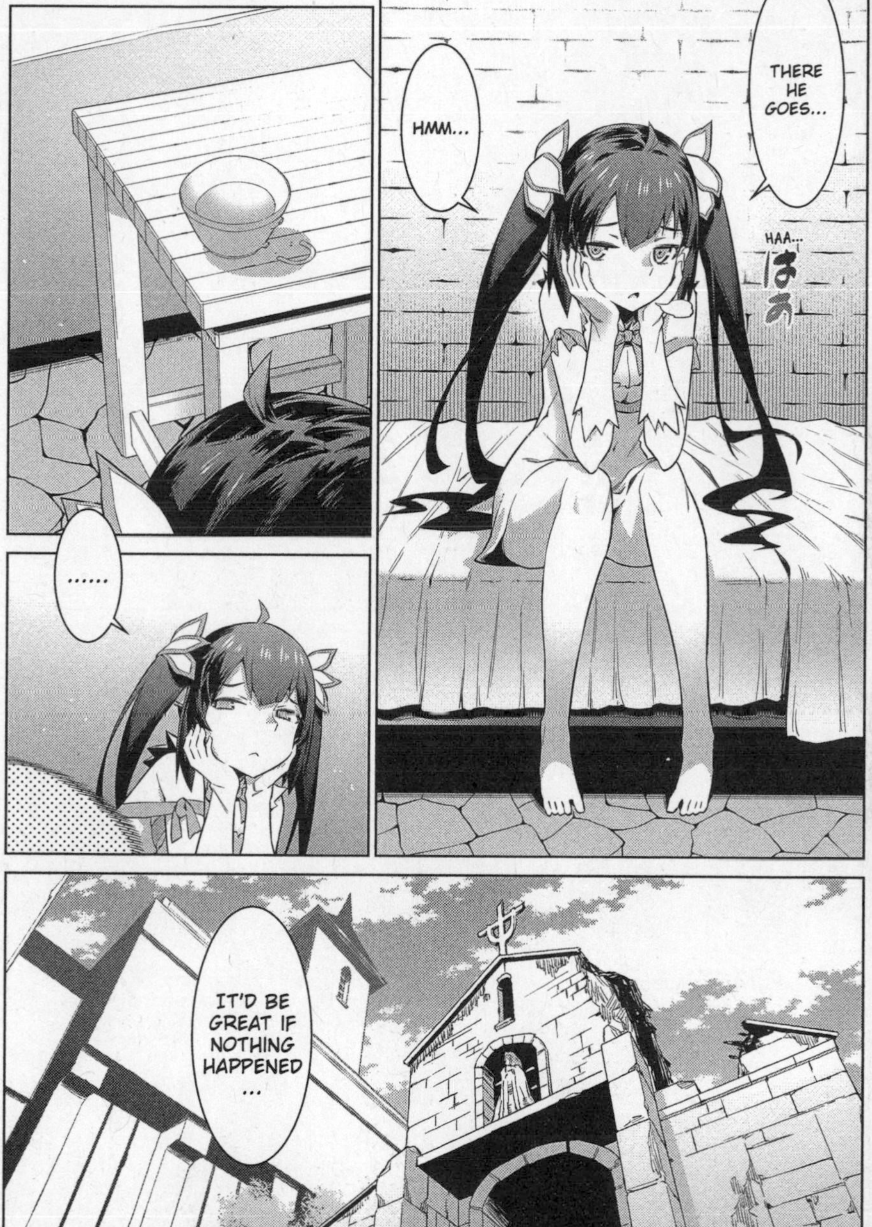
THERE HE GOES...
HMM...
HAA... はぁ
......
IT'D BE GREAT IF NOTHING HAPPENED...

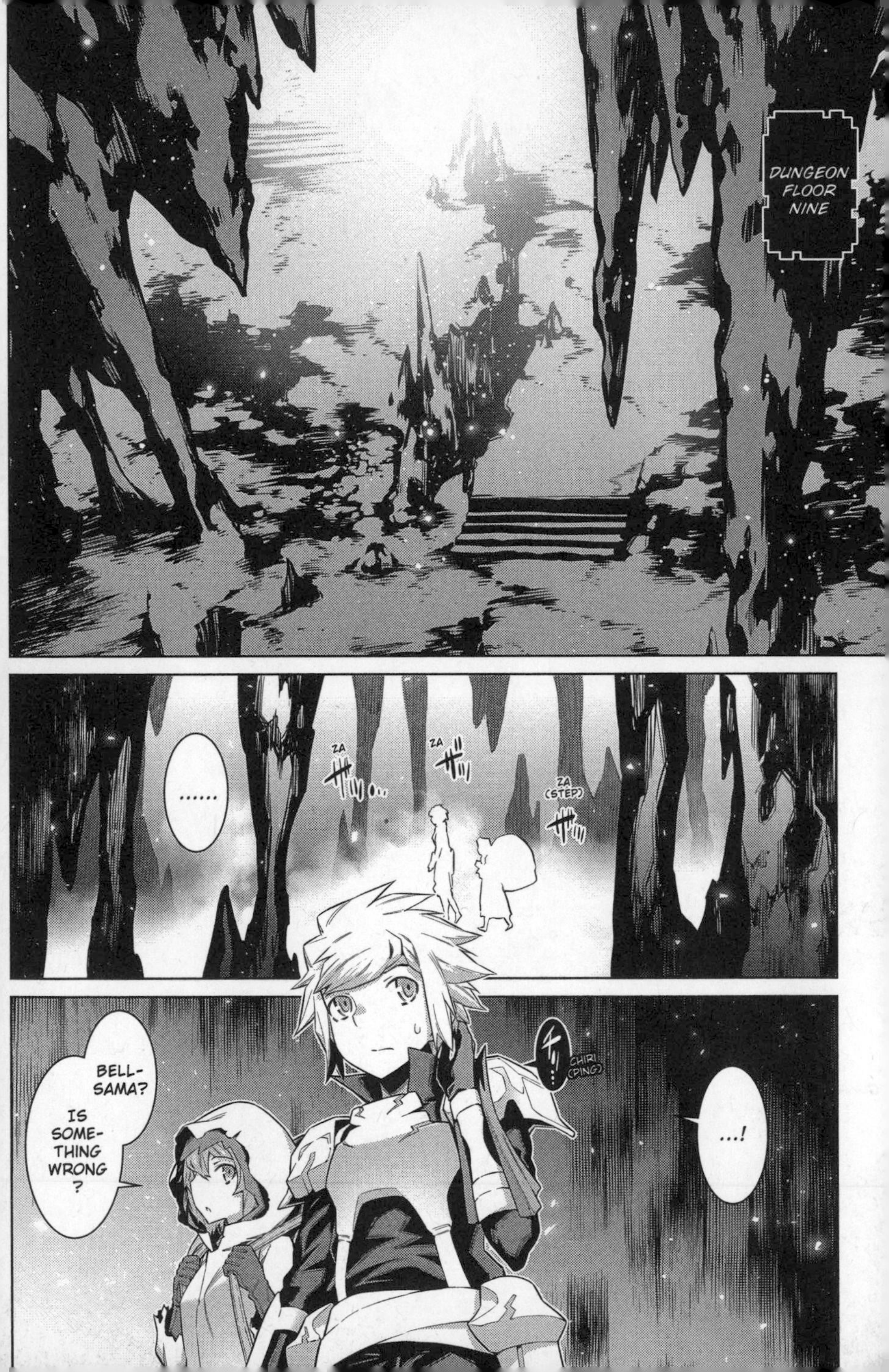
DUNGEON FLOOR NINE
ZA (STEP)
ZA
ZA
......
CHIRI (PING)
...!
BELL-SAMA?
IS SOMETHING WRONG?

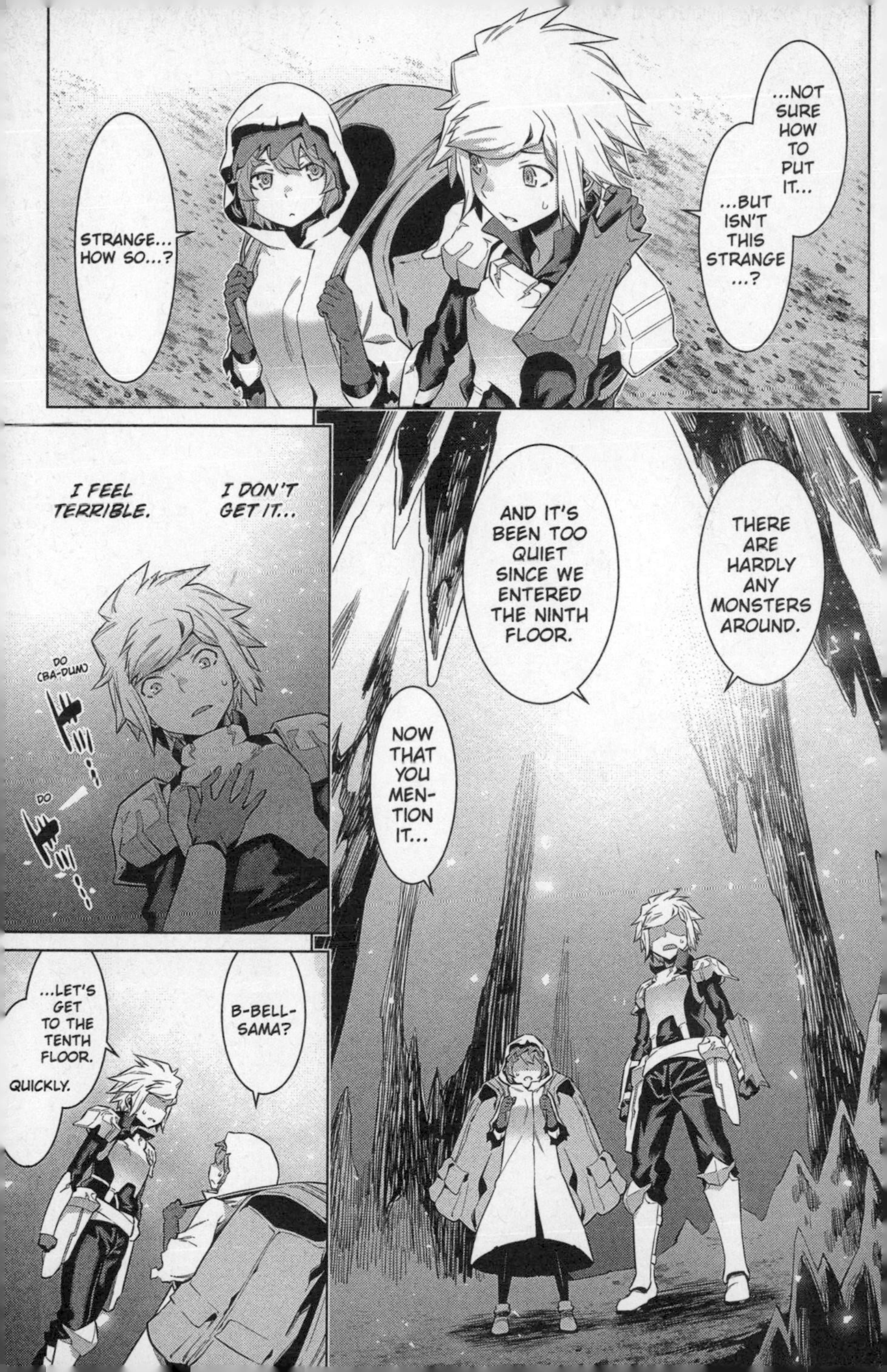
...NOT SURE HOW TO PUT IT...
...BUT ISN'T THIS STRANGE ...?
STRANGE... HOW SO...?
THERE ARE HARDLY ANY MONSTERS AROUND.
AND IT'S BEEN TOO QUIET SINCE WE ENTERED THE NINTH FLOOR.
NOW THAT YOU MEN-TION IT...
I DON'T GET IT...
I FEEL TERRIBLE.
DO (BA-DUM)
DO
B-BELL-SAMA?
...LET'S GET TO THE TENTH FLOOR.
QUICKLY.

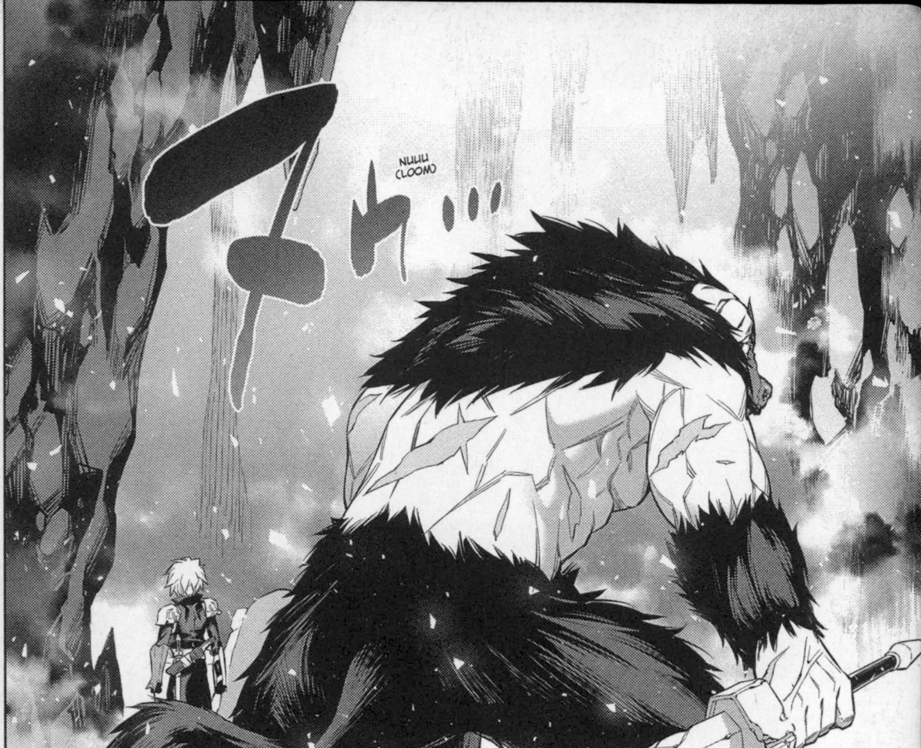
NUUU
(LOOM)
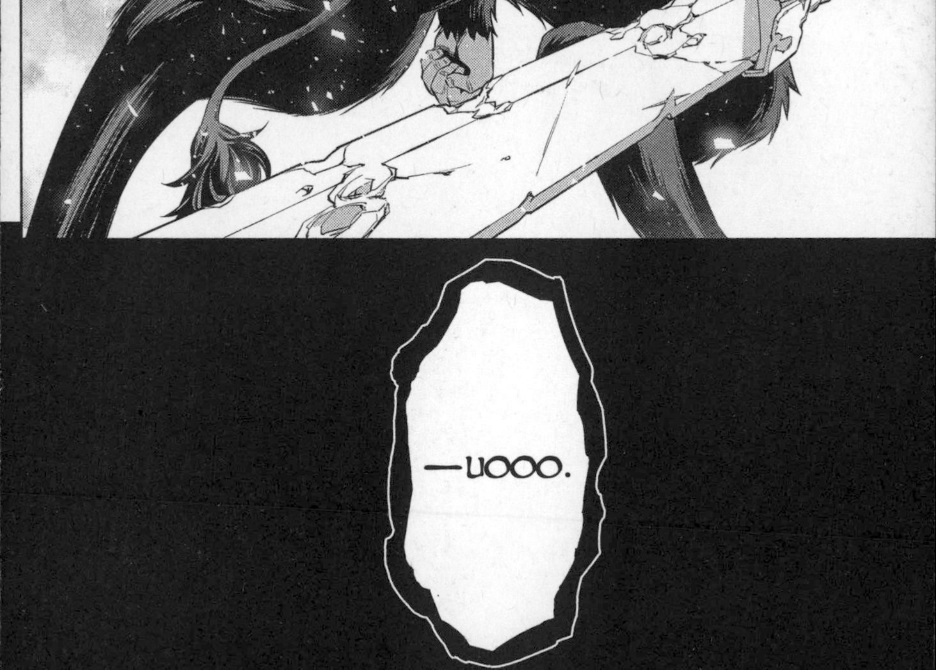
—UOOO.

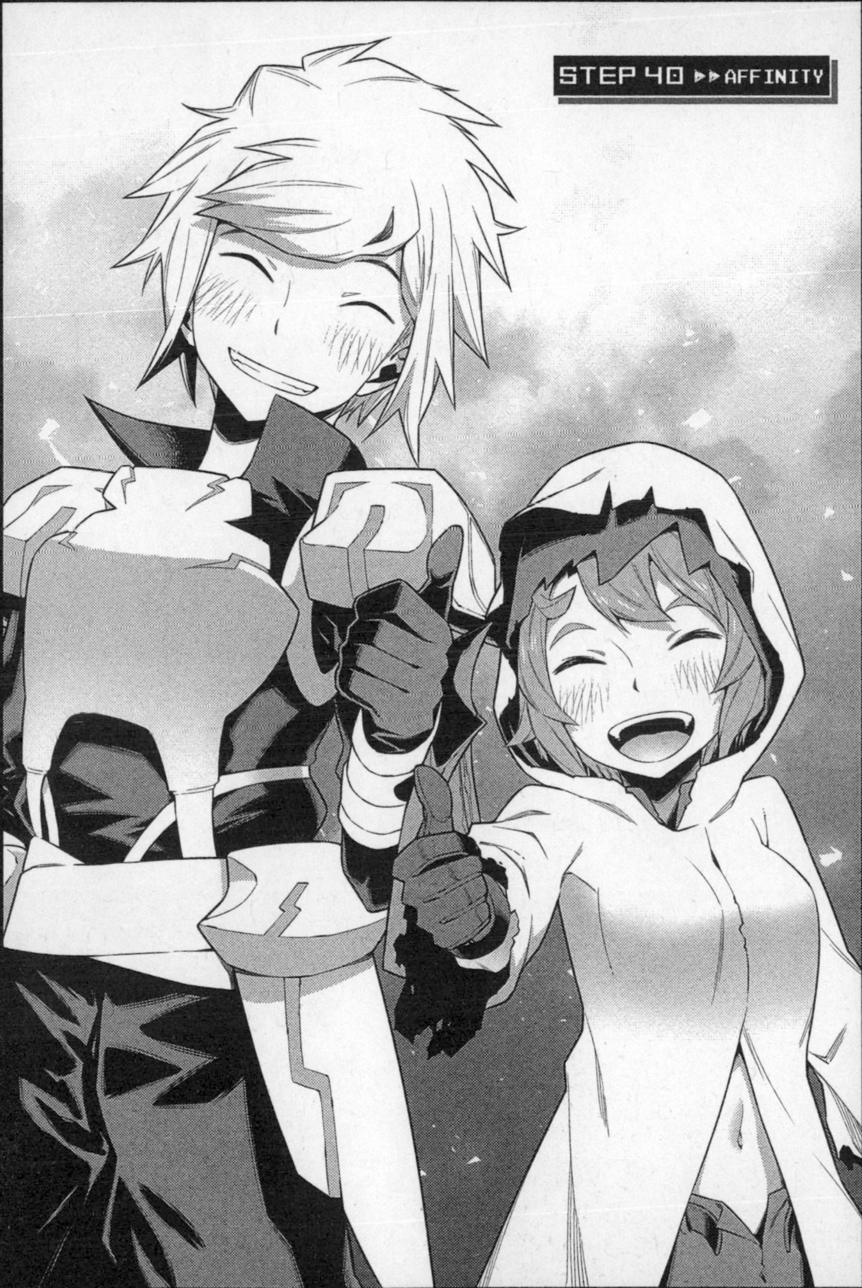
STEP 40 ▶▶ AFFINITY

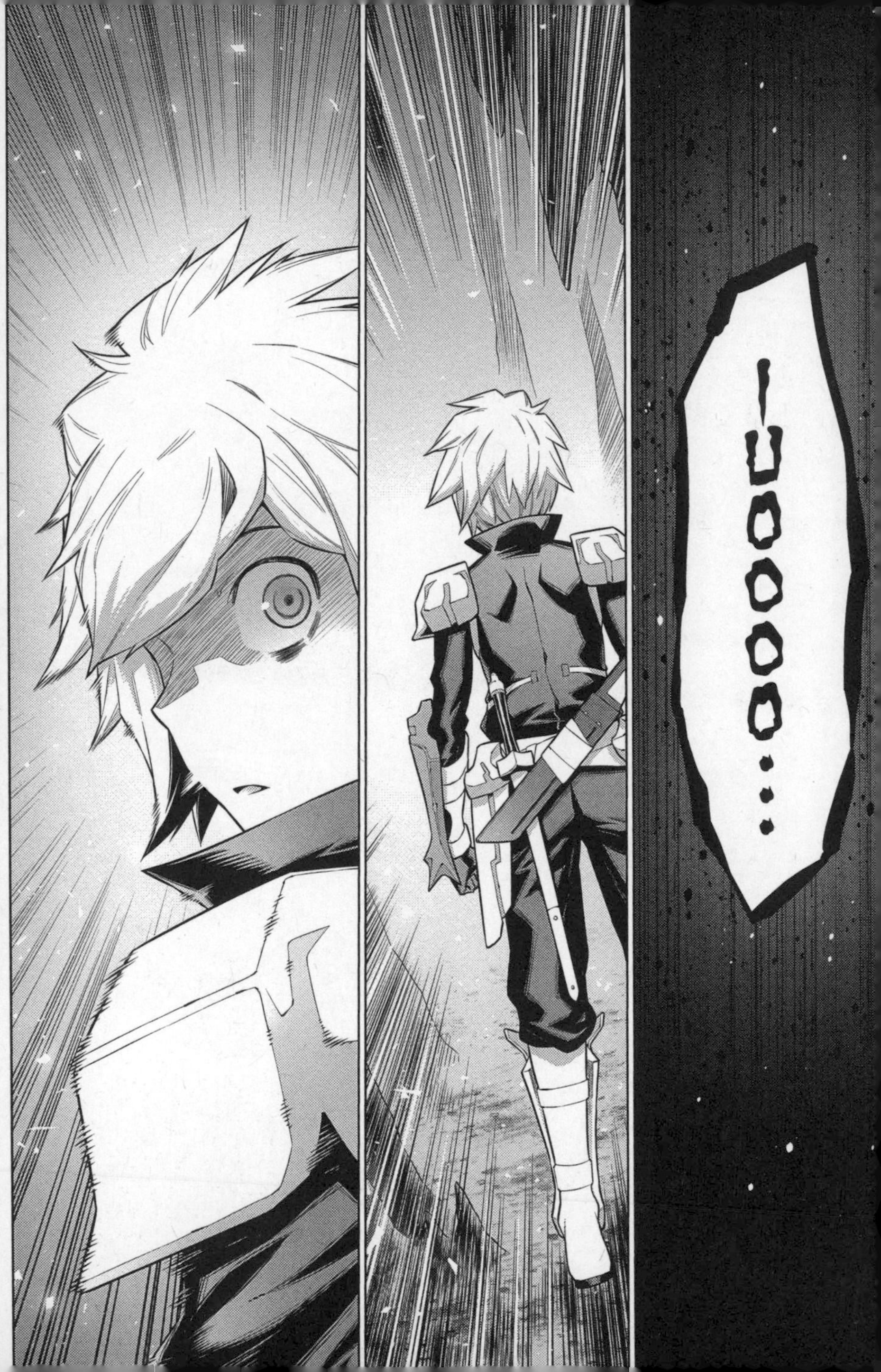
UOOOO...

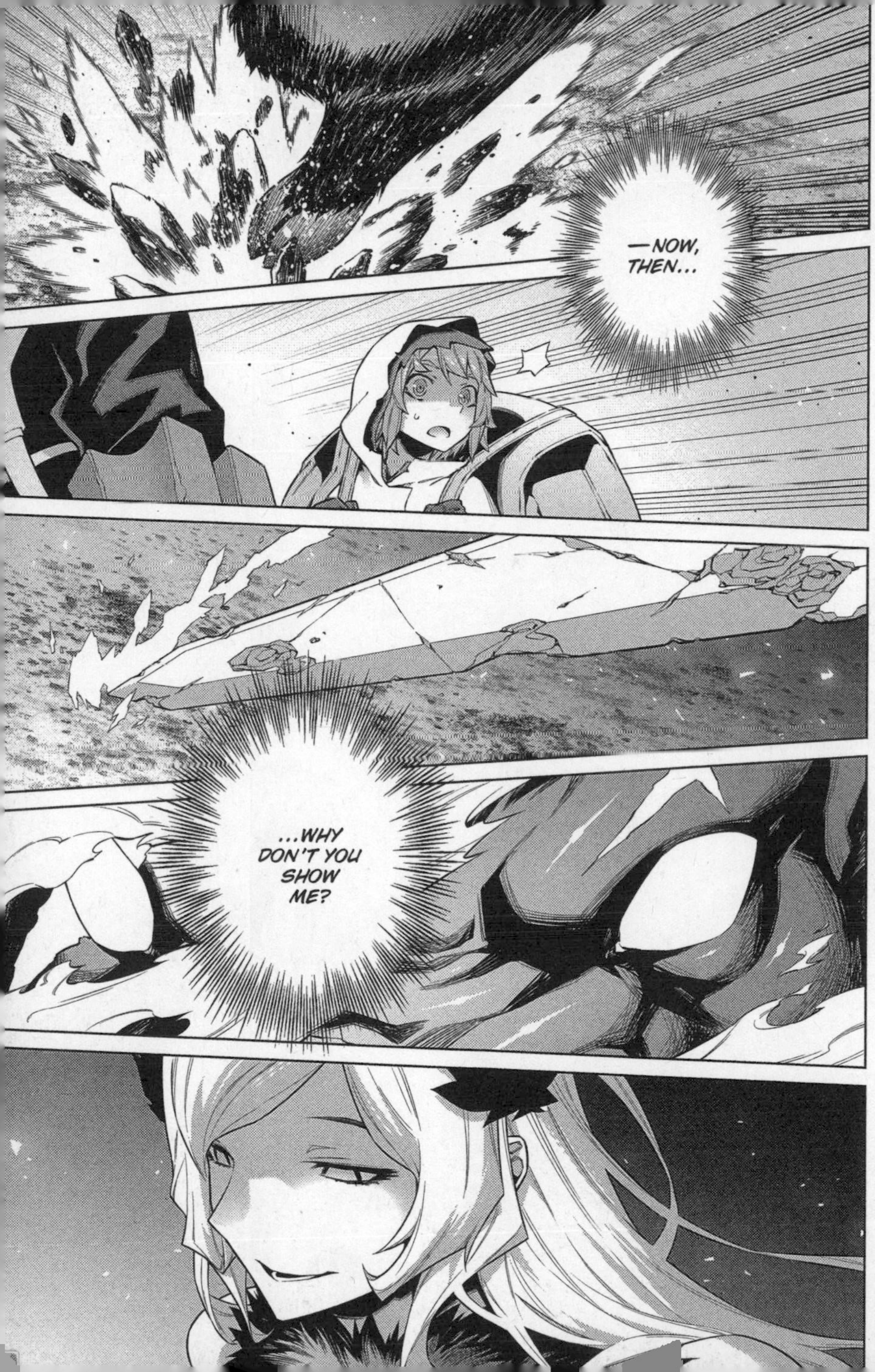
—NOW, THEN...
...WHY DON'T YOU SHOW ME?

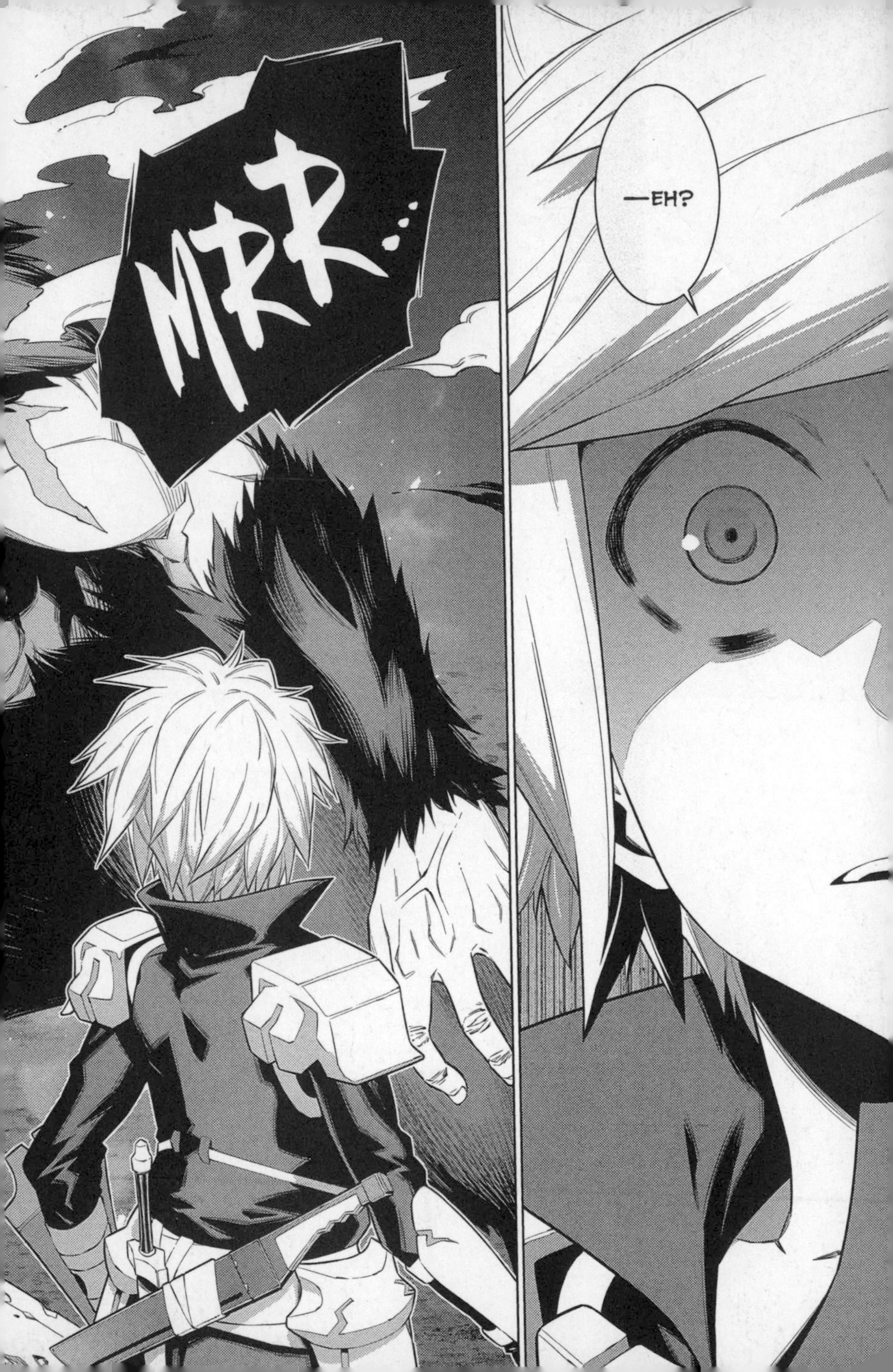
—EH?
MRR...

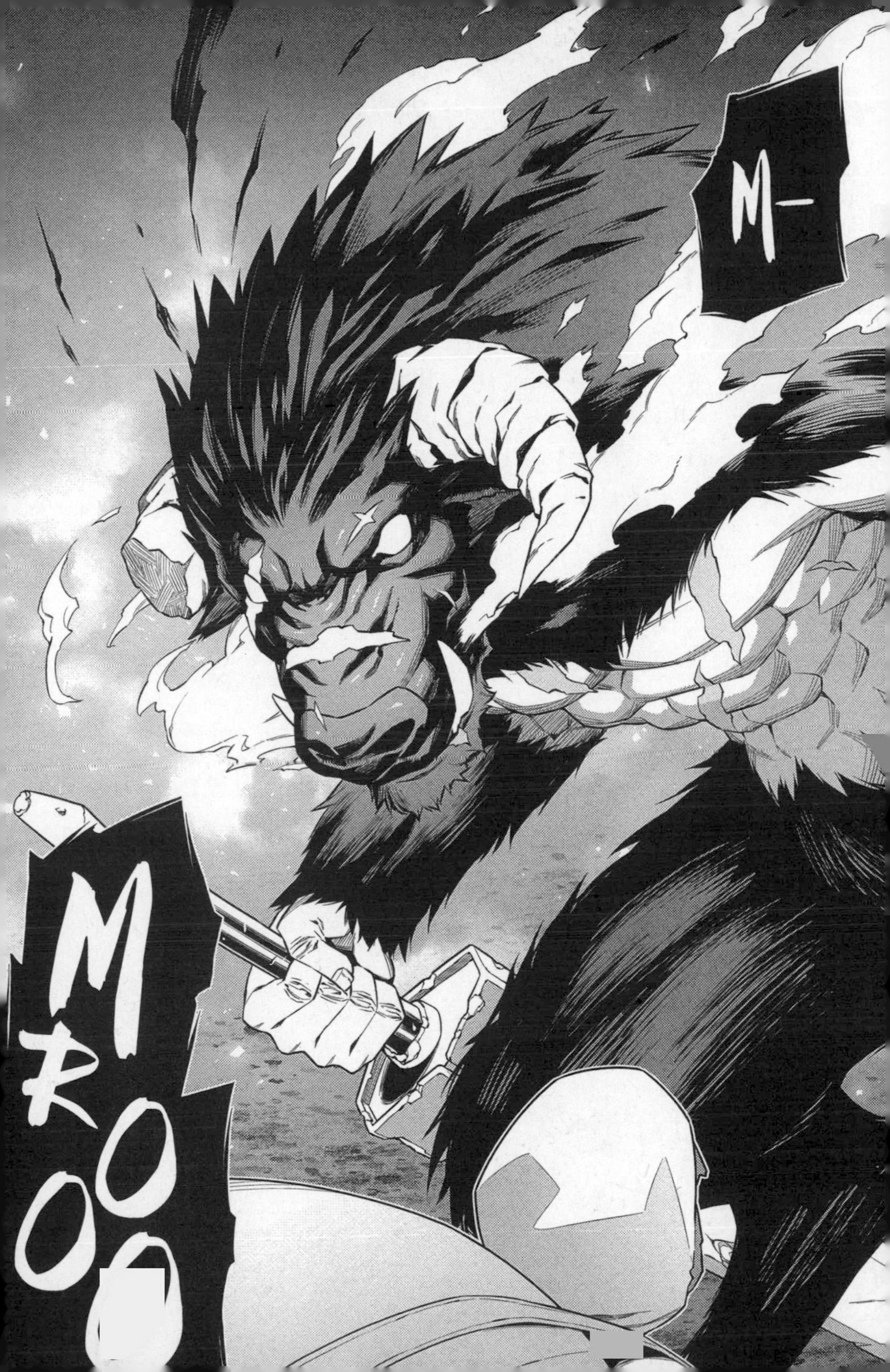
M—
MROOOO

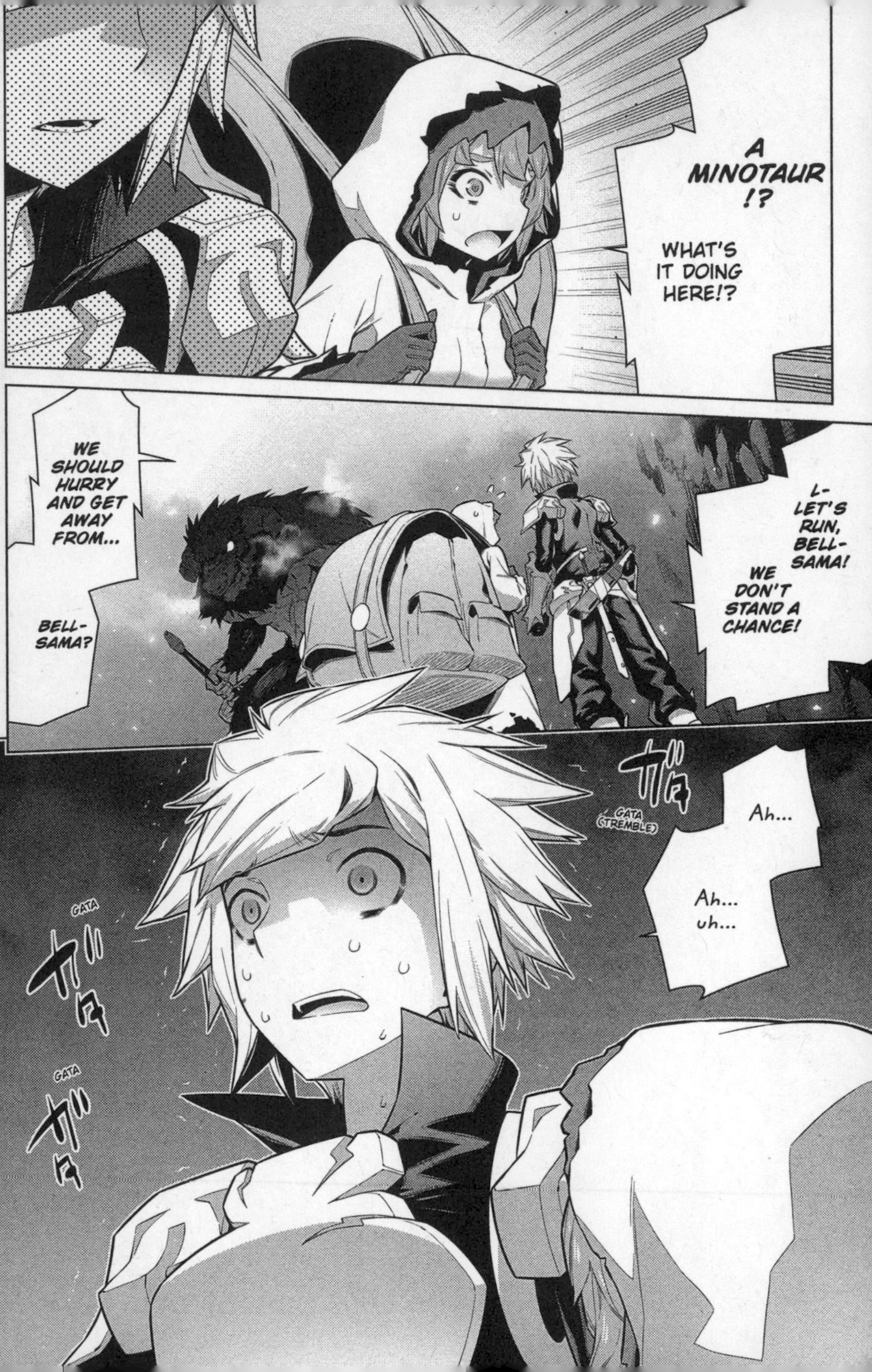
A MINOTAUR !?
WHAT'S IT DOING HERE!?
L-LET'S RUN, BELL-SAMA!
WE DON'T STAND A CHANCE!
WE SHOULD HURRY AND GET AWAY FROM...
BELL-SAMA?
GATA (TREMBLE)
Ah...
Ah... uh...
GATA
GATA

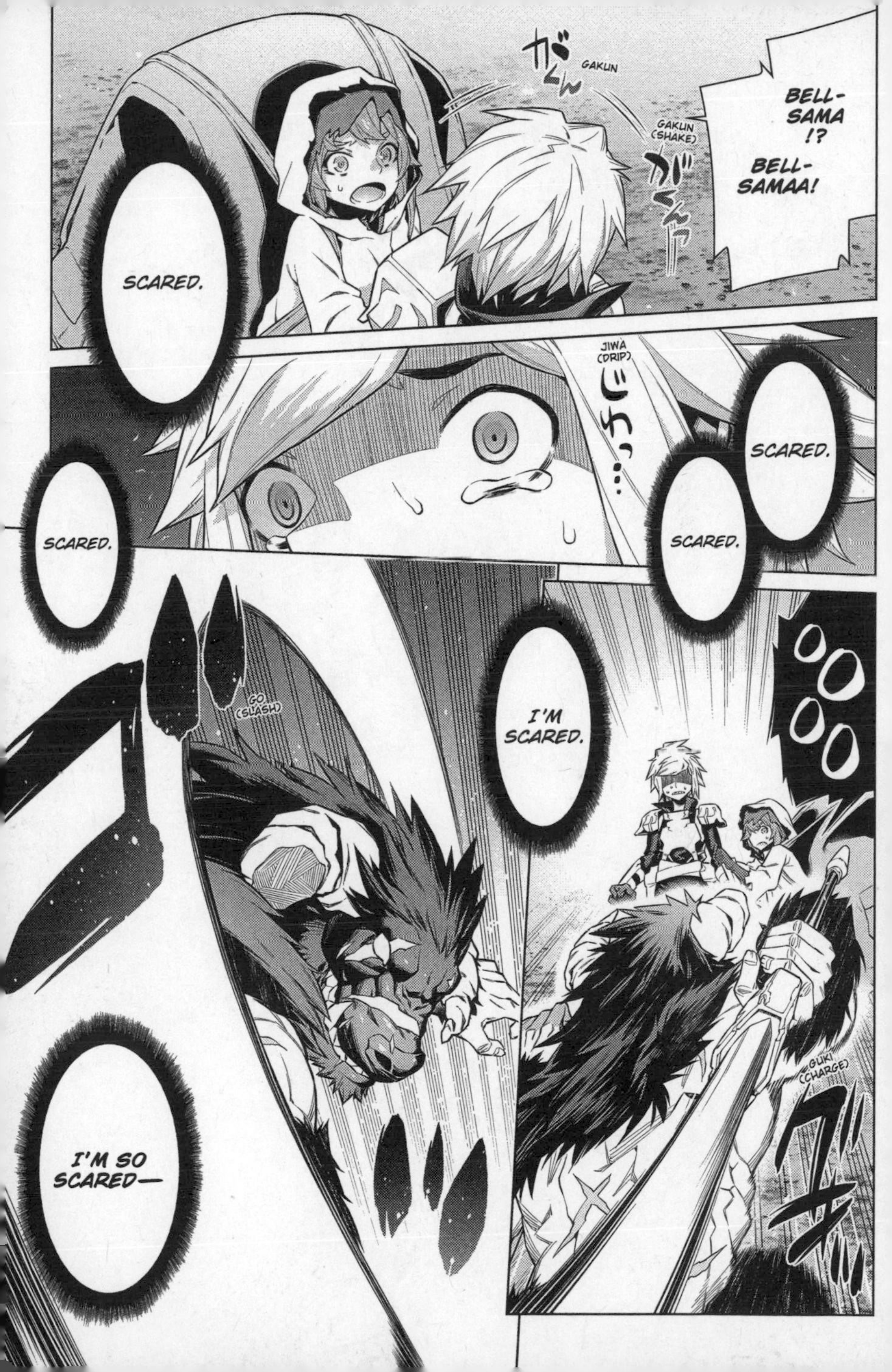

BELL-SAMA!?
BELL-SAMAA!
GAKUN (SHAKE)
がくん
GAKUN
がくん
SCARED.
SCARED.
JIWA (DRIP)
じわっ…
SCARED.
SCARED.
I'M SCARED.
GUKI (CHARGE)
GO (SLASH)
I'M SO SCARED—

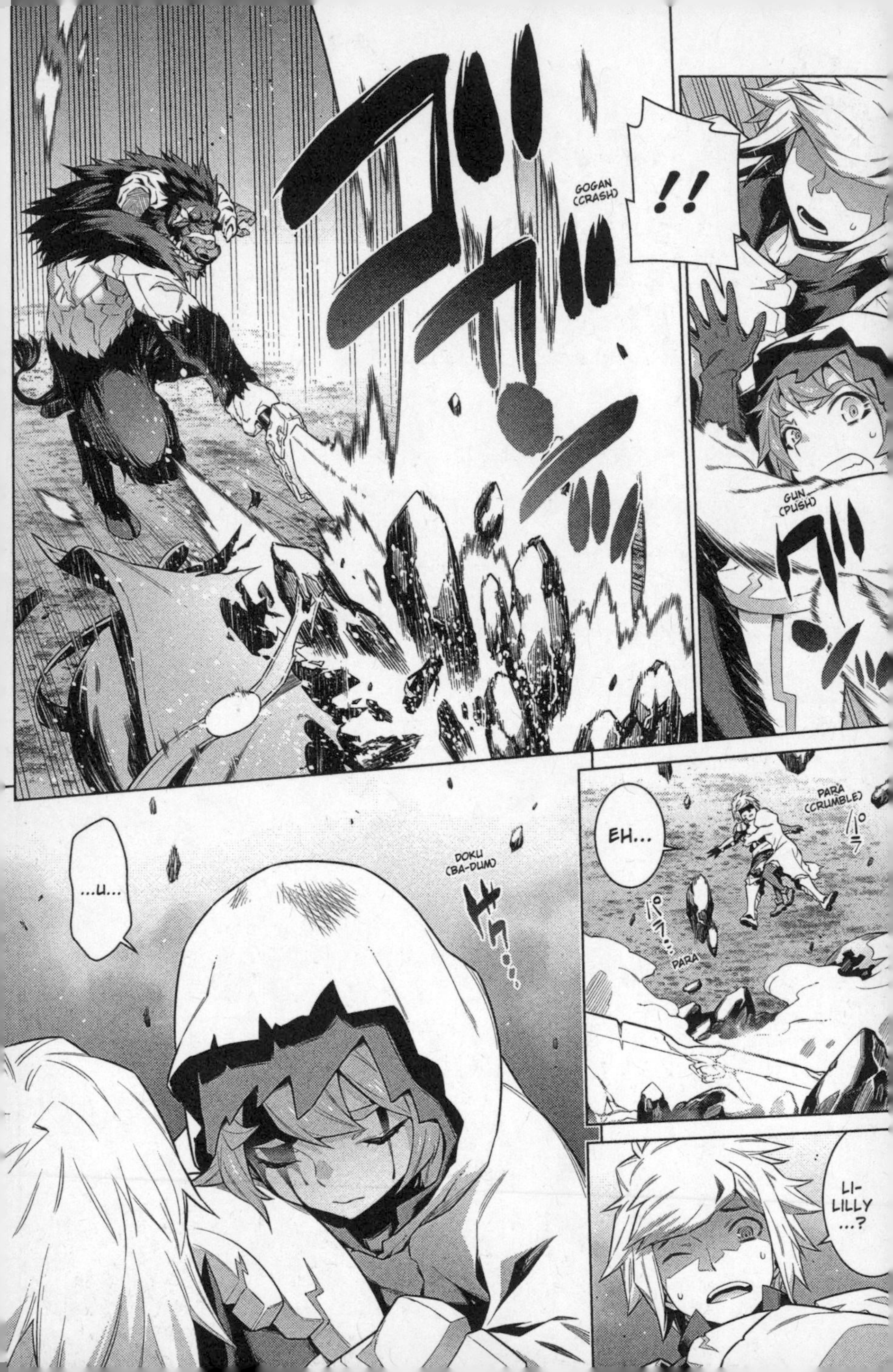
!!
GUN (PUSH)
GOGAN (CRASH)
PARA (CRUMBLE)
EH...
PARA
LI-LILLY...?
...U...
DOKU (BA-DUM)

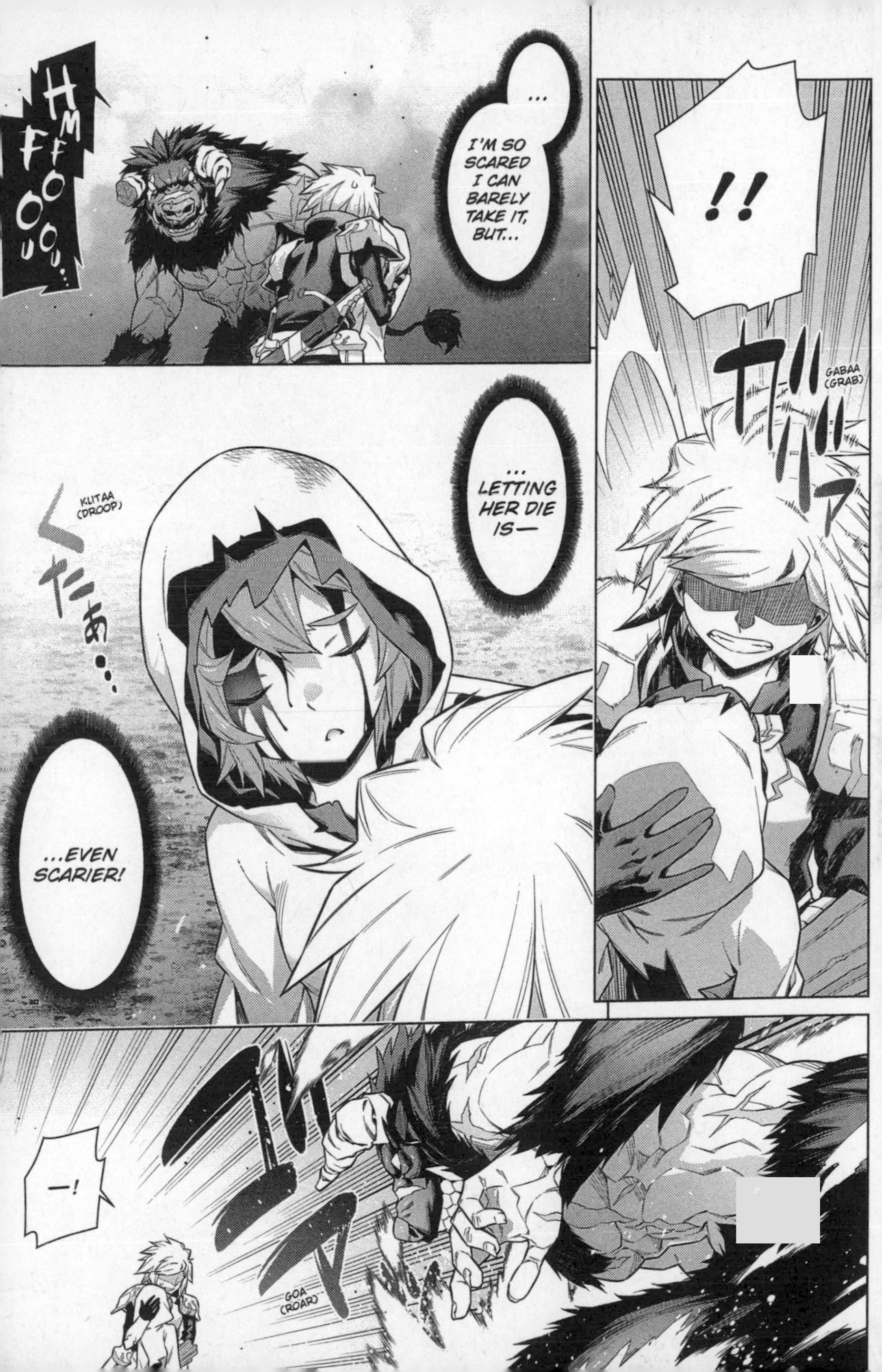
!!
GABAA (GRAB)
... I'M SO SCARED I CAN BARELY TAKE IT, BUT...
HMFFOOOOU...
... LETTING HER DIE IS—
KUTAA (DROOP)
...EVEN SCARIER!
GOA (ROAR)
—!

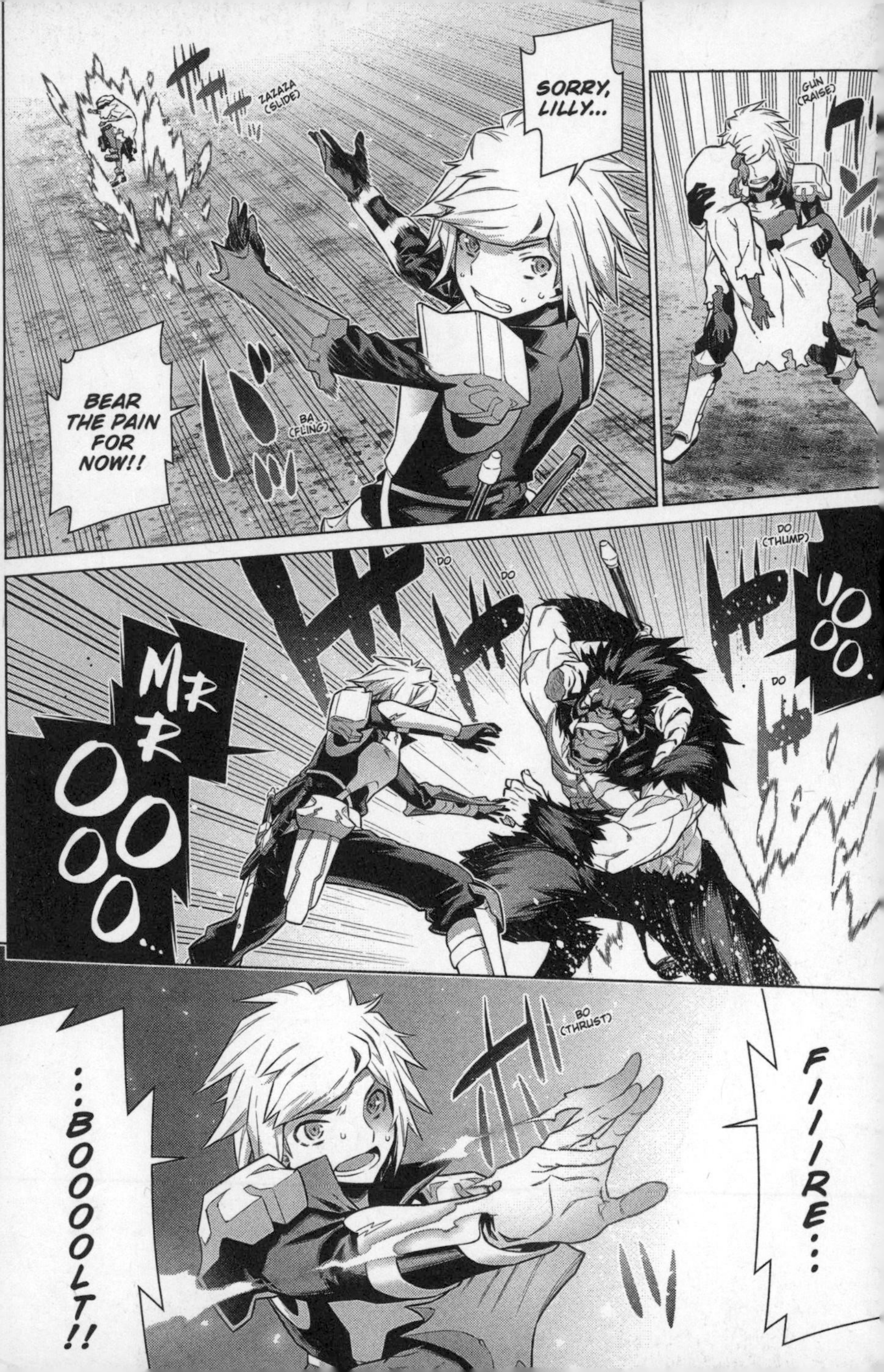

GUN (RAISE)
SORRY, LILLY...
ZAZAZA (SLIDE)
BEAR THE PAIN FOR NOW!!
BA (FLING)
DO (THUMP)
UOOO
DO
DO
DO
MRROOOOO...
FIIIRE...
BO (THRUST)
...BOOOOOLT!!

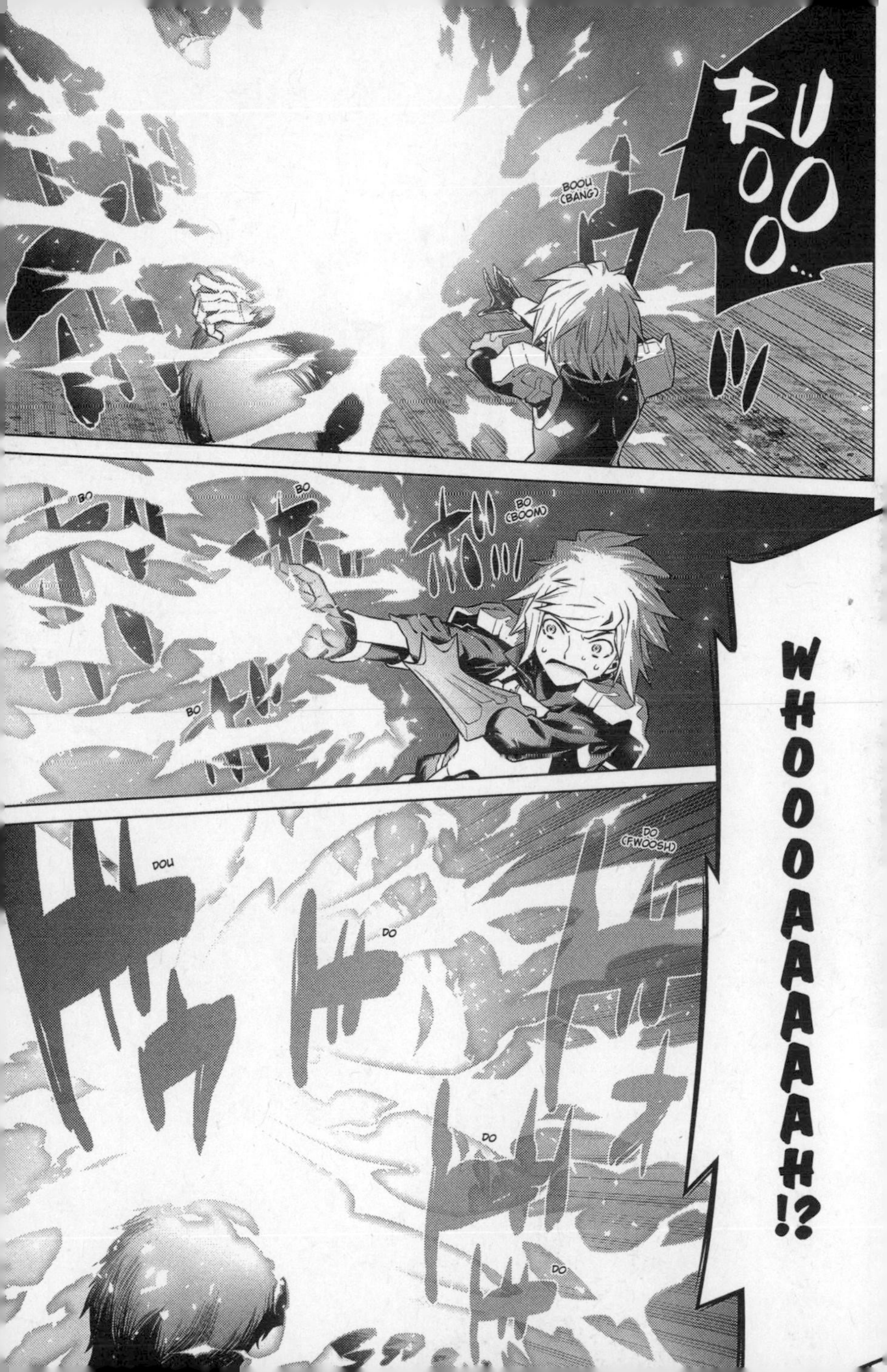
RUOOO...
BOOU (BANG)
WHOOOOAAAAAH!?
BO (BOOM)
BO
BO
BO
DO (FWOOSH)
DOU
DO
DO
DO

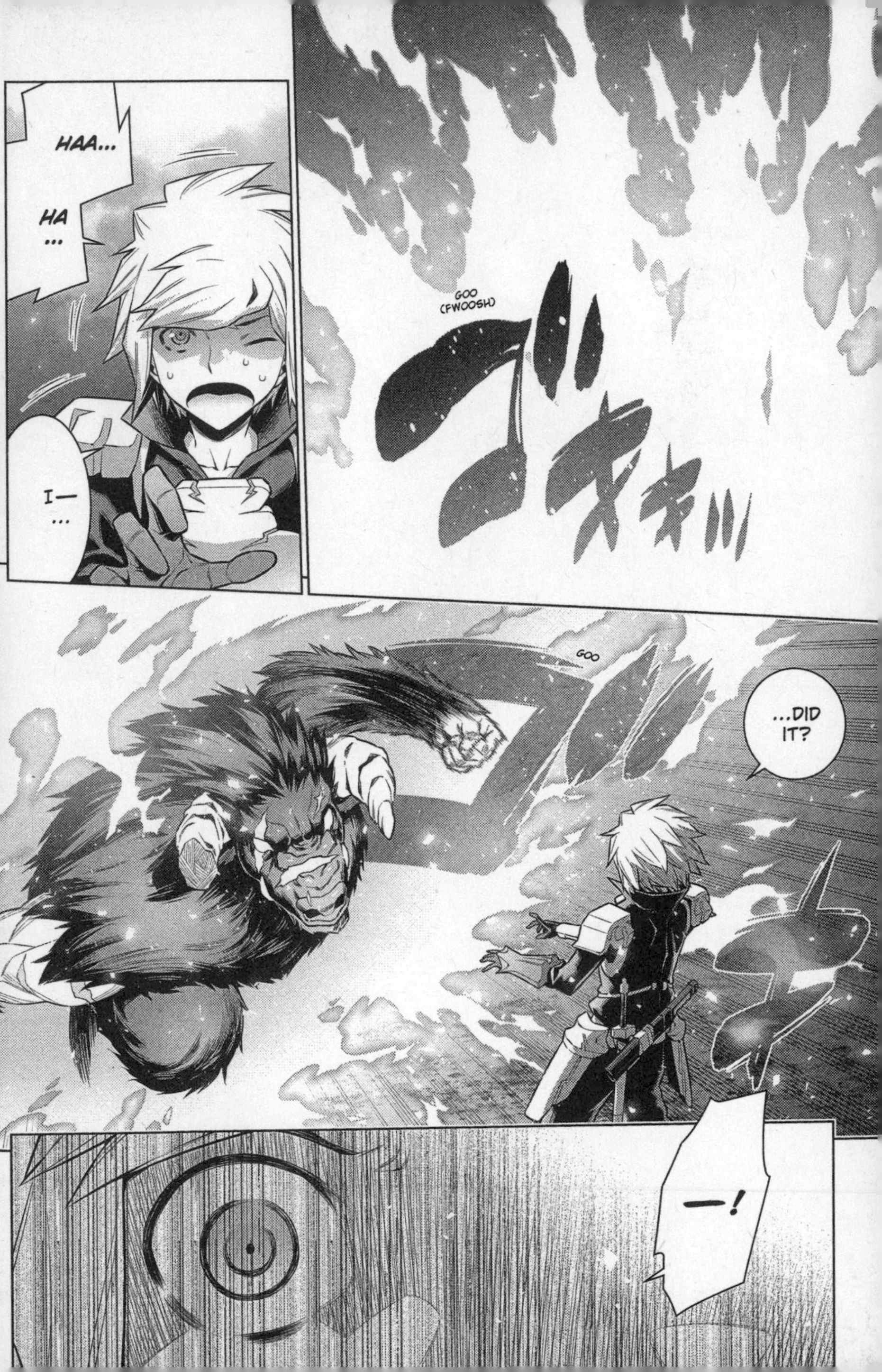
GOO (FWOOSH)
HAA...
HA...
I—...
GOO
...DID IT?
—!

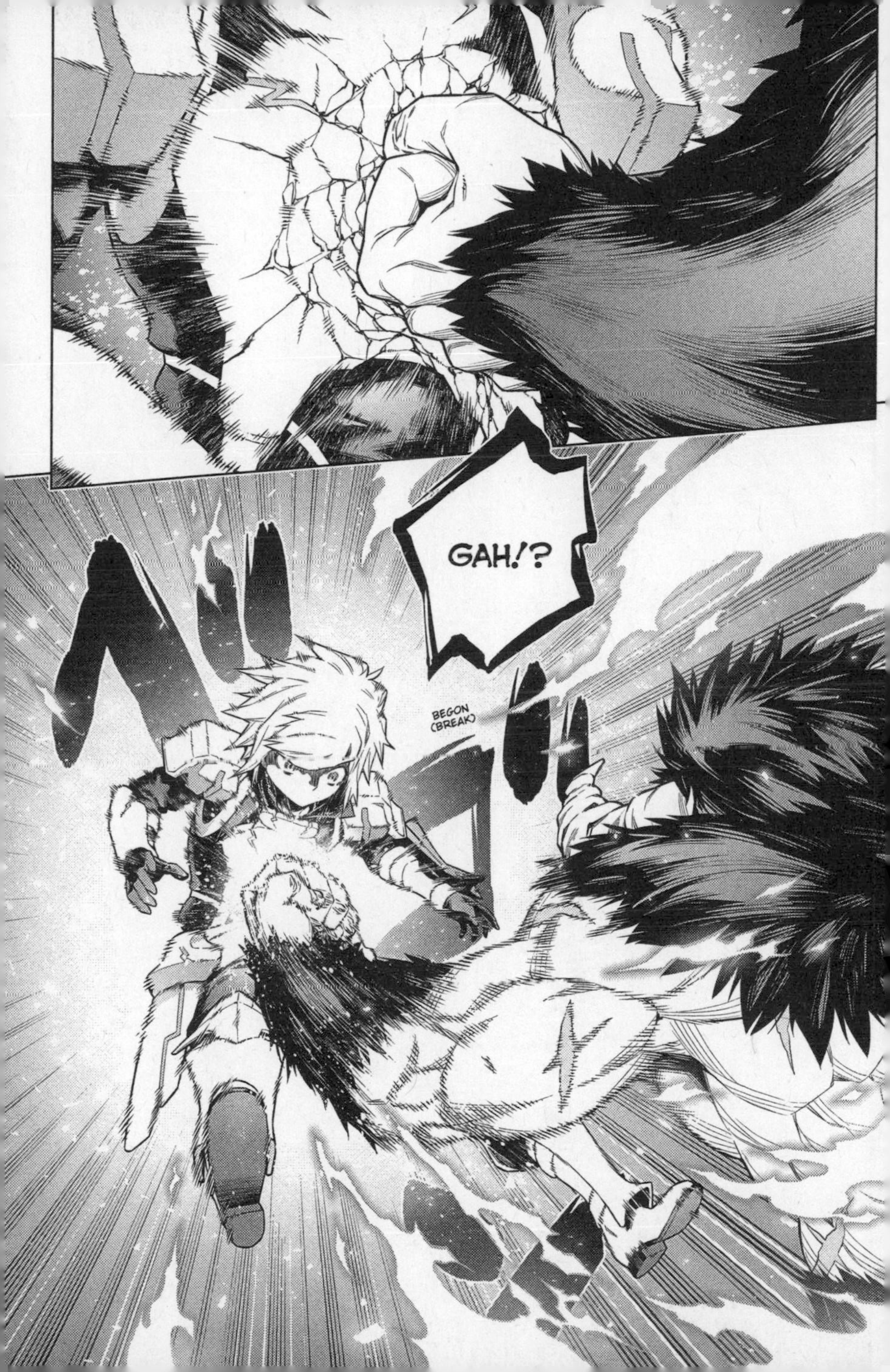
GAH!?
BEGON
(BREAK)

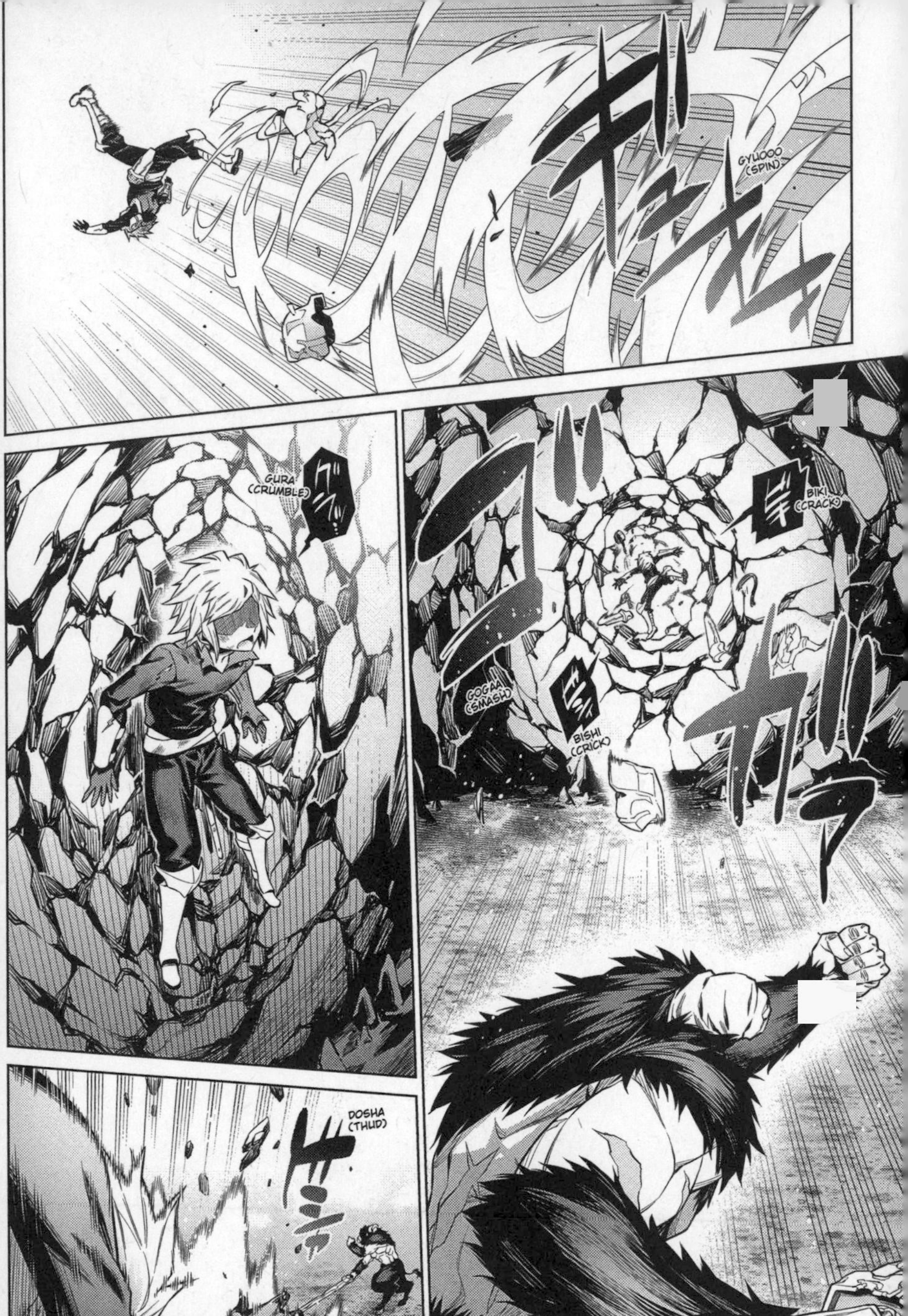
GYUOOO (SPIN)
BIKI (CRACK)
GOGAA (SMASH)
BISHI (CRICK)
GURA (CRUMBLE)
DOSHA (THUD)

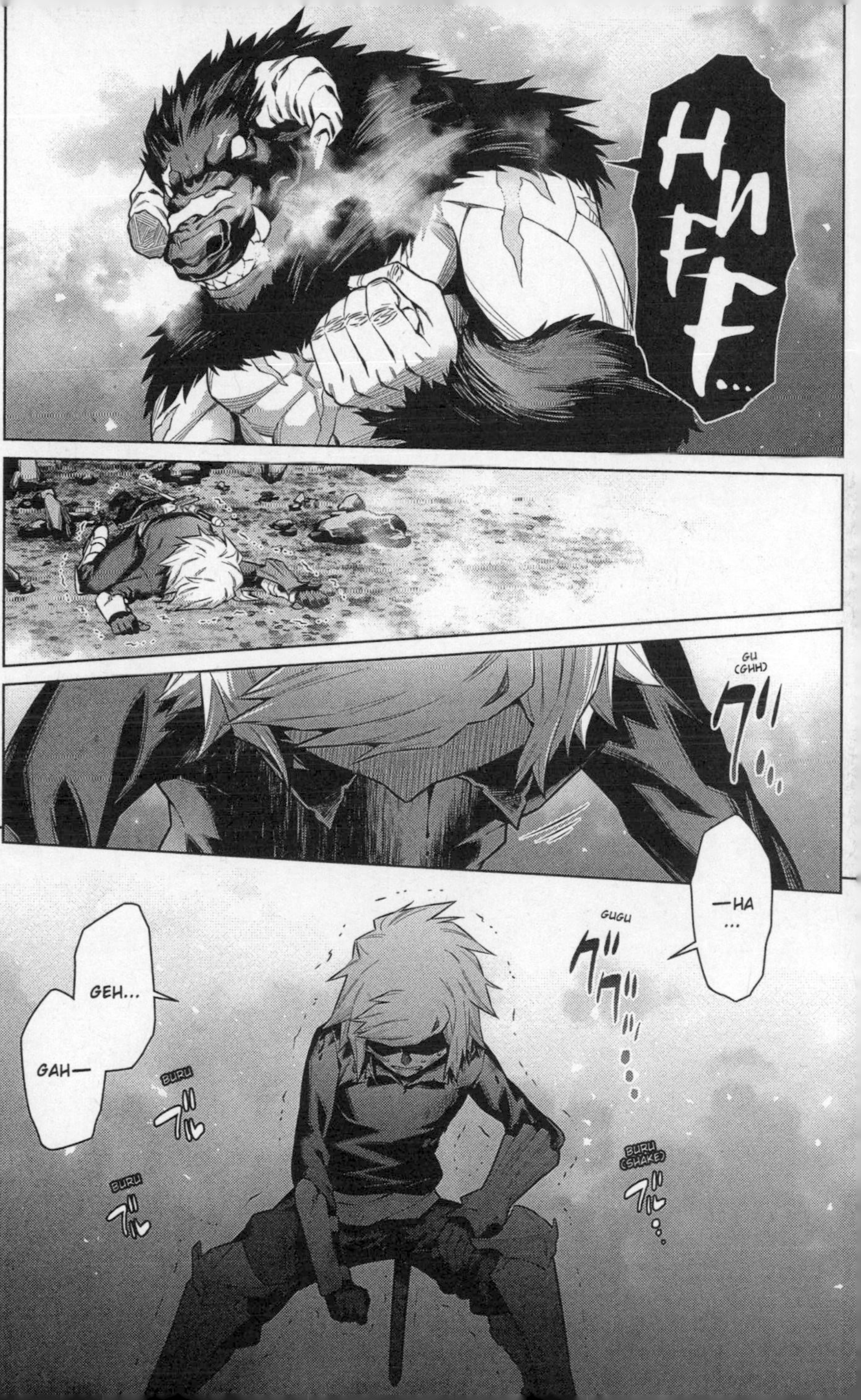
Hufff...
GU (GHH)
グ...
—HA...
GUGU
ググ...
GEH...
GAH—
BURU (SHAKE)
ブル...
BURU
ブル
BURU
ブル

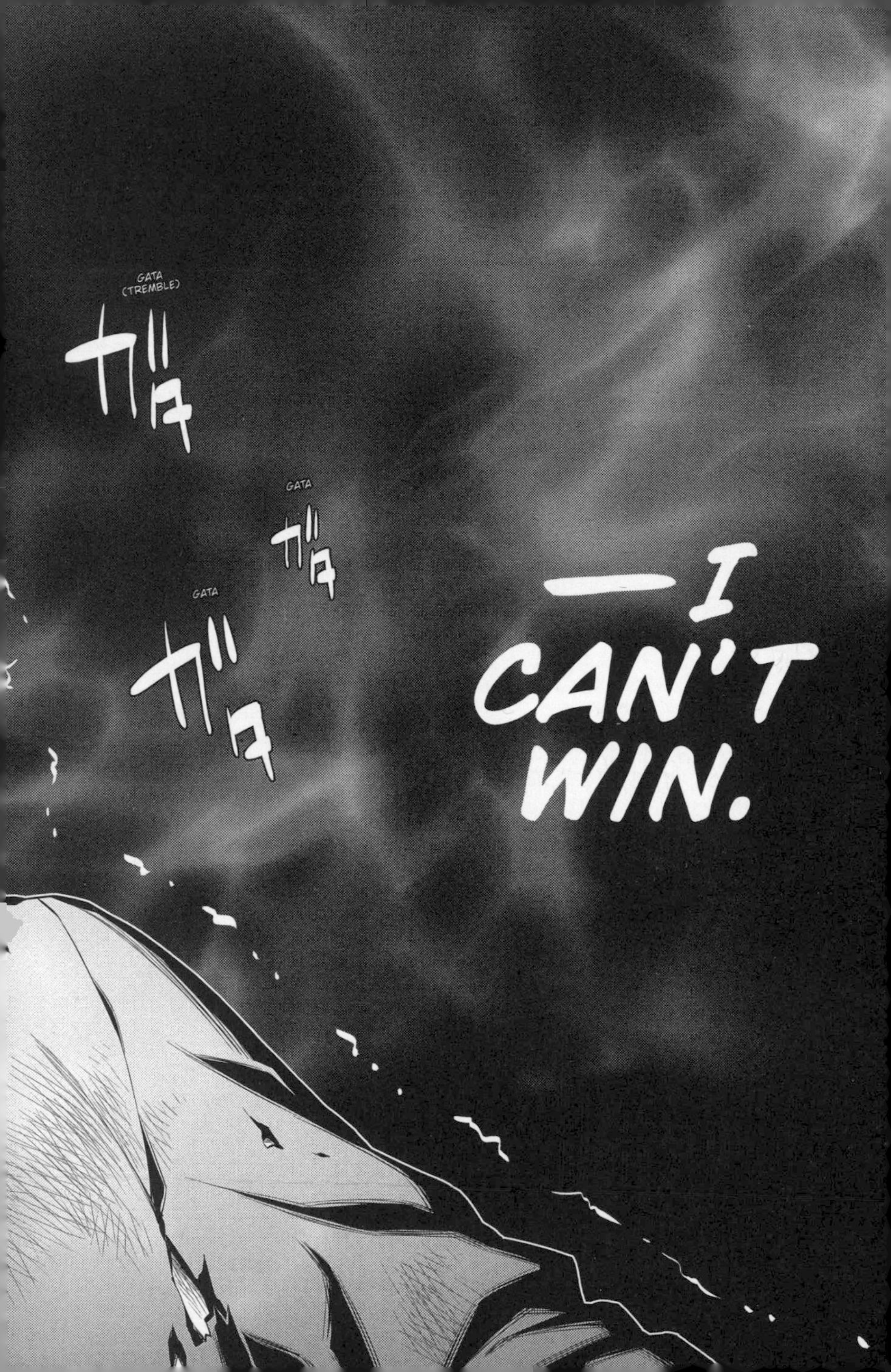
GATA (TREMBLE)
ガタ
GATA
ガタ
GATA
ガタ
—I CAN'T WIN.

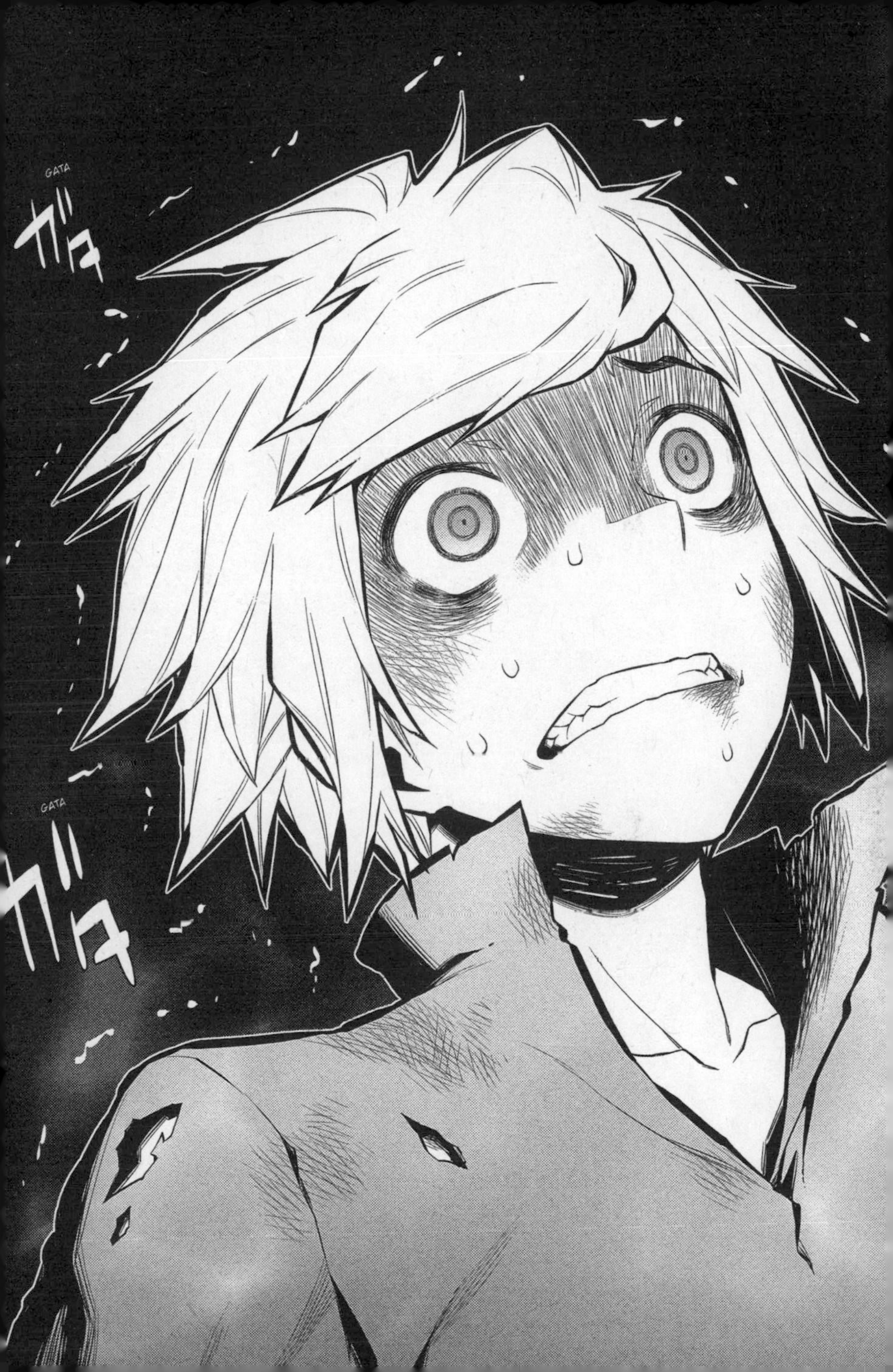
GATA
ガタ
GATA
ガタ

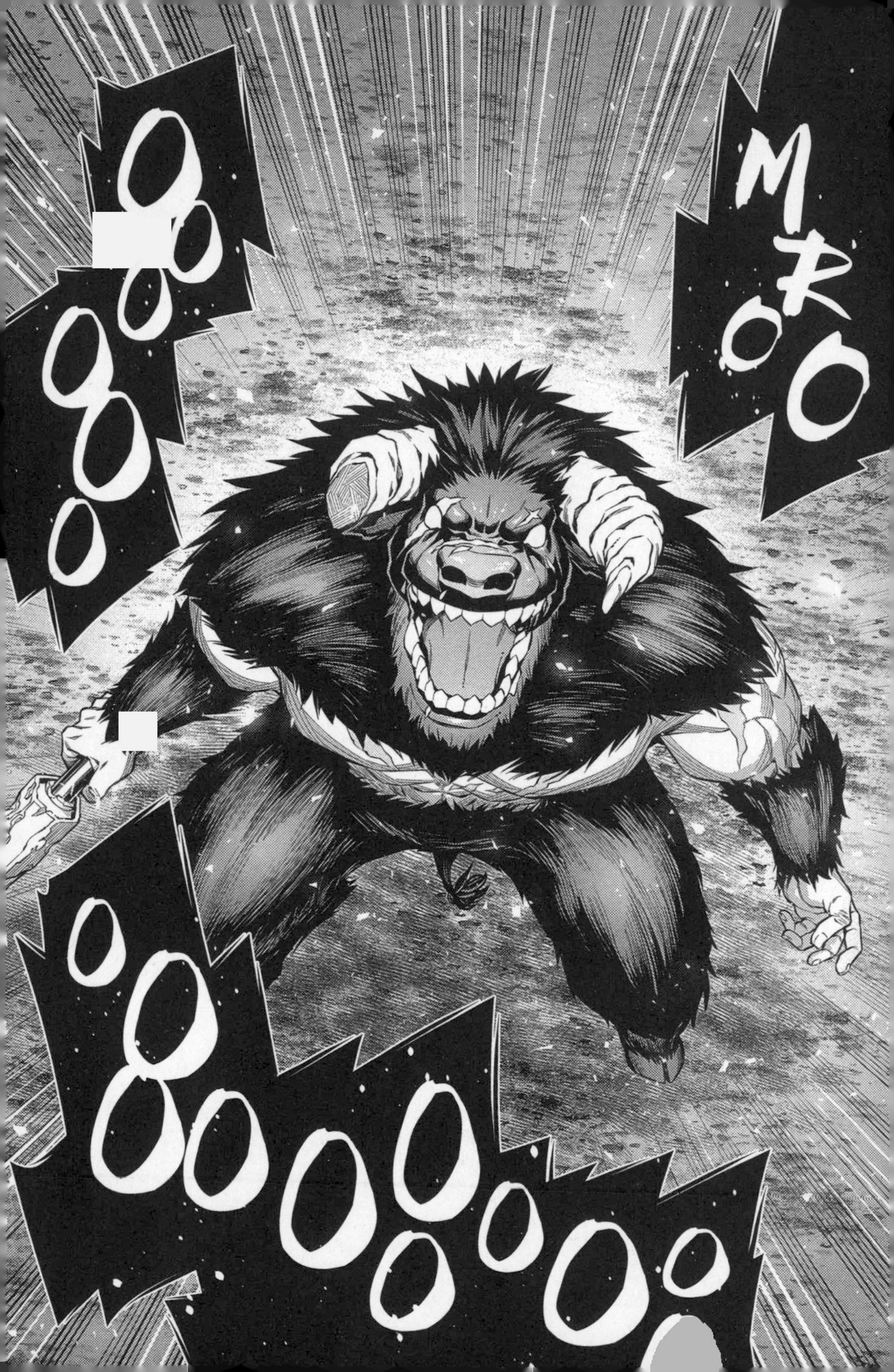
MROO
OOOOOOOOO
OOOOOOOOOOOOOO

IS it WRONG to TRY to PiCK UP GiRLS in A DUNGEON?

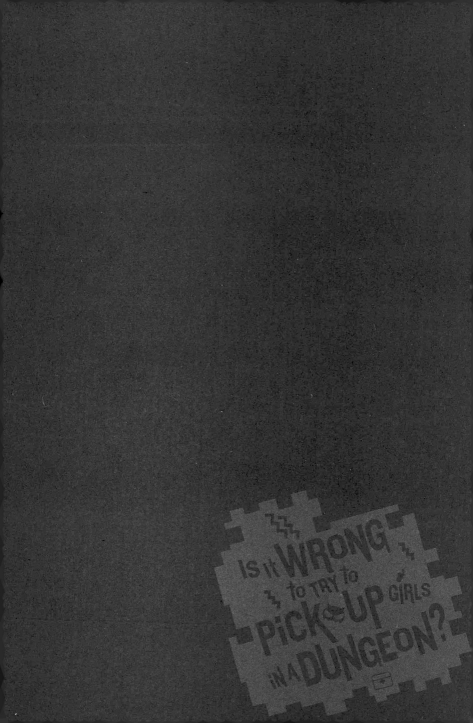

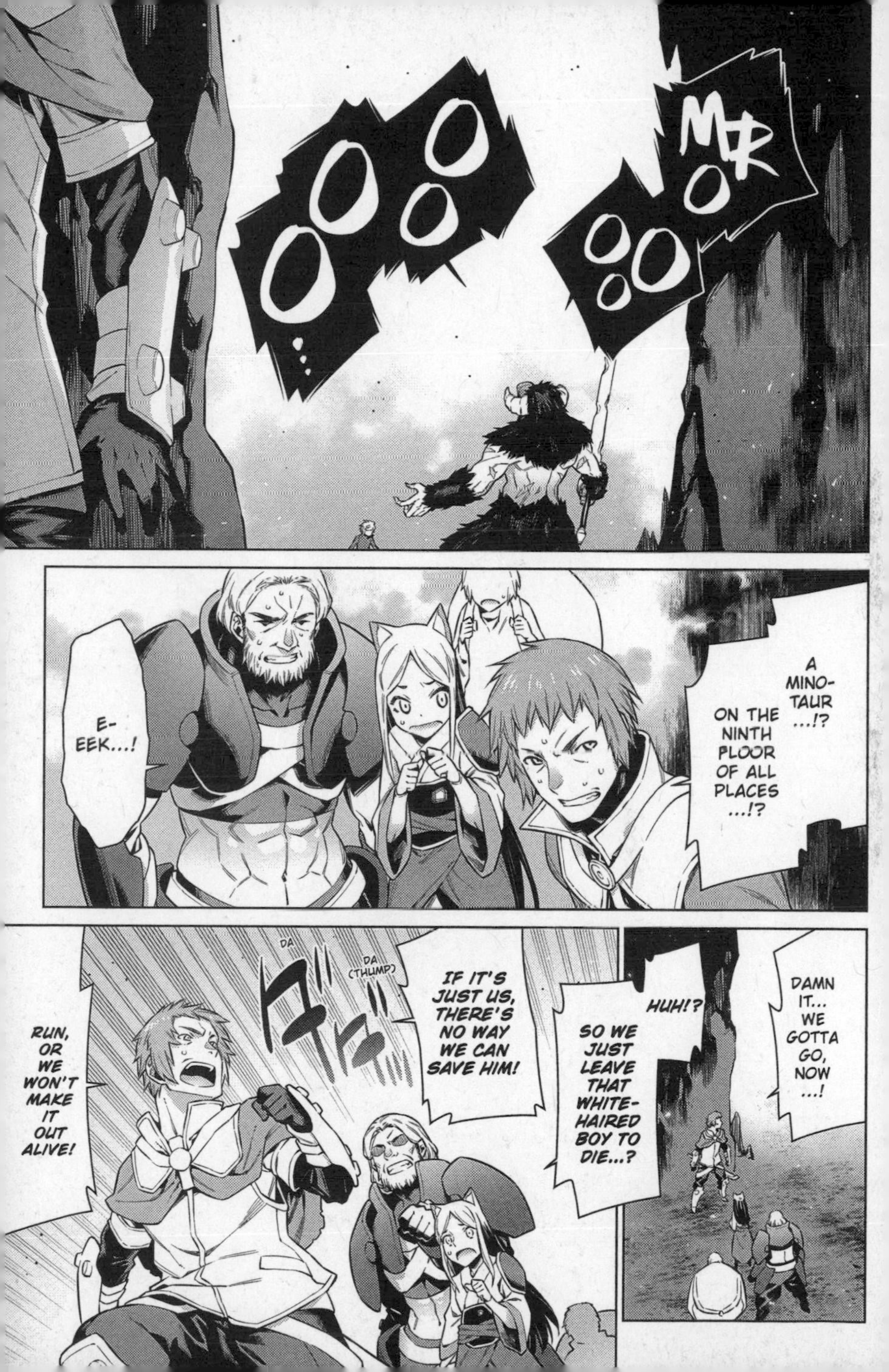
MOOOOO
OOOOO...
A MINOTAUR...!?
ON THE NINTH FLOOR OF ALL PLACES...!?
E-EEK...!
DAMN IT... WE GOTTA GO, NOW...!
HUH!?
SO WE JUST LEAVE THAT WHITE-HAIRED BOY TO DIE...?
IF IT'S JUST US, THERE'S NO WAY WE CAN SAVE HIM!
DA
DA (THUMP)
RUN, OR WE WON'T MAKE IT OUT ALIVE!

STEP 41 ▶▶THE MAKING O A HERO

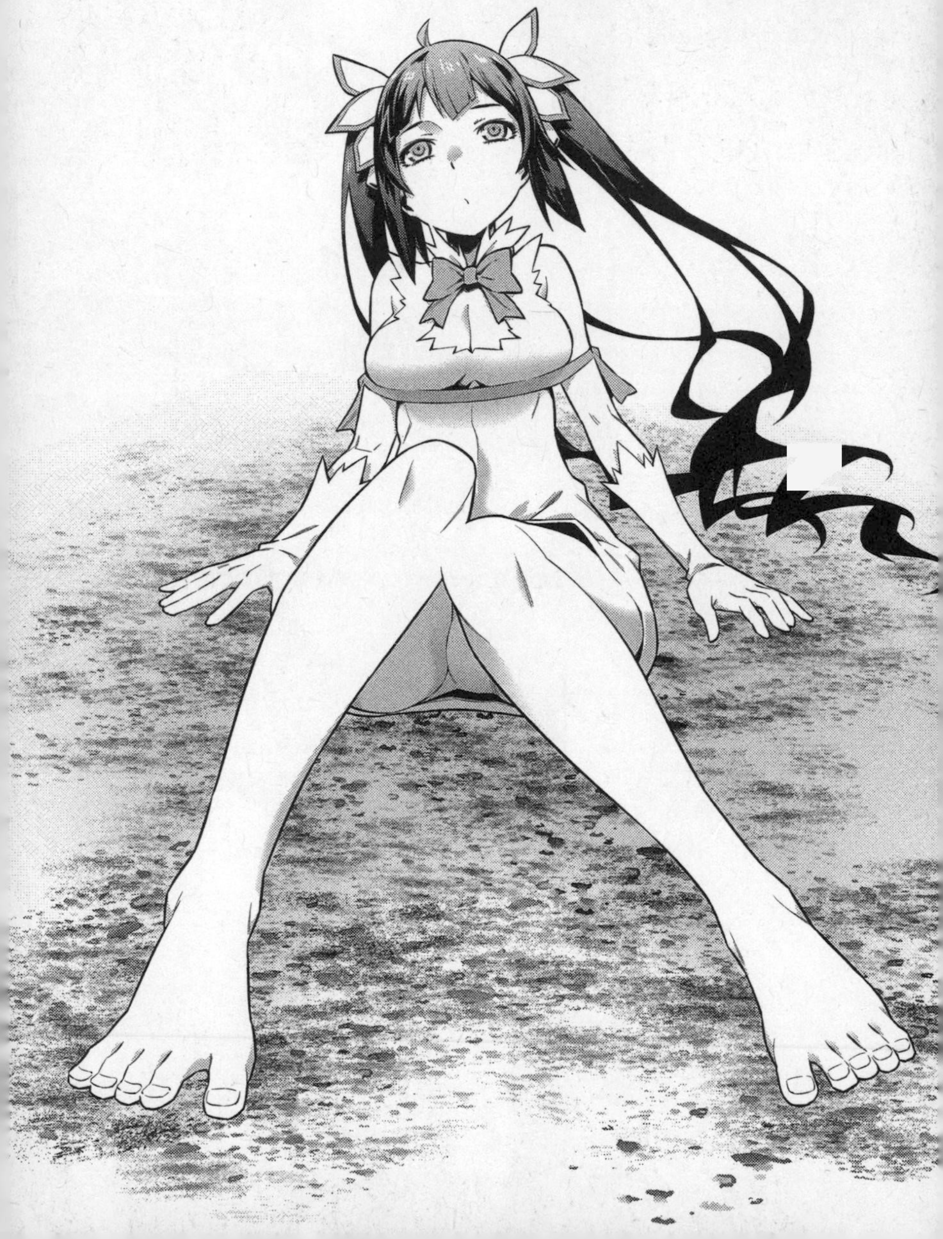

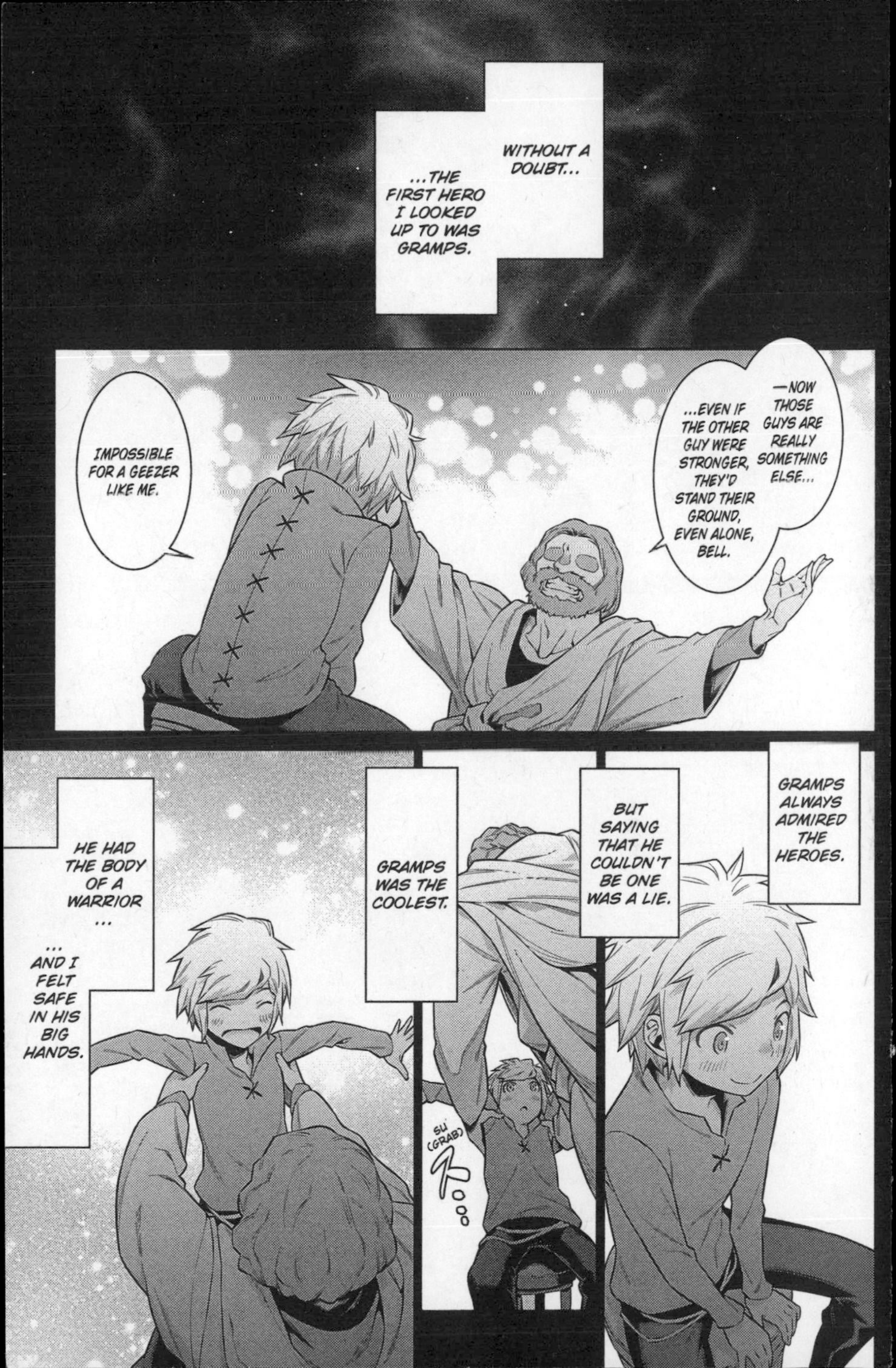
WITHOUT A DOUBT...
...THE FIRST HERO I LOOKED UP TO WAS GRAMPS.
—NOW THOSE GUYS ARE REALLY SOMETHING ELSE...
...EVEN IF THE OTHER GUY WERE STRONGER, THEY'D STAND THEIR GROUND, EVEN ALONE, BELL.
IMPOSSIBLE FOR A GEEZER LIKE ME.
GRAMPS ALWAYS ADMIRED THE HEROES.
BUT SAYING THAT HE COULDN'T BE ONE WAS A LIE.
GRAMPS WAS THE COOLEST.
SU (GRAB)
HE HAD THE BODY OF A WARRIOR...
...AND I FELT SAFE IN HIS BIG HANDS.

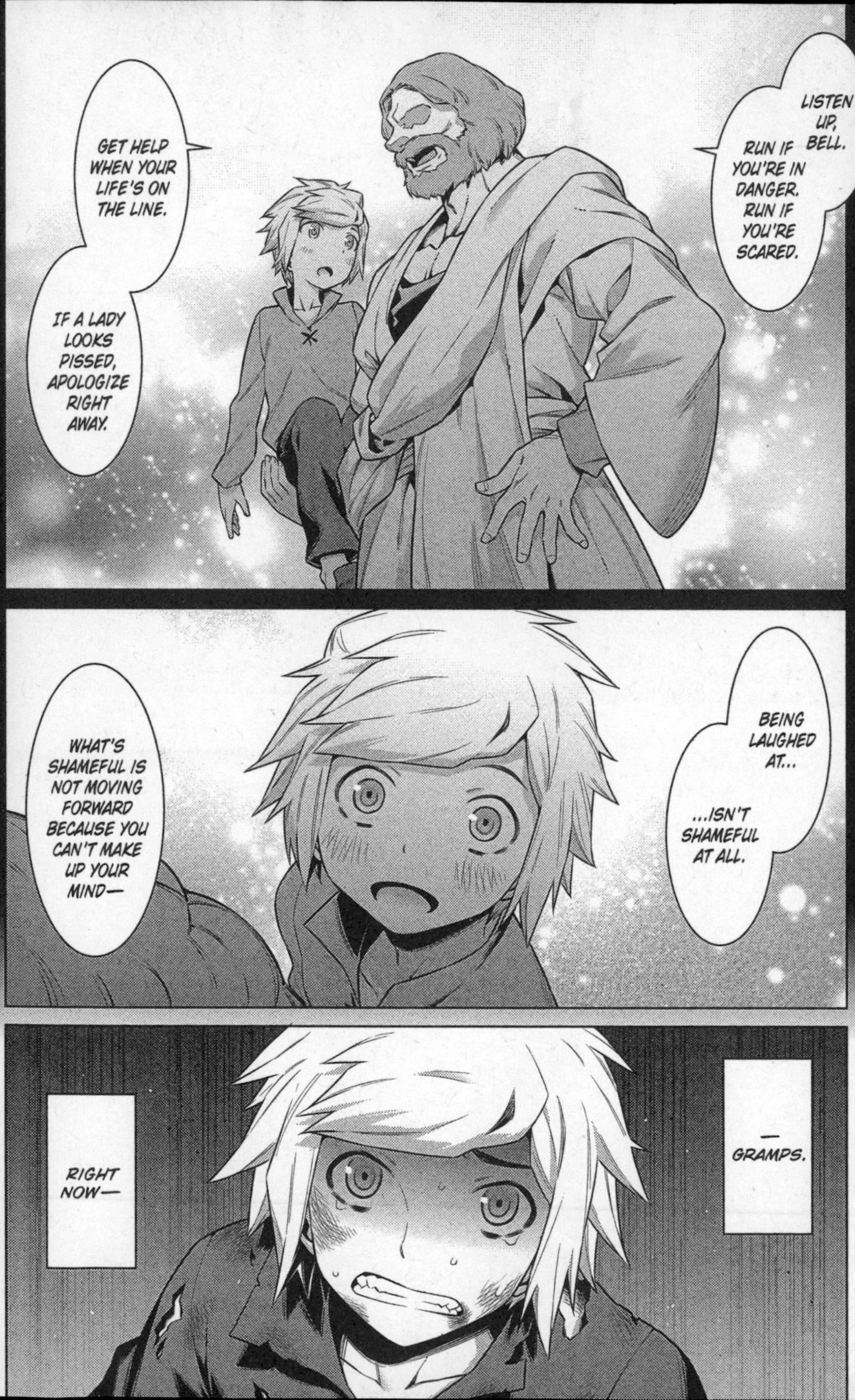
LISTEN UP, BELL.
RUN IF YOU'RE IN DANGER. RUN IF YOU'RE SCARED.
GET HELP WHEN YOUR LIFE'S ON THE LINE.
IF A LADY LOOKS PISSED, APOLOGIZE RIGHT AWAY.
BEING LAUGHED AT...
...ISN'T SHAMEFUL AT ALL.
WHAT'S SHAMEFUL IS NOT MOVING FORWARD BECAUSE YOU CAN'T MAKE UP YOUR MIND—
—GRAMPS.
RIGHT NOW—

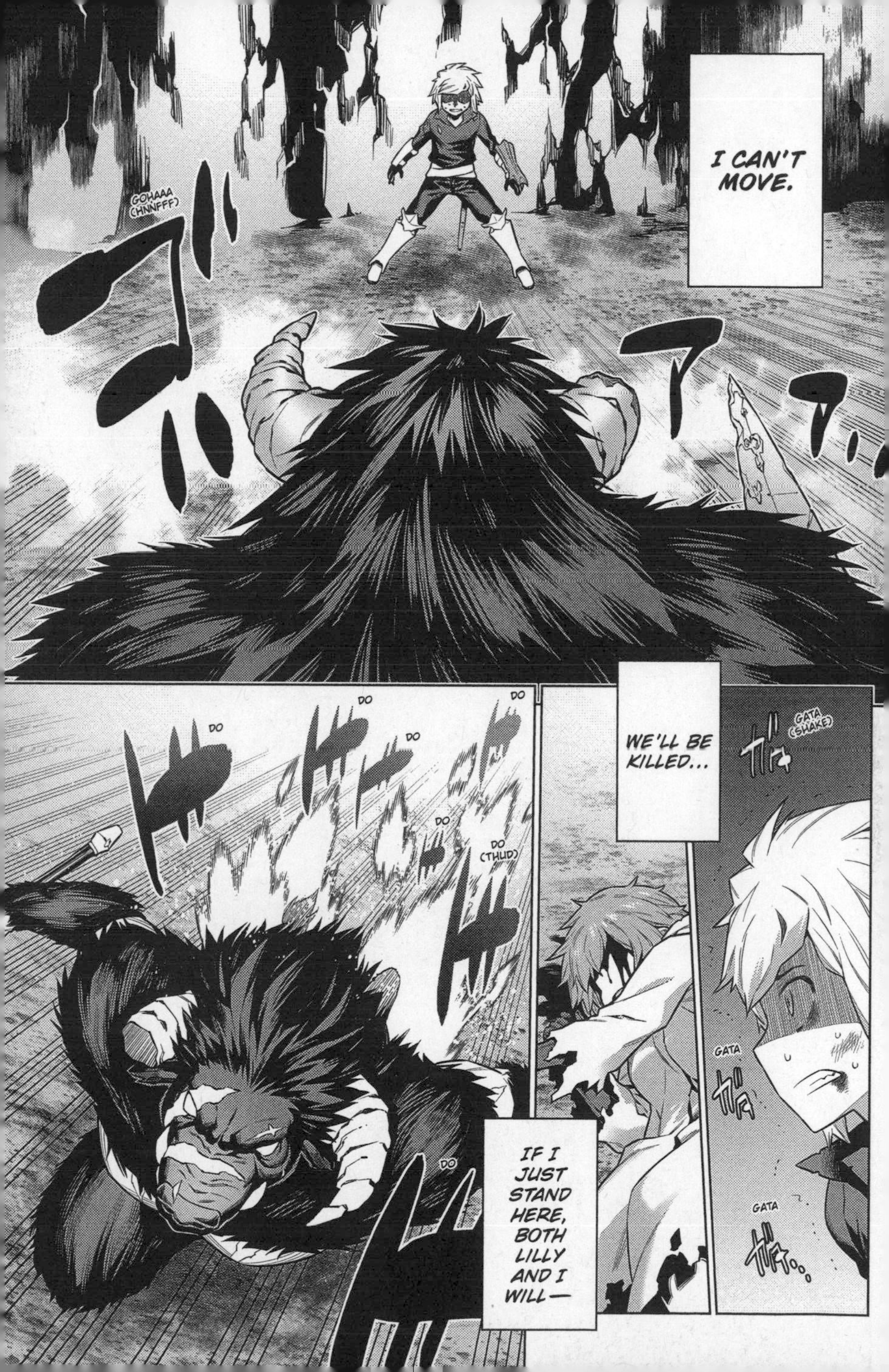
I CAN'T MOVE.
GOHAAA (HNNFFF)
WE'LL BE KILLED...
GATA (SHAKE)
GATA
GATA
IF I JUST STAND HERE, BOTH LILLY AND I WILL—
DO
DO
DO
DO
DO (THUD)
DO

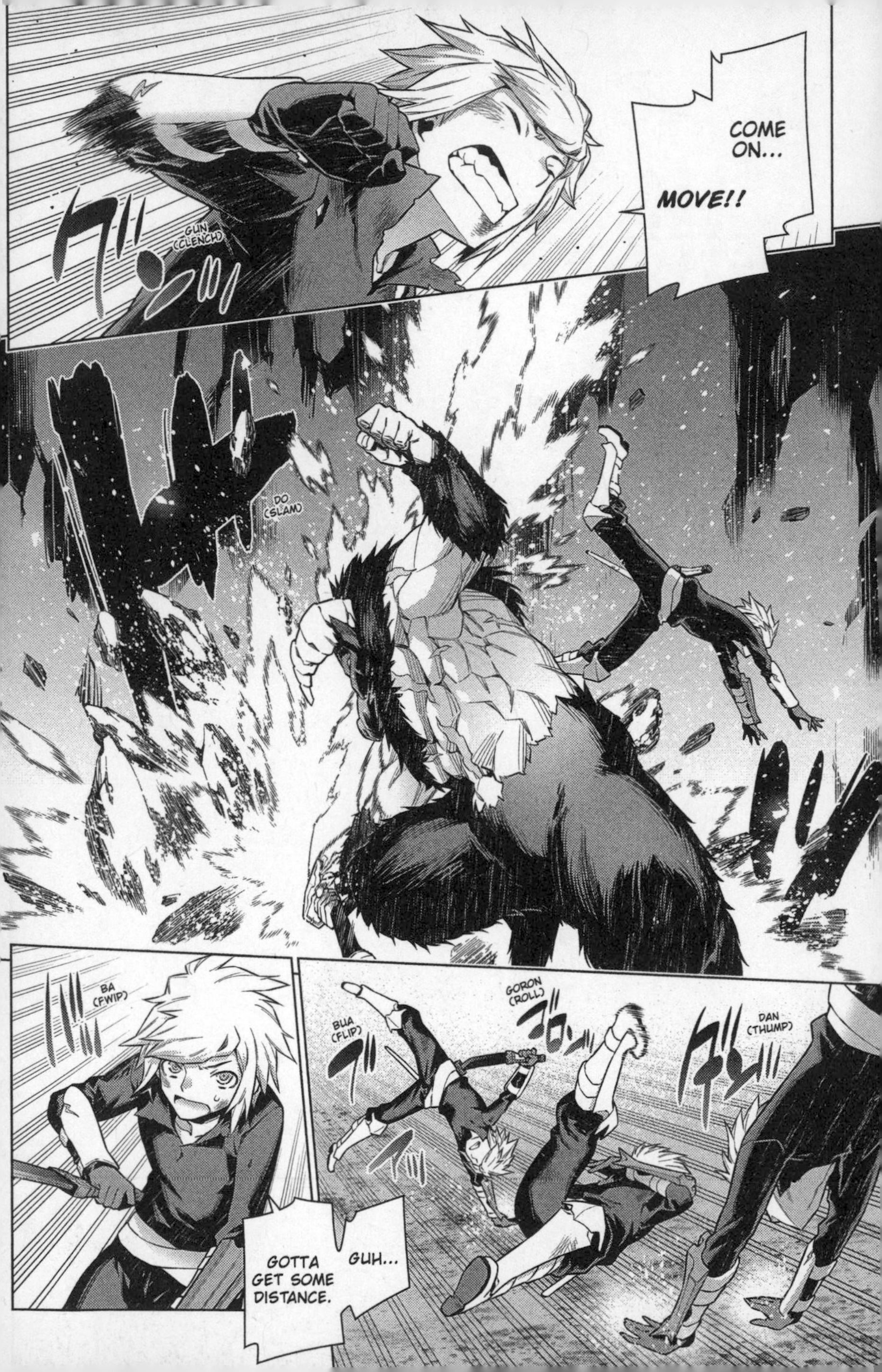
COME ON...
MOVE!!
GUN (CLENCH)
DO (SLAM)
DAN (THUMP)
GORON (ROLL)
BUA (FLIP)
BA (FWIP)
GUH...
GOTTA GET SOME DISTANCE.

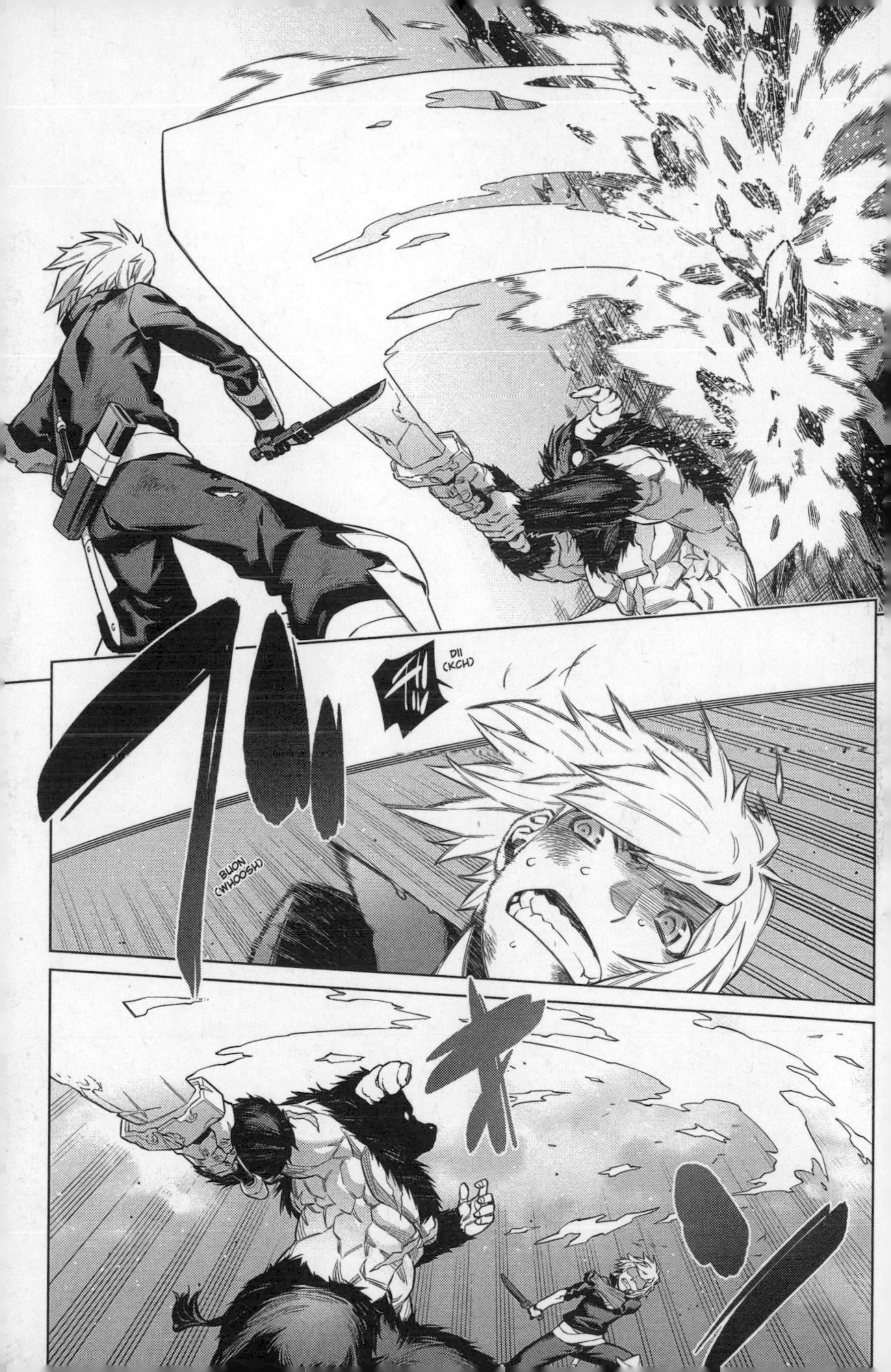
DII (KCH)
BUON (WHOOSH)

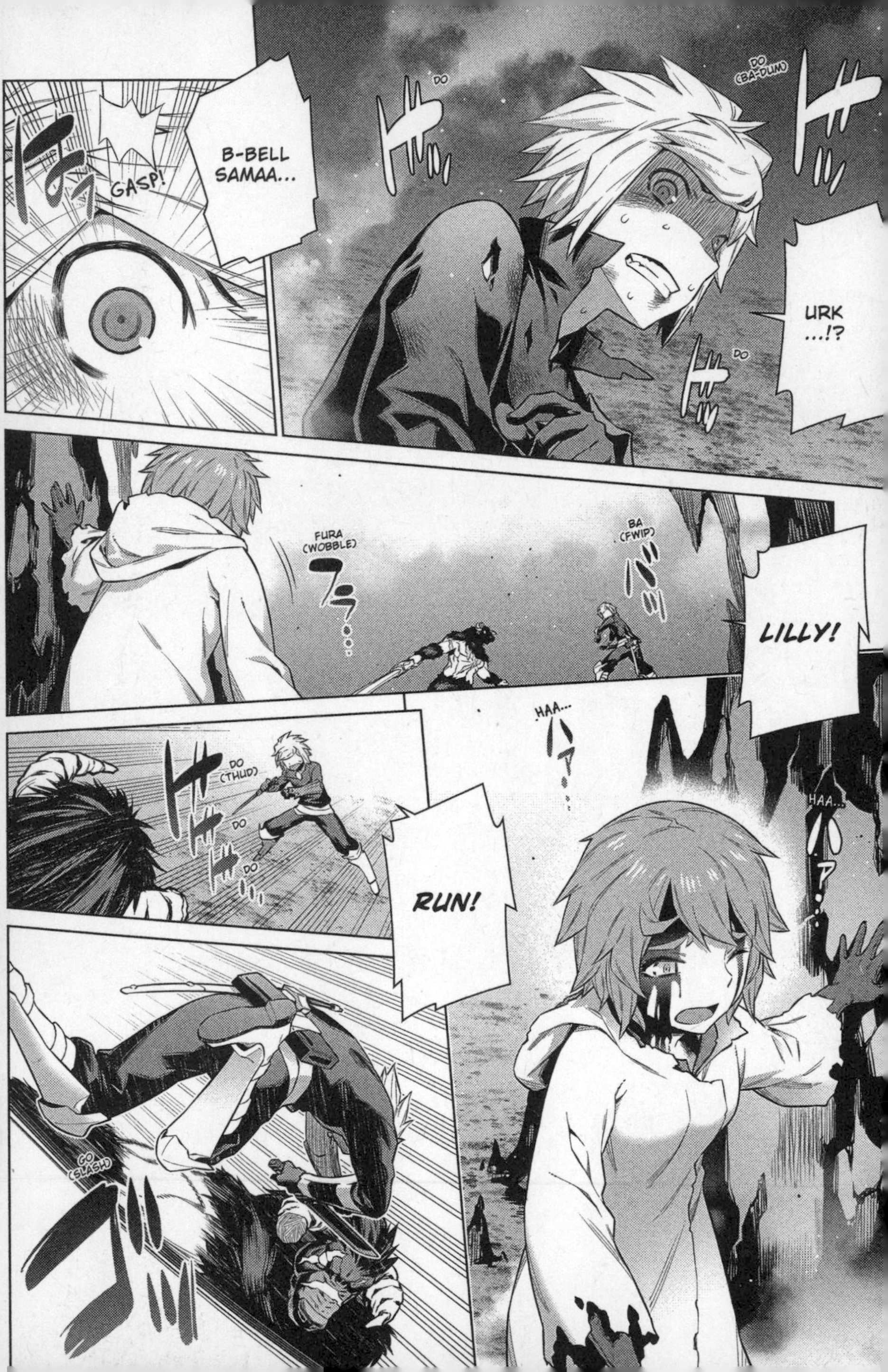
DO (BA-DUM)
DO
URK ...!?
DO
B-BELL SAMAA...
GASP!
LILLY!
BA (FWIP)
FURA (WOBBLE)
HAA...
HAA...
RUN!
DO (THUD)
DO
DO
GO (SLASH)

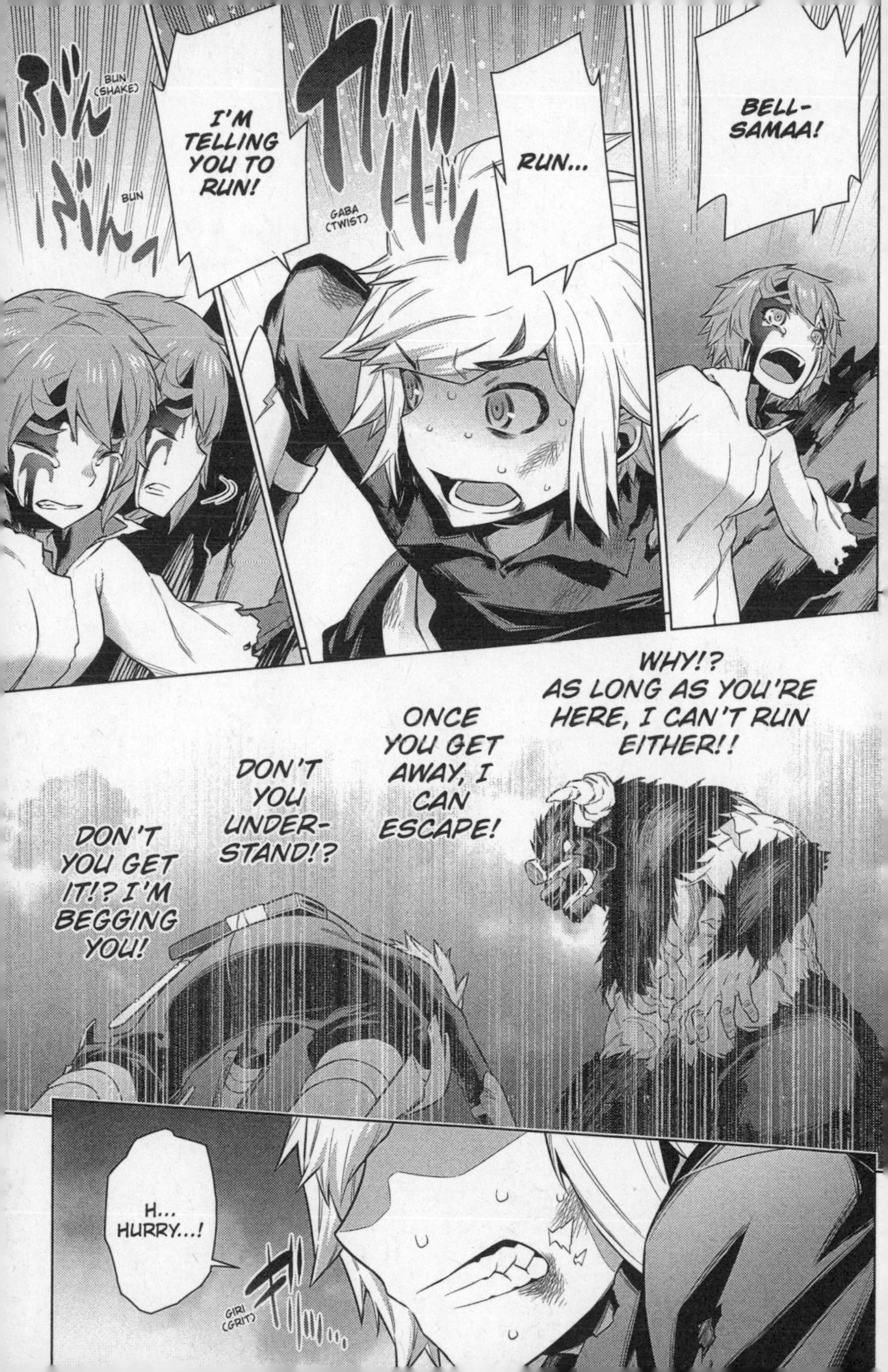

BELL-SAMAA!
RUN...
GABA (TWIST)
I'M TELLING YOU TO RUN!
BUN (SHAKE)
BUN
WHY!? AS LONG AS YOU'RE HERE, I CAN'T RUN EITHER!!
ONCE YOU GET AWAY, I CAN ESCAPE!
DON'T YOU UNDERSTAND!?
DON'T YOU GET IT!? I'M BEGGING YOU!
GIRI (GRIT)
H... HURRY...!

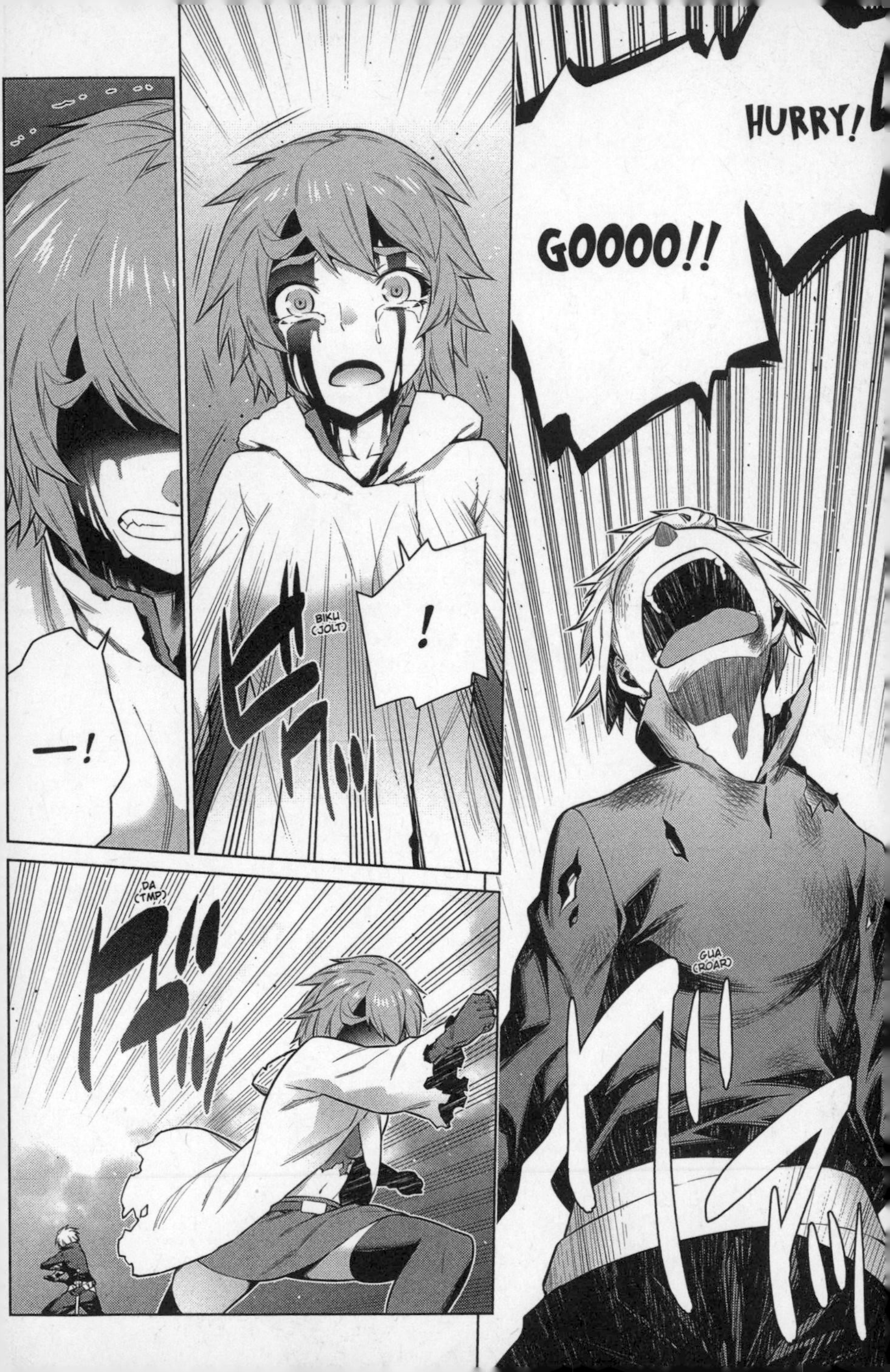
HURRY!
GOOOO!!
GUA (ROAR)
BIKU (JOLT)
!
—!
DA (TMP)

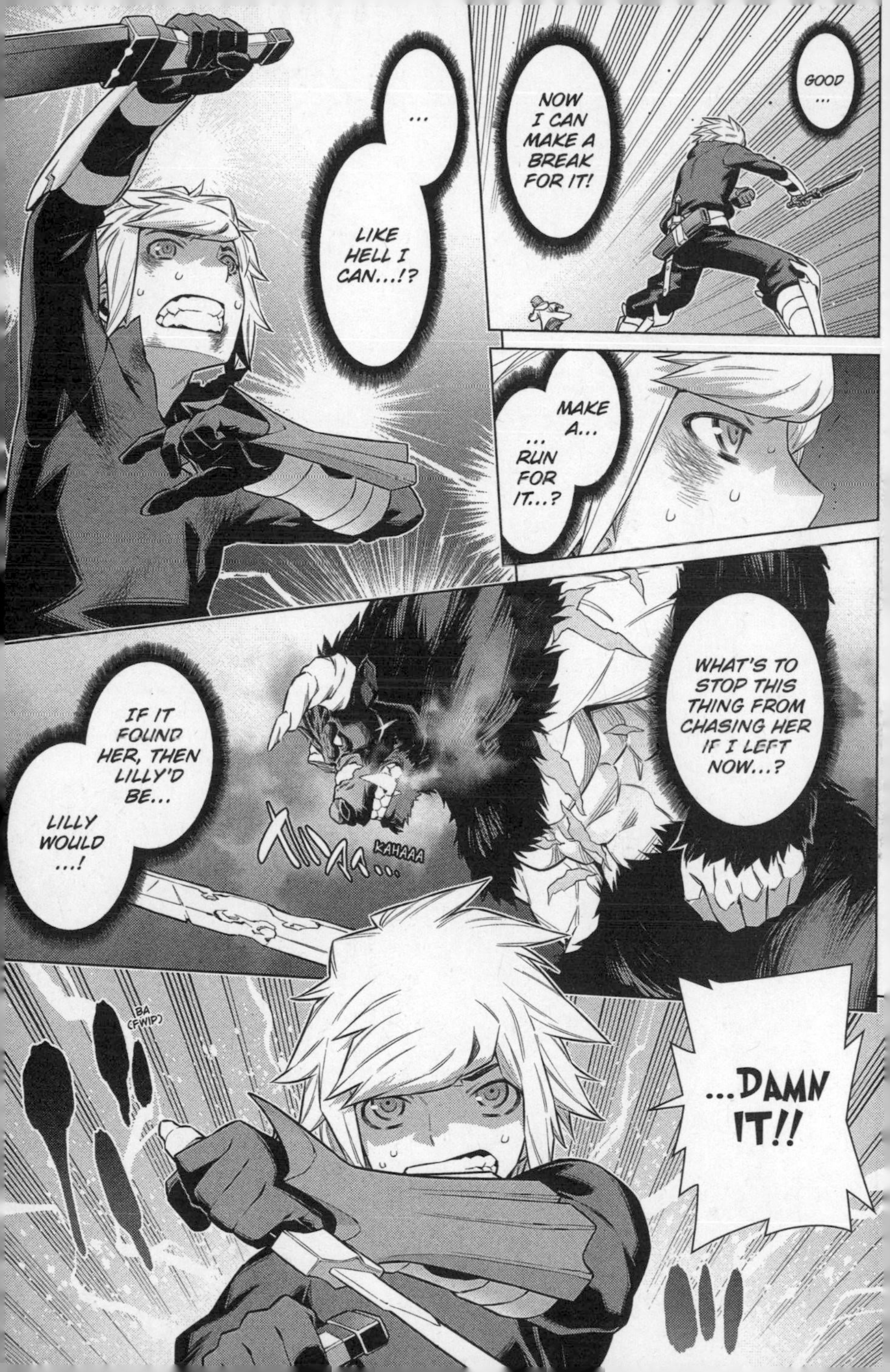
GOOD ...
NOW I CAN MAKE A BREAK FOR IT!
MAKE A...
... RUN FOR IT...?
...
LIKE HELL I CAN...!?
WHAT'S TO STOP THIS THING FROM CHASING HER IF I LEFT NOW...?
IF IT FOUND HER, THEN LILLY'D BE...
LILLY WOULD ...!
KAHAAA
...DAMN IT!!
BA (FWIP)

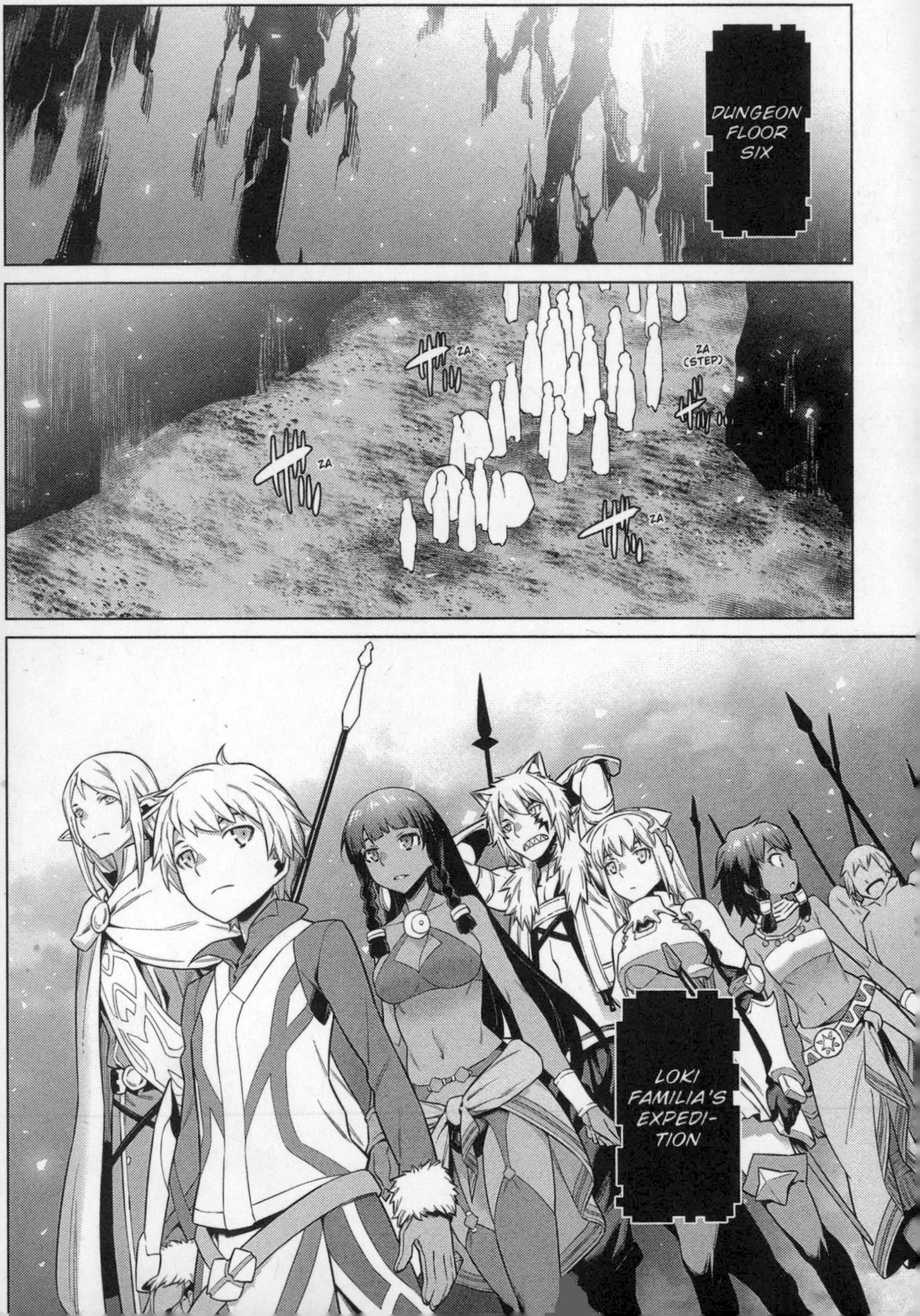
DUNGEON FLOOR SIX
ZA (STEP)
ZA
ZA
ZA
LOKI FAMILIA'S EXPEDITION

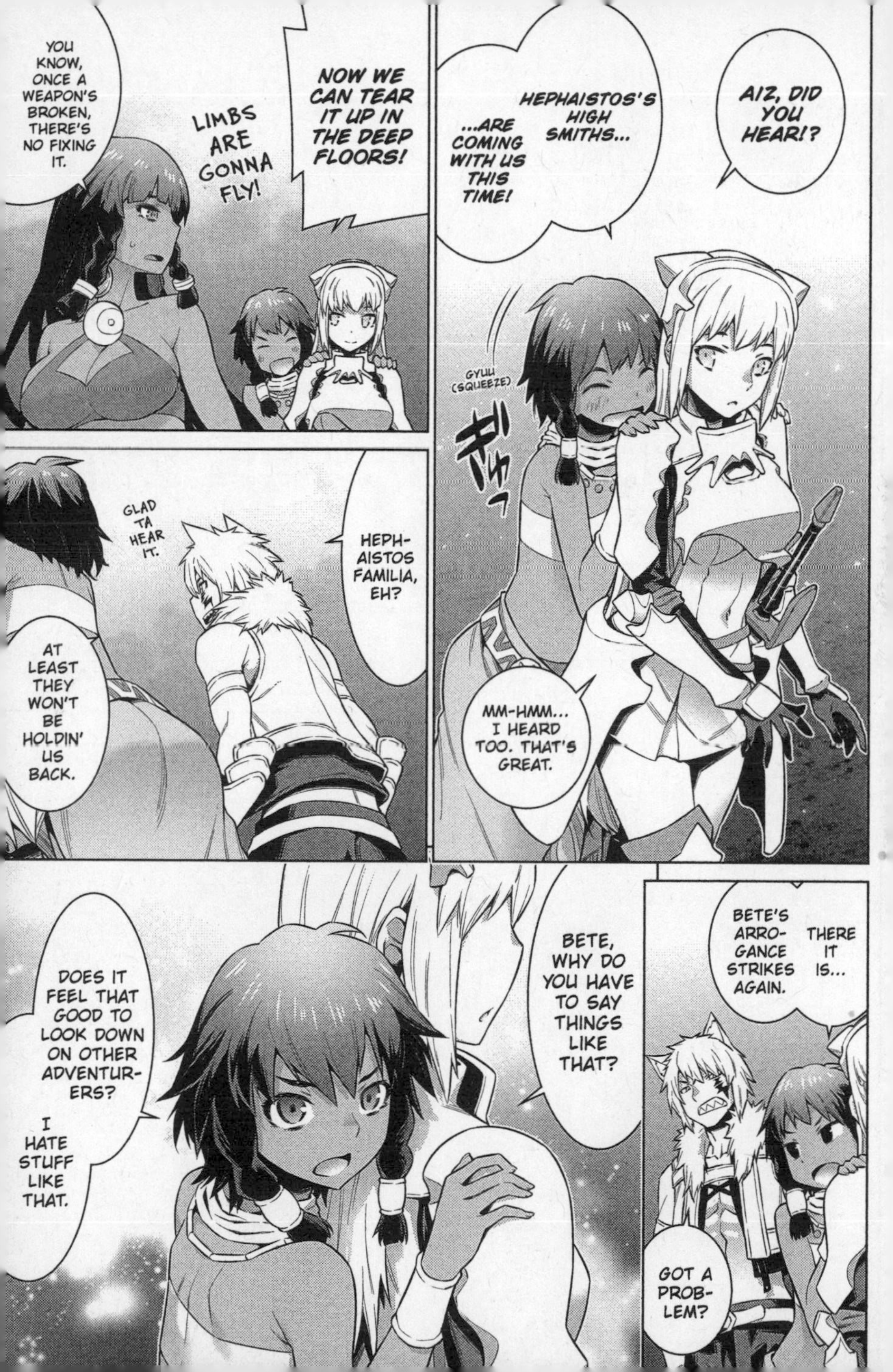
AIZ, DID YOU HEAR!?
HEPHAISTOS'S HIGH SMITHS...
...ARE COMING WITH US THIS TIME!
GYUU (SQUEEZE)
ぎゅっ
MM-HMM... I HEARD TOO. THAT'S GREAT.
NOW WE CAN TEAR IT UP IN THE DEEP FLOORS!
LIMBS ARE GONNA FLY!
YOU KNOW, ONCE A WEAPON'S BROKEN, THERE'S NO FIXING IT.
HEPH-AISTOS FAMILIA, EH?
GLAD TA HEAR IT.
AT LEAST THEY WON'T BE HOLDIN' US BACK.
THERE IT IS...
BETE'S ARRO-GANCE STRIKES AGAIN.
GOT A PROB-LEM?
BETE, WHY DO YOU HAVE TO SAY THINGS LIKE THAT?
DOES IT FEEL THAT GOOD TO LOOK DOWN ON OTHER ADVENTUR-ERS?
I HATE STUFF LIKE THAT.

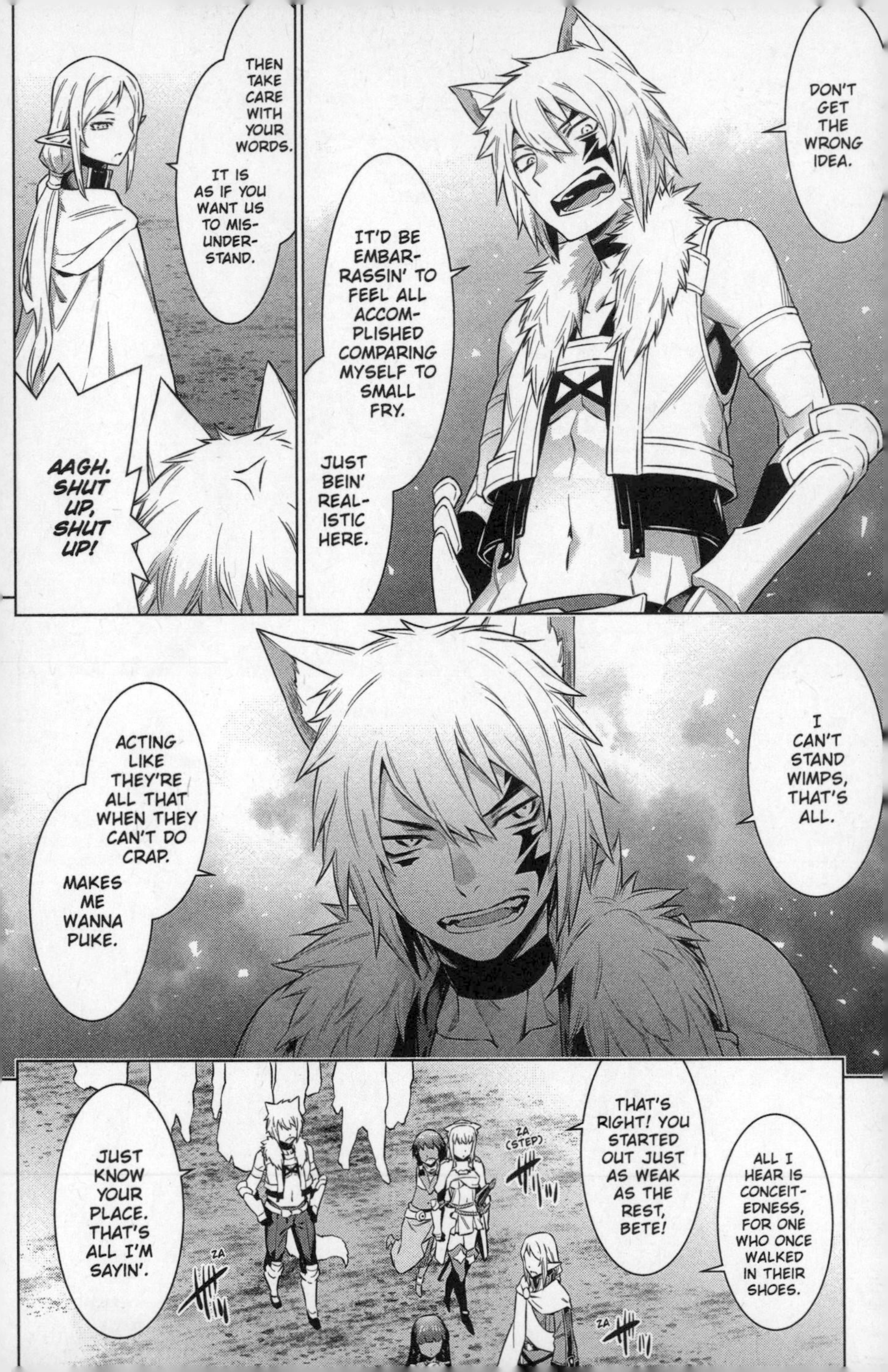
DON'T GET THE WRONG IDEA.
IT'D BE EMBARRASSIN' TO FEEL ALL ACCOMPLISHED COMPARING MYSELF TO SMALL FRY.
JUST BEIN' REALISTIC HERE.
THEN TAKE CARE WITH YOUR WORDS.
IT IS AS IF YOU WANT US TO MISUNDERSTAND.
AAGH. SHUT UP, SHUT UP!
I CAN'T STAND WIMPS, THAT'S ALL.
ACTING LIKE THEY'RE ALL THAT WHEN THEY CAN'T DO CRAP.
MAKES ME WANNA PUKE.
ALL I HEAR IS CONCEITEDNESS, FOR ONE WHO ONCE WALKED IN THEIR SHOES.
ZA
THAT'S RIGHT! YOU STARTED OUT JUST AS WEAK AS THE REST, BETE!
ZA (STEP)
JUST KNOW YOUR PLACE. THAT'S ALL I'M SAYIN'.
ZA

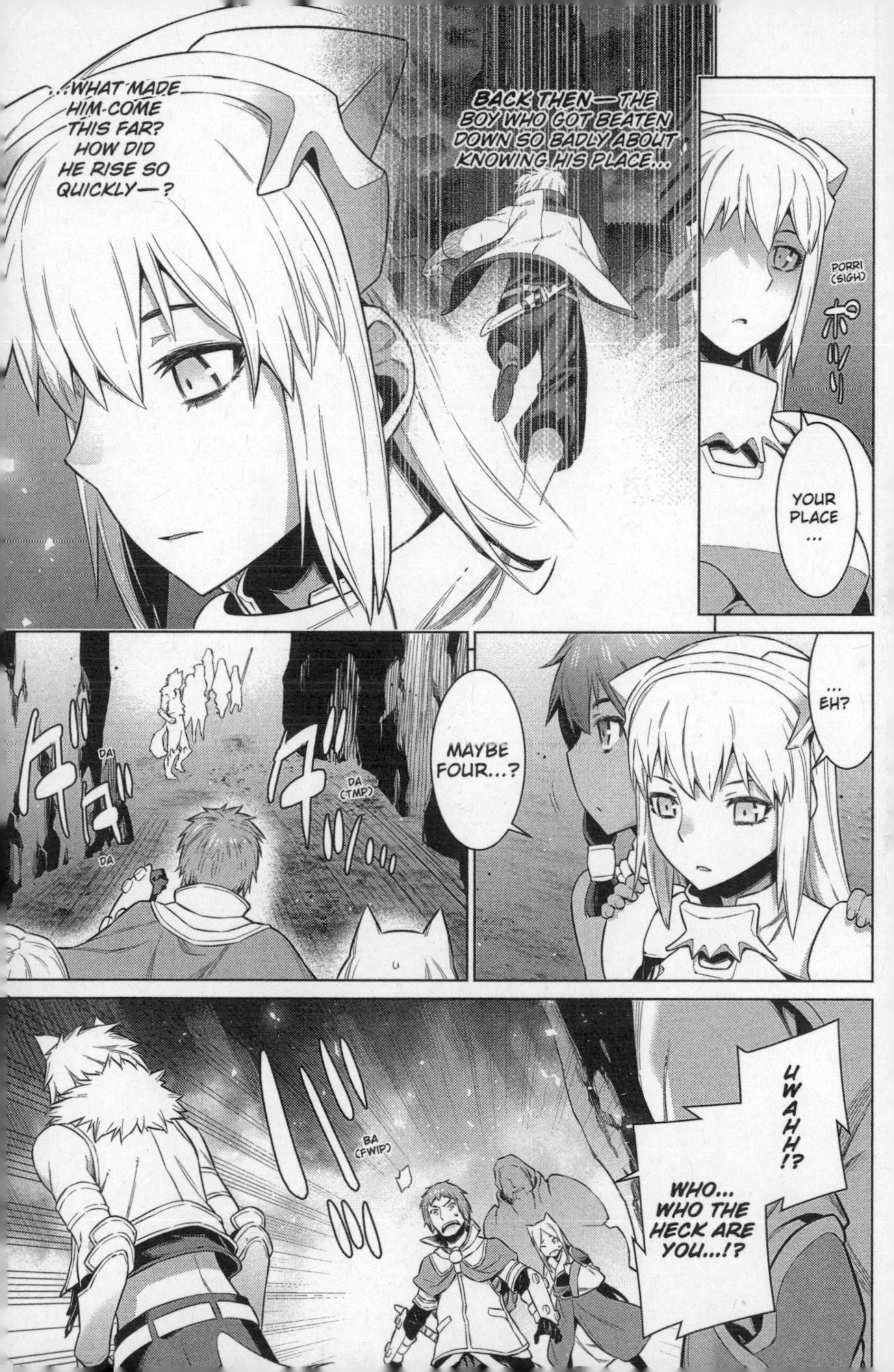
PORRI (SIGH)
YOUR PLACE ...
BACK THEN—THE BOY WHO GOT BEATEN DOWN SO BADLY ABOUT KNOWING HIS PLACE...
...WHAT MADE HIM COME THIS FAR? HOW DID HE RISE SO QUICKLY—?
... EH?
MAYBE FOUR...?
DA (TMP)
DA
DA
UWAHH!?
WHO... WHO THE HECK ARE YOU...!?
BA (FWIP)

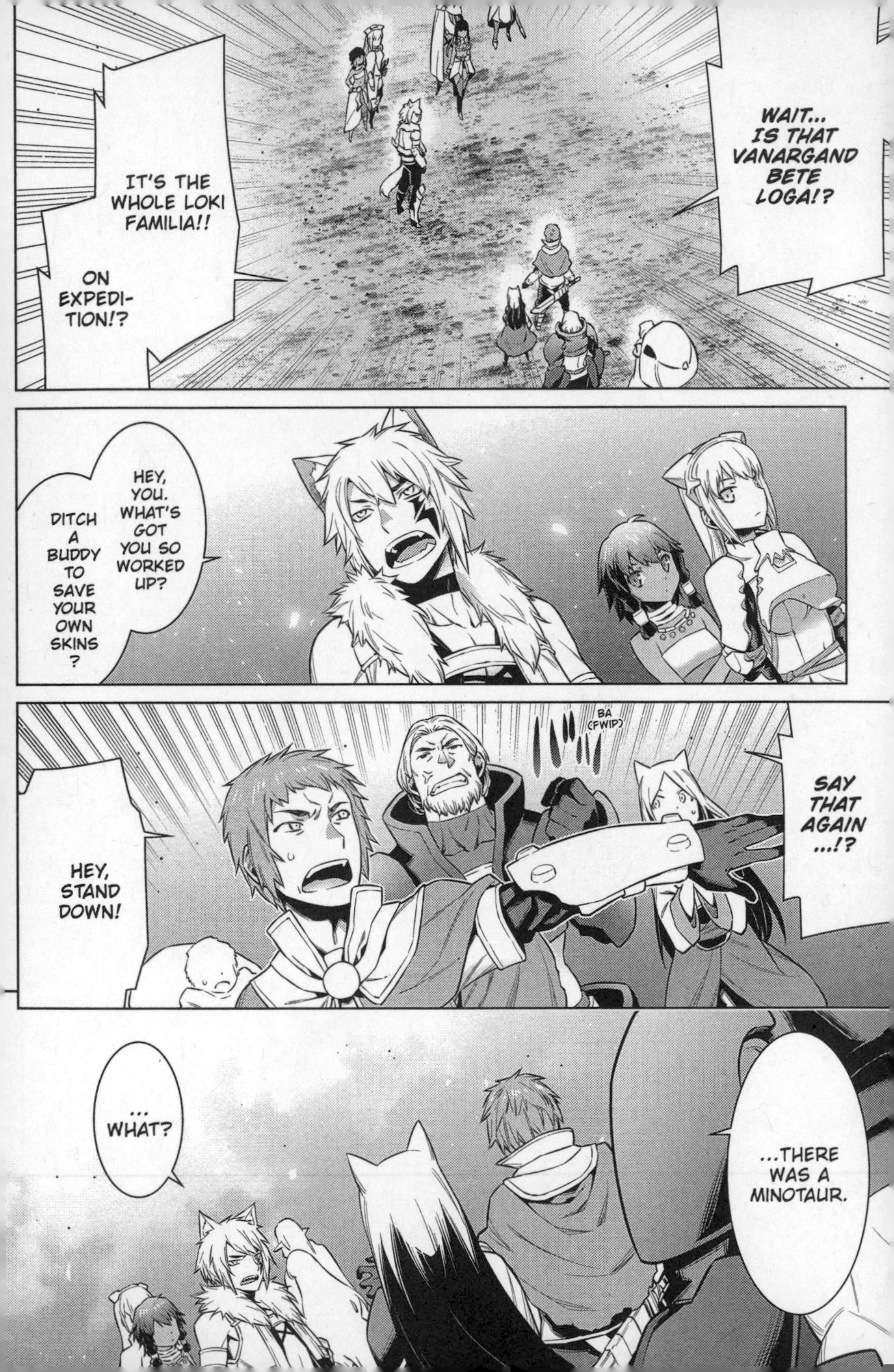
WAIT... IS THAT VANARGAND BETE LOGA!?
IT'S THE WHOLE LOKI FAMILIA!!
ON EXPEDITION!?
HEY, YOU. WHAT'S GOT YOU SO WORKED UP?
DITCH A BUDDY TO SAVE YOUR OWN SKINS?
SAY THAT AGAIN...!?
BA (FWIP)
HEY, STAND DOWN!
...THERE WAS A MINOTAUR.
... WHAT?

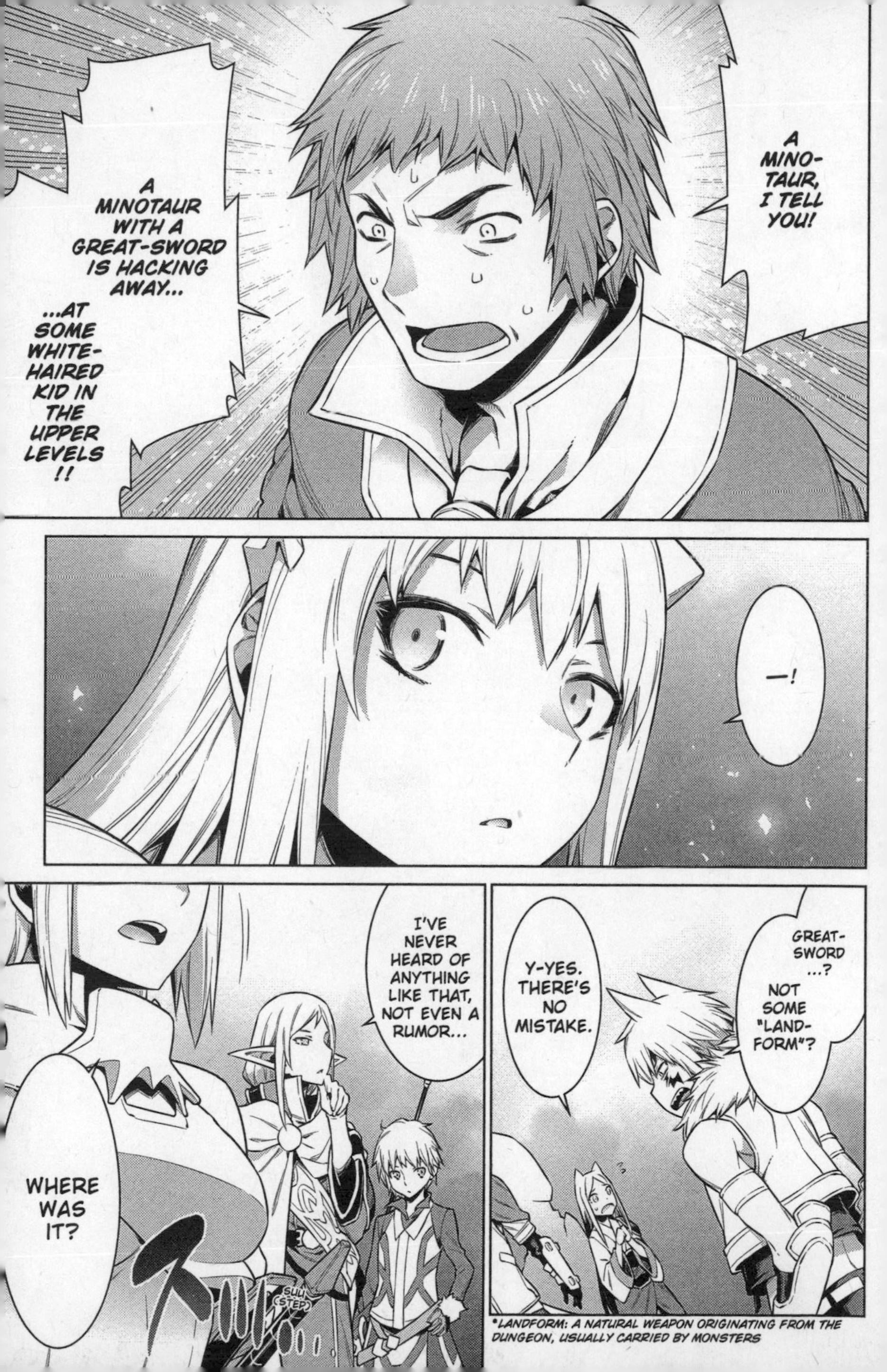
A MINOTAUR, I TELL YOU!
A MINOTAUR WITH A GREAT-SWORD IS HACKING AWAY...
...AT SOME WHITE-HAIRED KID IN THE UPPER LEVELS!!
—!
GREAT-SWORD...?
NOT SOME "LANDFORM"?
Y-YES. THERE'S NO MISTAKE.
I'VE NEVER HEARD OF ANYTHING LIKE THAT, NOT EVEN A RUMOR...
WHERE WAS IT?
SUU (STEP)

*LANDFORM: A NATURAL WEAPON ORIGINATING FROM THE DUNGEON, USUALLY CARRIED BY MONSTERS

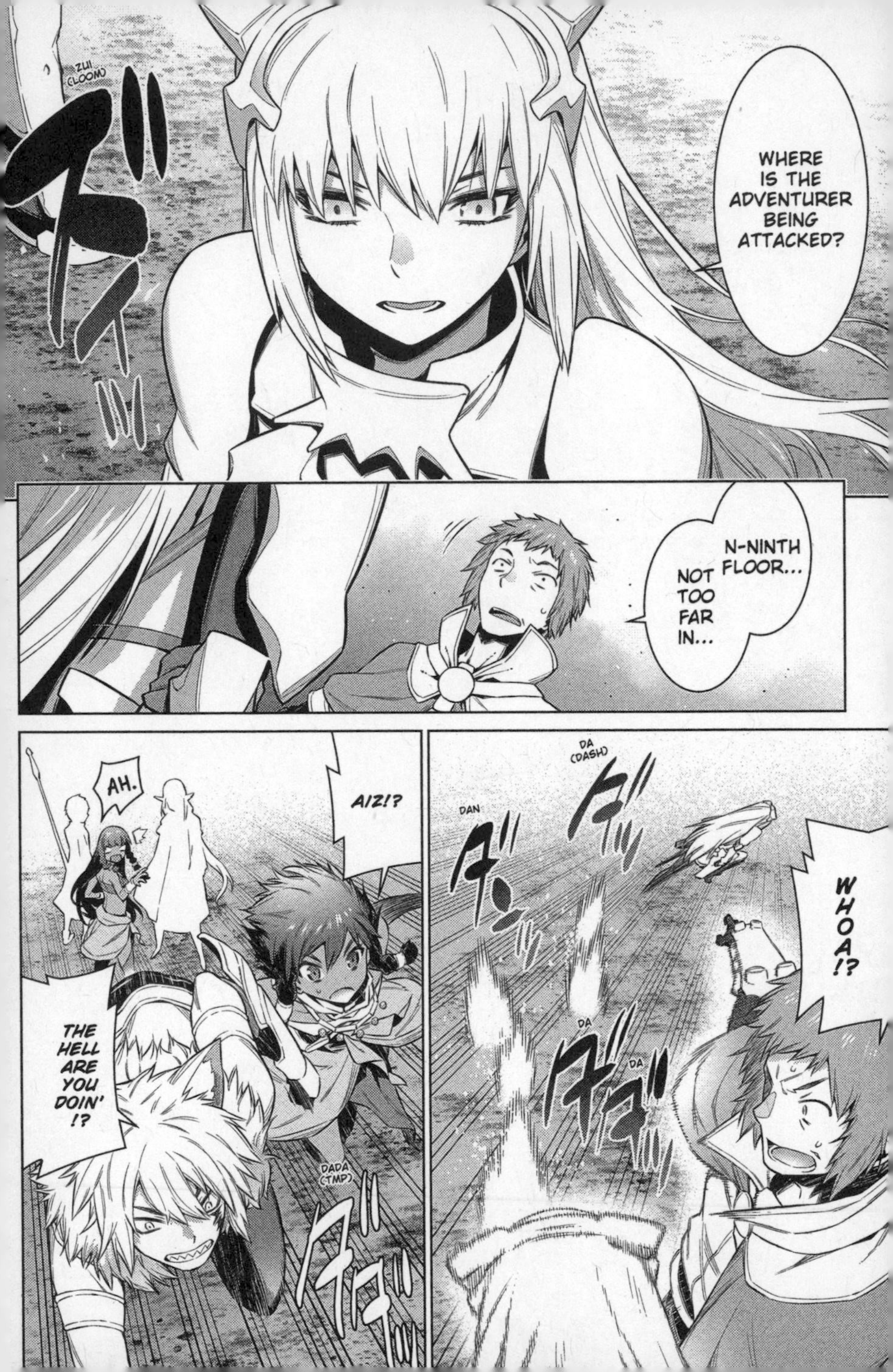
WHERE IS THE ADVENTURER BEING ATTACKED?
ZUI (LOOM)
N-NINTH FLOOR... NOT TOO FAR IN...
DA (DASH)
DAN
WHOA!?
DA
DA
AIZ!?
AH.
THE HELL ARE YOU DOIN'!?
DADA (TMP)

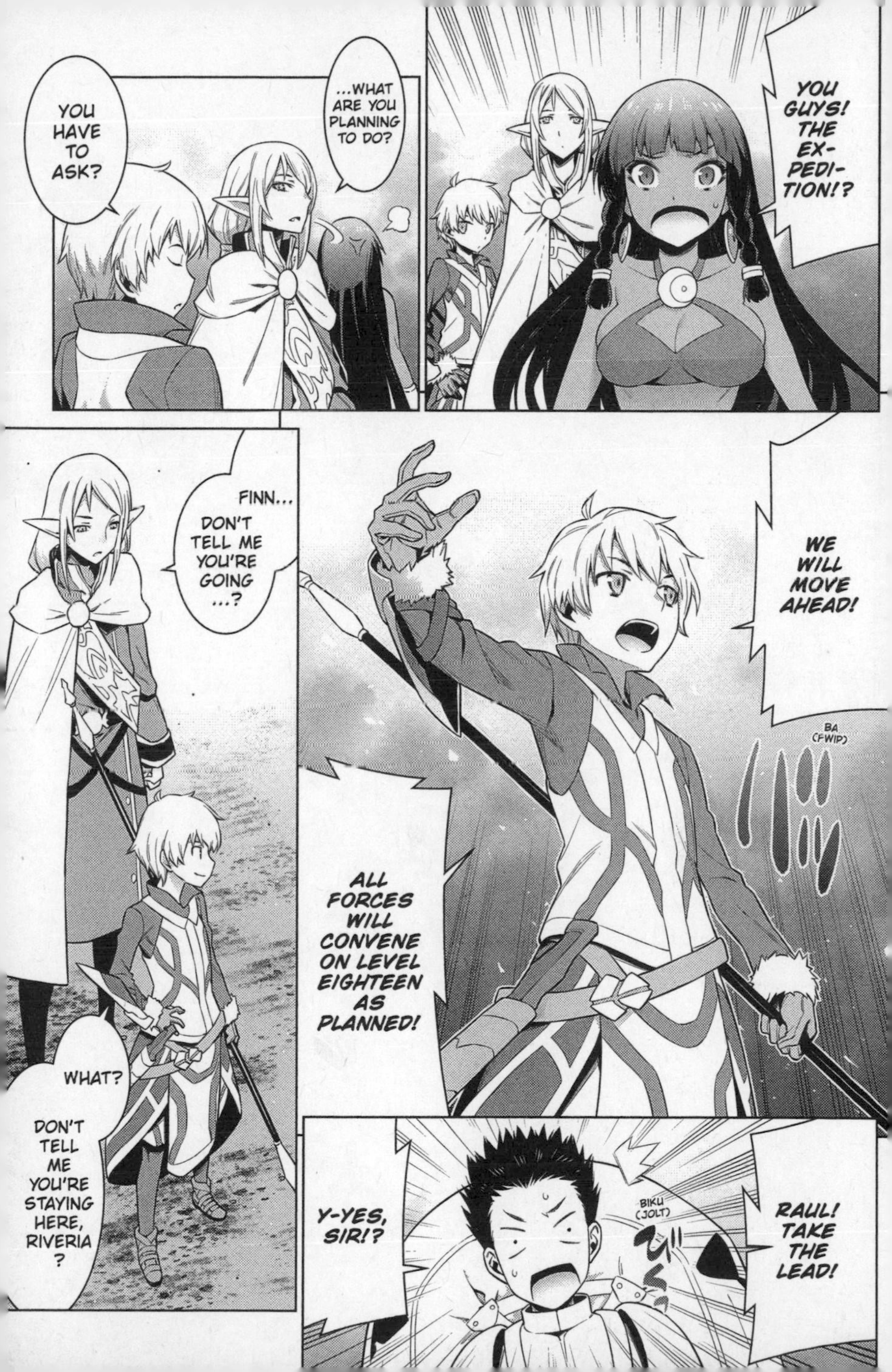
YOU GUYS! THE EX-PEDI-TION!?
...WHAT ARE YOU PLANNING TO DO?
YOU HAVE TO ASK?
WE WILL MOVE AHEAD!
BA (FWIP)
ALL FORCES WILL CONVENE ON LEVEL EIGHTEEN AS PLANNED!
RAUL! TAKE THE LEAD!
BIKU (JOLT)
Y-YES, SIR!?
FINN... DON'T TELL ME YOU'RE GOING ...?
WHAT?
DON'T TELL ME YOU'RE STAYING HERE, RIVERIA ?

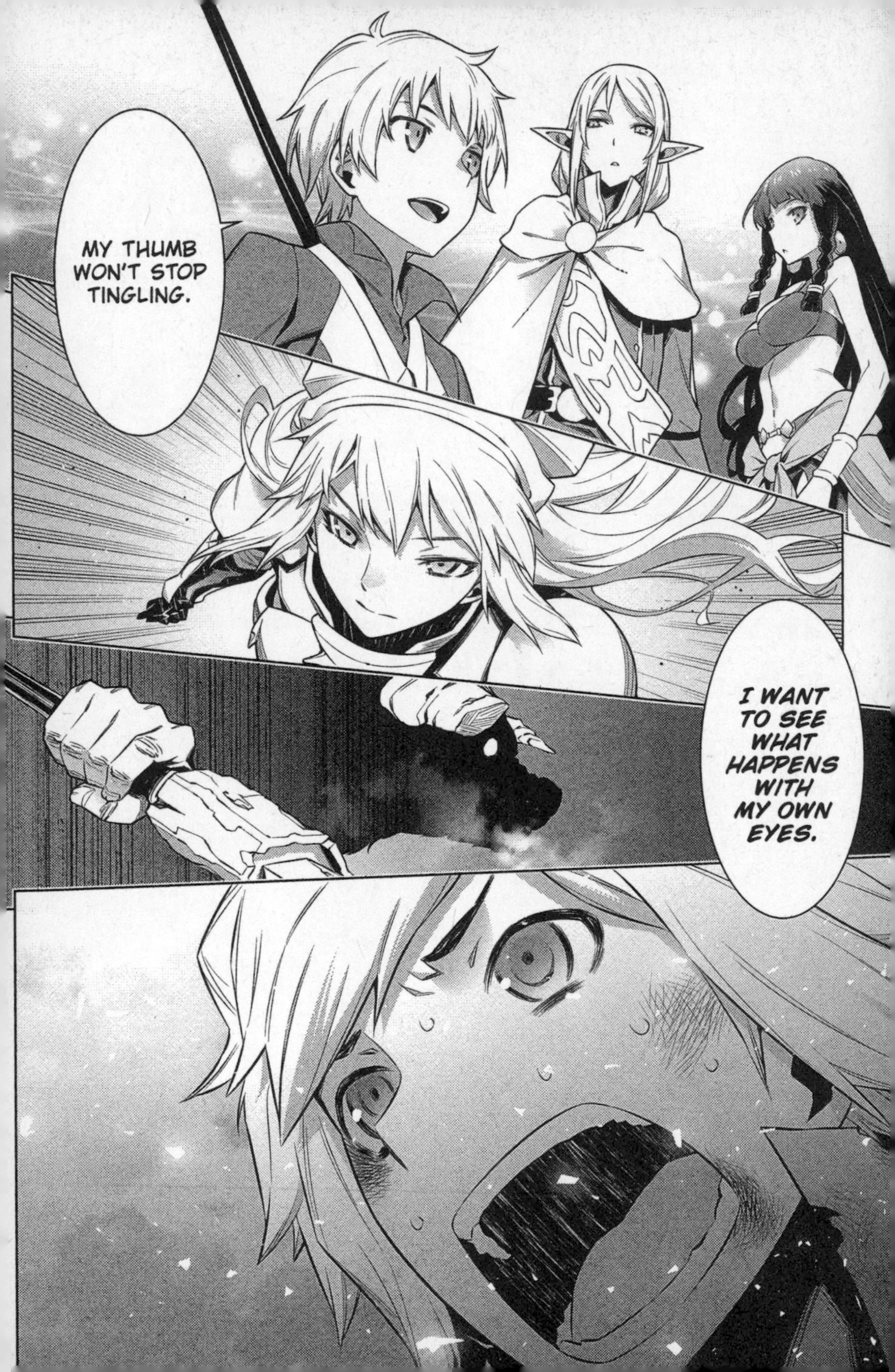
MY THUMB WON'T STOP TINGLING.
I WANT TO SEE WHAT HAPPENS WITH MY OWN EYES.

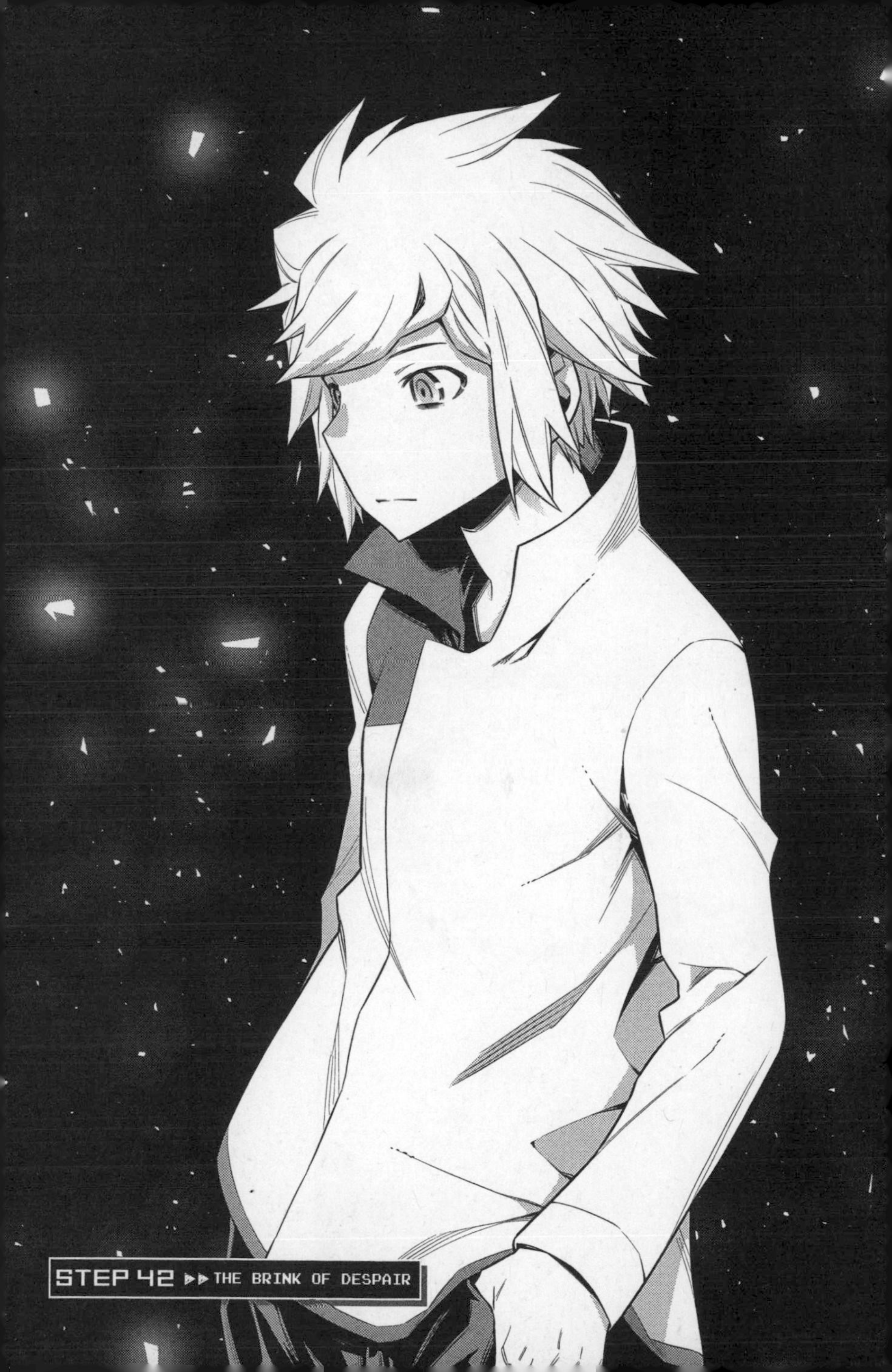
STEP 42 ▶▶ THE BRINK OF DESPAIR

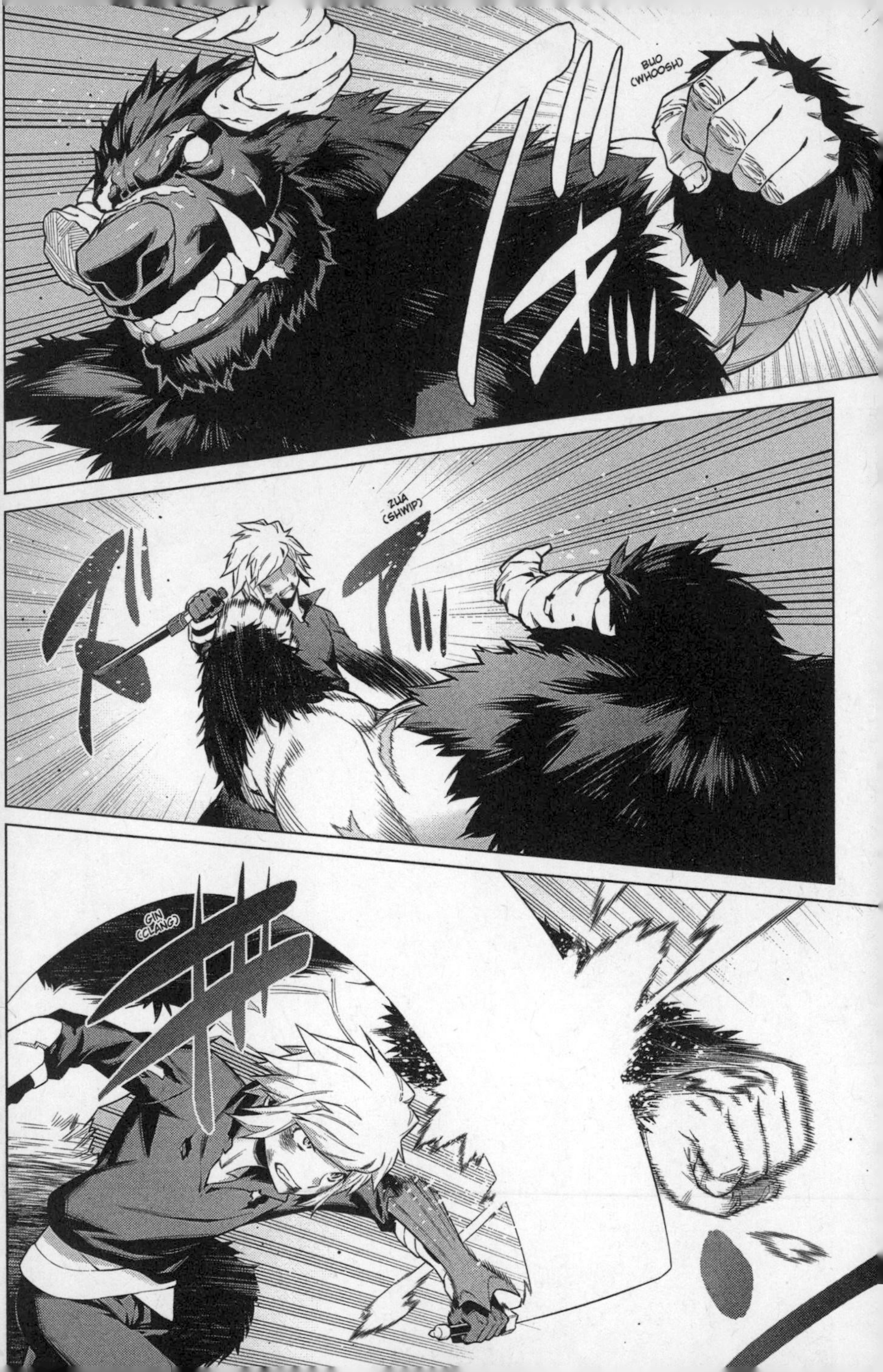
BUO (WHOOSH)
ZUA (SHWIP)
GIN (CLANG)

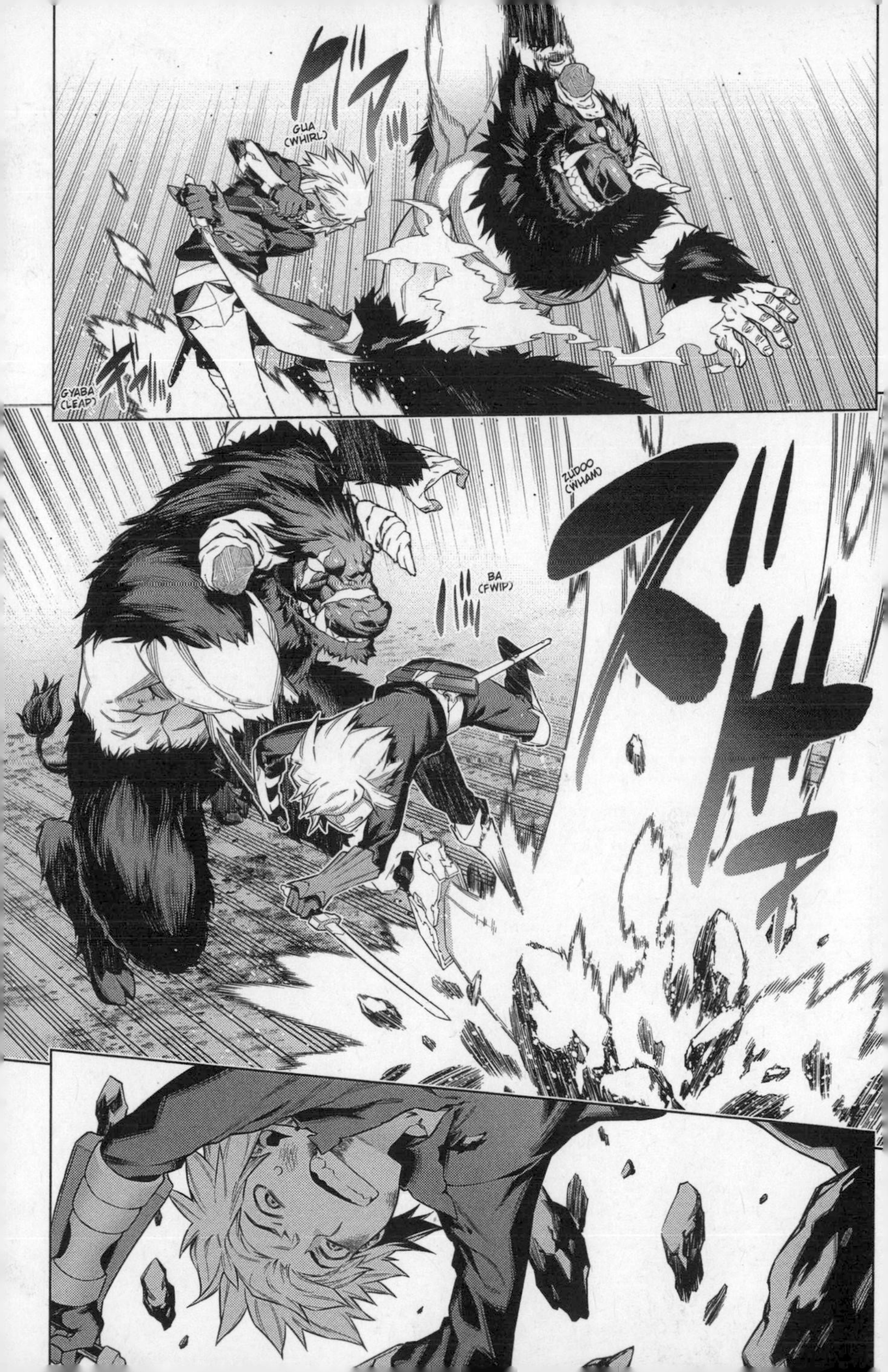
GUA (WHIRL)
GYABA (LEAP)
ZUDOO (WHAM)
BA (FWIP)

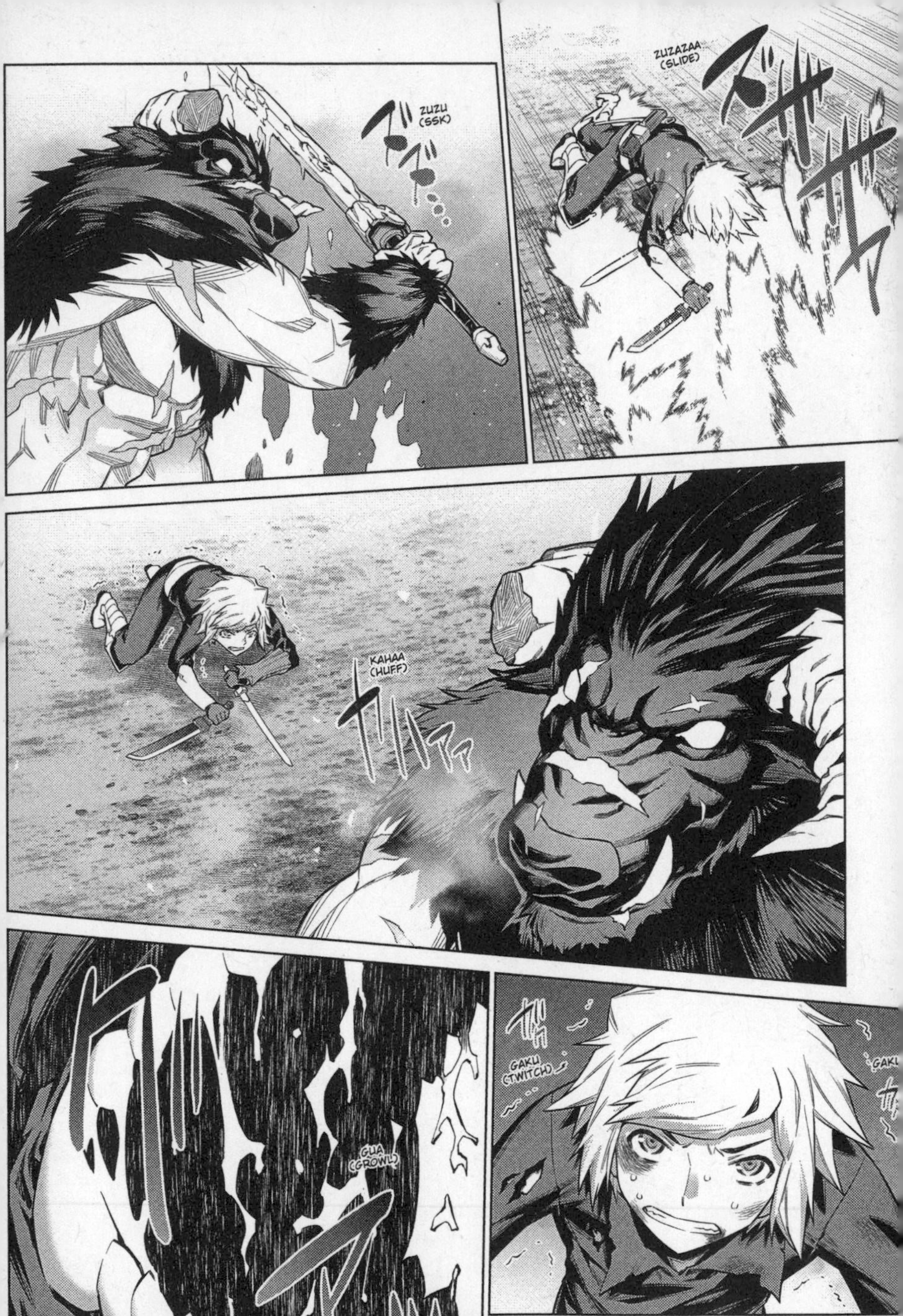
ZUZAZAA (SLIDE)
ZUZU (SSK)
KAHAA (HUFF)
GAKU (TWITCH)
GAKU
GUA (GROWL)

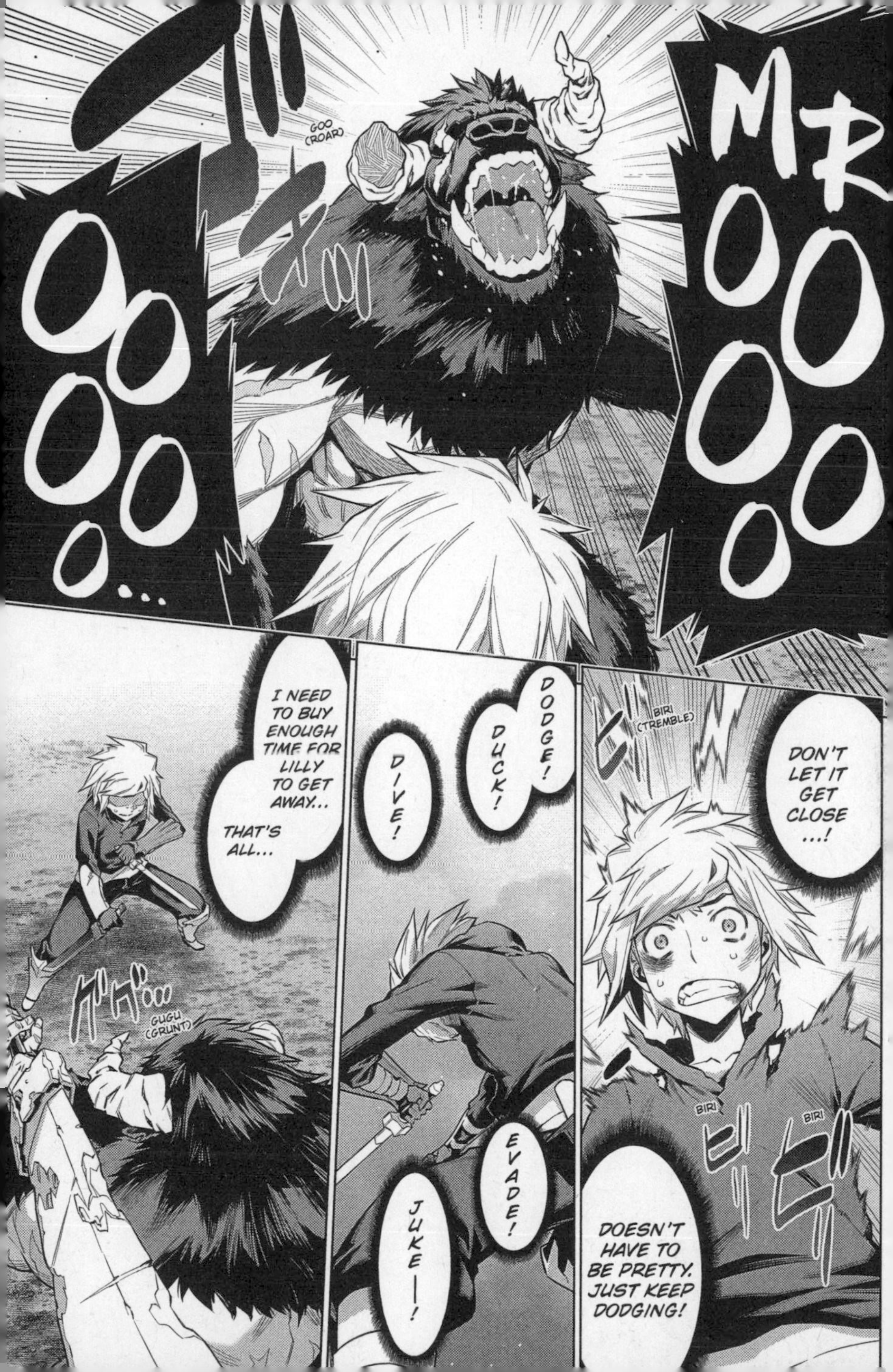
MROOOOOOOO
OOOOOO...
GOO (ROAR)
BIRI (TREMBLE)
DON'T LET IT GET CLOSE ...!
BIRI
BIRI
DOESN'T HAVE TO BE PRETTY. JUST KEEP DODGING!
DODGE!
DUCK!
DIVE!
EVADE!
JUKE—!
I NEED TO BUY ENOUGH TIME FOR LILLY TO GET AWAY...
THAT'S ALL...
GUGU (GRUNT)

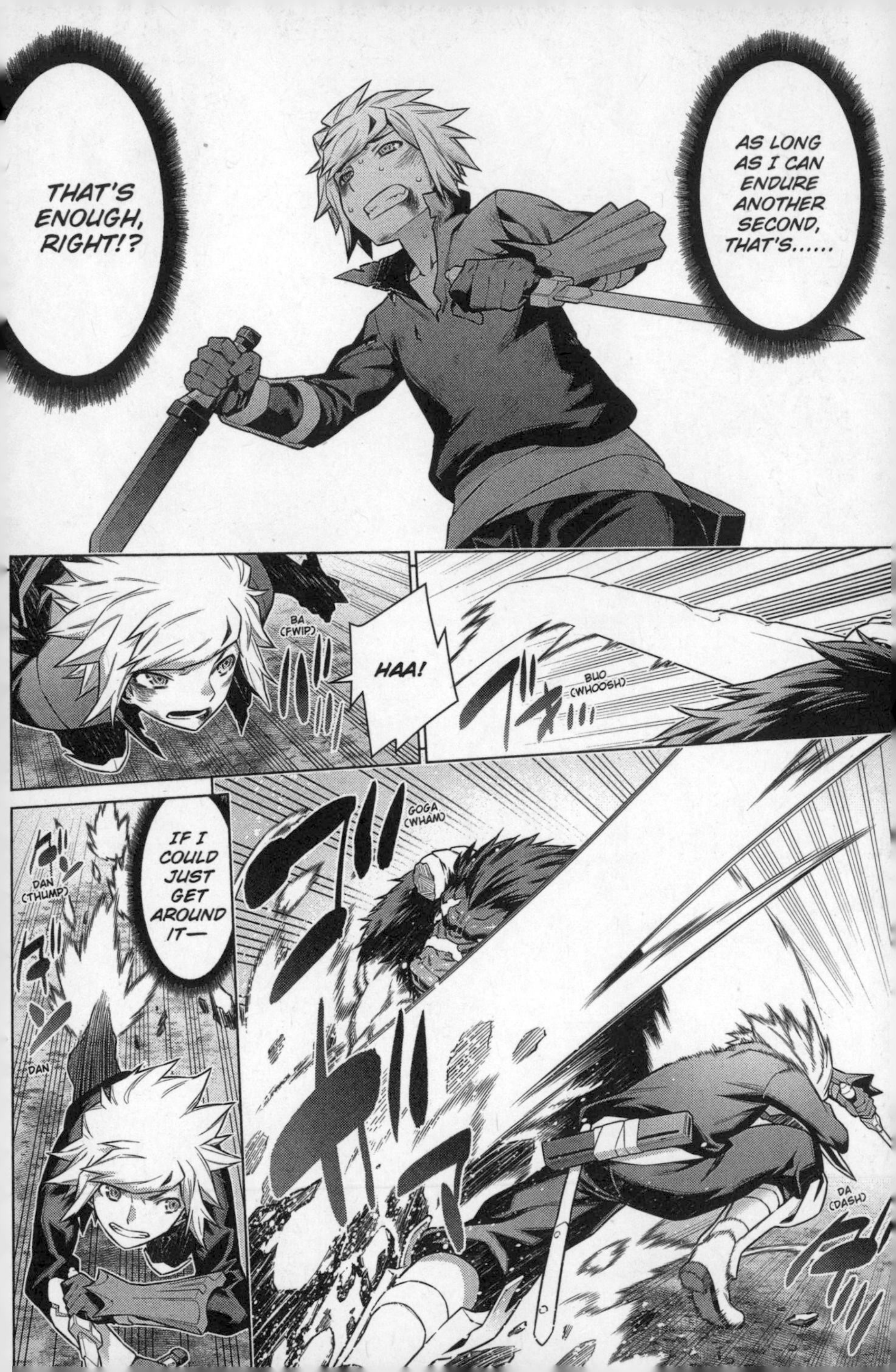
AS LONG AS I CAN ENDURE ANOTHER SECOND, THAT'S......
THAT'S ENOUGH, RIGHT!?
BUO (WHOOSH)
HAA!
BA (FWIP)
GOGA (WHAM)
DA (DASH)
IF I COULD JUST GET AROUND IT—
DAN (THUMP)
DAN

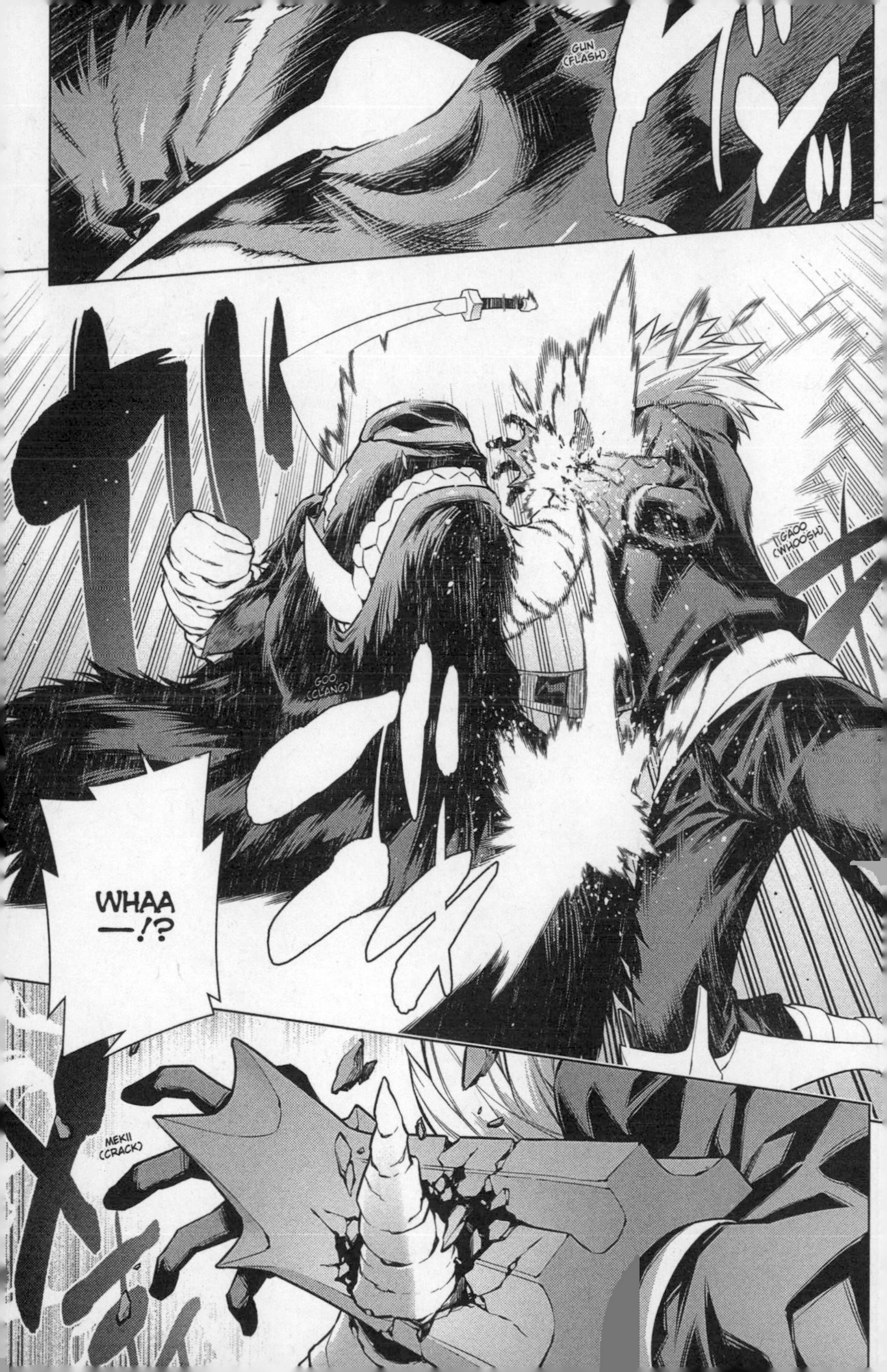
GUN (FLASH)
GAOO (WHOOSH)
GOO (CLANG)
WHAA—!?
MEKII (CRACK)

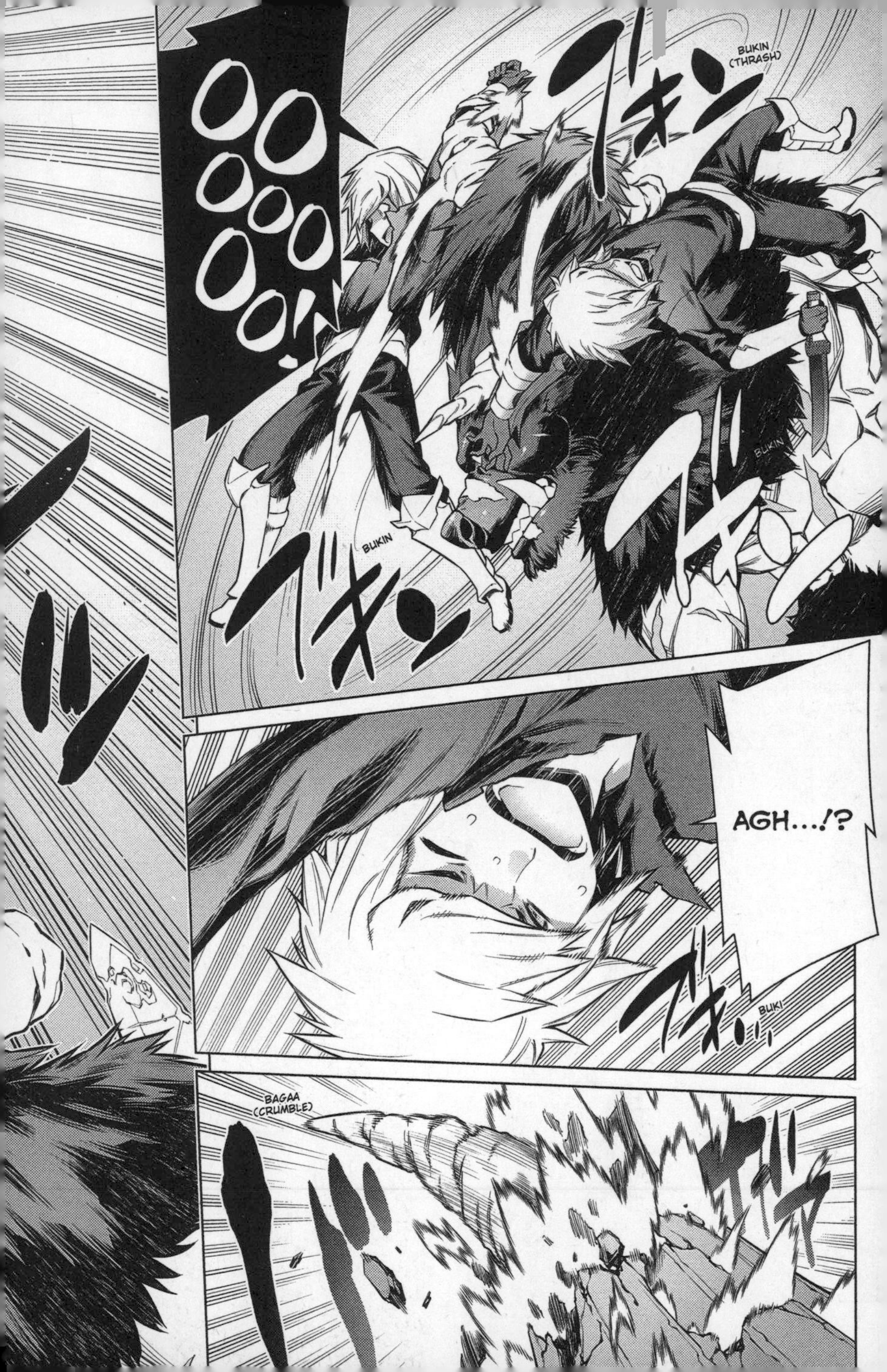
BUKIN (THRASH)
OOOOOOOOOO!!
BUKIN
BUKIN
AGH...!?
BUKI
BAGAA (CRUMBLE)

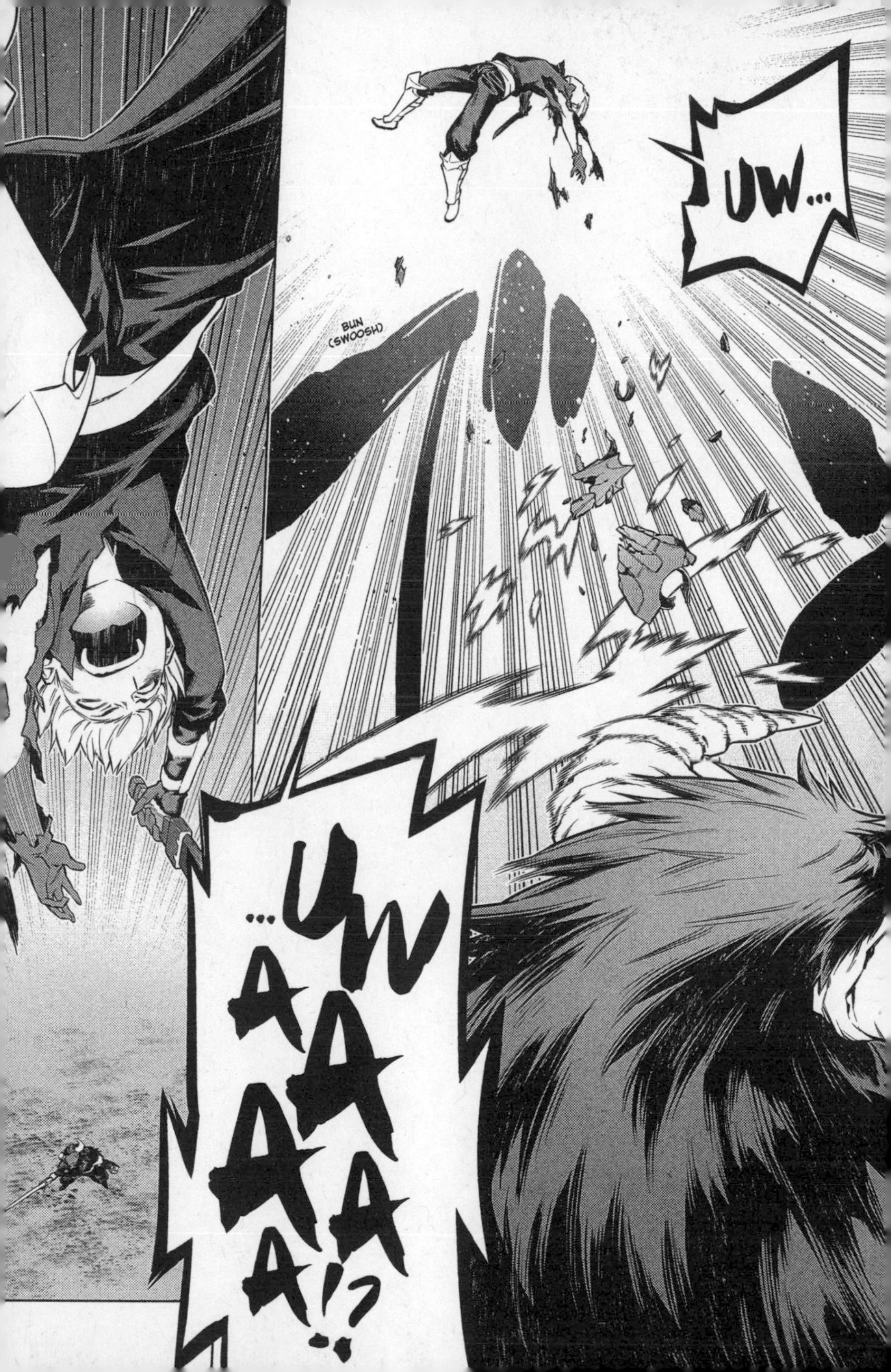
UW...
BUN (SWOOSH)
...UWAAAAAA!?

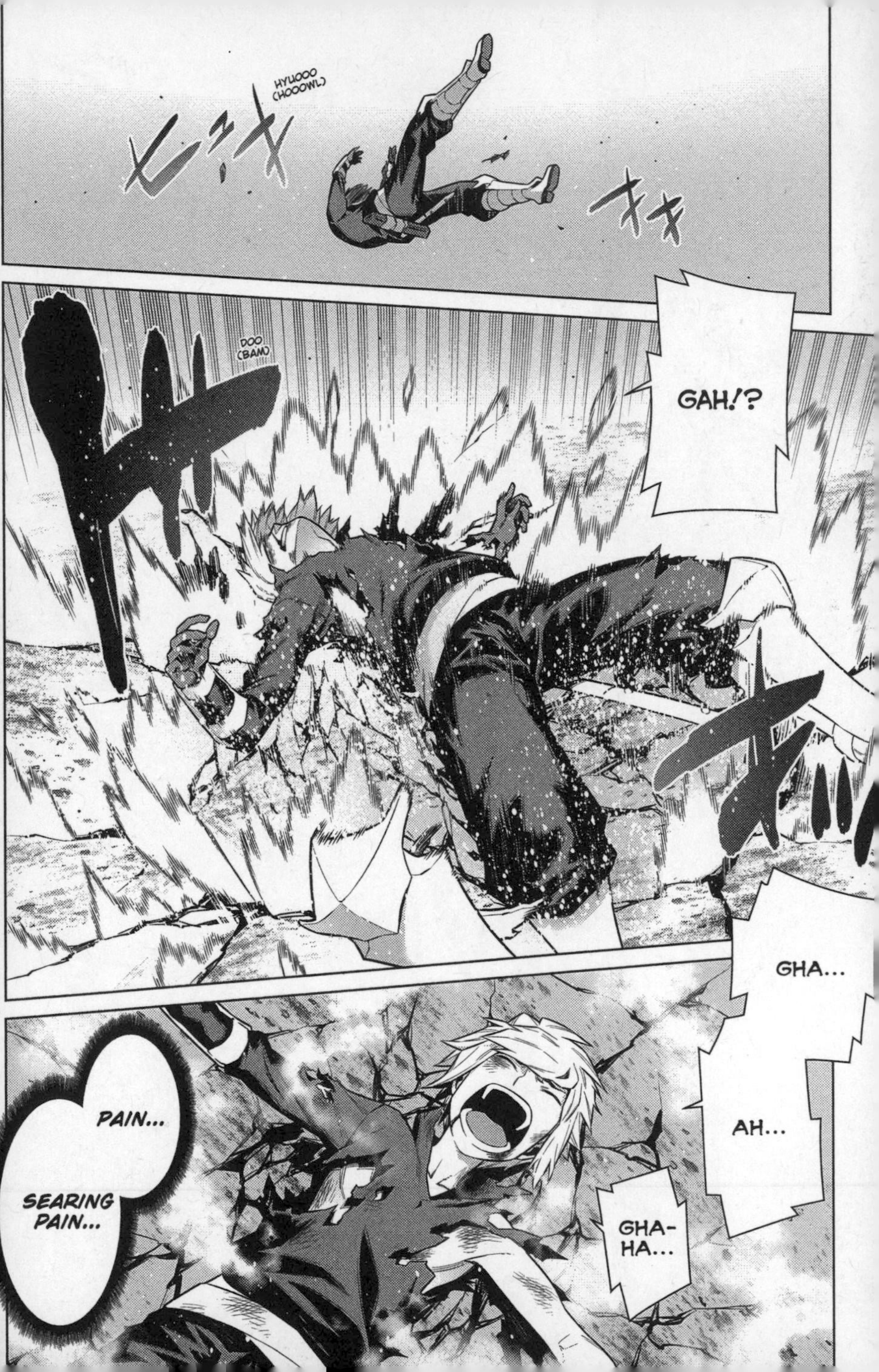
HYUOOO (HOOOWL)
GAH!?
DOO (BAM)
GHA...
AH...
GHA-HA...
PAIN...
SEARING PAIN...

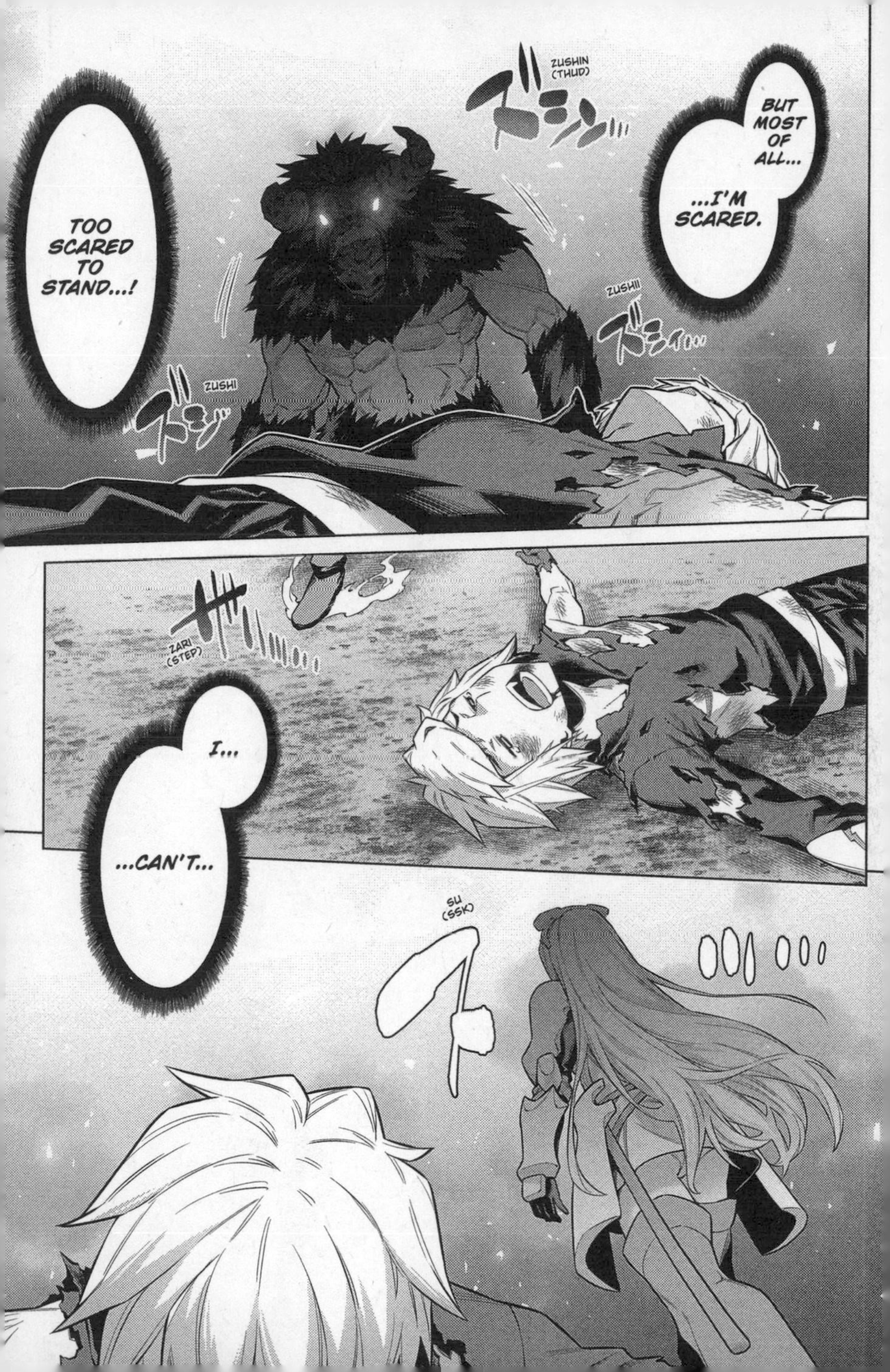
BUT MOST OF ALL...
...I'M SCARED.
ZUSHIN (THUD)
TOO SCARED TO STAND...!
ZUSHII
ZUSHI
ZARI (STEP)
I...
...CAN'T...
SU (SSK)

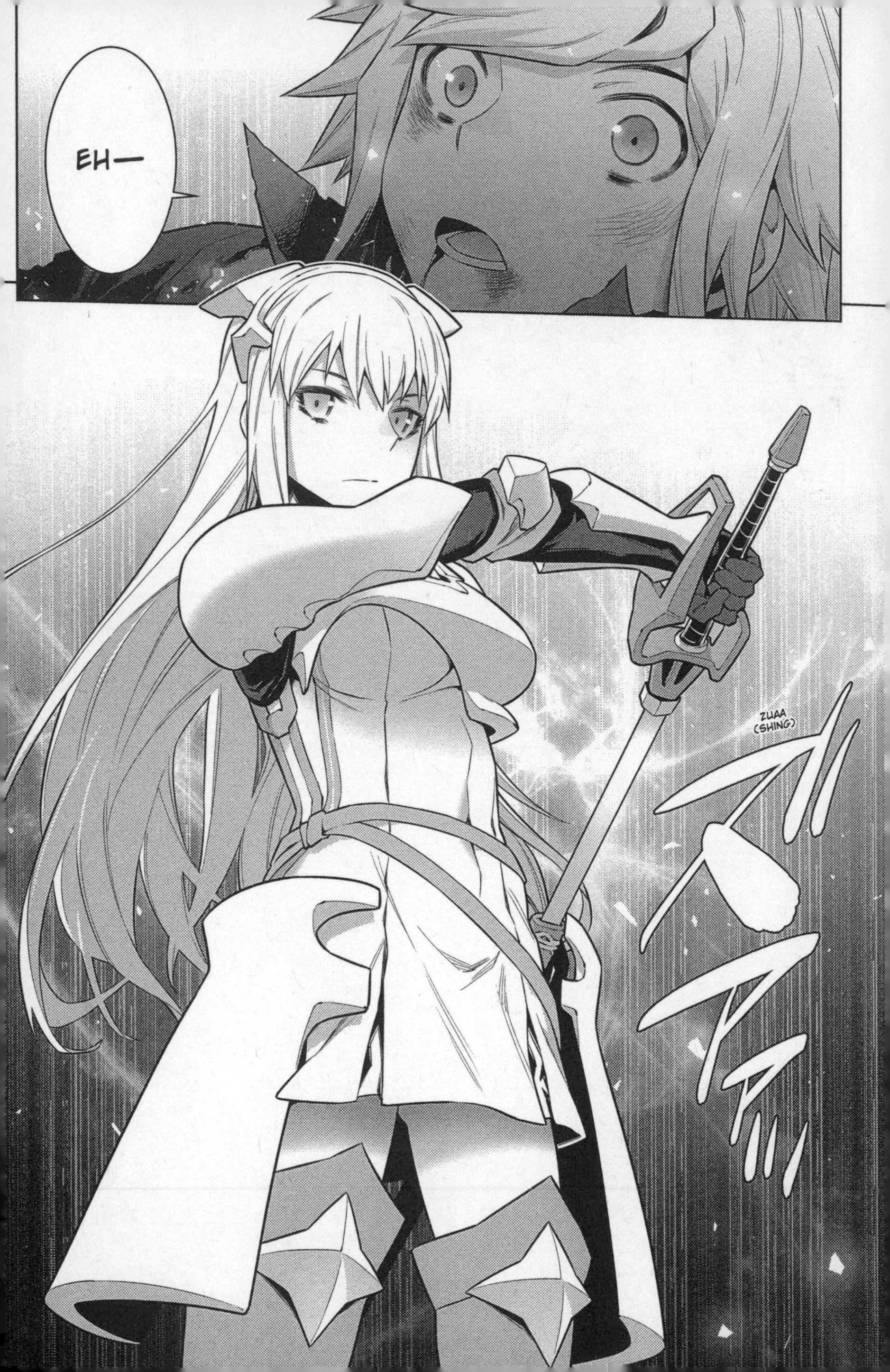
EH—
ZUAA
(SHING)

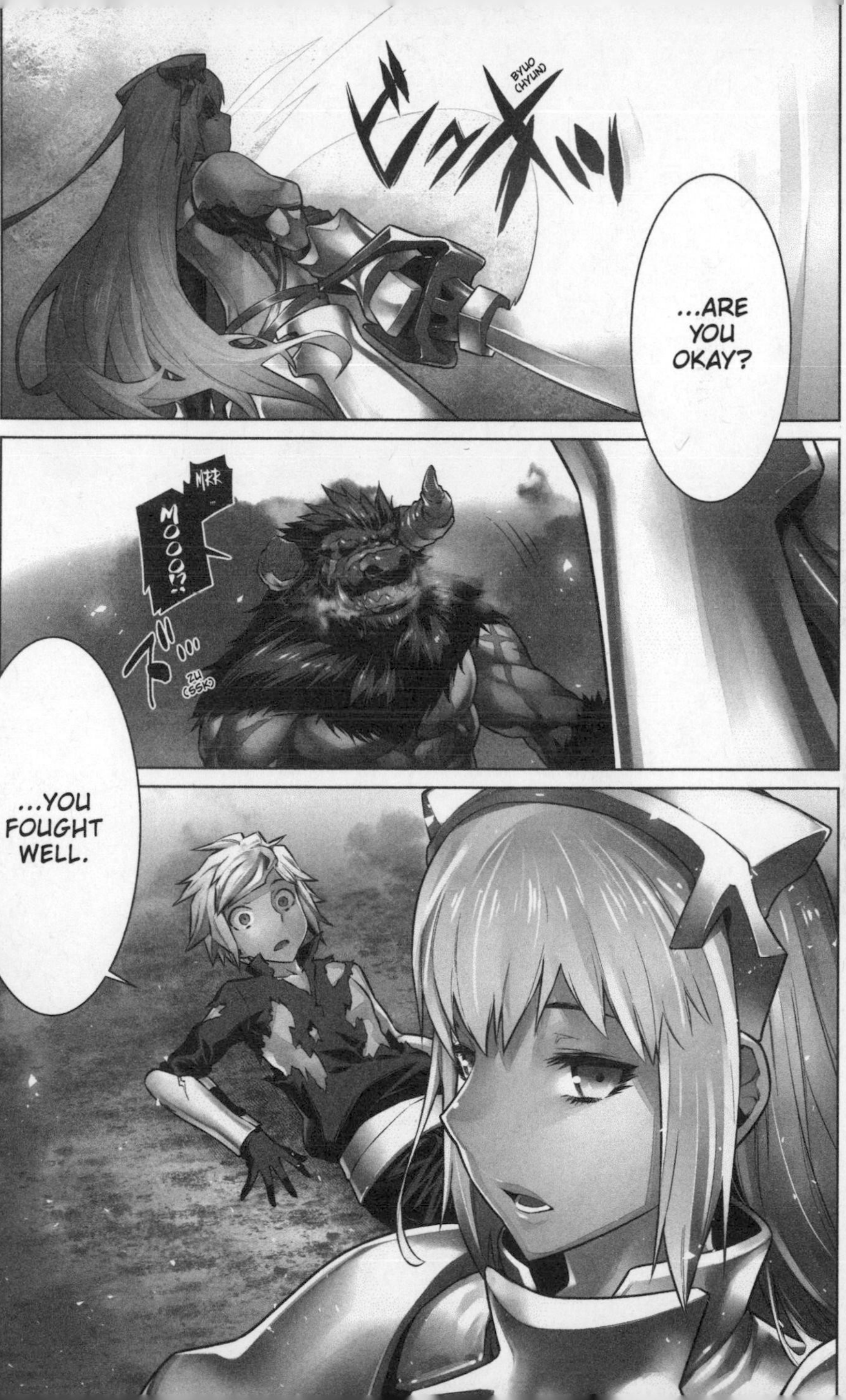
BYUO (HYUN)
...ARE YOU OKAY?
MRR...
MOOOO!?
ZU (SSK)
...YOU FOUGHT WELL.

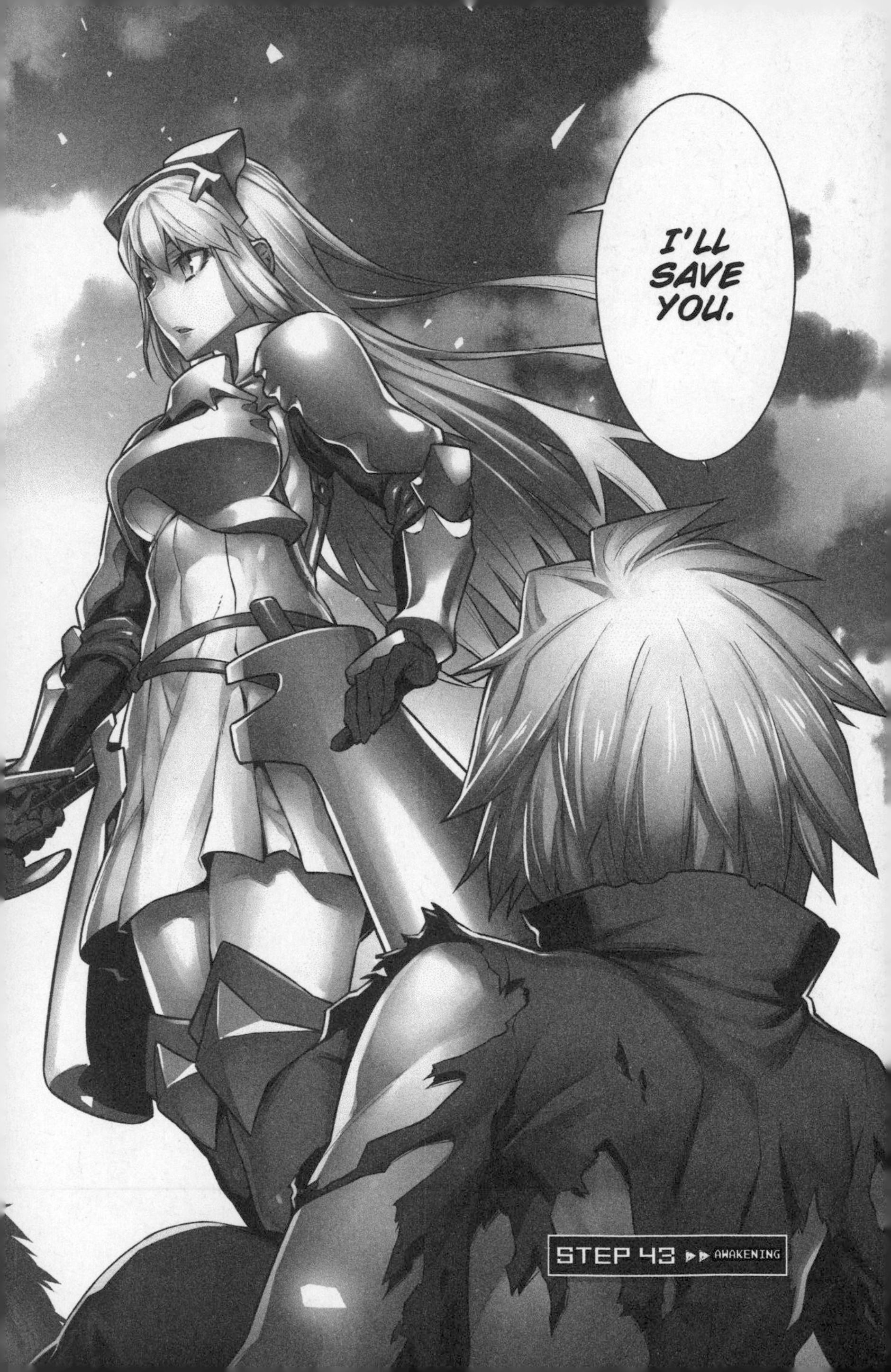
I'LL SAVE YOU.
STEP 43 ▶▶ AWAKENING

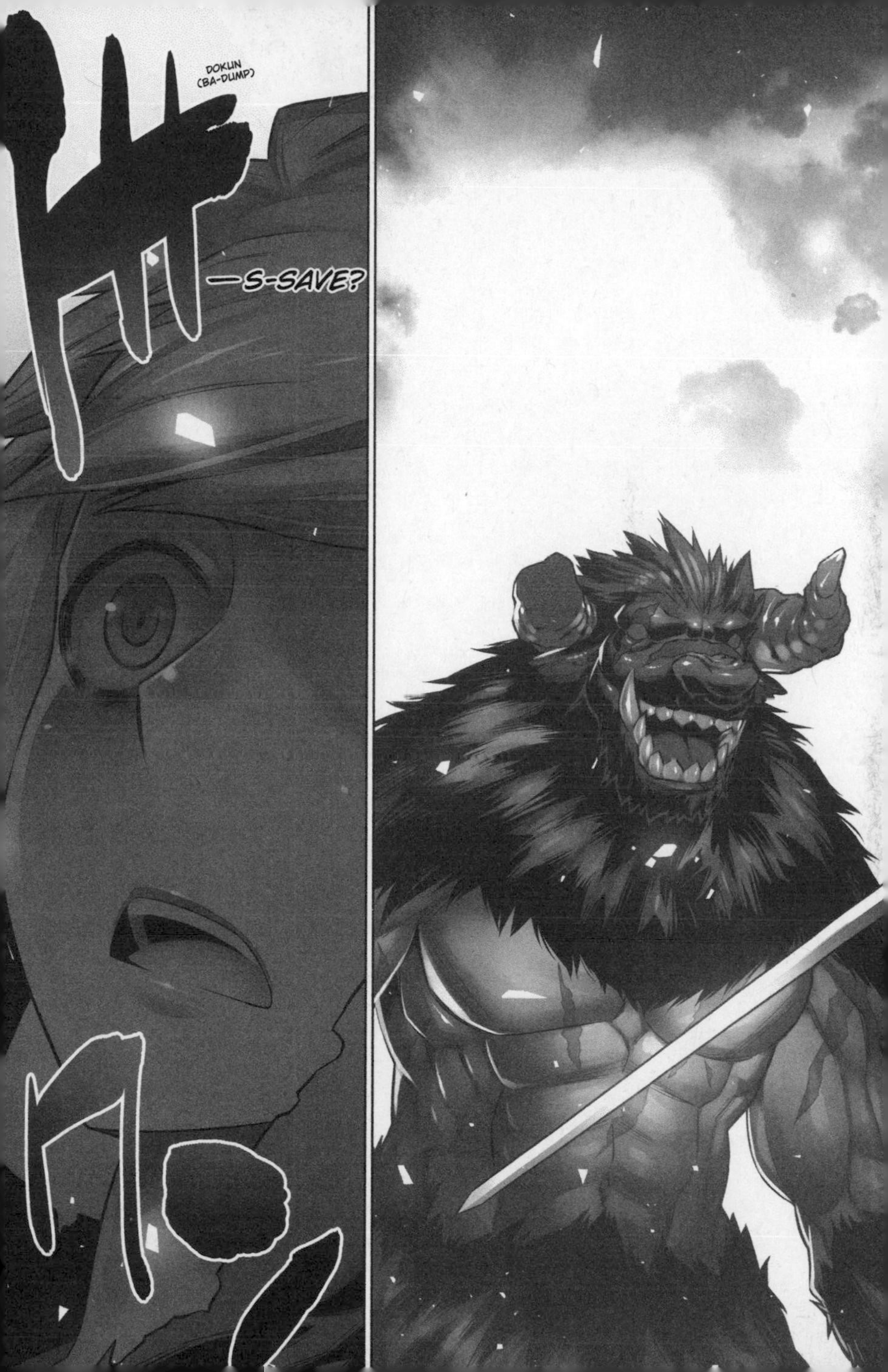
DOKUN (BA-DUMP)
—S-SAVE?

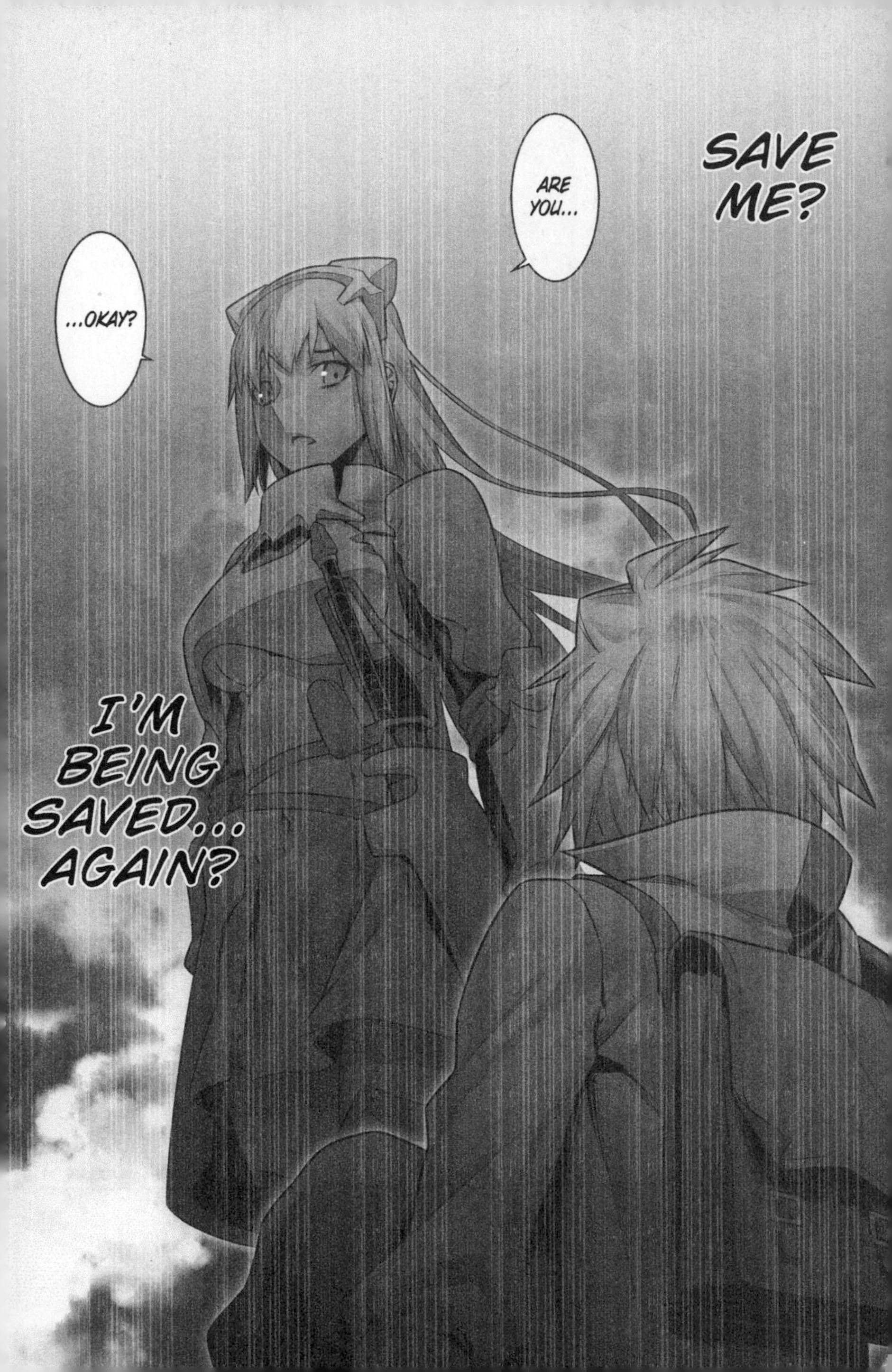

SAVE ME?
ARE YOU...
...OKAY?
I'M BEING SAVED... AGAIN?

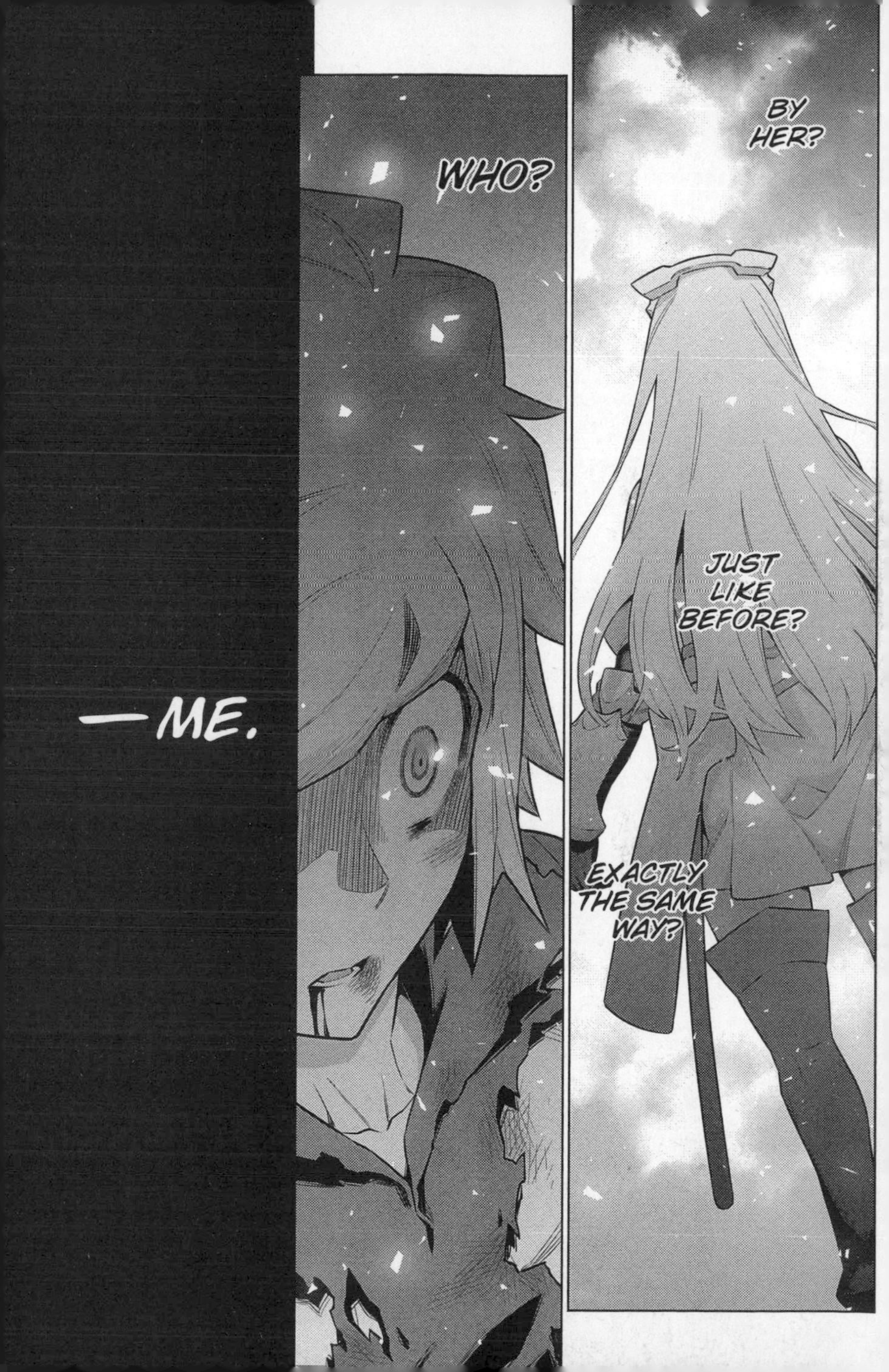
BY HER?
JUST LIKE BEFORE?
EXACTLY THE SAME WAY?
WHO?
—ME.

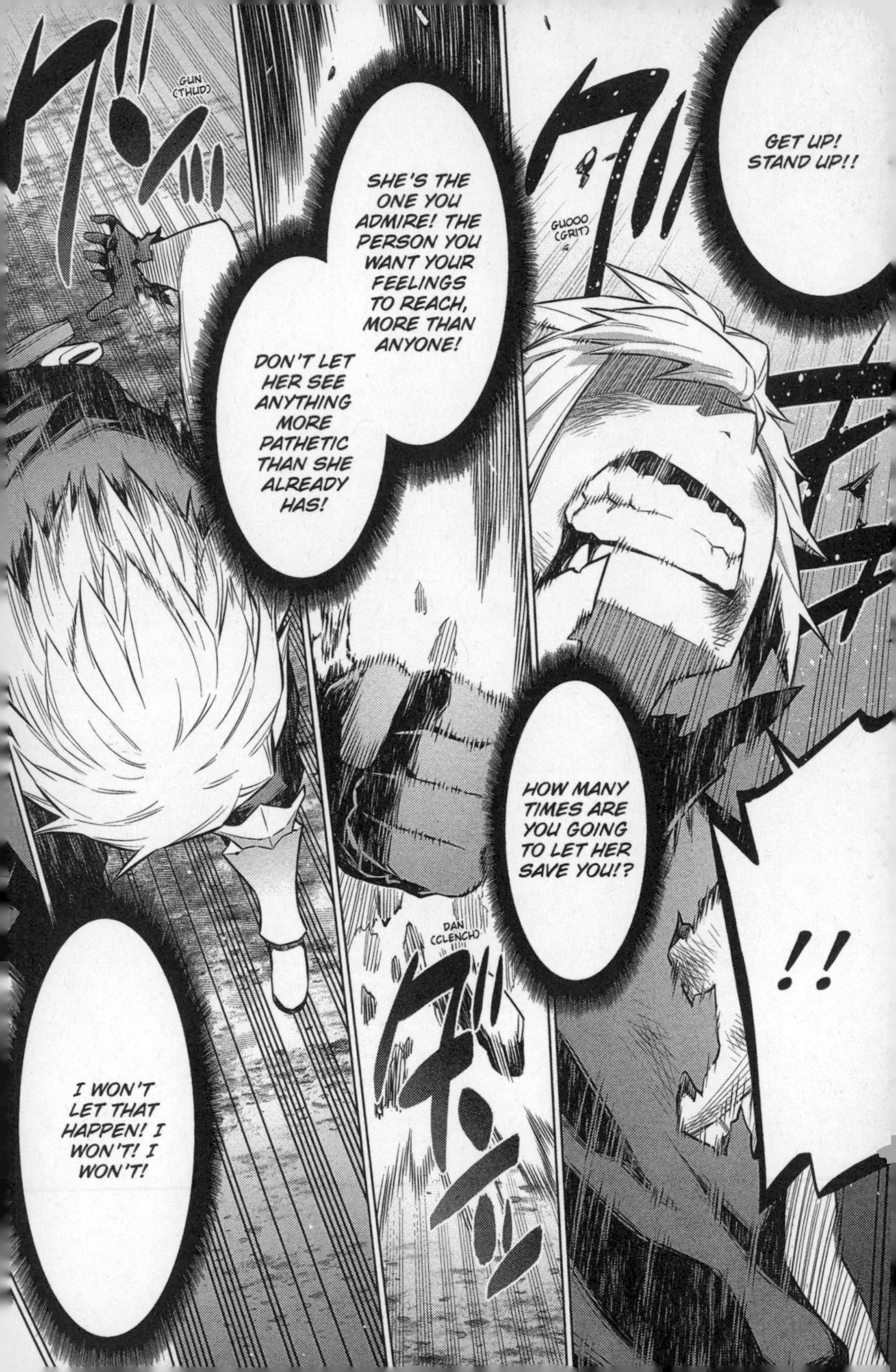
GET UP! STAND UP!!
GUOOO (GRIT)
HOW MANY TIMES ARE YOU GOING TO LET HER SAVE YOU!?
!!
SHE'S THE ONE YOU ADMIRE! THE PERSON YOU WANT YOUR FEELINGS TO REACH, MORE THAN ANYONE!
DON'T LET HER SEE ANYTHING MORE PATHETIC THAN SHE ALREADY HAS!
DAN (CLENCH)
GUN (THUD)
I WON'T LET THAT HAPPEN! I WON'T! I WON'T!

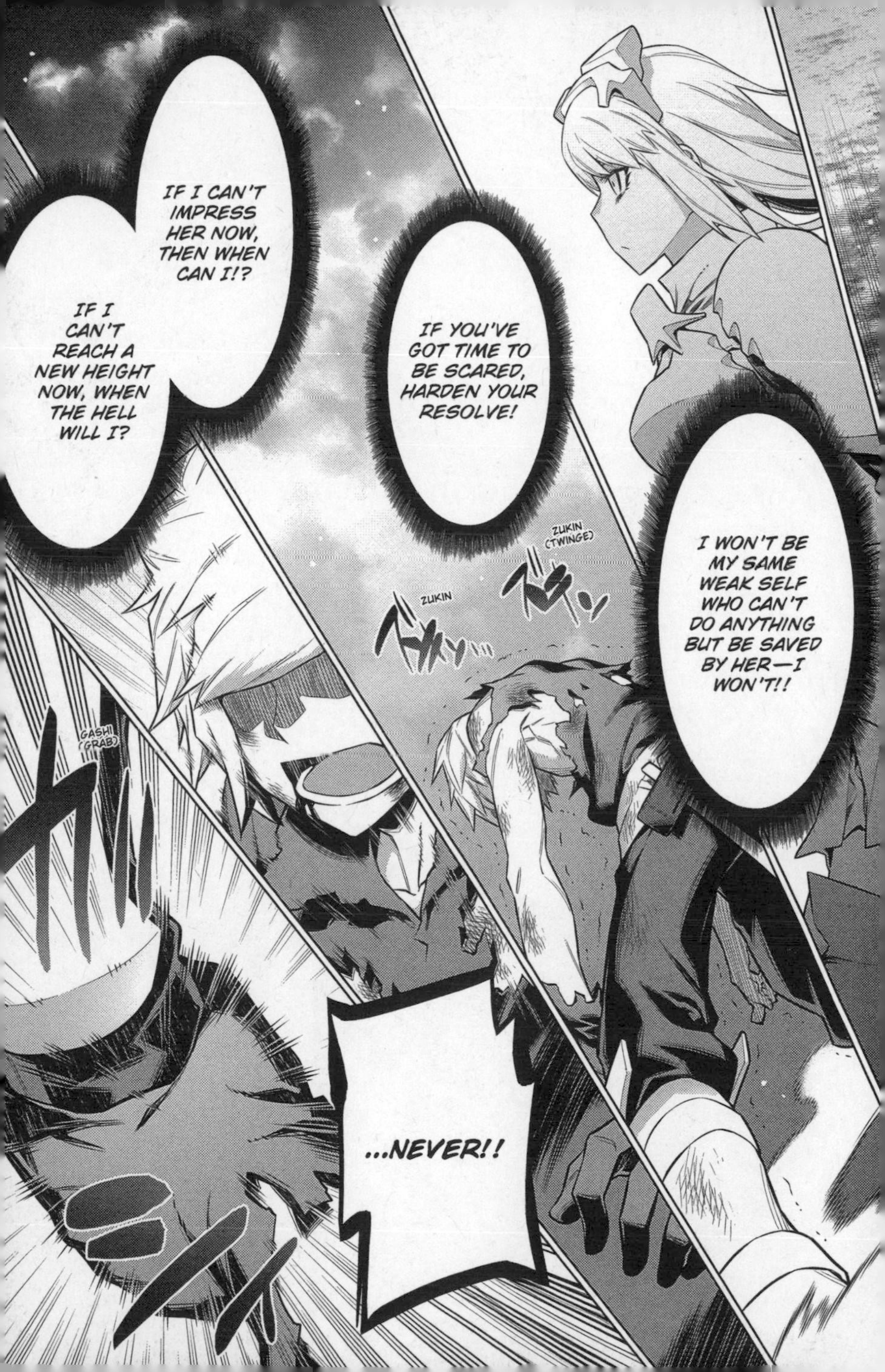
IF YOU'VE GOT TIME TO BE SCARED, HARDEN YOUR RESOLVE!
IF I CAN'T IMPRESS HER NOW, THEN WHEN CAN I!?
IF I CAN'T REACH A NEW HEIGHT NOW, WHEN THE HELL WILL I?
I WON'T BE MY SAME WEAK SELF WHO CAN'T DO ANYTHING BUT BE SAVED BY HER—I WON'T!!
ZUKIN (TWINGE)
ZUKIN
...NEVER!!
GASHI (GRAB)

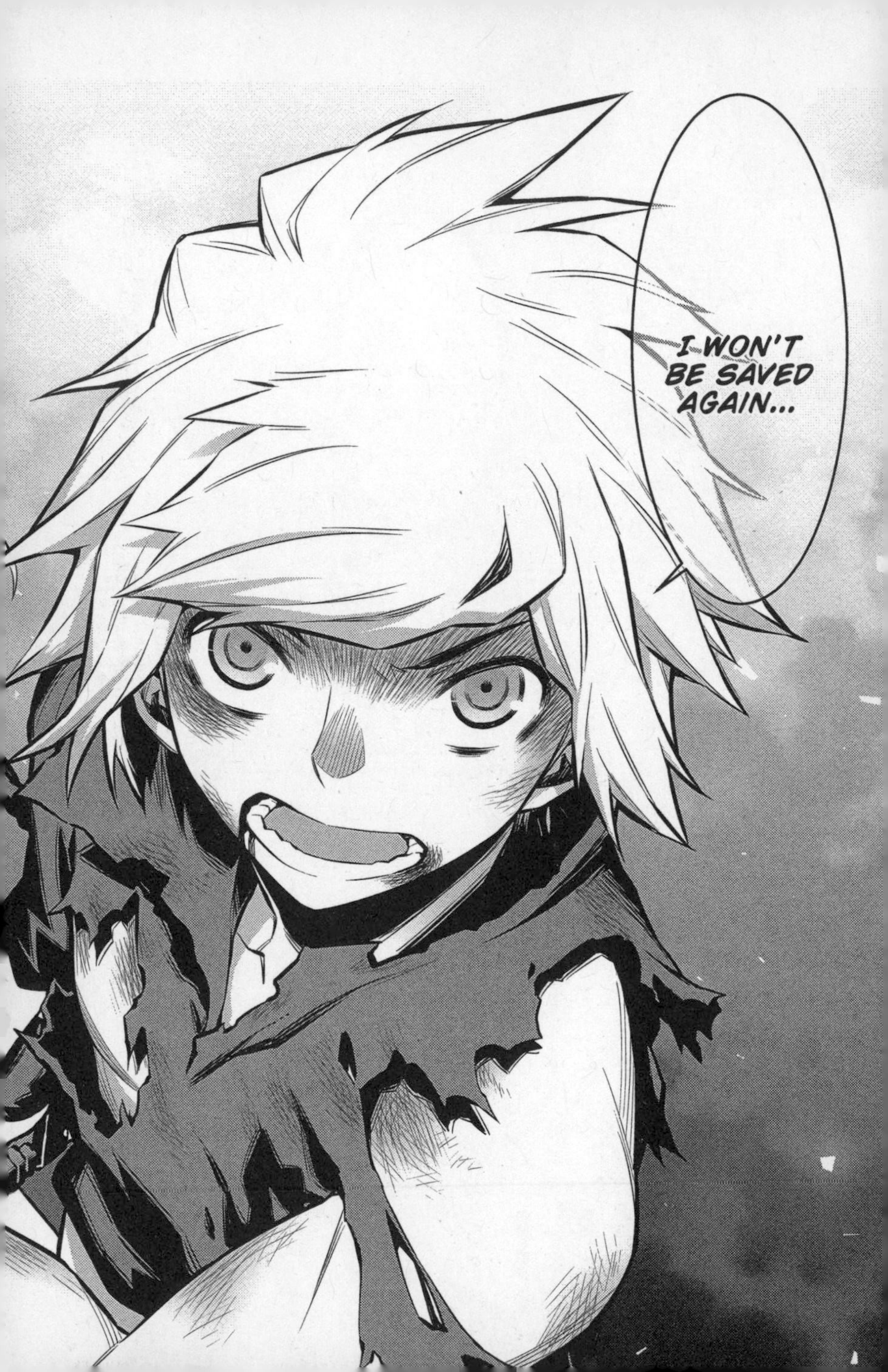
I WON'T BE SAVED AGAIN...

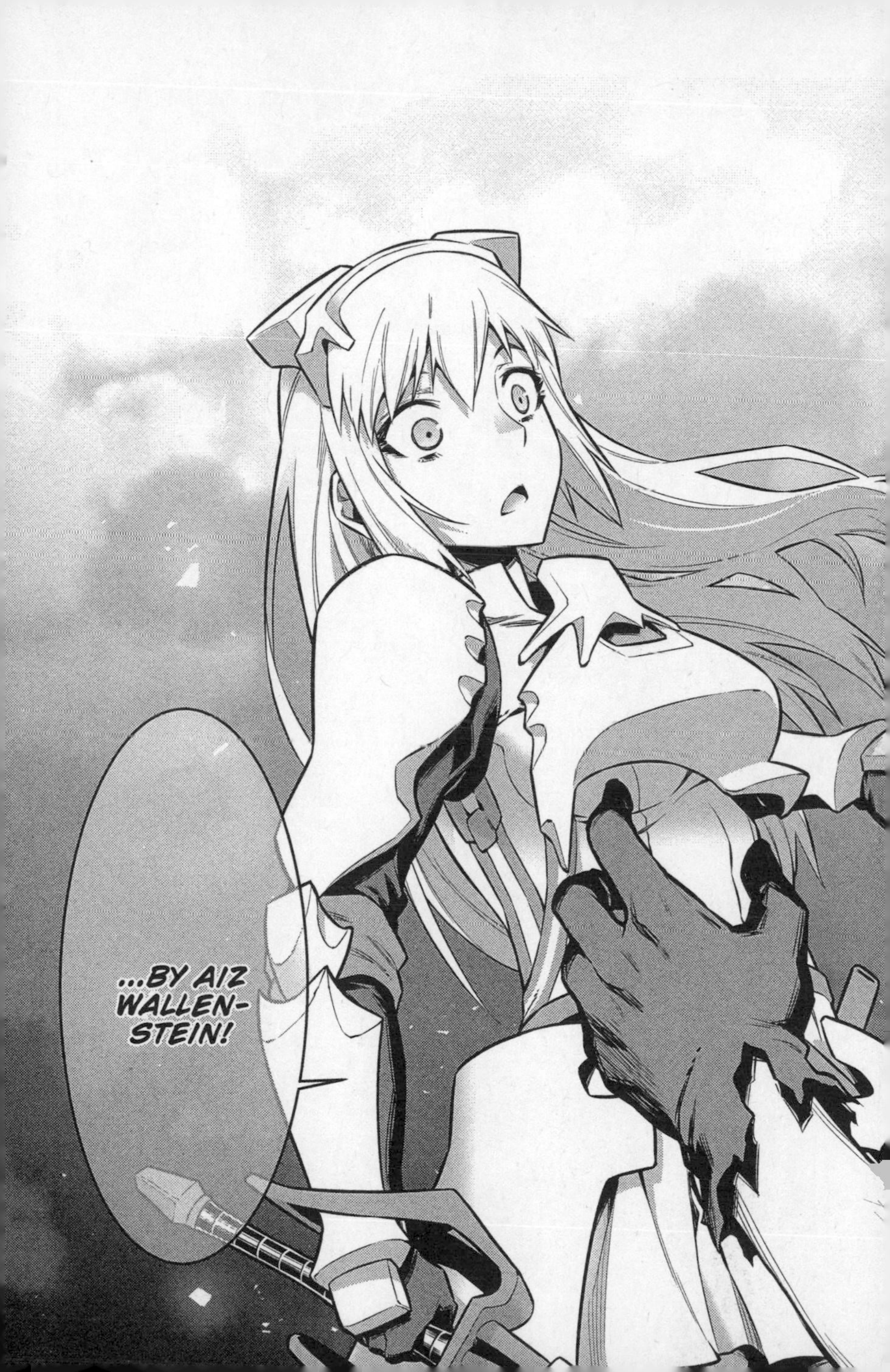
...BY AIZ WALLEN-STEIN!

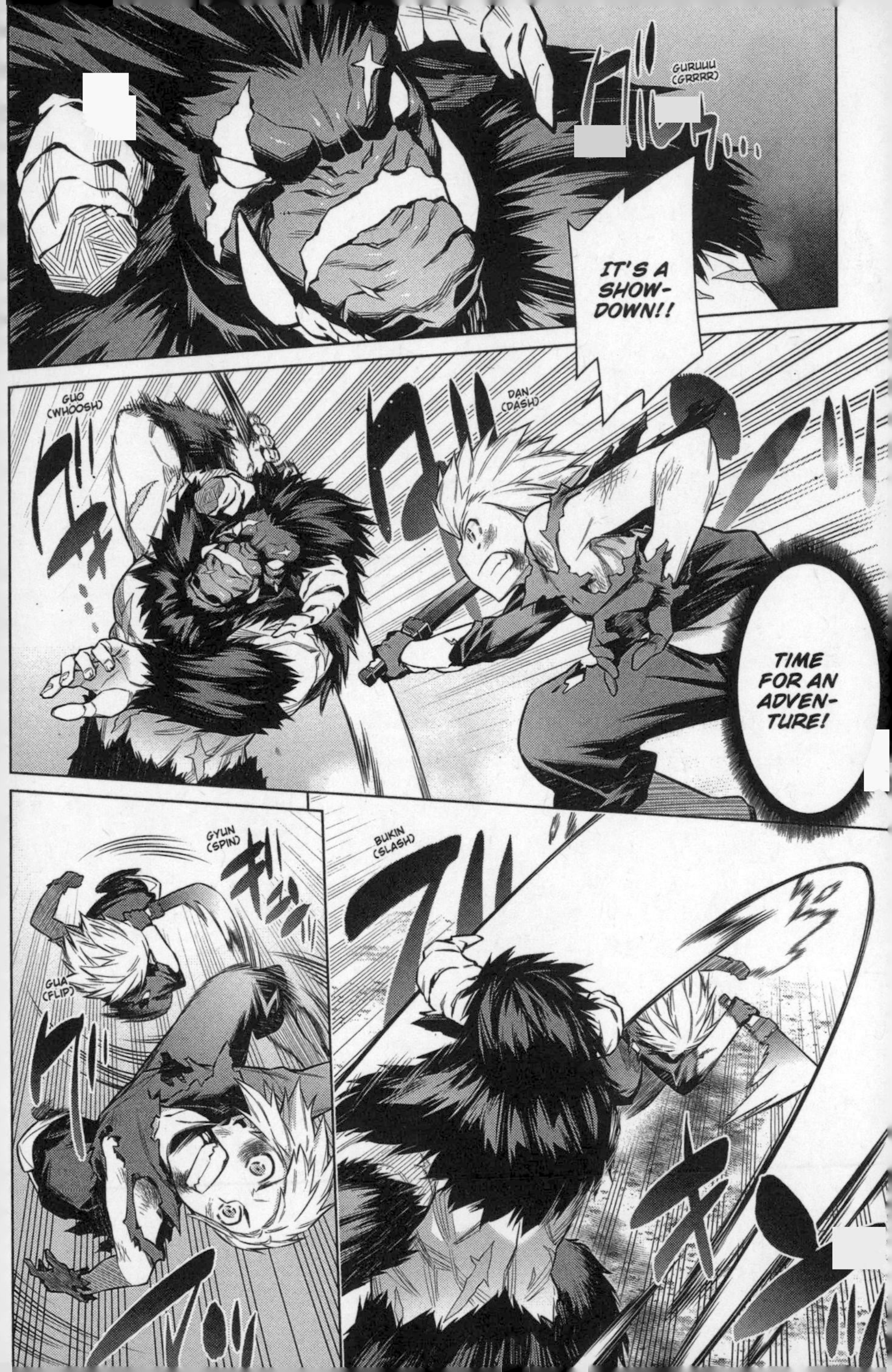
GURUUU (GRRRR)
IT'S A SHOW-DOWN!!
TIME FOR AN ADVEN-TURE!
DAN (DASH)
GUO (WHOOSH)
BUKIN (SLASH)
GYUN (SPIN)
GUA (FLIP)

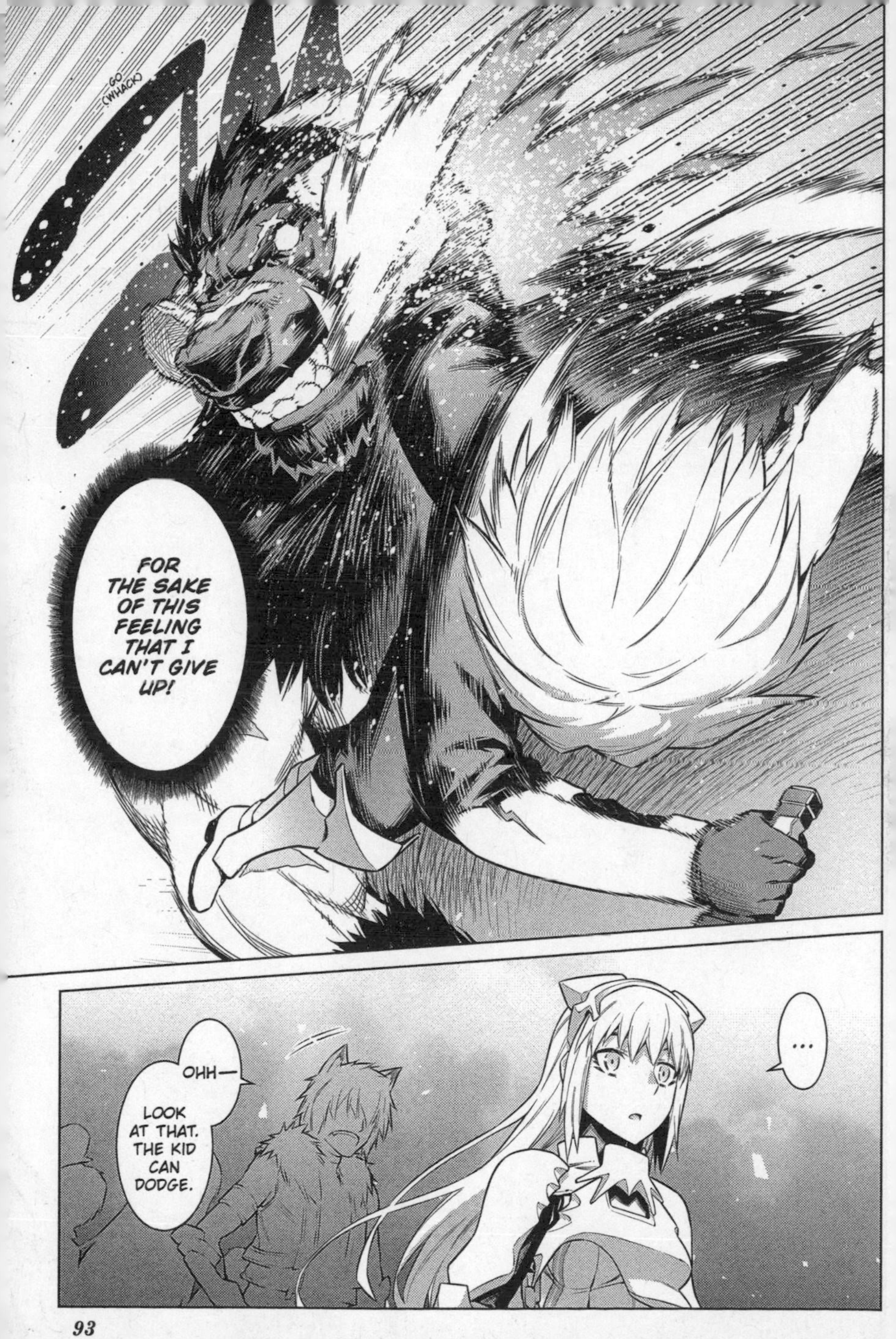
GO (WHACK)
FOR THE SAKE OF THIS FEELING THAT I CAN'T GIVE UP!
...
OHH—
LOOK AT THAT. THE KID CAN DODGE.

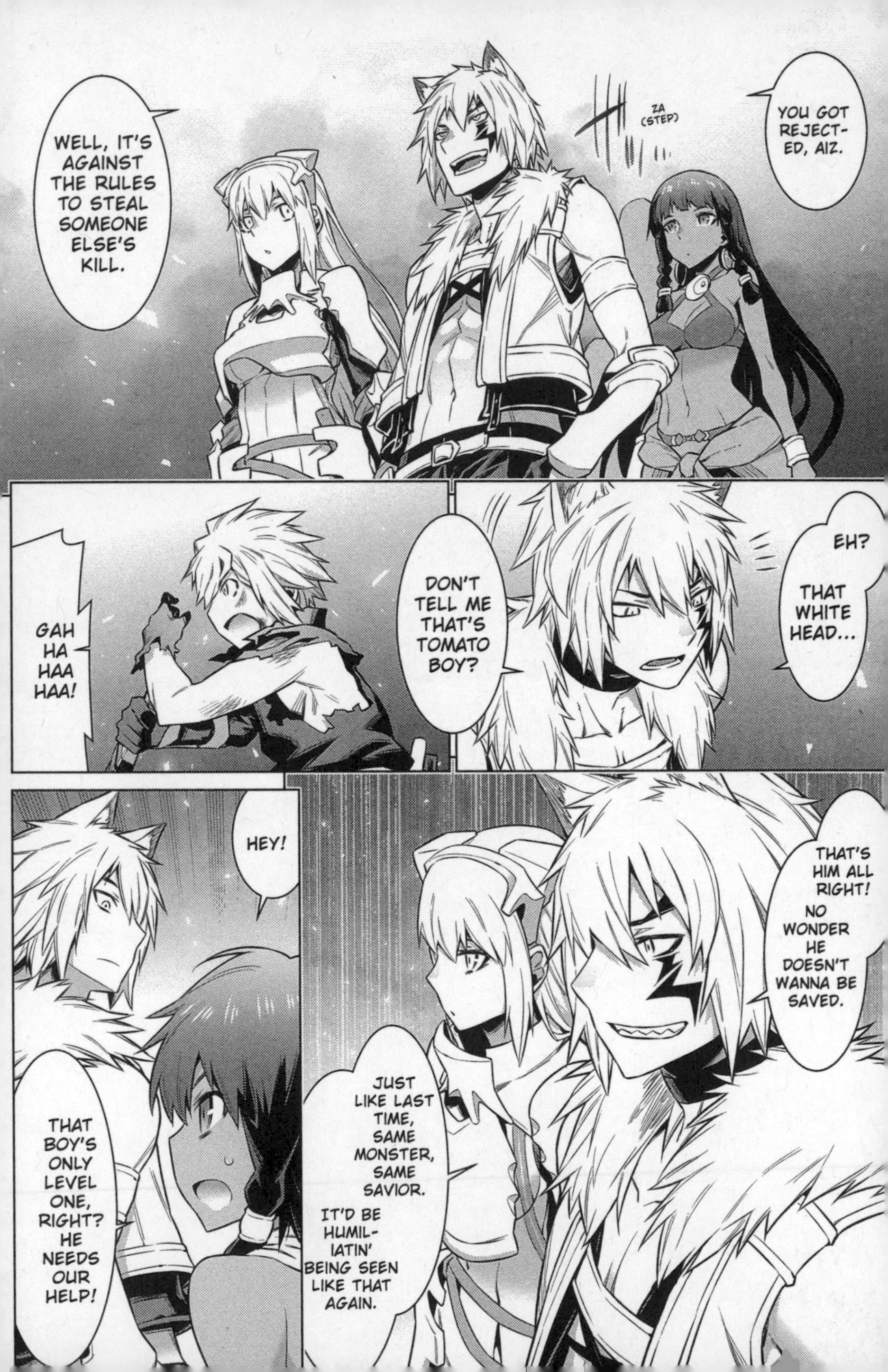
YOU GOT REJECT-ED, AIZ.
ZA (STEP)
WELL, IT'S AGAINST THE RULES TO STEAL SOMEONE ELSE'S KILL.
EH? THAT WHITE HEAD...
DON'T TELL ME THAT'S TOMATO BOY?
GAH HA HAA HAA!
THAT'S HIM ALL RIGHT!
NO WONDER HE DOESN'T WANNA BE SAVED.
JUST LIKE LAST TIME, SAME MONSTER, SAME SAVIOR.
IT'D BE HUMIL-IATIN' BEING SEEN LIKE THAT AGAIN.
HEY!
THAT BOY'S ONLY LEVEL ONE, RIGHT? HE NEEDS OUR HELP!

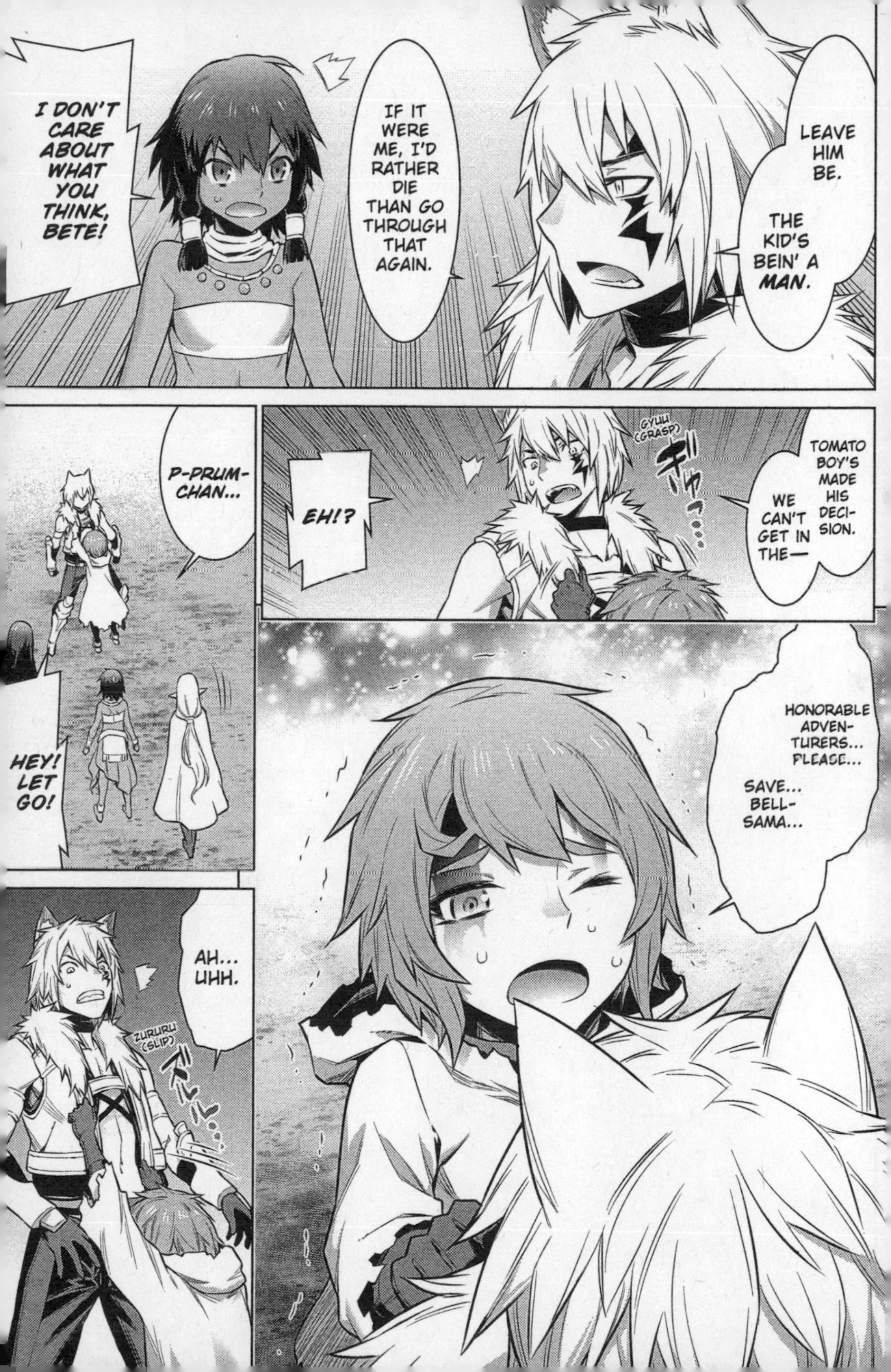
LEAVE HIM BE.
THE KID'S BEIN' A MAN.
IF IT WERE ME, I'D RATHER DIE THAN GO THROUGH THAT AGAIN.
I DON'T CARE ABOUT WHAT YOU THINK, BETE!
TOMATO BOY'S MADE HIS DECISION.
WE CAN'T GET IN THE—
GYUU (GRASP)
EH!?
HONORABLE ADVENTURERS... PLEASE...
SAVE... BELL-SAMA...
P-PRUM-CHAN...
HEY! LET GO!
AH... UHH.
ZURURU (SLIP)

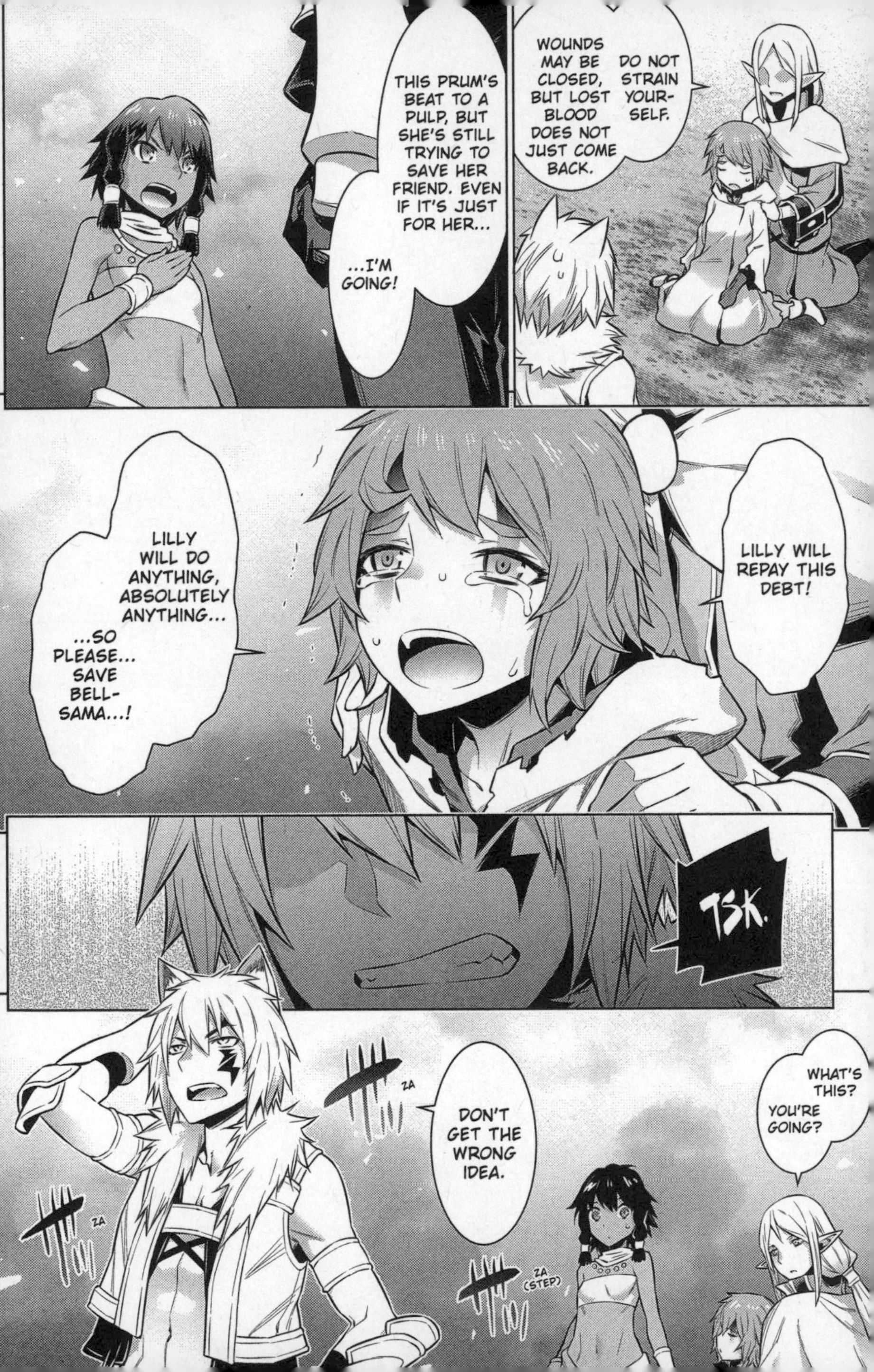
WOUNDS MAY BE CLOSED, BUT LOST BLOOD DOES NOT JUST COME BACK.
DO NOT STRAIN YOURSELF.
THIS PRUM'S BEAT TO A PULP, BUT SHE'S STILL TRYING TO SAVE HER FRIEND. EVEN IF IT'S JUST FOR HER...
...I'M GOING!
LILLY WILL REPAY THIS DEBT!
LILLY WILL DO ANYTHING, ABSOLUTELY ANYTHING...
...SO PLEASE... SAVE BELL-SAMA...!
TSK.
WHAT'S THIS?
YOU'RE GOING?
DON'T GET THE WRONG IDEA.
ZA
ZA (STEP)
ZA

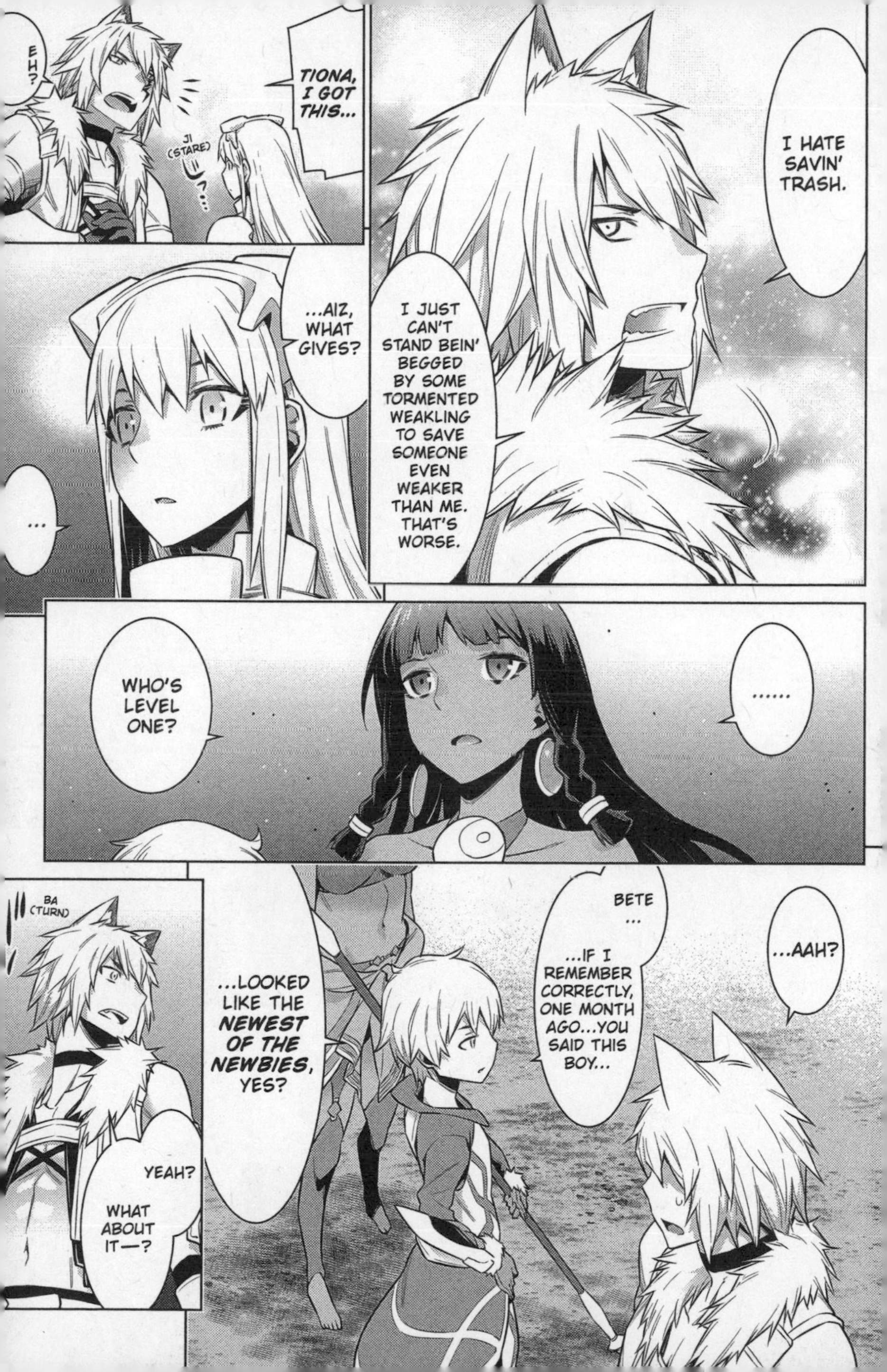
I HATE SAVIN' TRASH.
I JUST CAN'T STAND BEIN' BEGGED BY SOME TORMENTED WEAKLING TO SAVE SOMEONE EVEN WEAKER THAN ME. THAT'S WORSE.
TIONA, I GOT THIS...
EH?
JI (STARE)
...AIZ, WHAT GIVES?
...
......
WHO'S LEVEL ONE?
...AAH?
BETE ...
...IF I REMEMBER CORRECTLY, ONE MONTH AGO...YOU SAID THIS BOY...
...LOOKED LIKE THE *NEWEST OF THE NEWBIES*, YES?
BA (TURN)
YEAH?
WHAT ABOUT IT—?

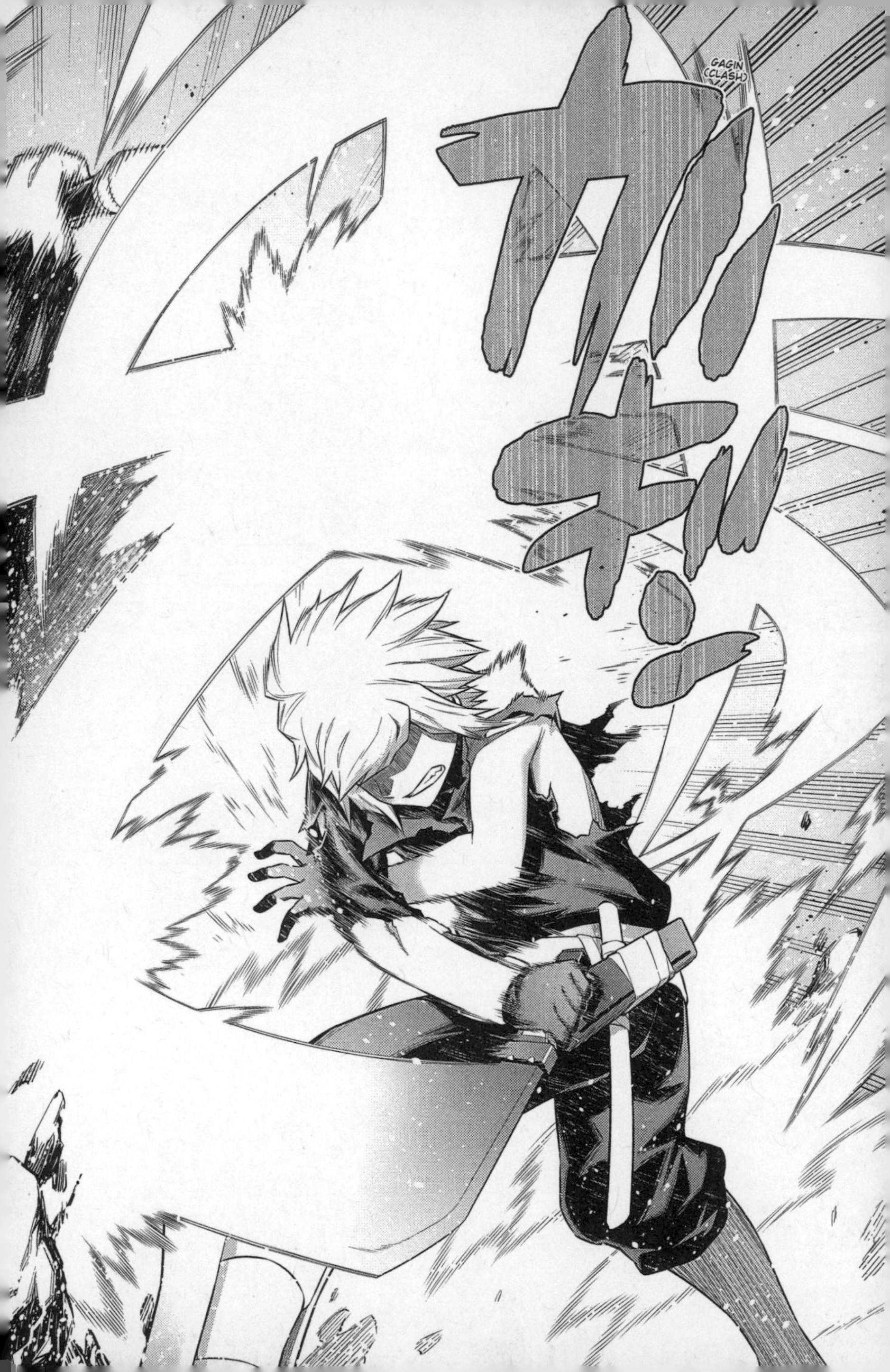
GAGIN (CLASH)
ガギン!!

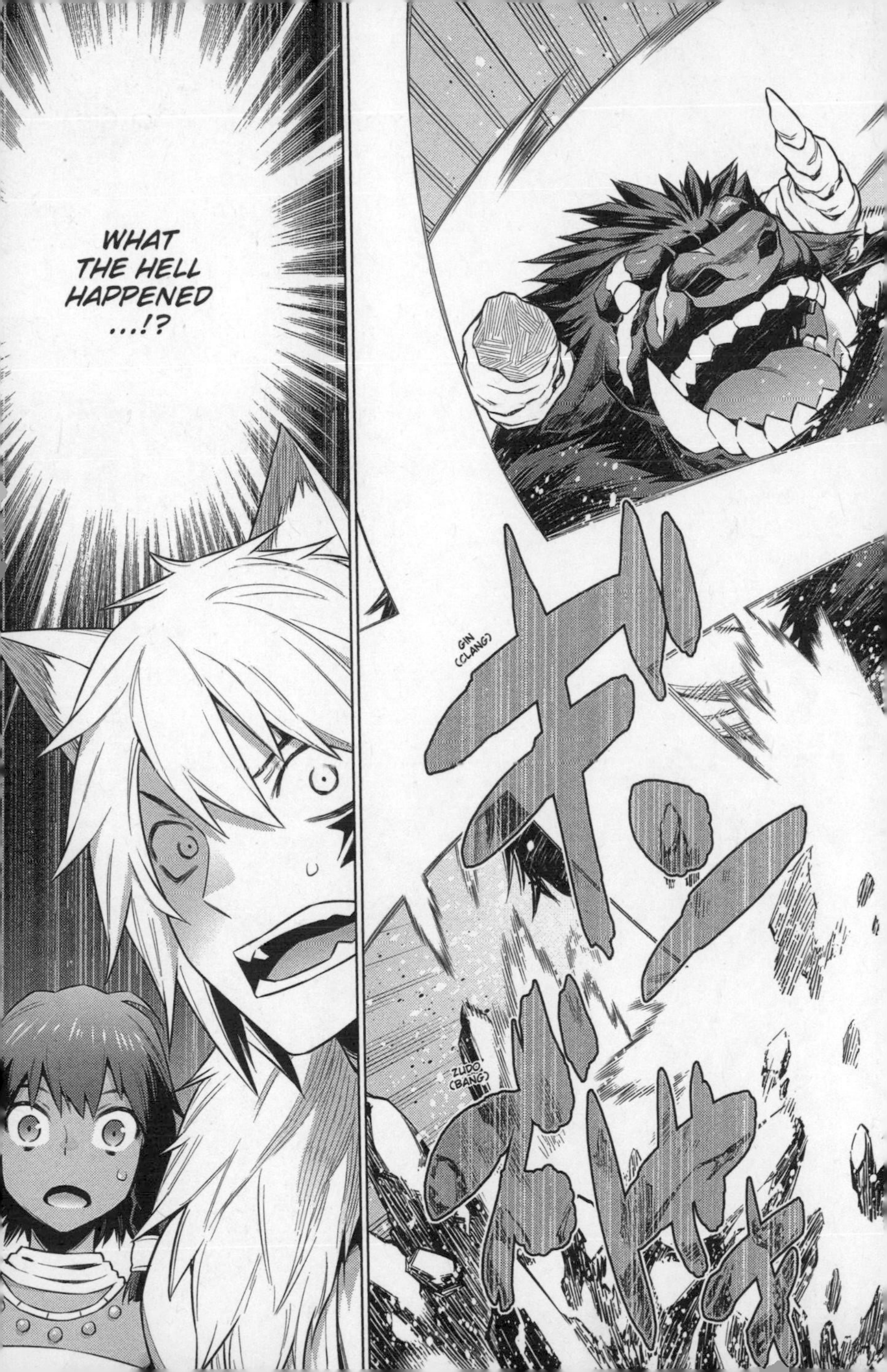
GIN (CLANG)
ZUDO (BANG)
WHAT THE HELL HAPPENED ...!?

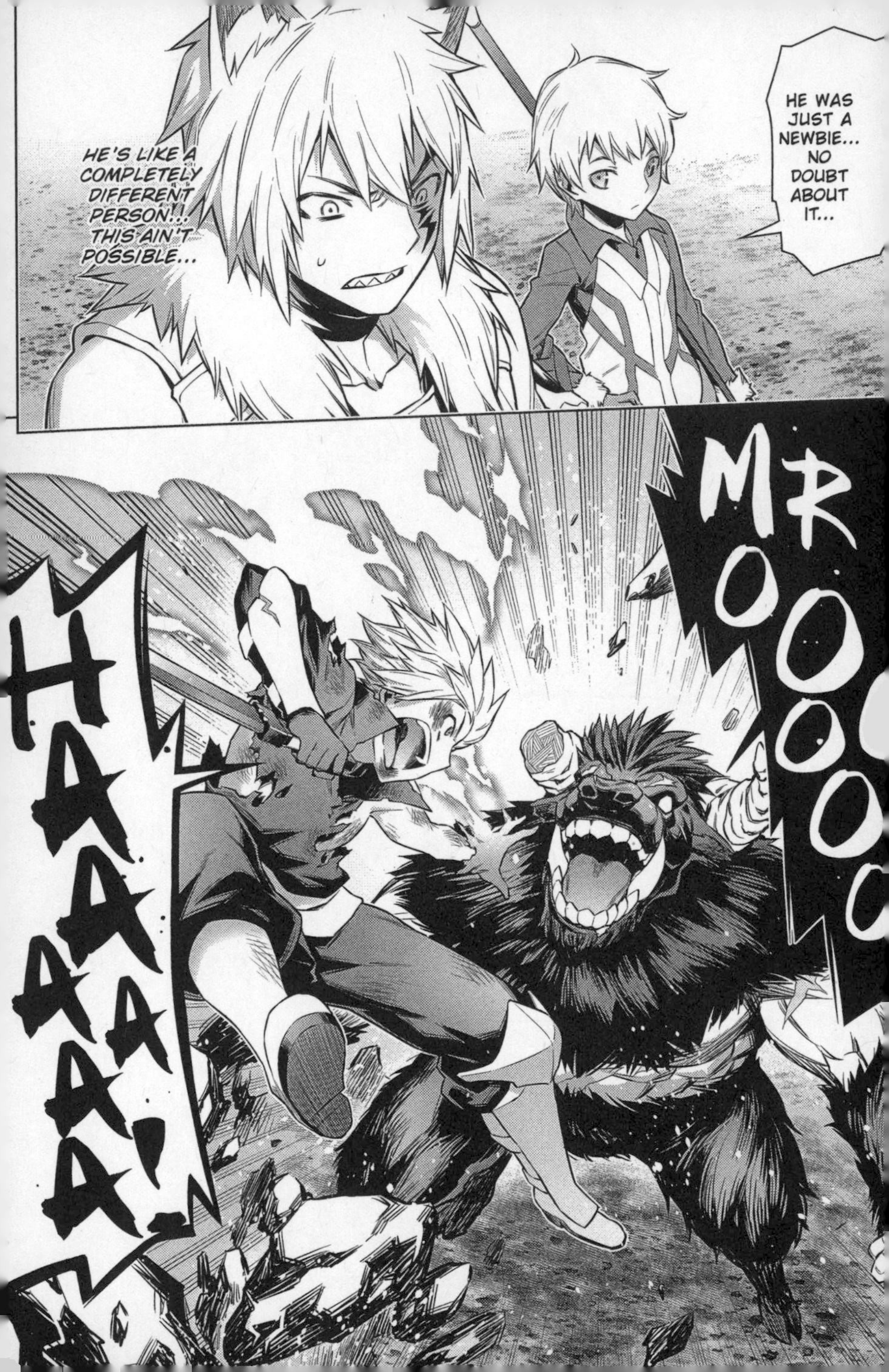
HE WAS JUST A NEWBIE... NO DOUBT ABOUT IT...
HE'S LIKE A COMPLETELY DIFFERENT PERSON!! THIS AIN'T POSSIBLE...
MROOOOOO
HAAAAAA

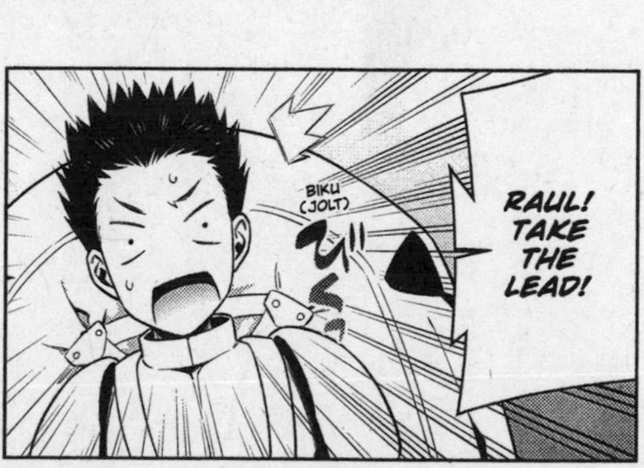
RAUL! TAKE THE LEAD!
BIKU (JOLT)

Is it WRONG to TRY to PICK UP GIRLS in a DUNGEON?

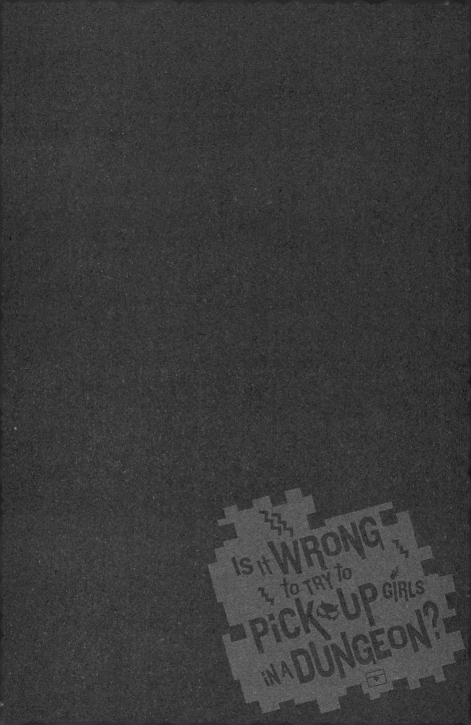

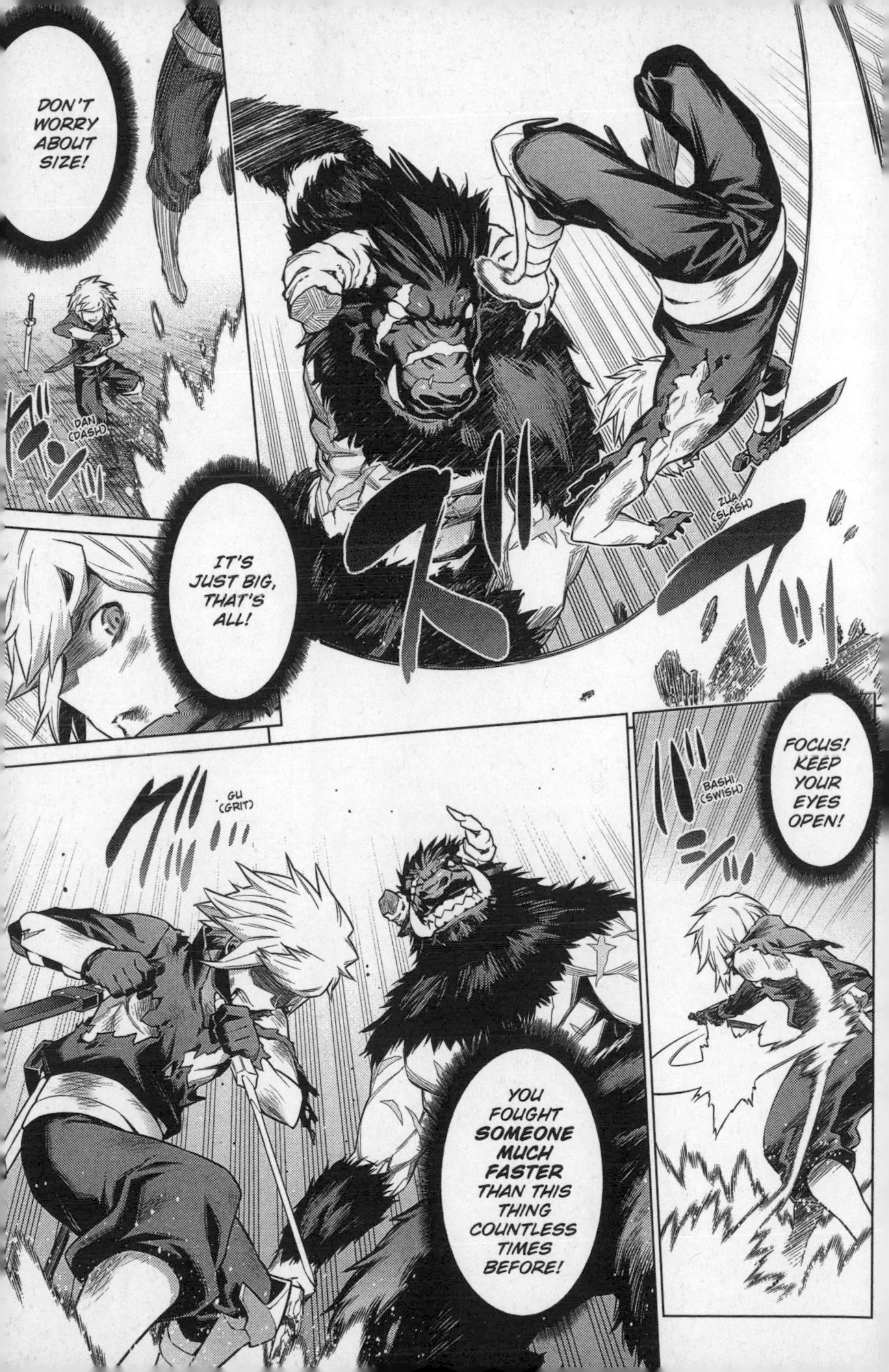
ZUA (SLASH)
DON'T WORRY ABOUT SIZE!
DAN (DASH)
IT'S JUST BIG, THAT'S ALL!
FOCUS! KEEP YOUR EYES OPEN!
BASHI (SWISH)
GU (GRIT)
YOU FOUGHT SOMEONE MUCH FASTER THAN THIS THING COUNTLESS TIMES BEFORE!

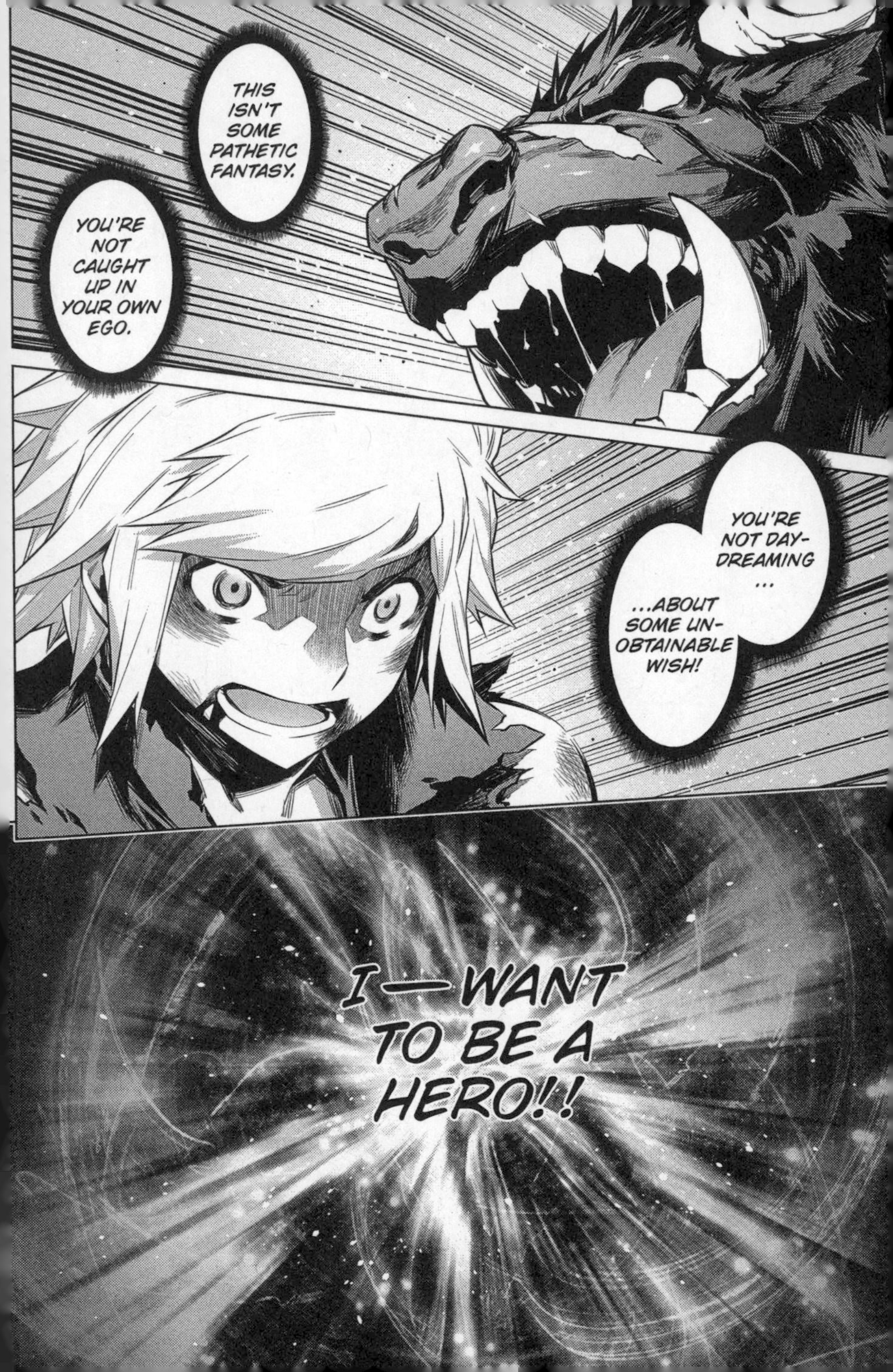
THIS ISN'T SOME PATHETIC FANTASY.
YOU'RE NOT CAUGHT UP IN YOUR OWN EGO.
YOU'RE NOT DAY-DREAMING...
...ABOUT SOME UN-OBTAINABLE WISH!
I—WANT TO BE A HERO!!

STEP 44 ▸▸ ARGONAUT

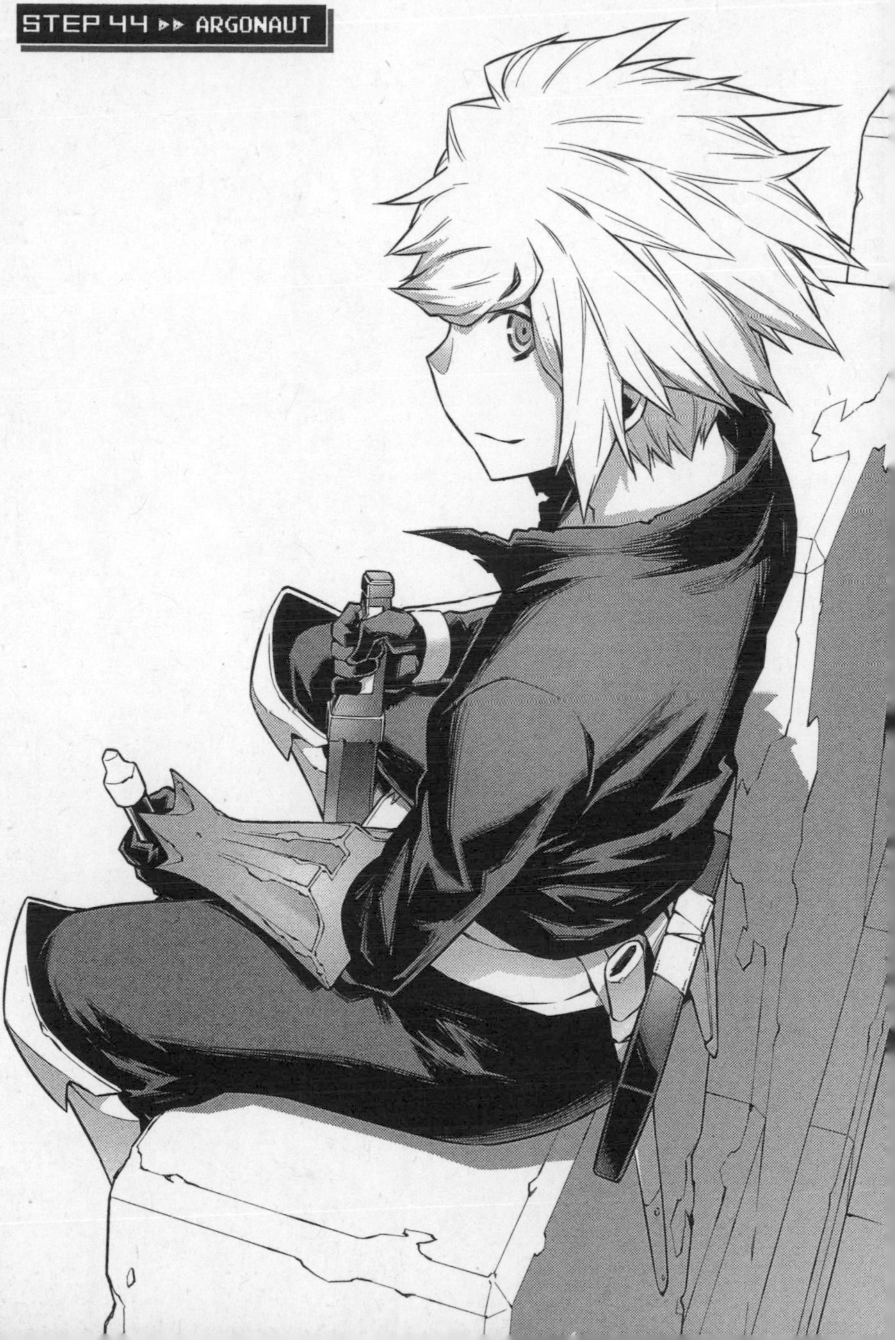

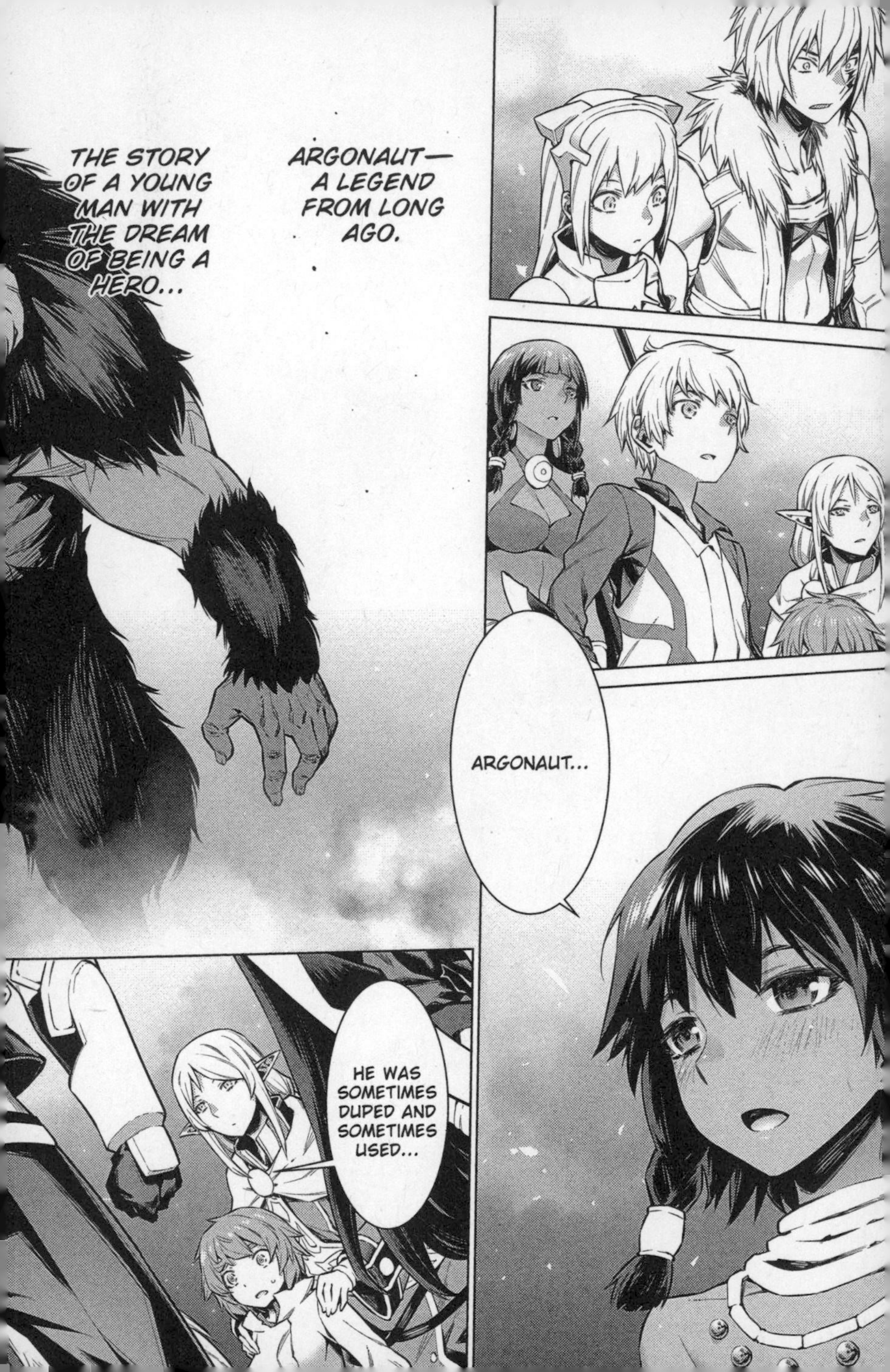
ARGONAUT...
ARGONAUT—A LEGEND FROM LONG AGO.
THE STORY OF A YOUNG MAN WITH THE DREAM OF BEING A HERO...
HE WAS SOMETIMES DUPED AND SOMETIMES USED...

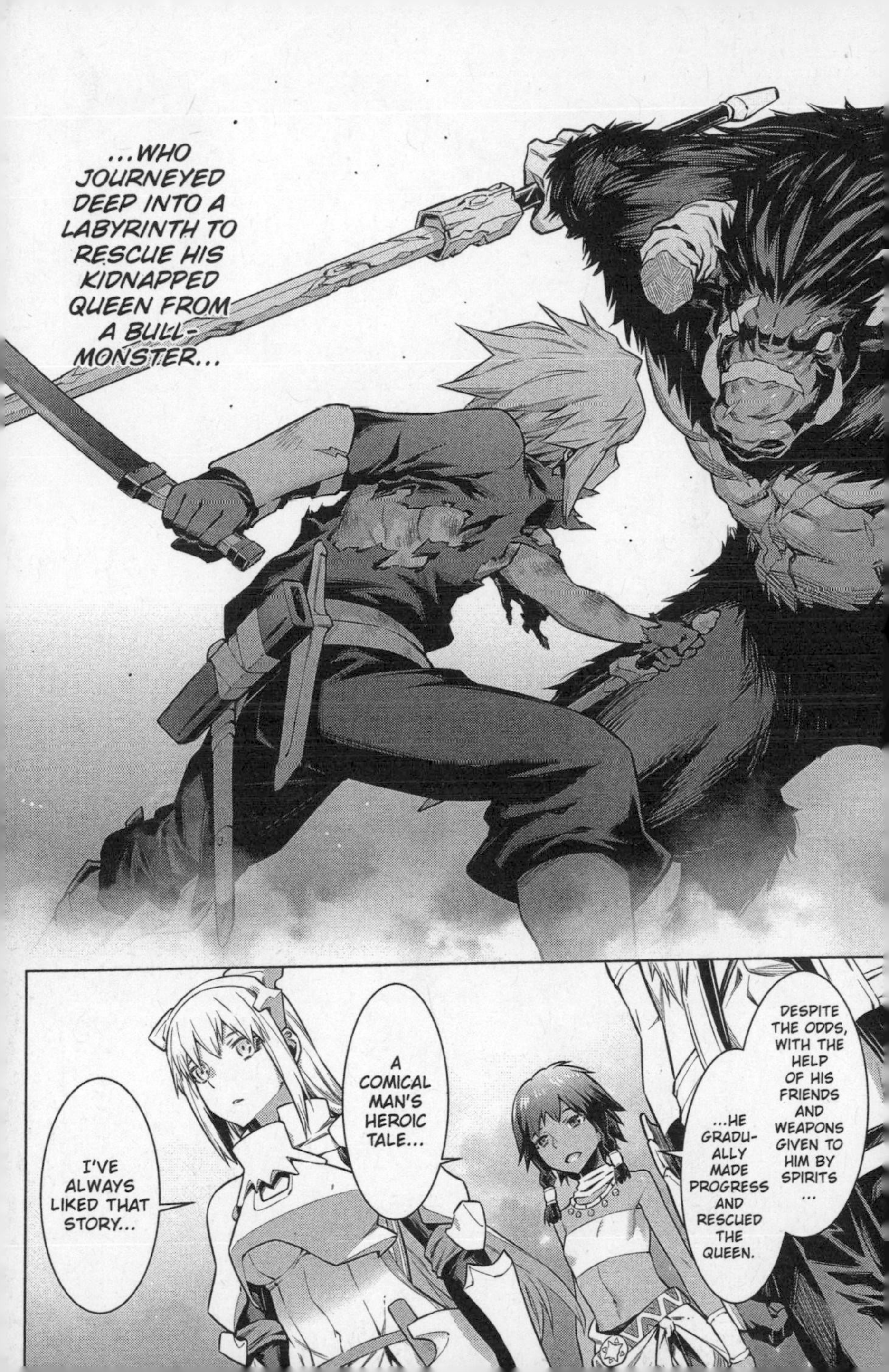
...WHO JOURNEYED DEEP INTO A LABYRINTH TO RESCUE HIS KIDNAPPED QUEEN FROM A BULL-MONSTER...
DESPITE THE ODDS, WITH THE HELP OF HIS FRIENDS AND WEAPONS GIVEN TO HIM BY SPIRITS ...
...HE GRADUALLY MADE PROGRESS AND RESCUED THE QUEEN.
A COMICAL MAN'S HEROIC TALE...
I'VE ALWAYS LIKED THAT STORY...

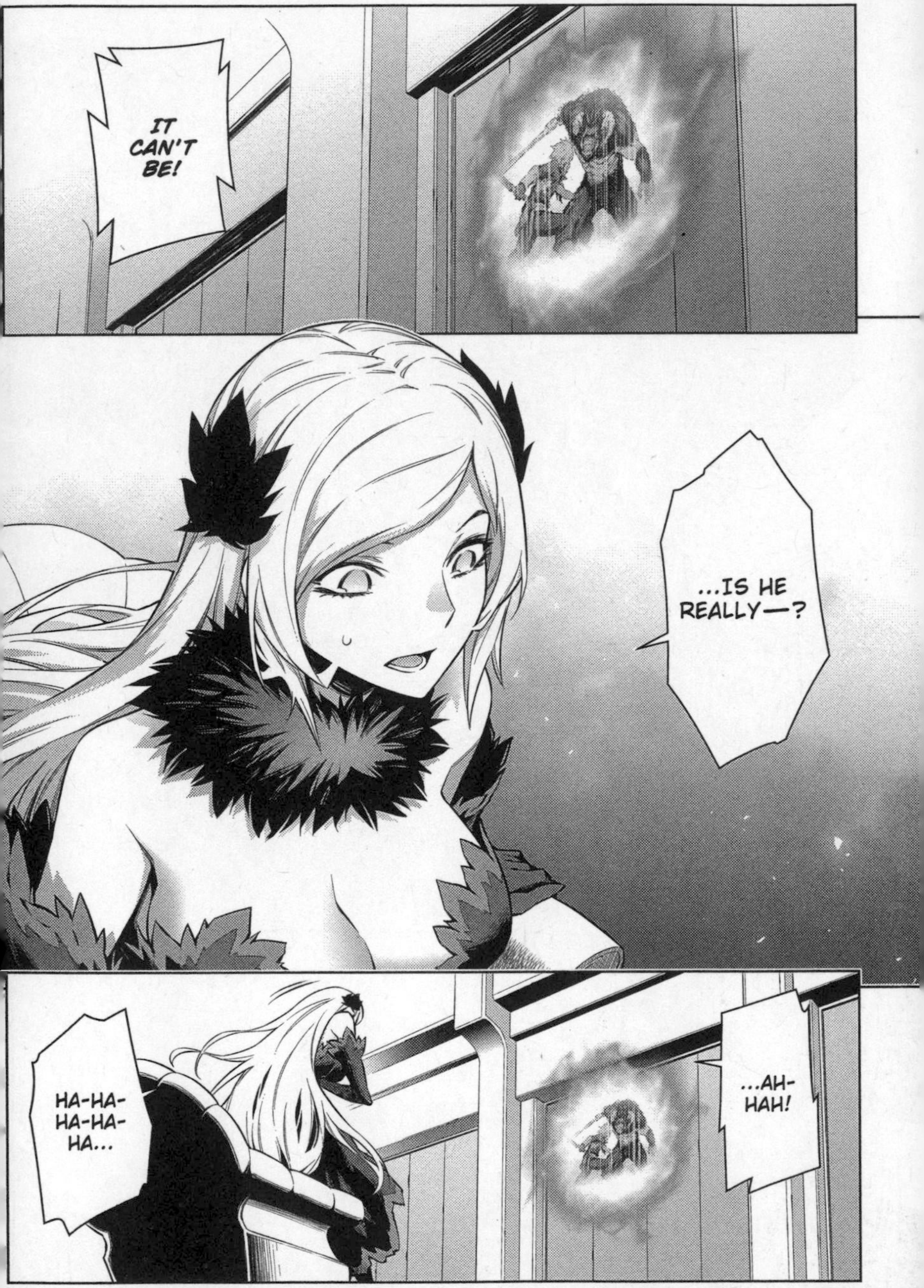
IT CAN'T BE!
...IS HE REALLY—?
...AH-HAH!
HA-HA-HA-HA-HA...

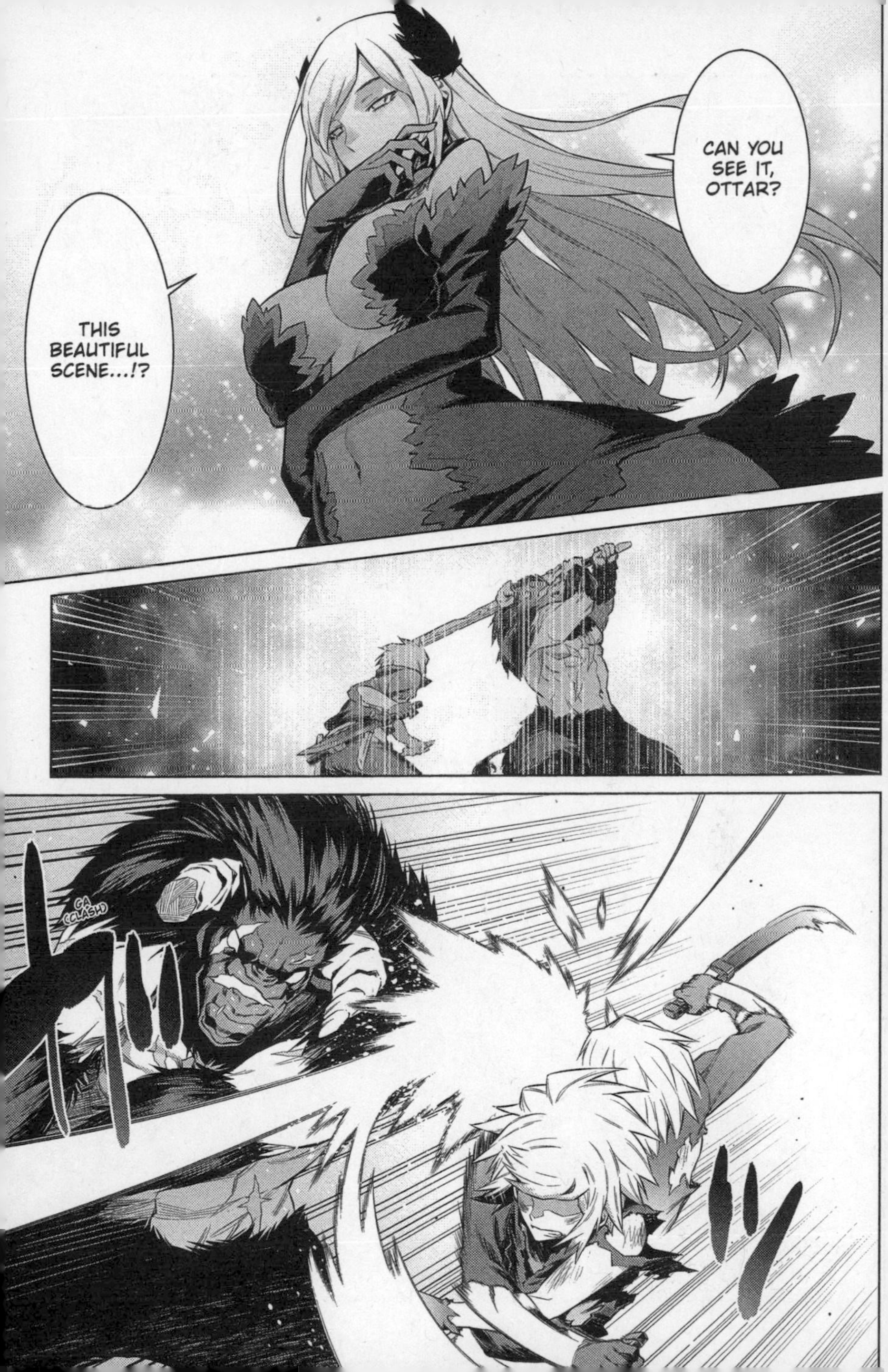
CAN YOU SEE IT, OTTAR?
THIS BEAUTIFUL SCENE...!?
GA (CLASH)

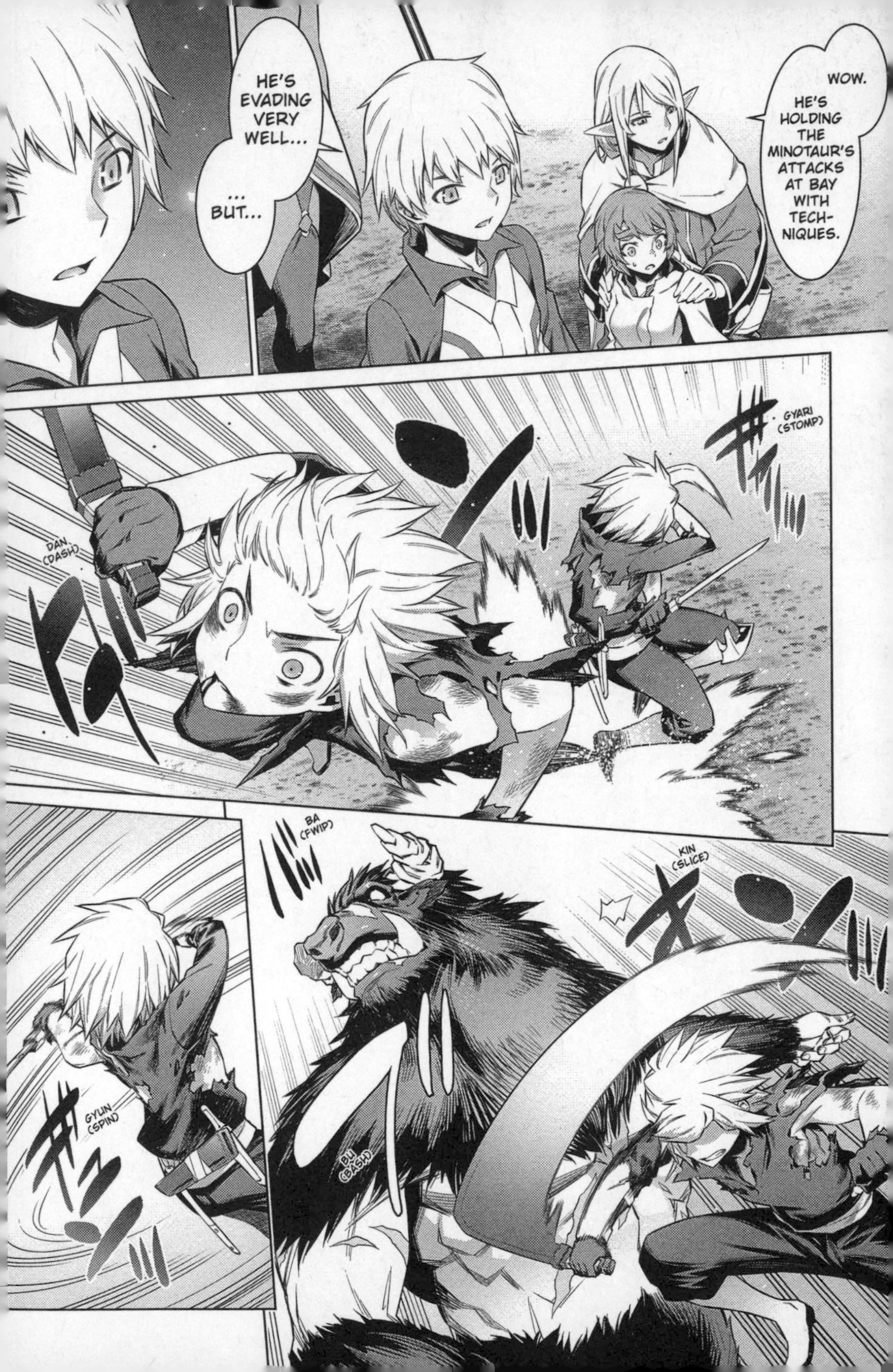
WOW. HE'S HOLDING THE MINOTAUR'S ATTACKS AT BAY WITH TECH-NIQUES.
HE'S EVADING VERY WELL...
... BUT...
GYARI (STOMP)
DAN (DASH)
KIN (SLICE)
BA (FWIP)
BU (BASH)
GYUN (SPIN)

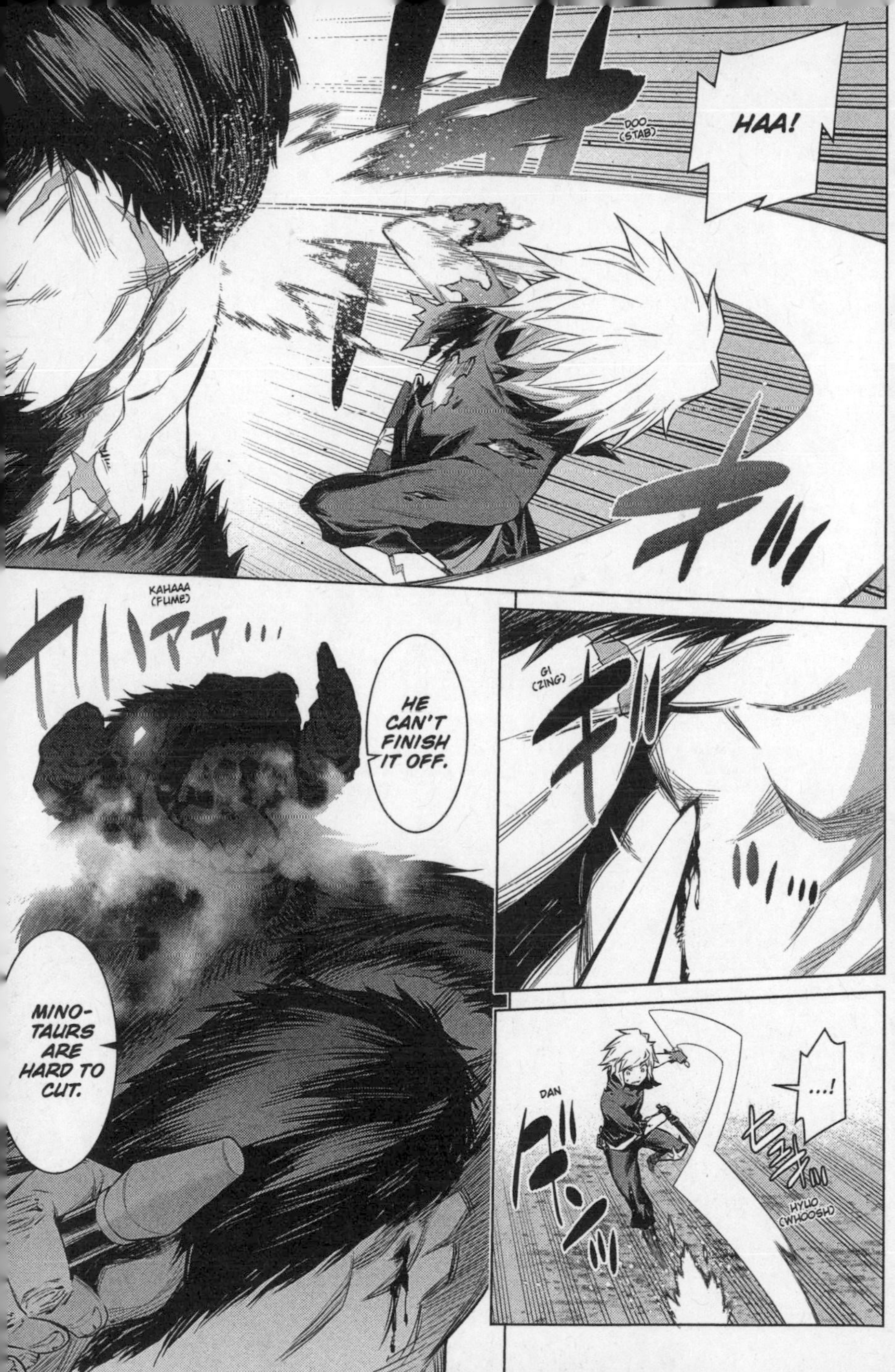
HAA!
DOO (STAB)
GI (ZING)
...!
HYUO (WHOOSH)
DAN
KAHAAA (FUME)
HE CAN'T FINISH IT OFF.
MINO-TAURS ARE HARD TO CUT.

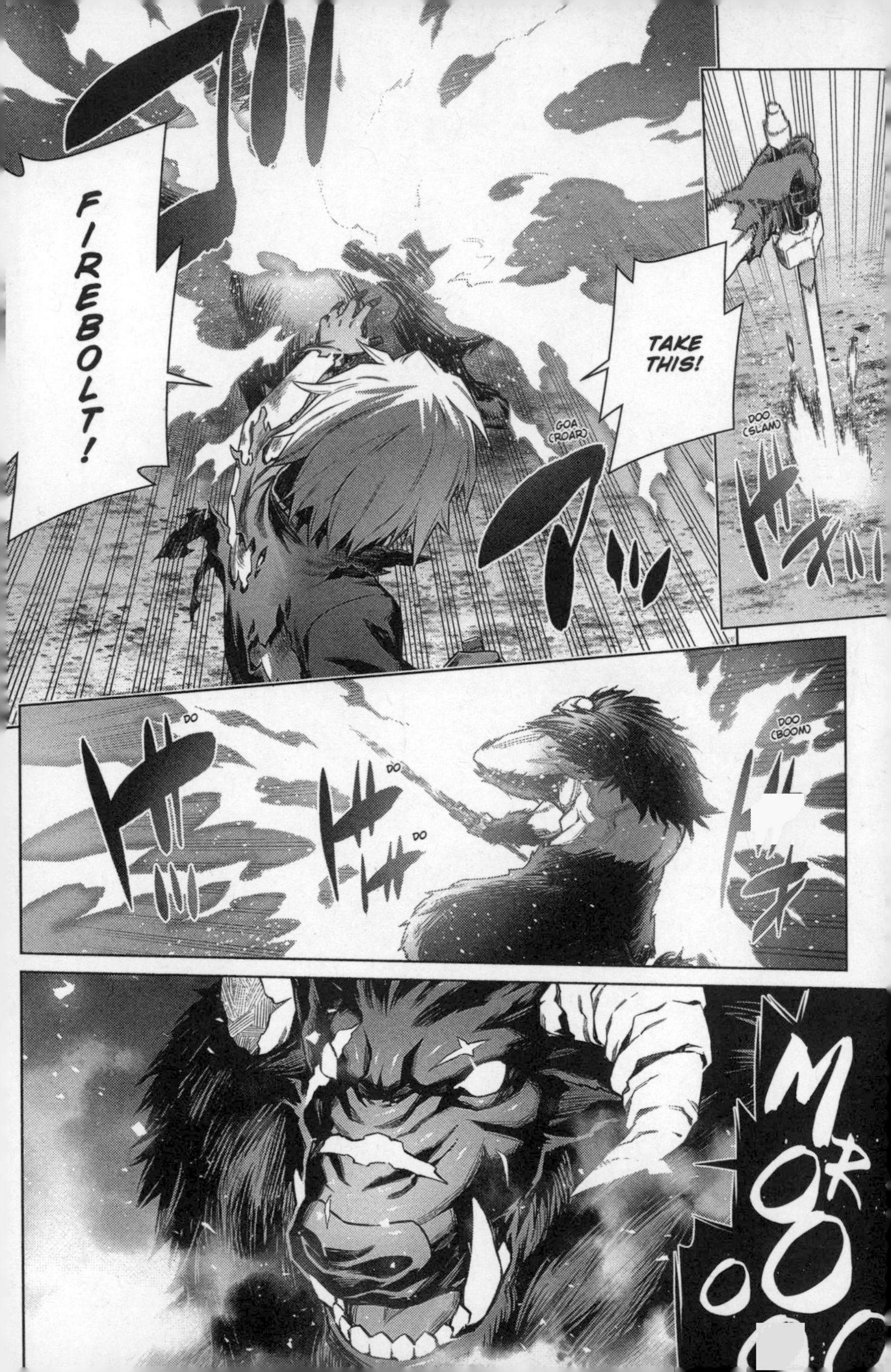
DOO (SLAM)
TAKE THIS!
GOA (ROAR)
FIREBOLT!
DOO (BOOM)
DO
DO
DO

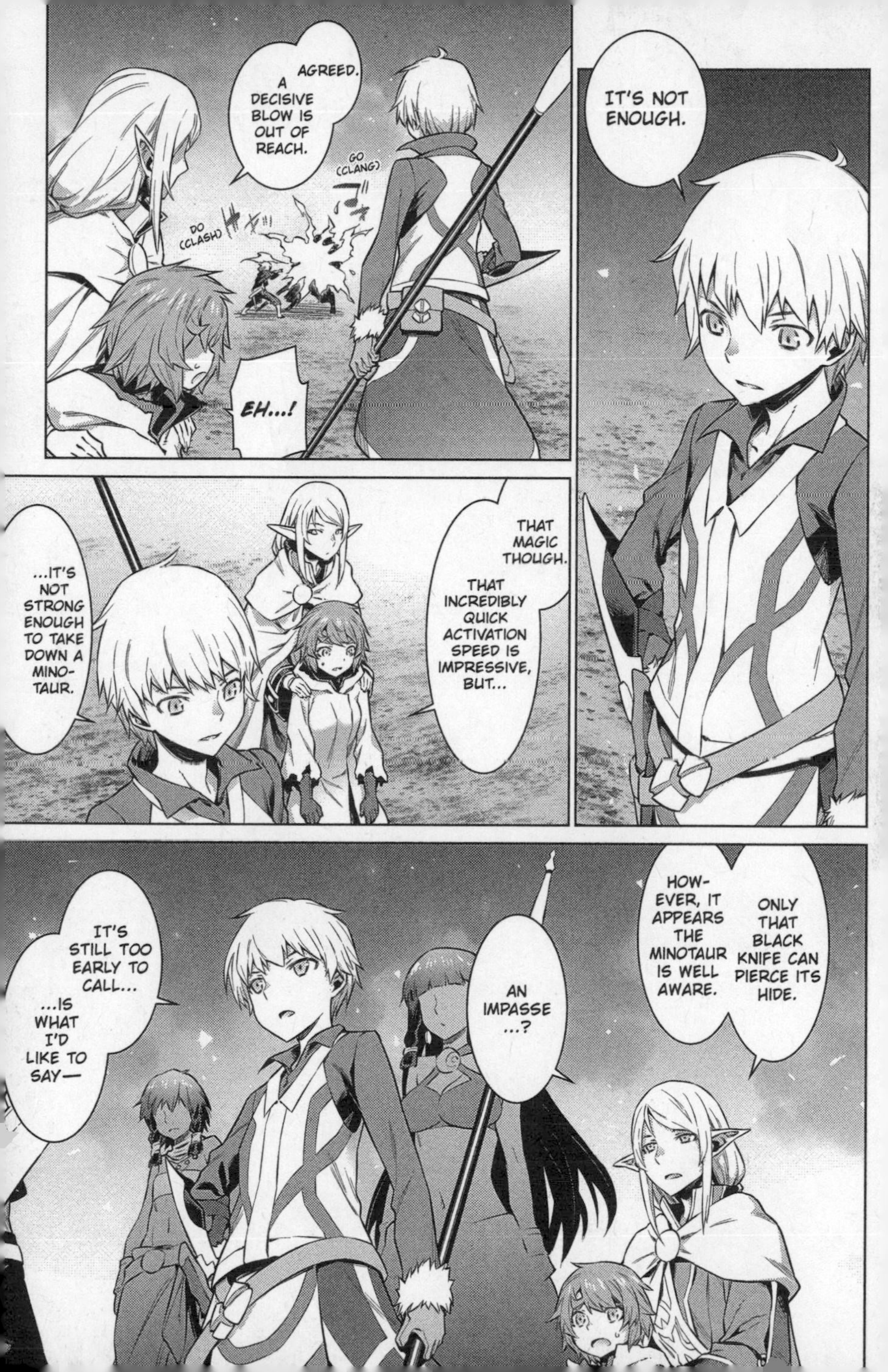
IT'S NOT ENOUGH.
AGREED. A DECISIVE BLOW IS OUT OF REACH.
GO (CLANG)
DO (CLASH)
EH...!
THAT MAGIC THOUGH.
THAT INCREDIBLY QUICK ACTIVATION SPEED IS IMPRESSIVE, BUT...
...IT'S NOT STRONG ENOUGH TO TAKE DOWN A MINO-TAUR.
ONLY THAT BLACK KNIFE CAN PIERCE ITS HIDE.
HOW-EVER, IT APPEARS THE MINOTAUR IS WELL AWARE.
AN IMPASSE ...?
IT'S STILL TOO EARLY TO CALL...
...IS WHAT I'D LIKE TO SAY—

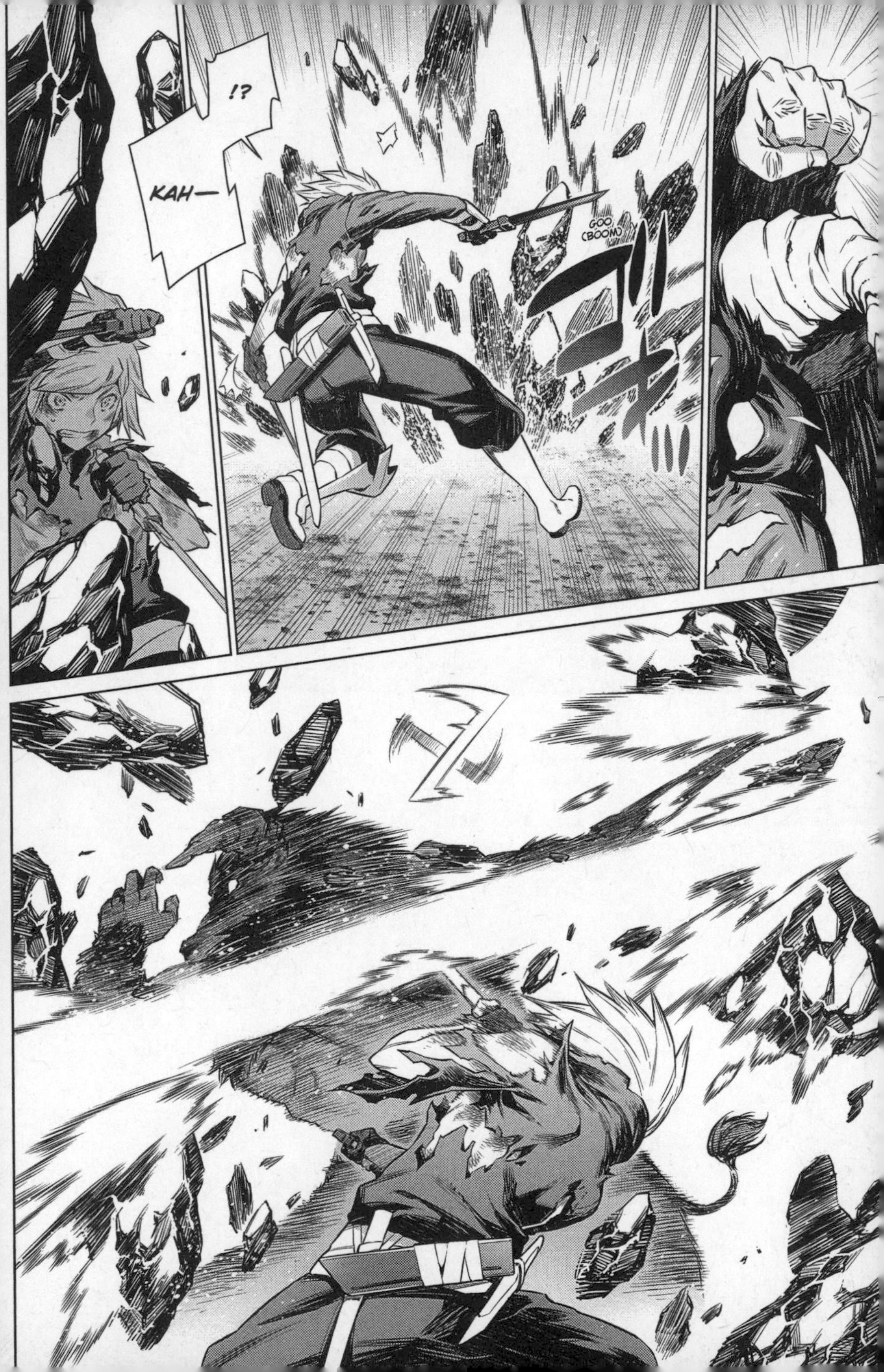
GOO (BOOM)
!?
KAH—

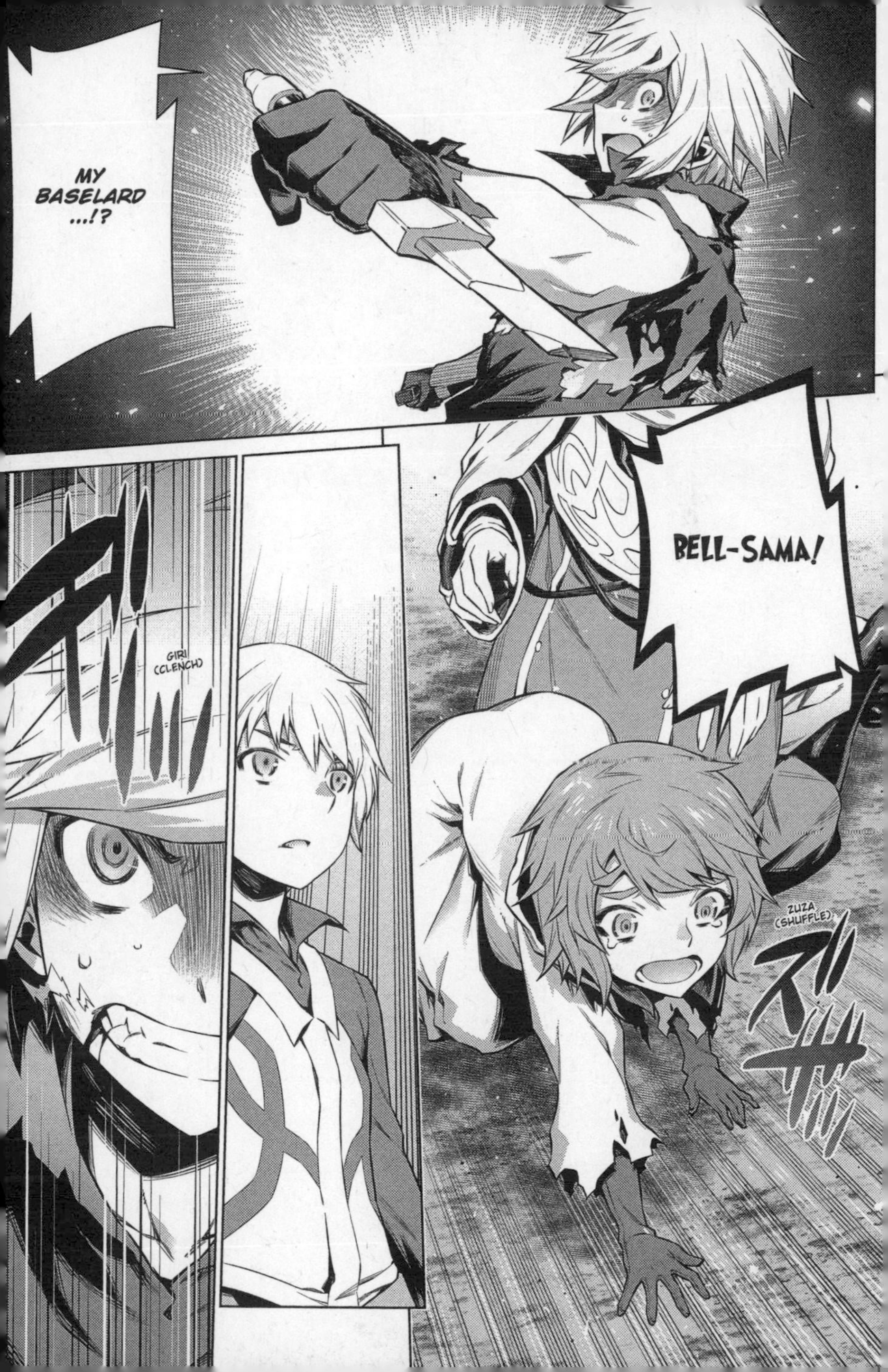
MY BASELARD ...!?
BELL-SAMA!
ZUZA (SHUFFLE)
GIRI (CLENCH)

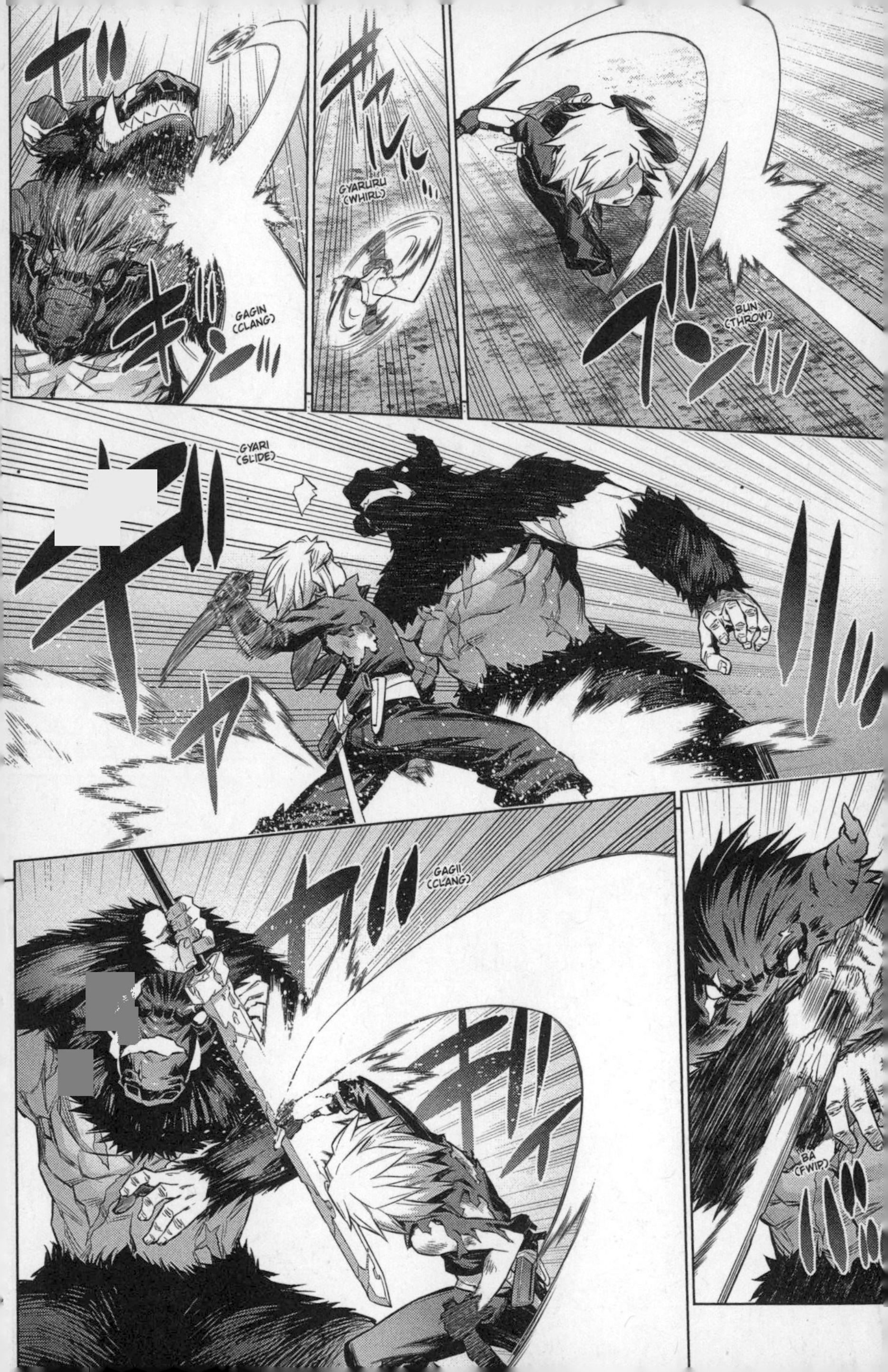
BUN
(THROW)
GYARURU
(WHIRL)
GAGIN
(CLANG)
GYARI
(SLIDE)
BA
(FWIP)
GAGII
(CLANG)

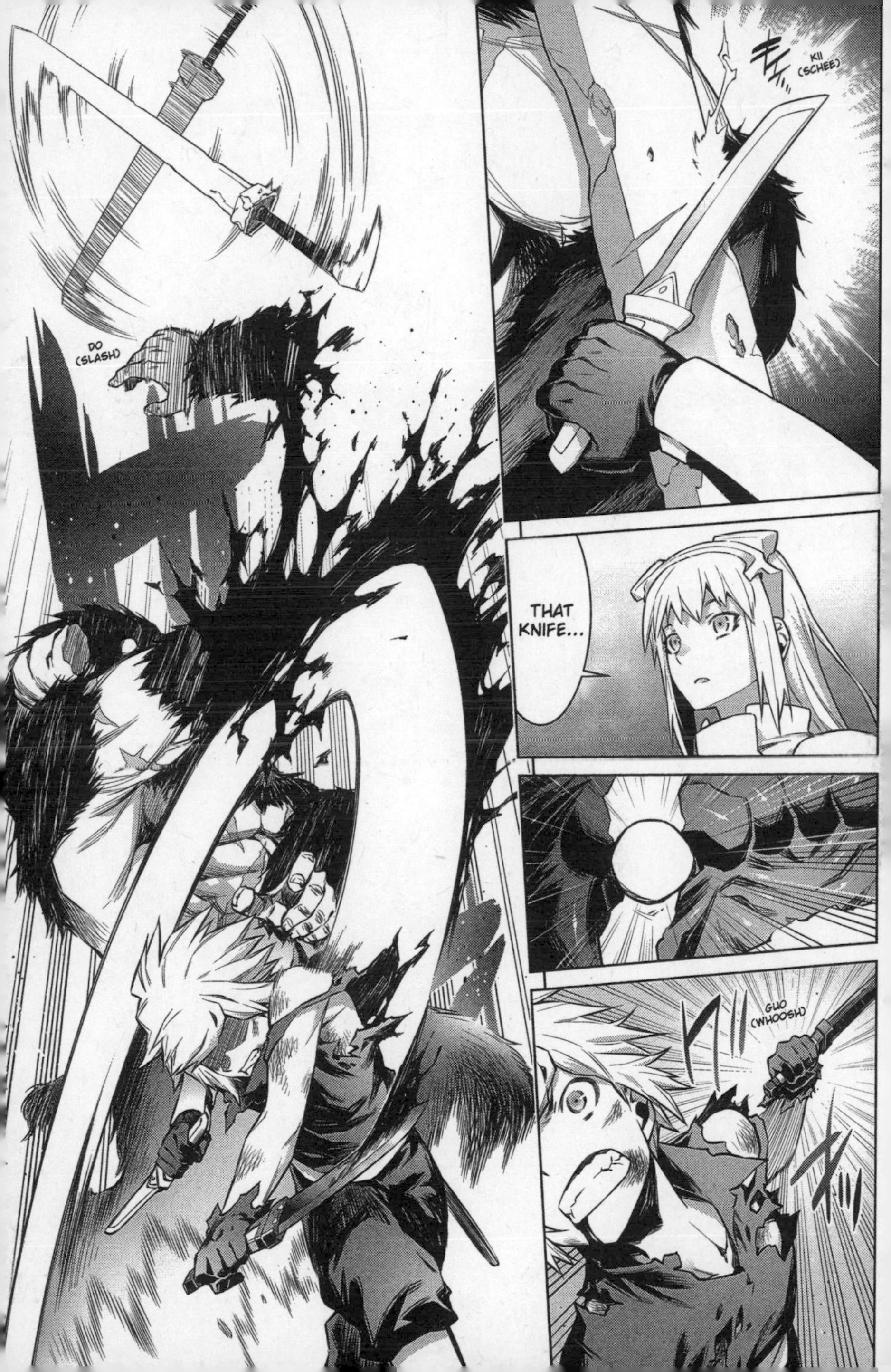
KII
(SCHEE)
THAT KNIFE...
GUO
(WHOOSH)
DO
(SLASH)

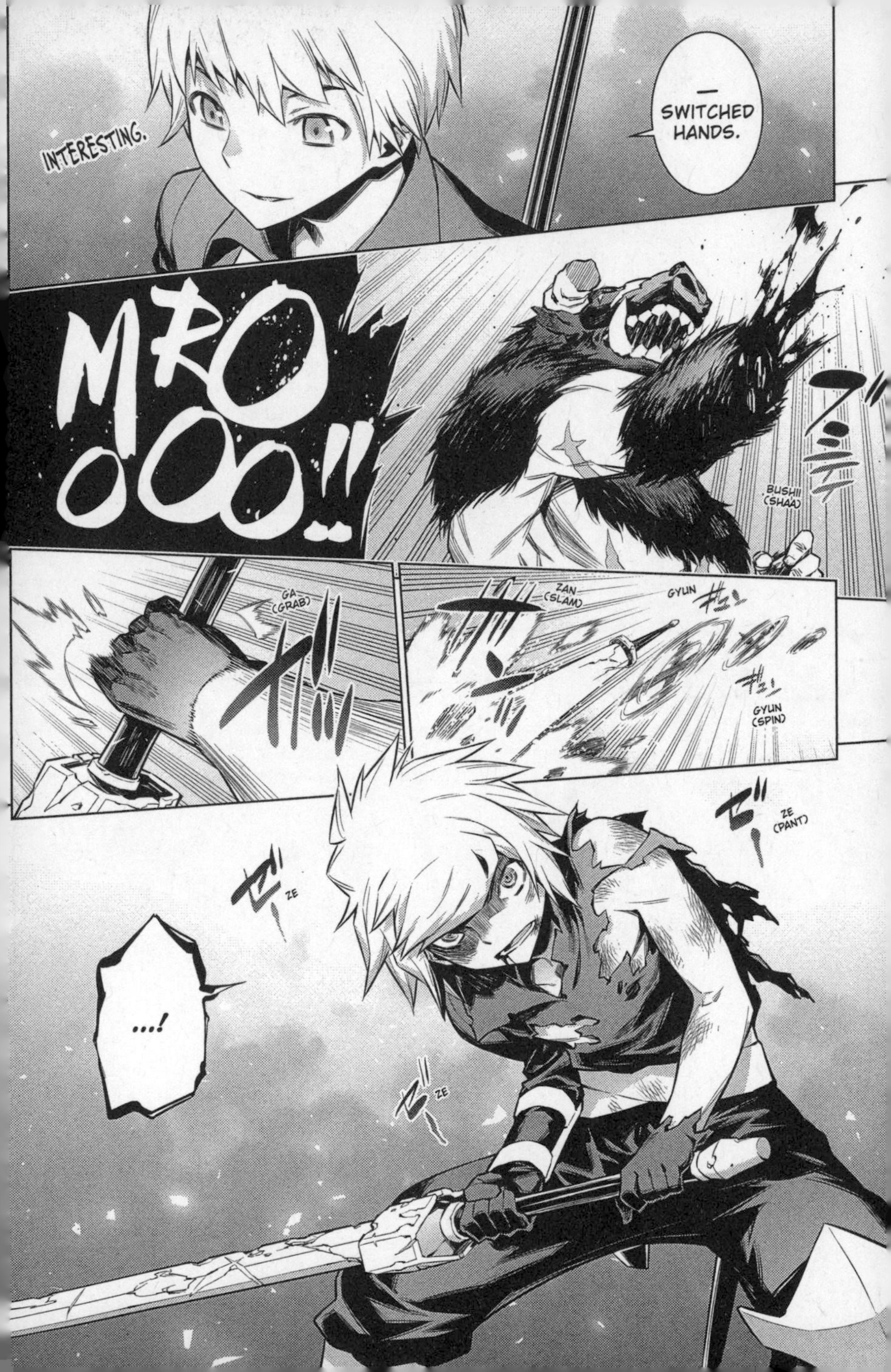
—SWITCHED HANDS.
INTERESTING.
BUSHII (SHAA)
MROOOO!!
ZAN (SLAM)
GYUN
GYUN (SPIN)
GA (GRAB)
ZE (PANT)
ZE
...!
ZE

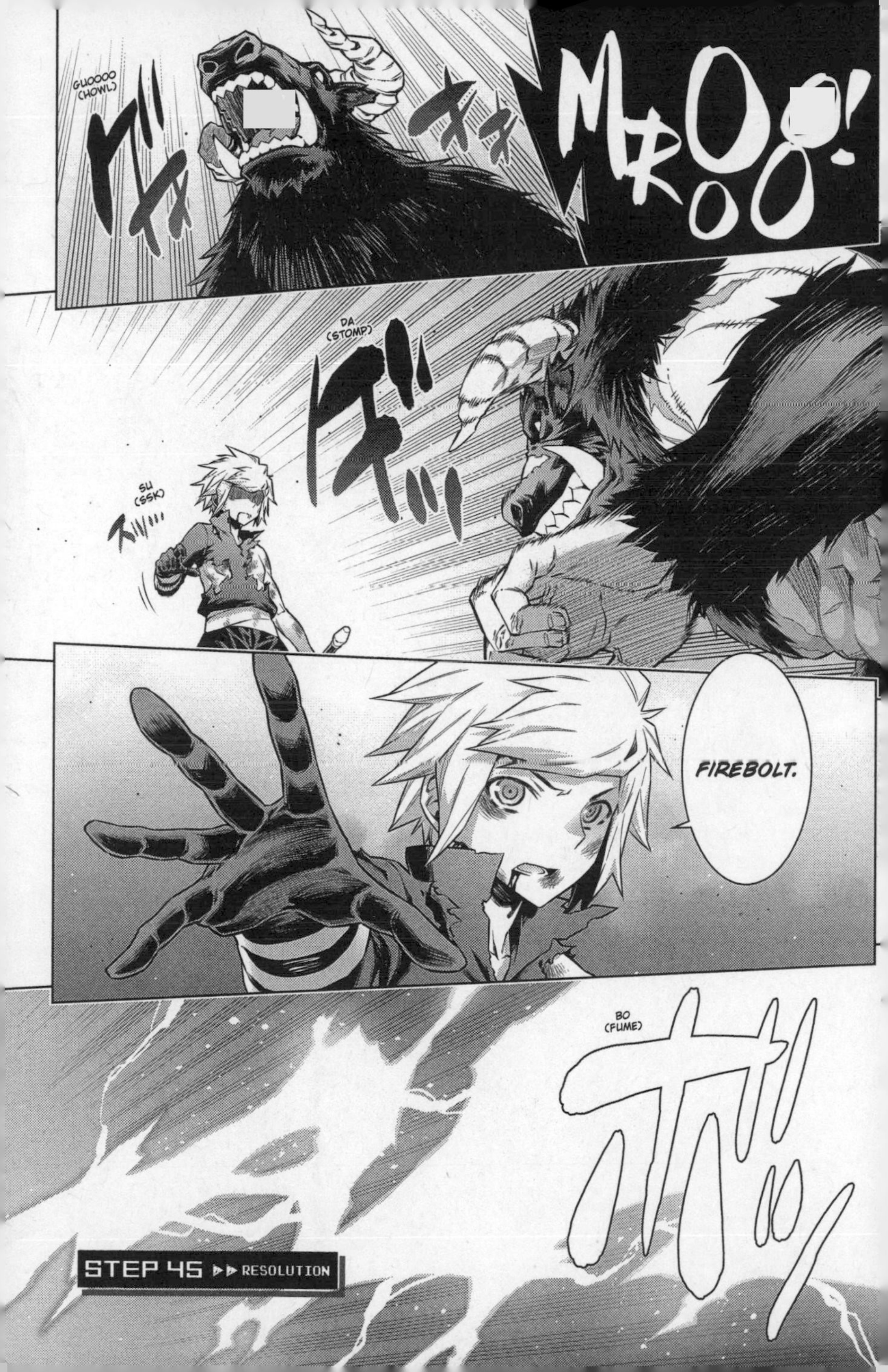
MROOOOO!
GUOOOO
(HOWL)
DA
(STOMP)
SU
(SSK)
FIREBOLT.
BO
(FUME)
STEP 45 ▶▶ RESOLUTION

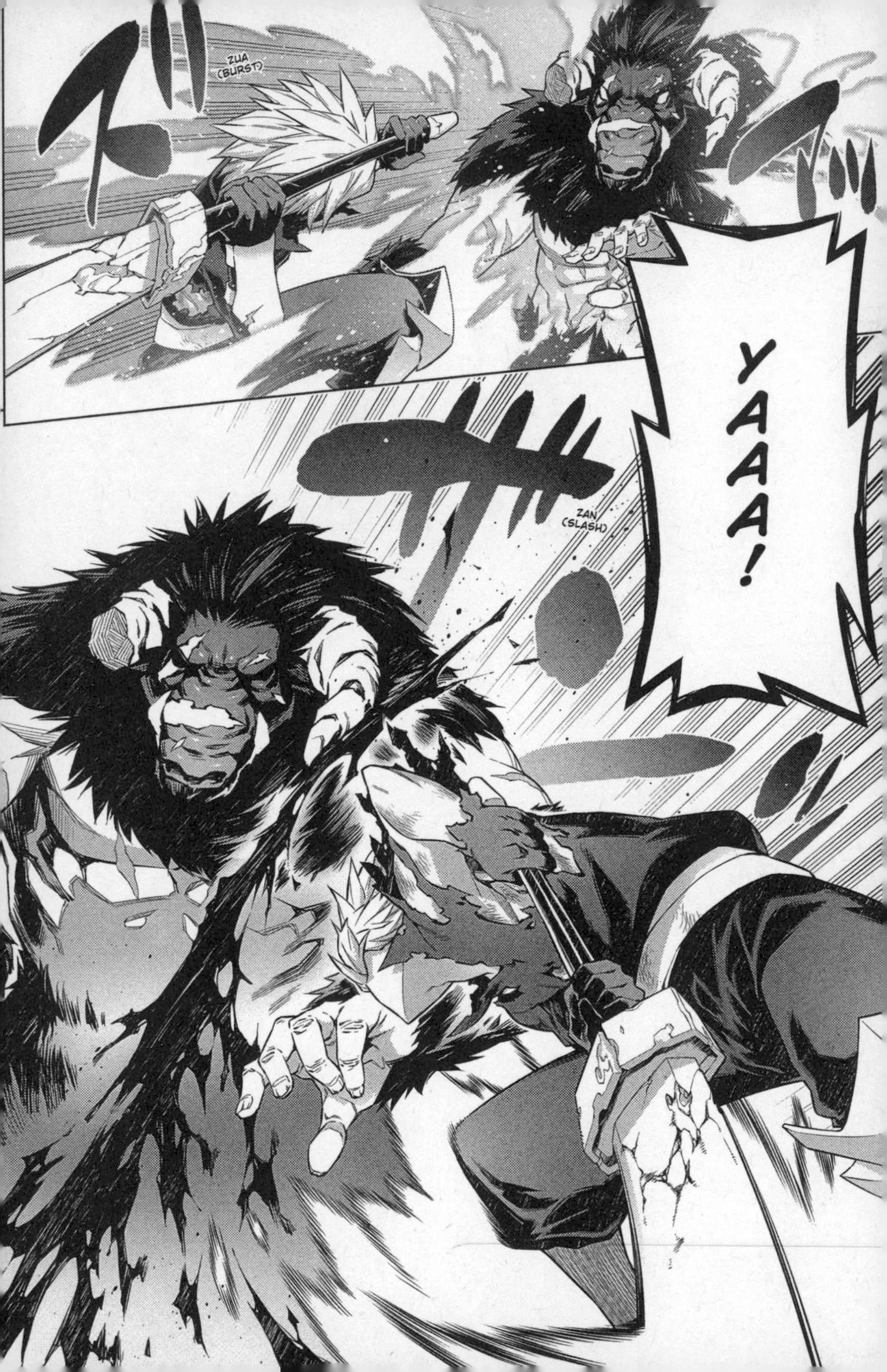
ZUA (BURST)
YAAAA!
ZAN (SLASH)

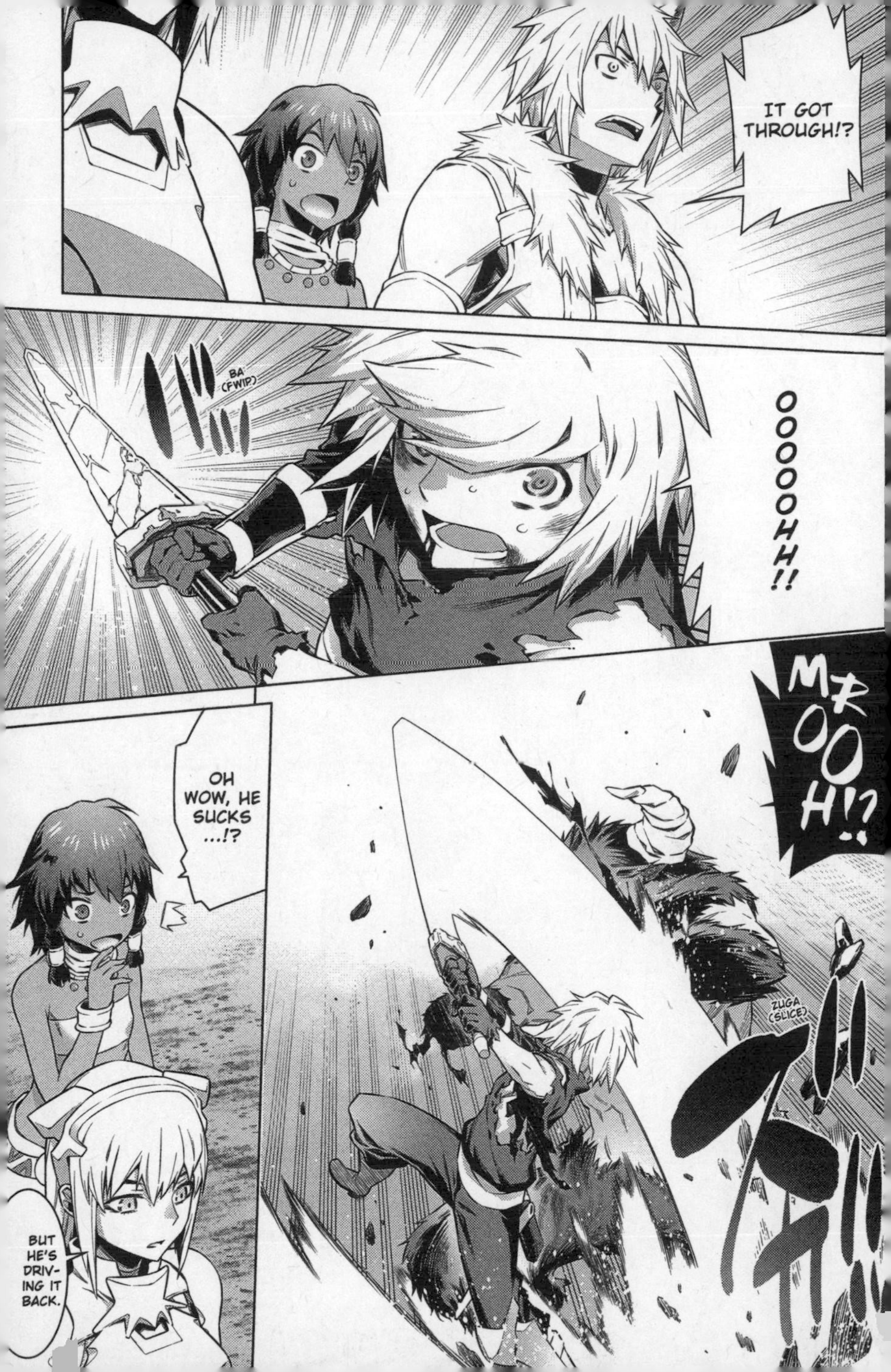
IT GOT THROUGH!?
OOOOOOHH!!
BA (FWIP)
MROOH!?
ZUGA (SLICE)
OH WOW, HE SUCKS ...!?
BUT HE'S DRIVING IT BACK.

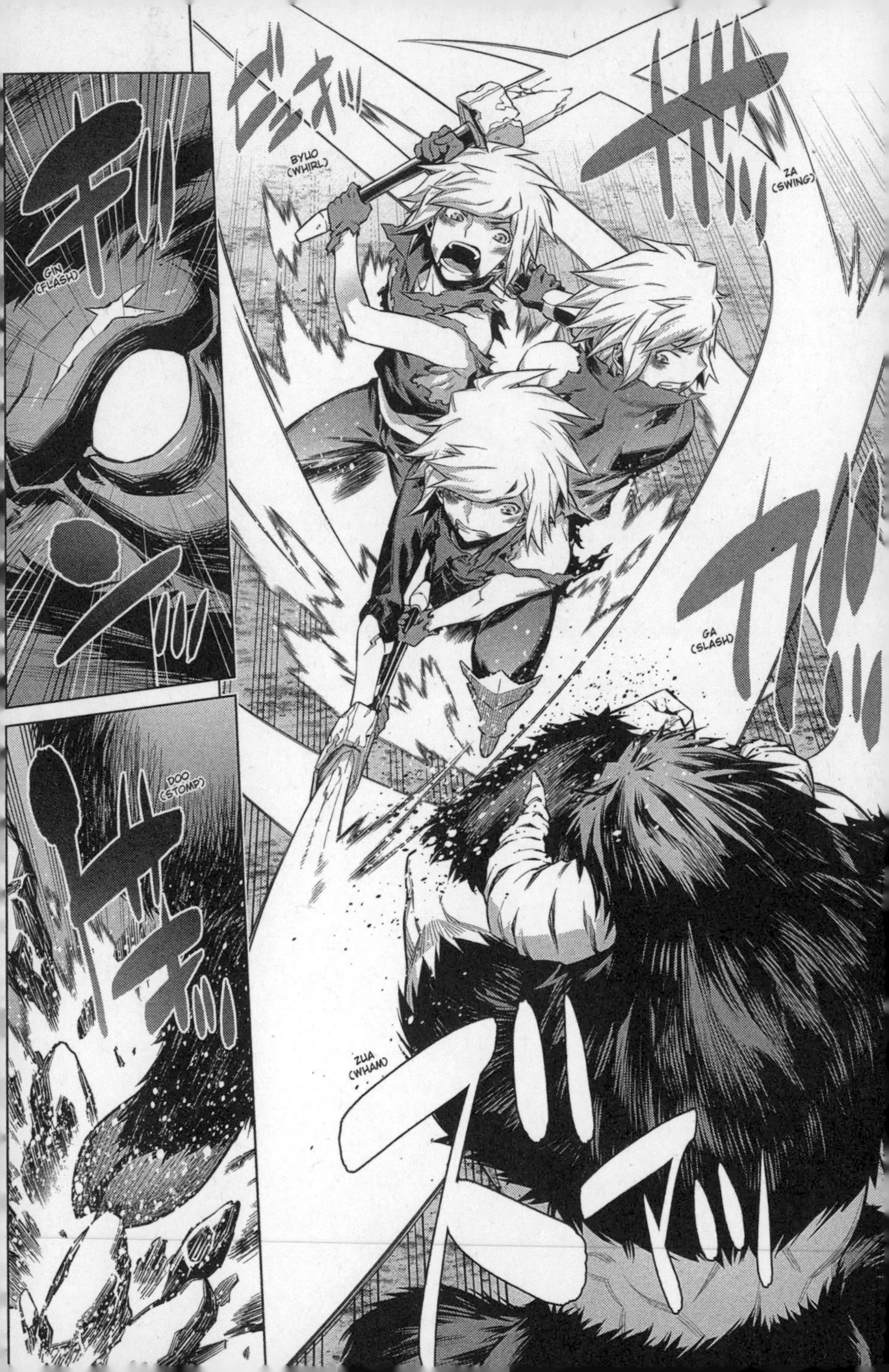
ZA (SWING)
BYUO (WHIRL)
GA (SLASH)
ZUA (WHAM)
GIN (FLASH)
DOO (STOMP)

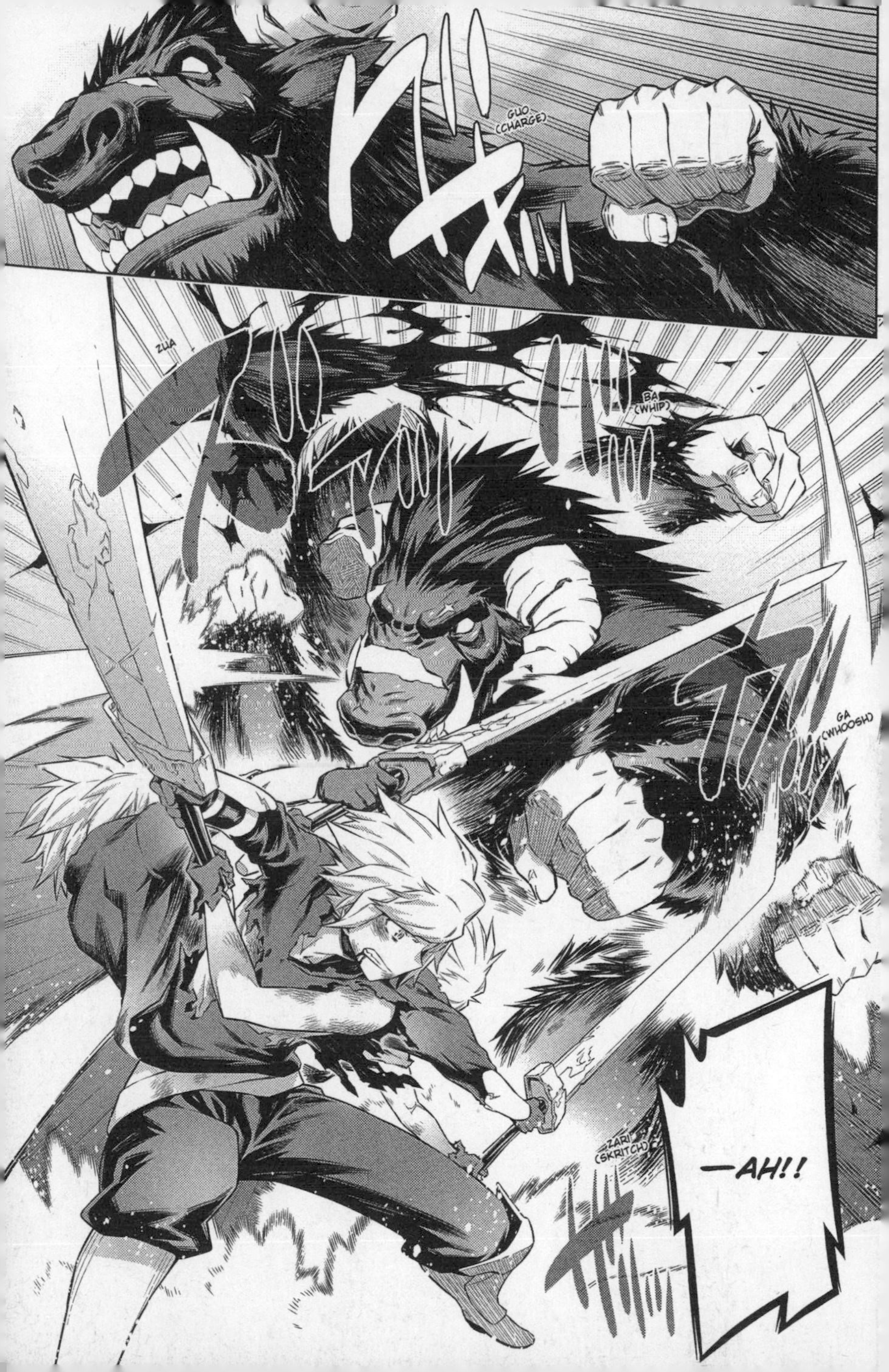
GUO (CHARGE)
BA (WHIP)
ZUA
GA (WHOOSH)
—AH!!
ZARI (SKRITCH)

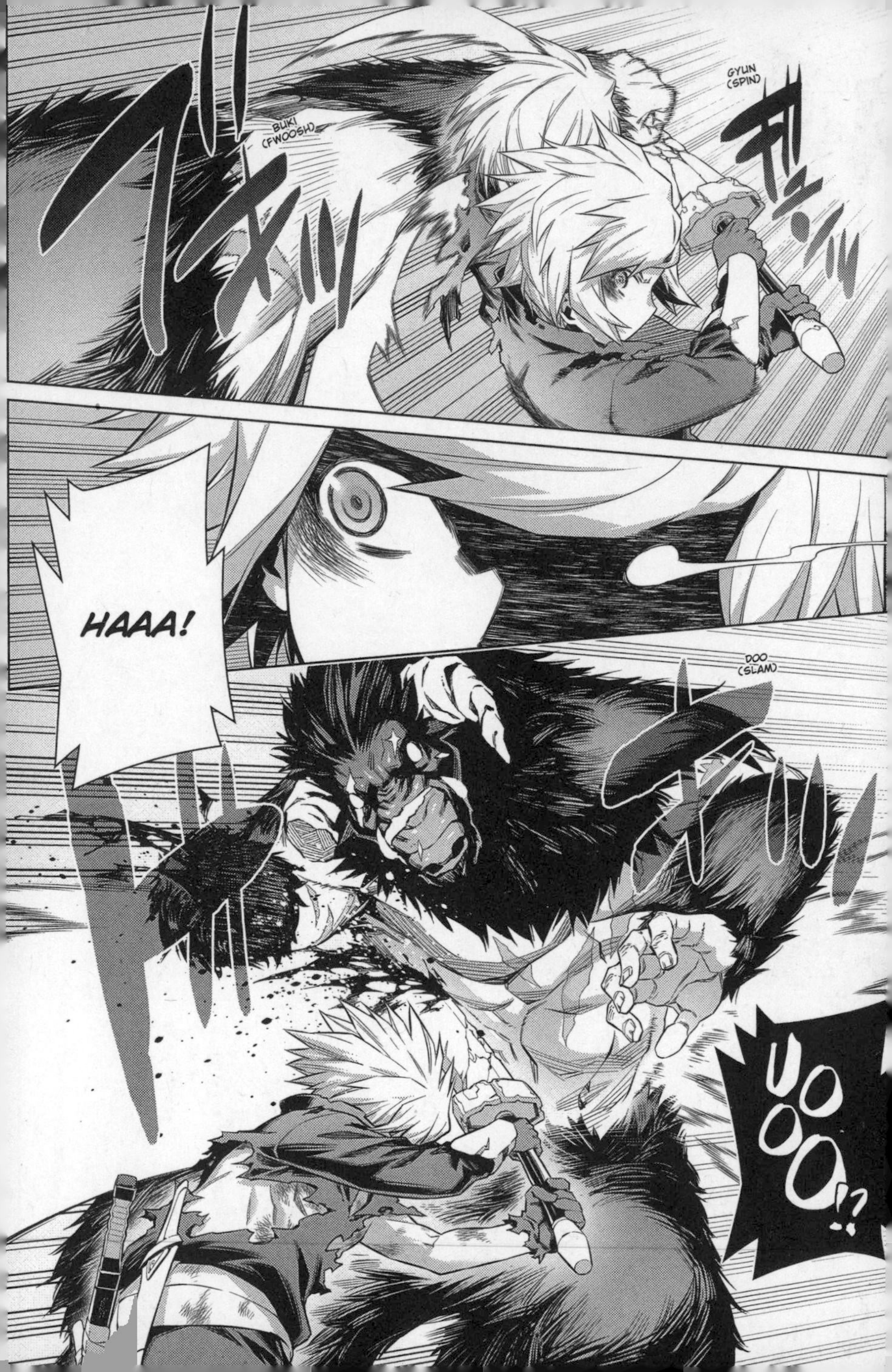
GYUN (SPIN)
BUKI (FWOOSH)
HAAA!
DOO (SLAM)
UOOO!?

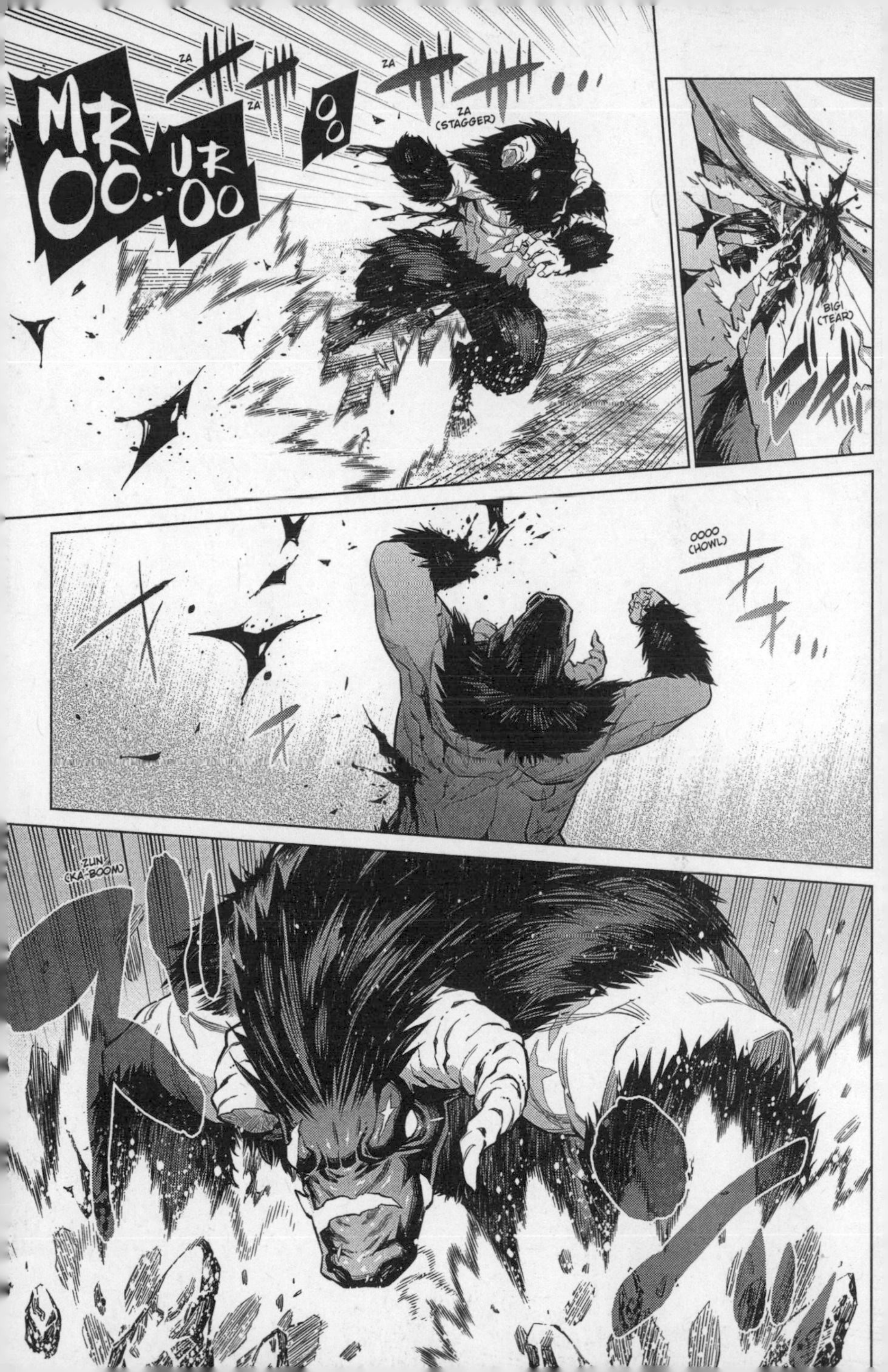
BIGI
(TEAR)
ZA
(STAGGER)
ZA
ZA
ZA
MROO... UROO
OOOO
(HOWL)
ZUN
(KA-BOOM)

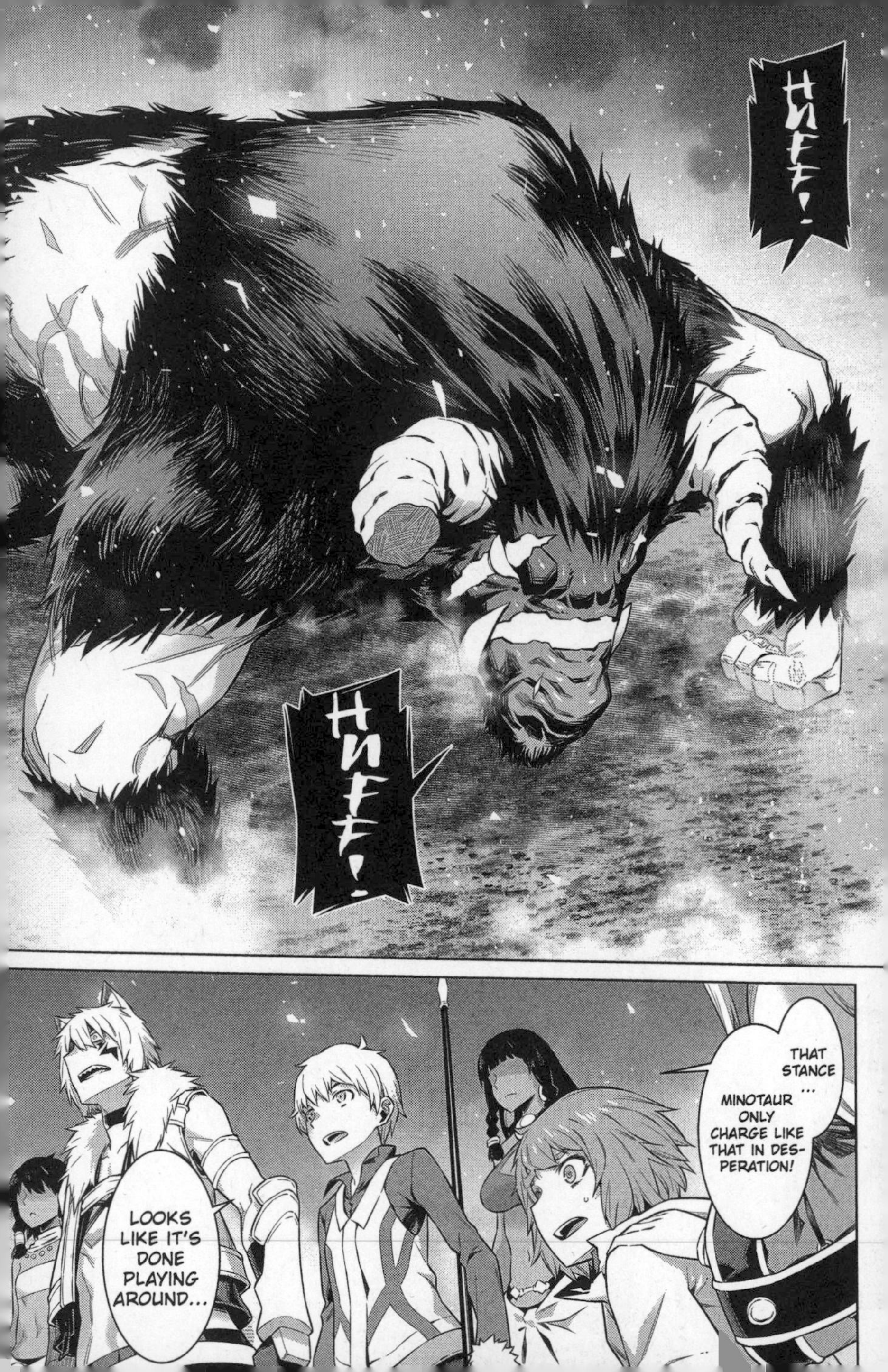
HUFF!
HUFF!
THAT STANCE... MINOTAUR ONLY CHARGE LIKE THAT IN DES-PERATION!
LOOKS LIKE IT'S DONE PLAYING AROUND...

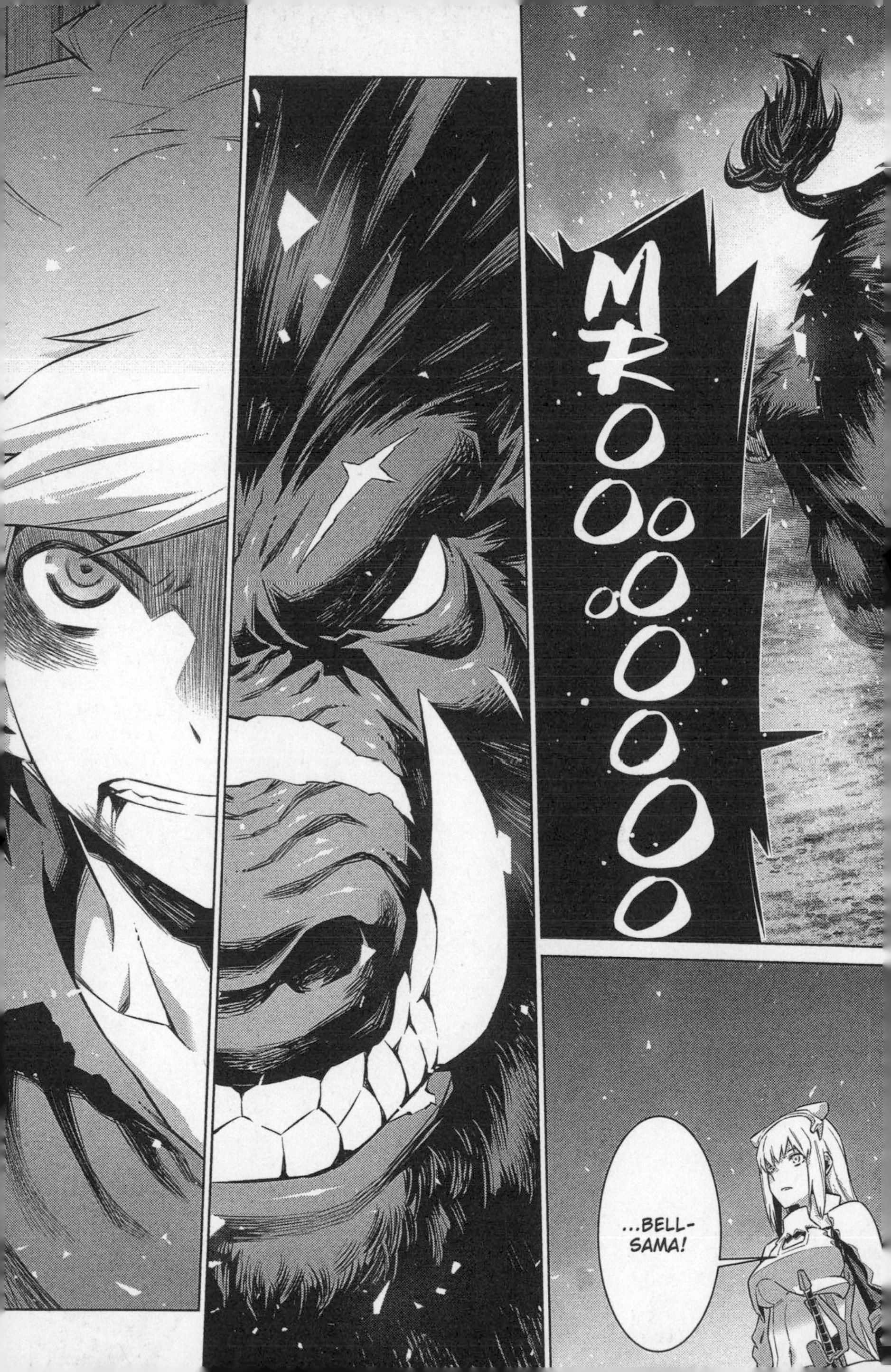
MROOOOOOOOOO
...BELL-SAMA!

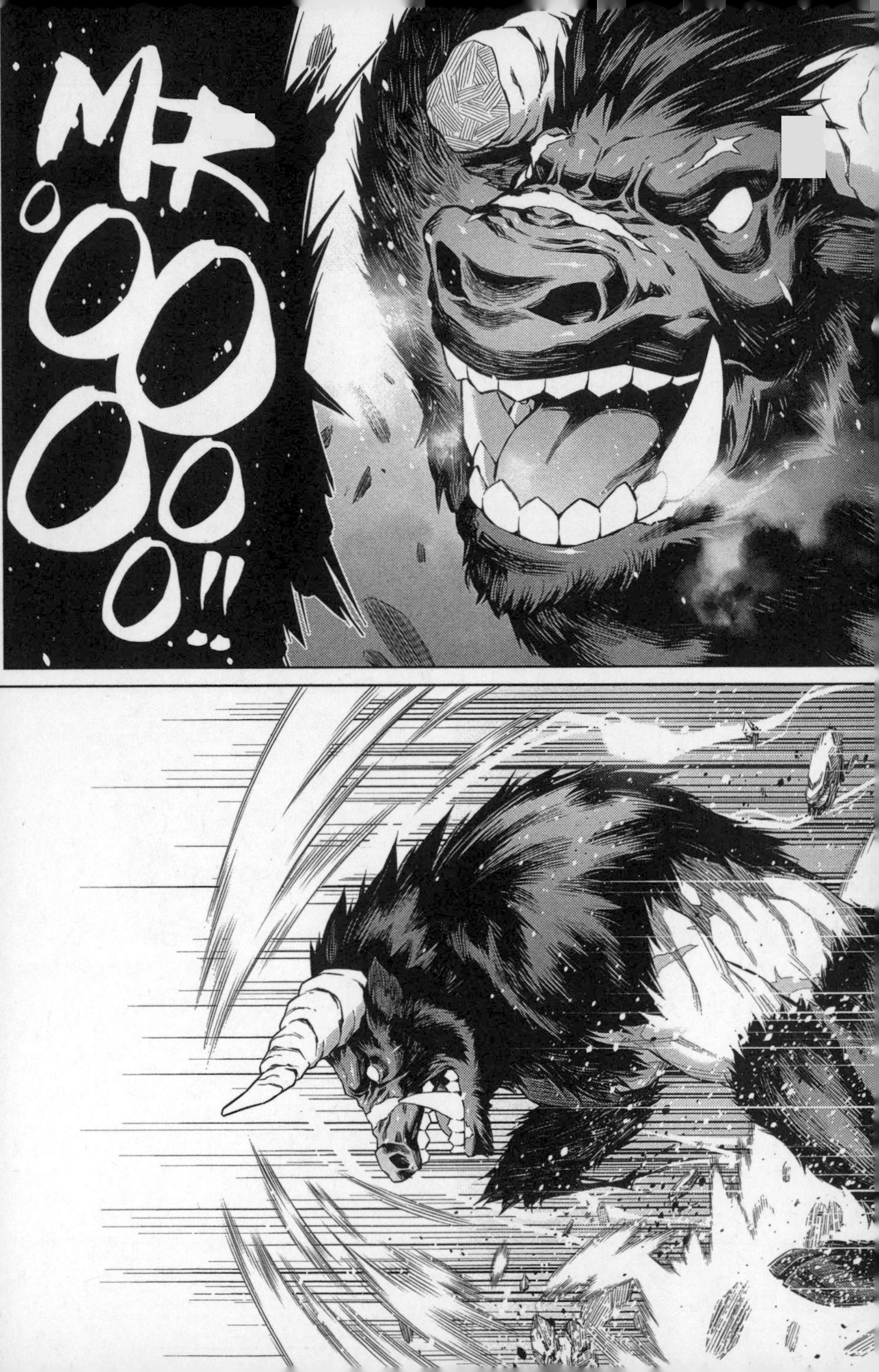
MROOOOOO!!

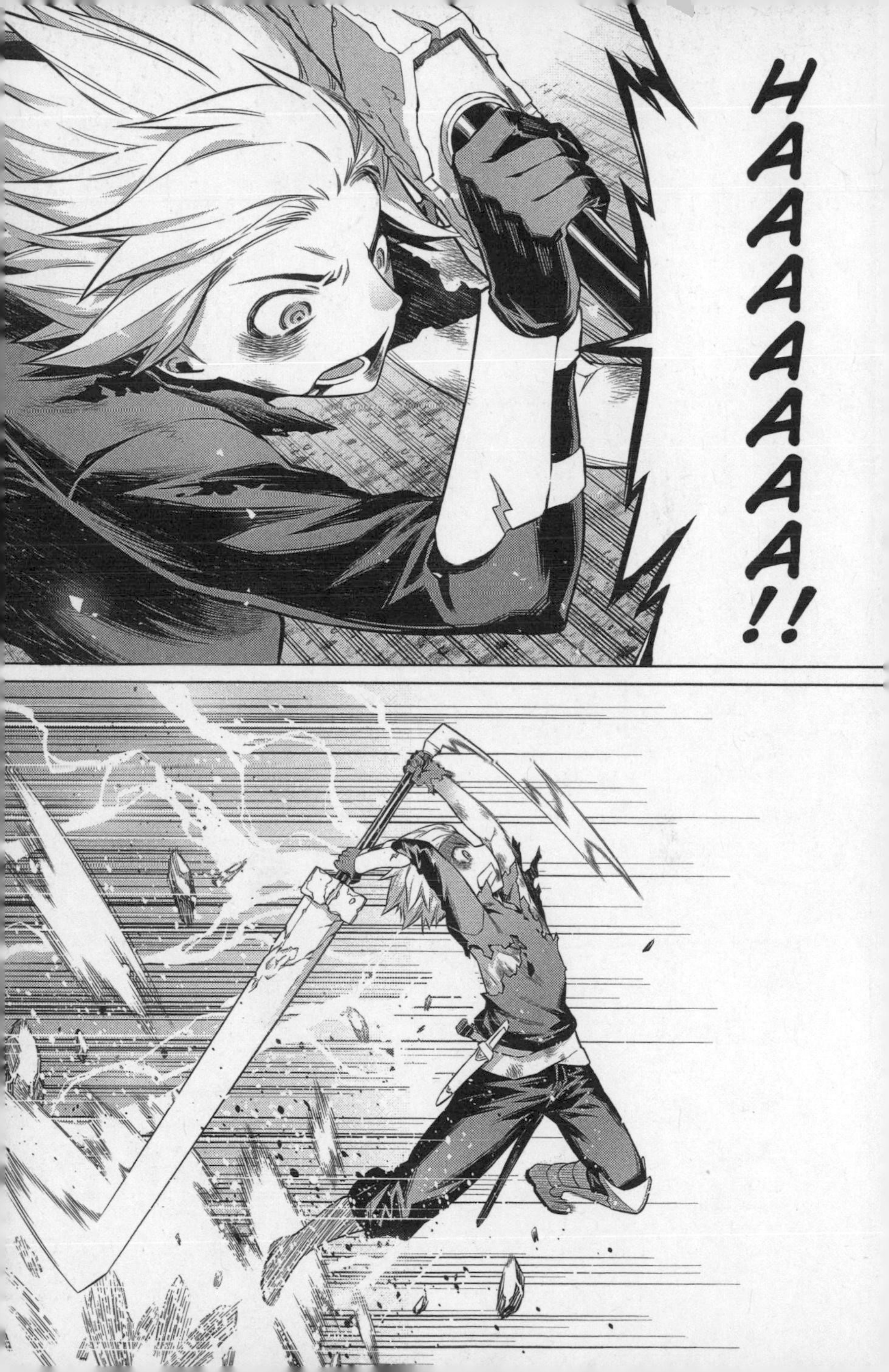
HAAAAAAA!!

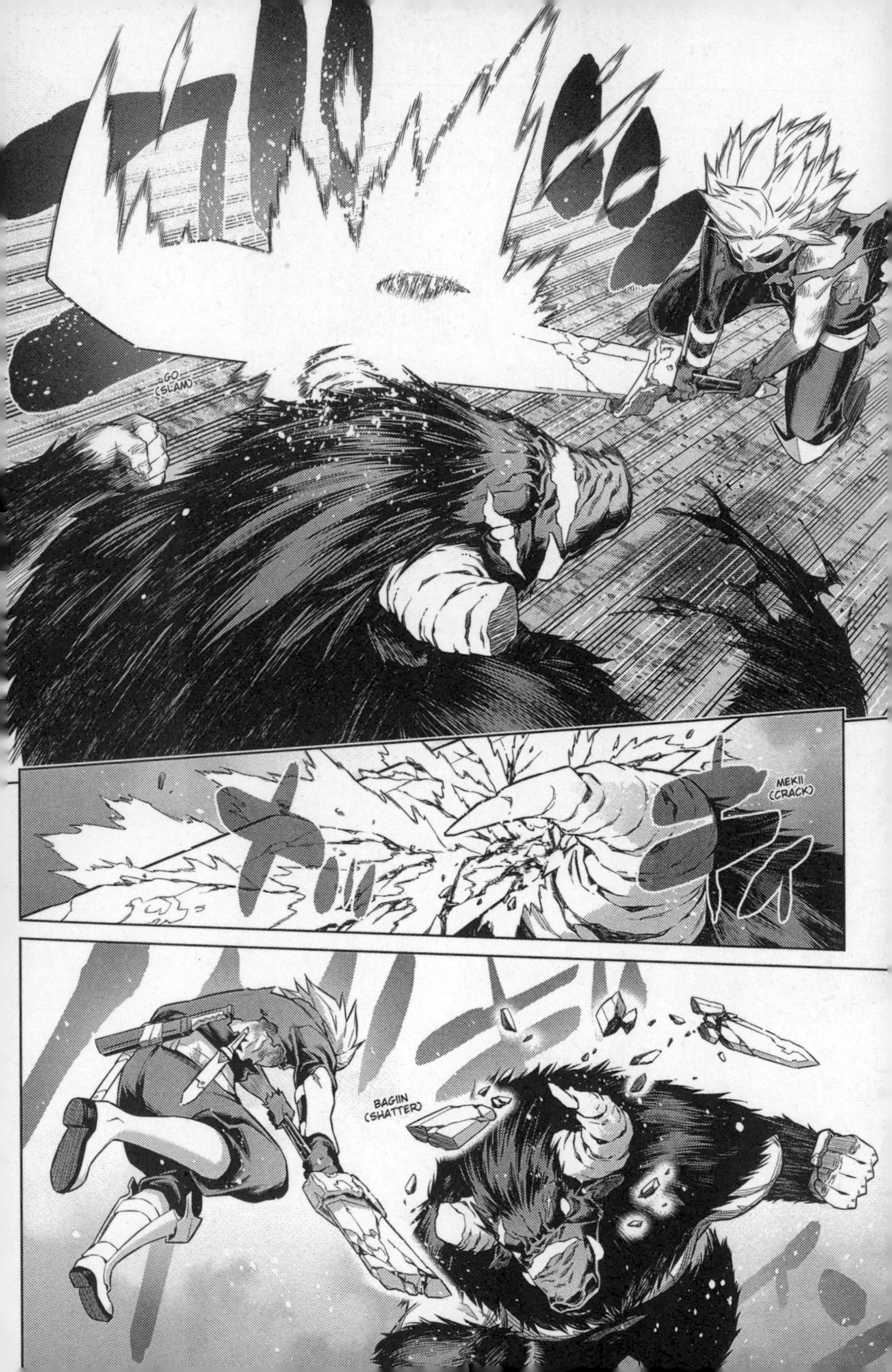
GO
(SLAM)
MEKII
(CRACK)
BAGIIN
(SHATTER)

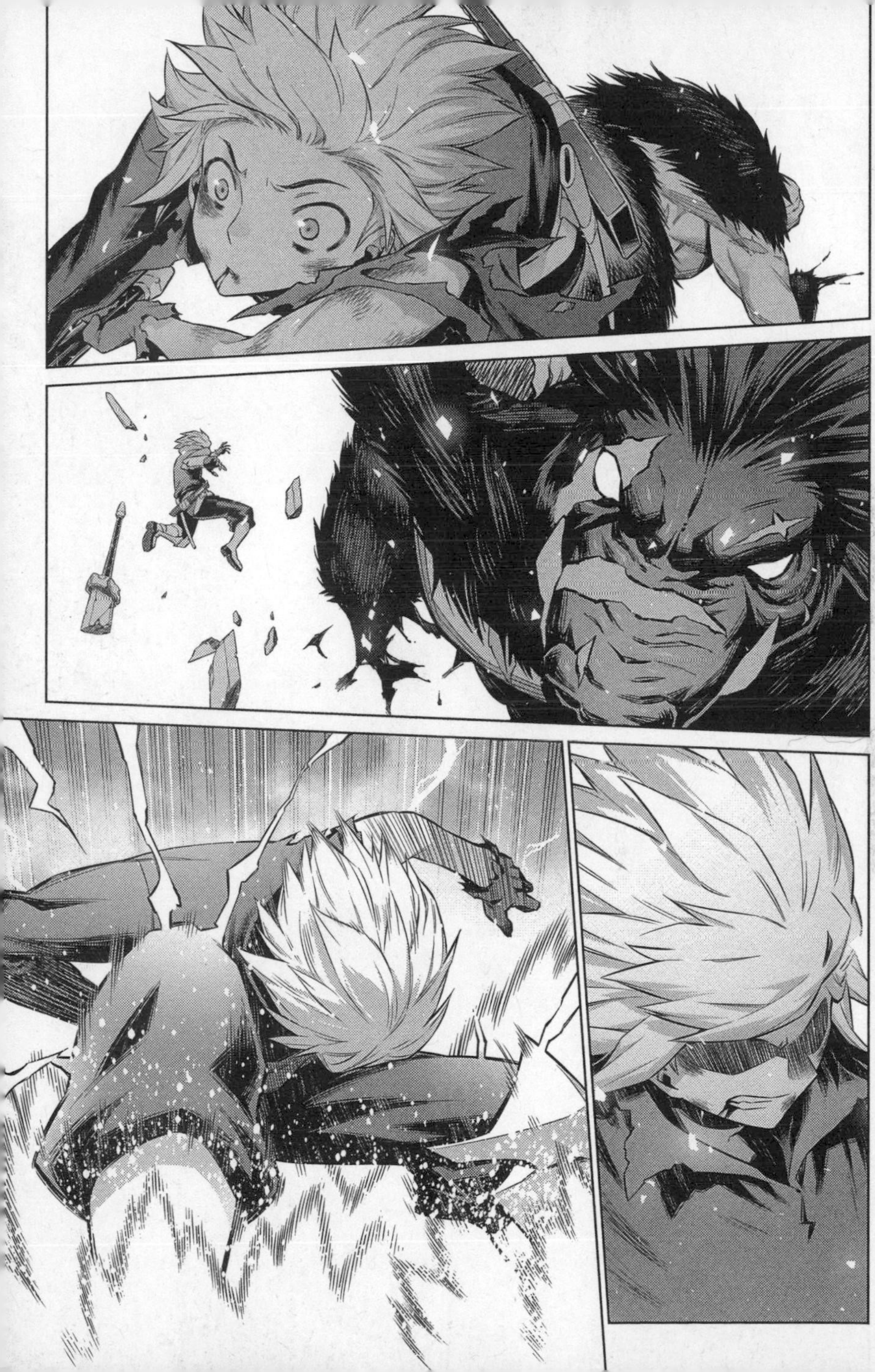

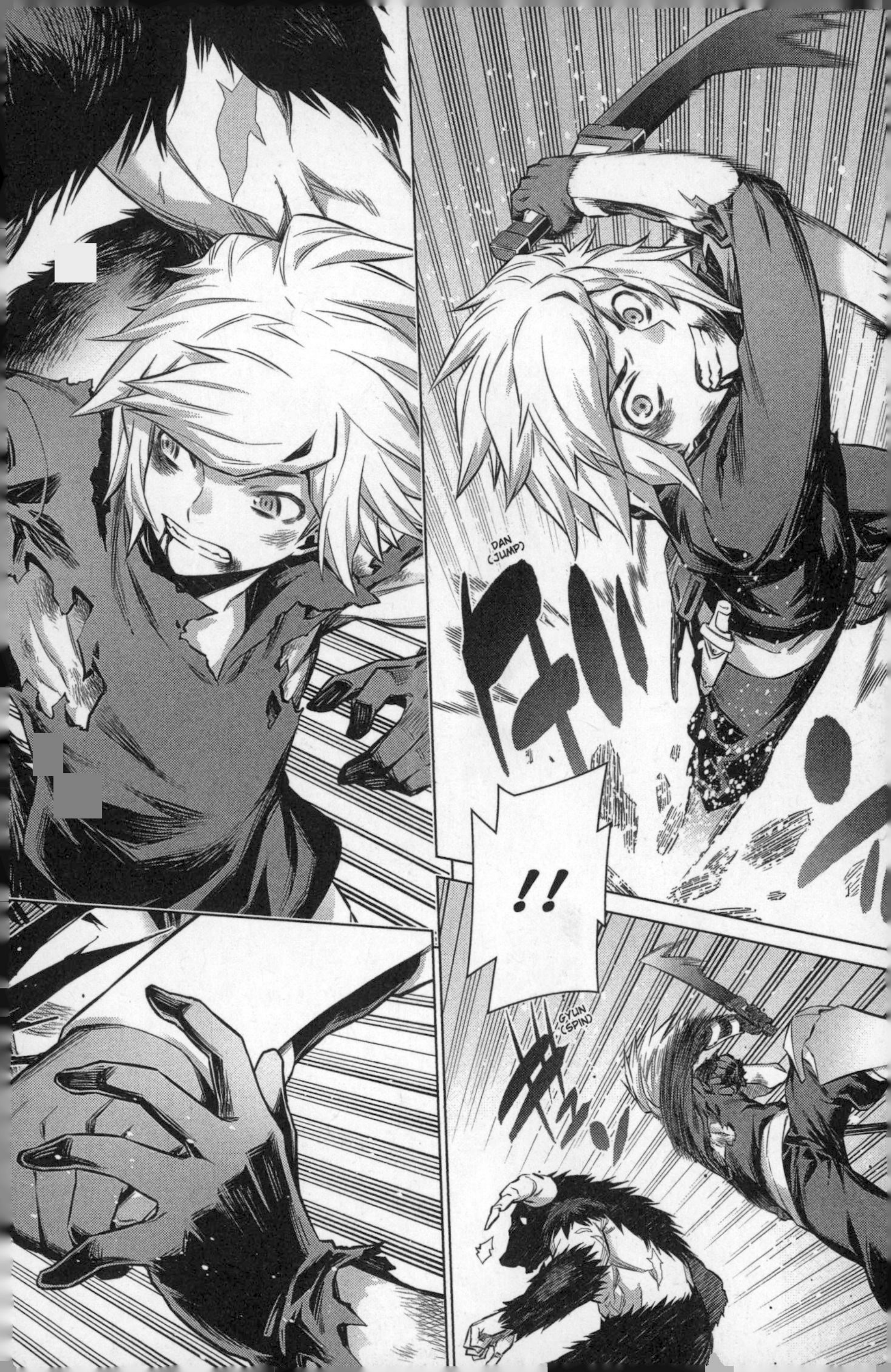
DAN (JUMP)
!!
GYUN (SPIN)

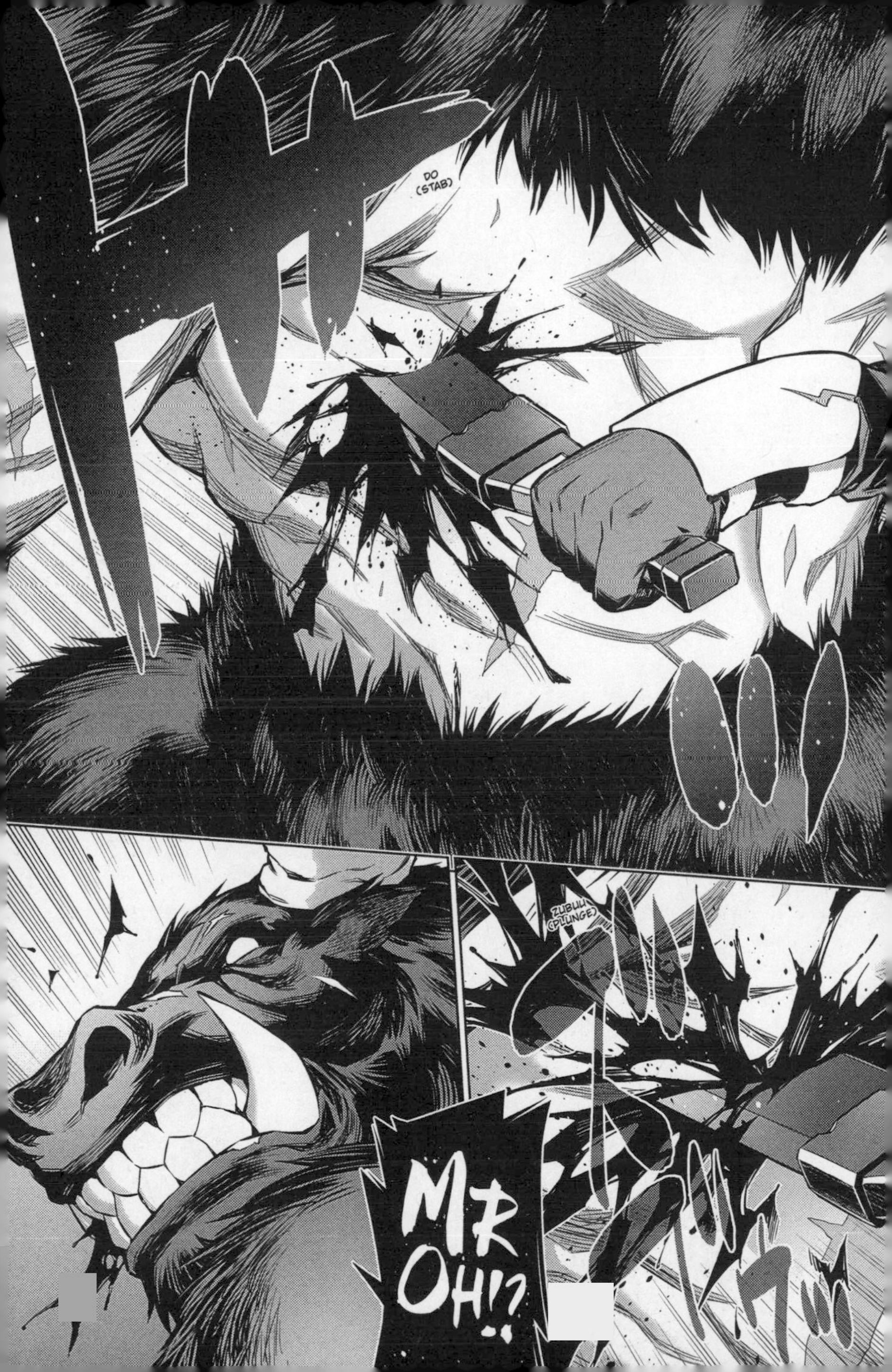
DO
(STAB)
ZUBUU
(PLUNGE)
MR OH!?

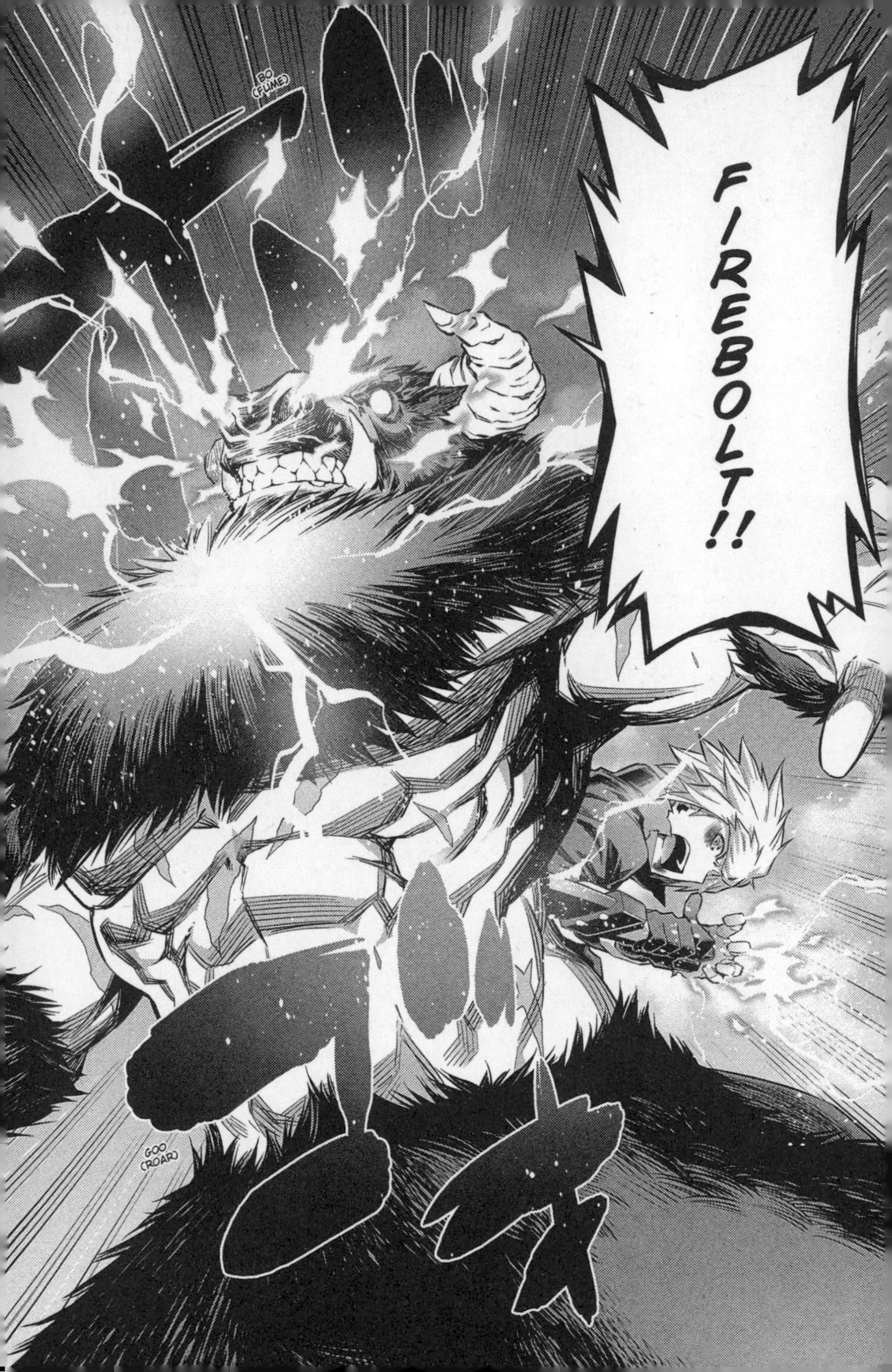
FIREBOLT!!
BO (FUME)
GOO (ROAR)

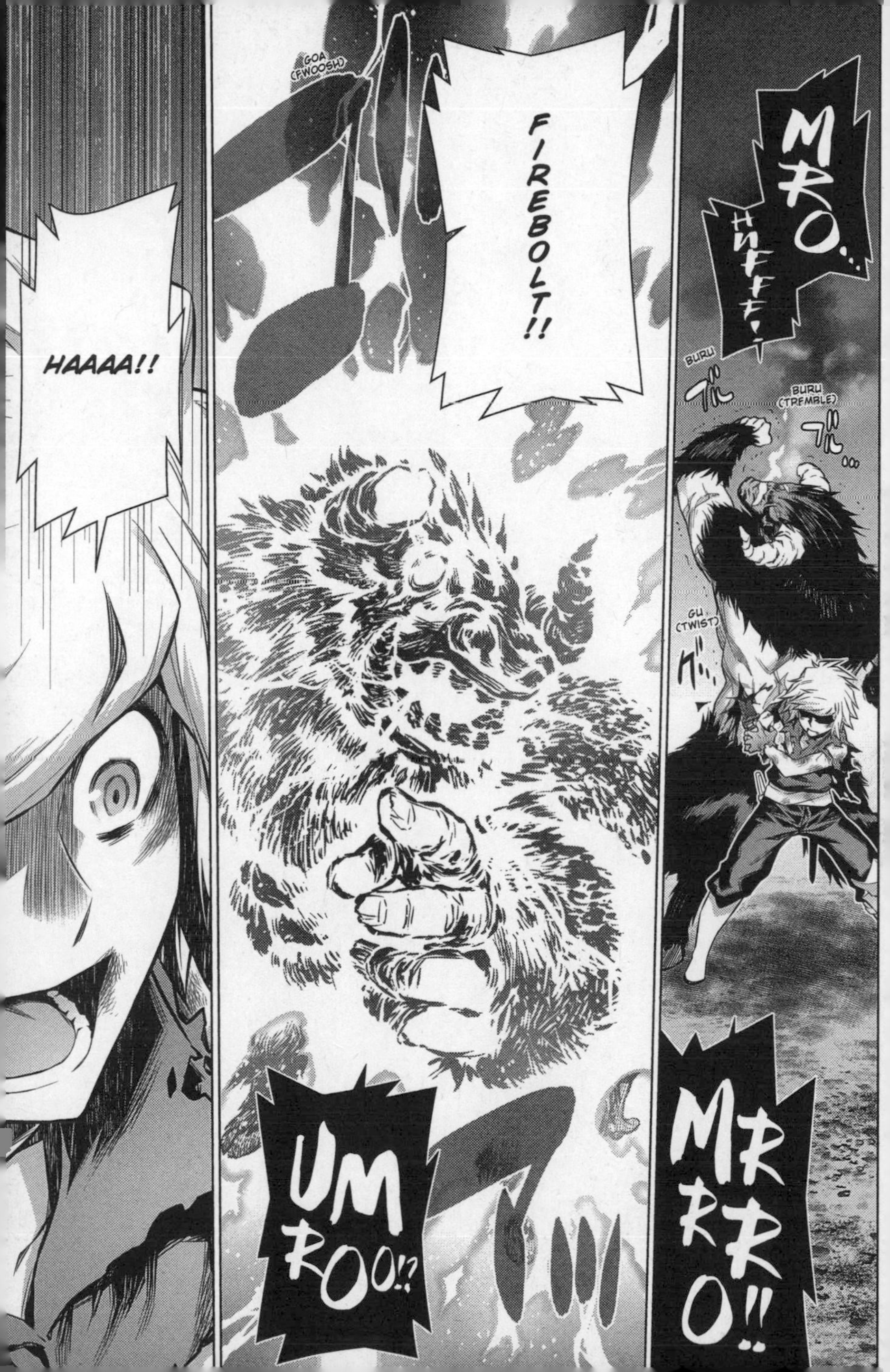

MRO...
HUFFF...
BURU
BURU (TREMBLE)
GU (TWIST)
MRRRO!!
FIREBOLT!!
GOA (FWOOSH)
UMROO!?
HAAAA!!

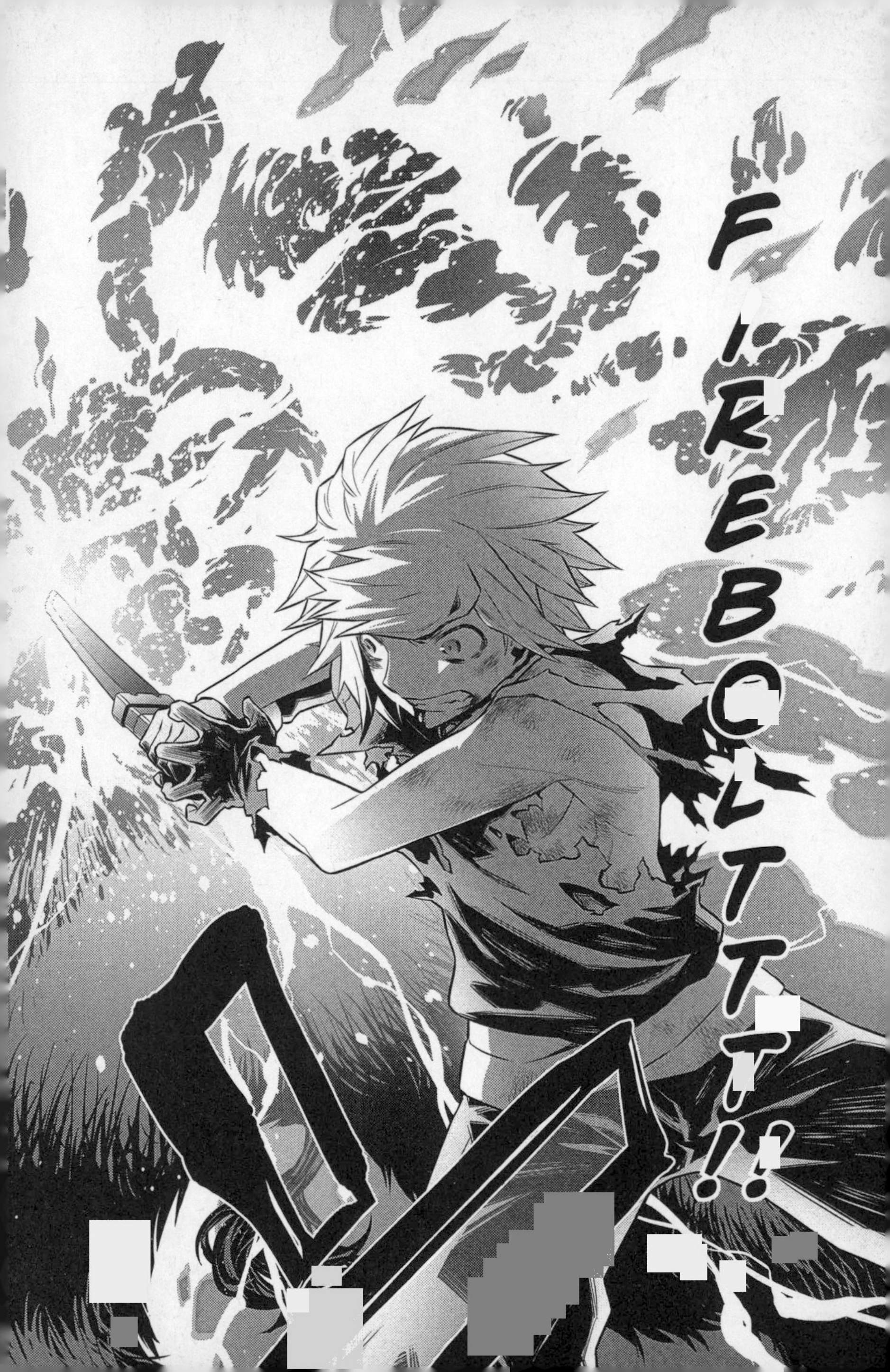
FIREBOLTTT!!

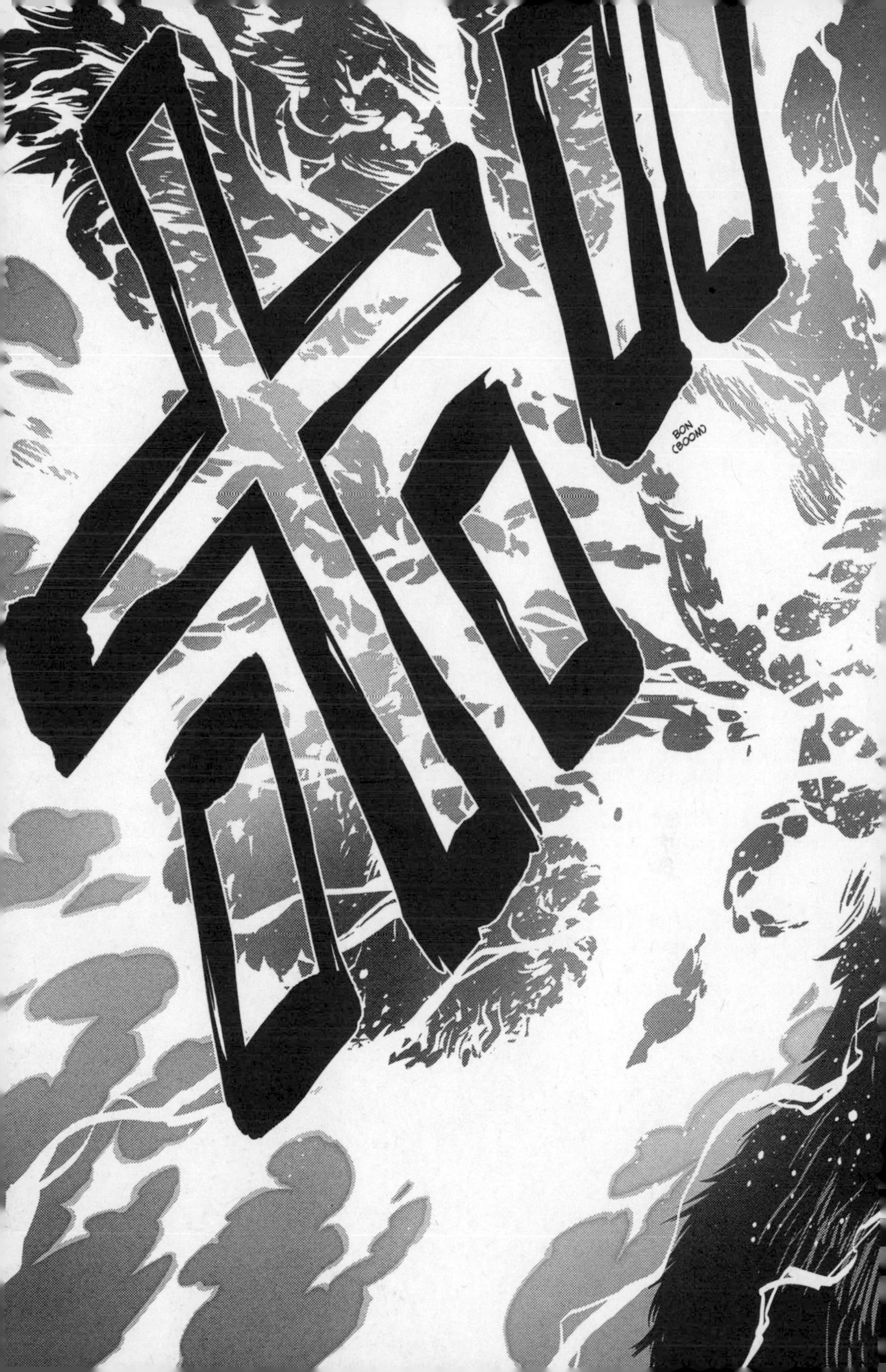
BON
(BOOM)

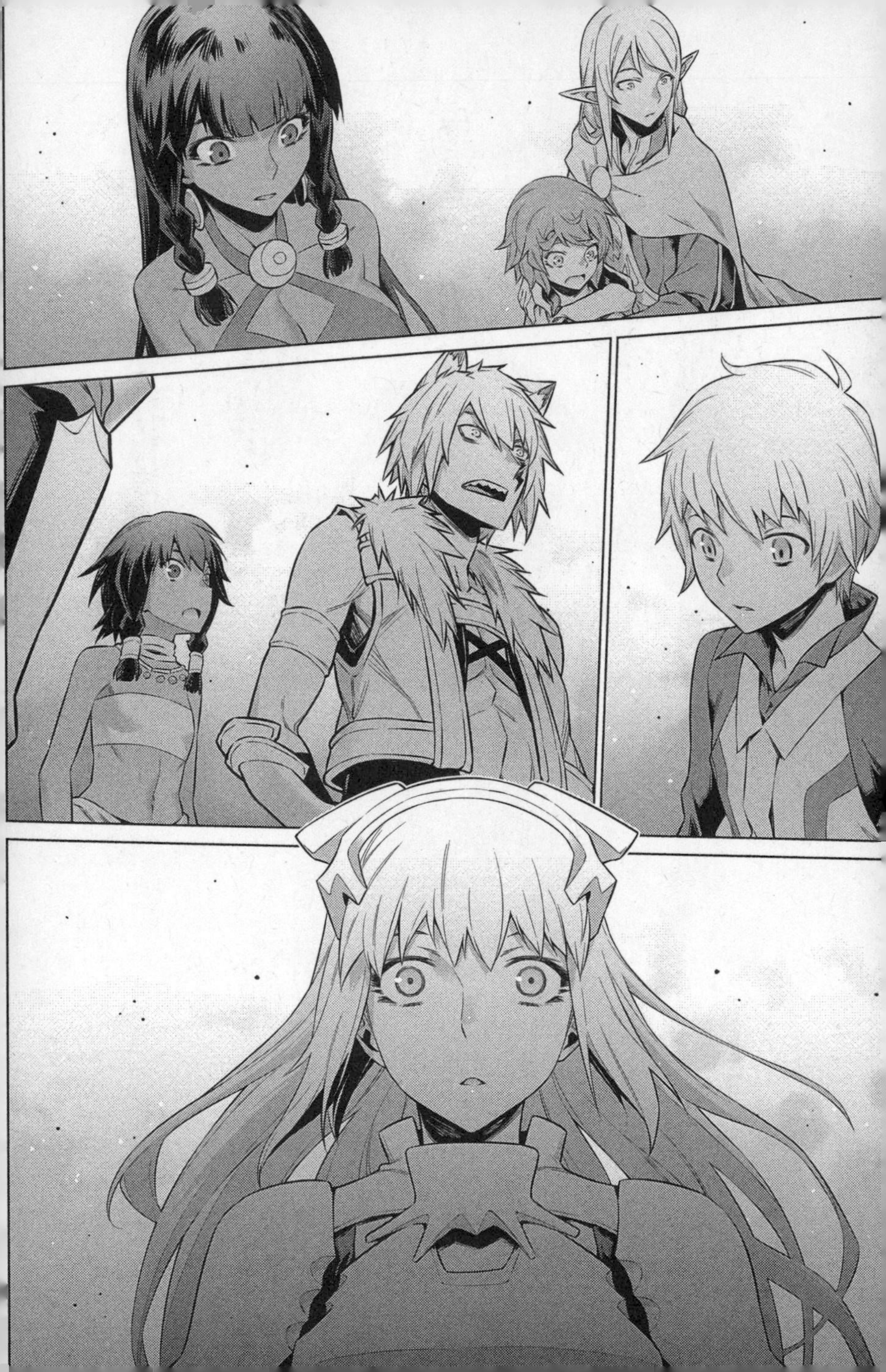

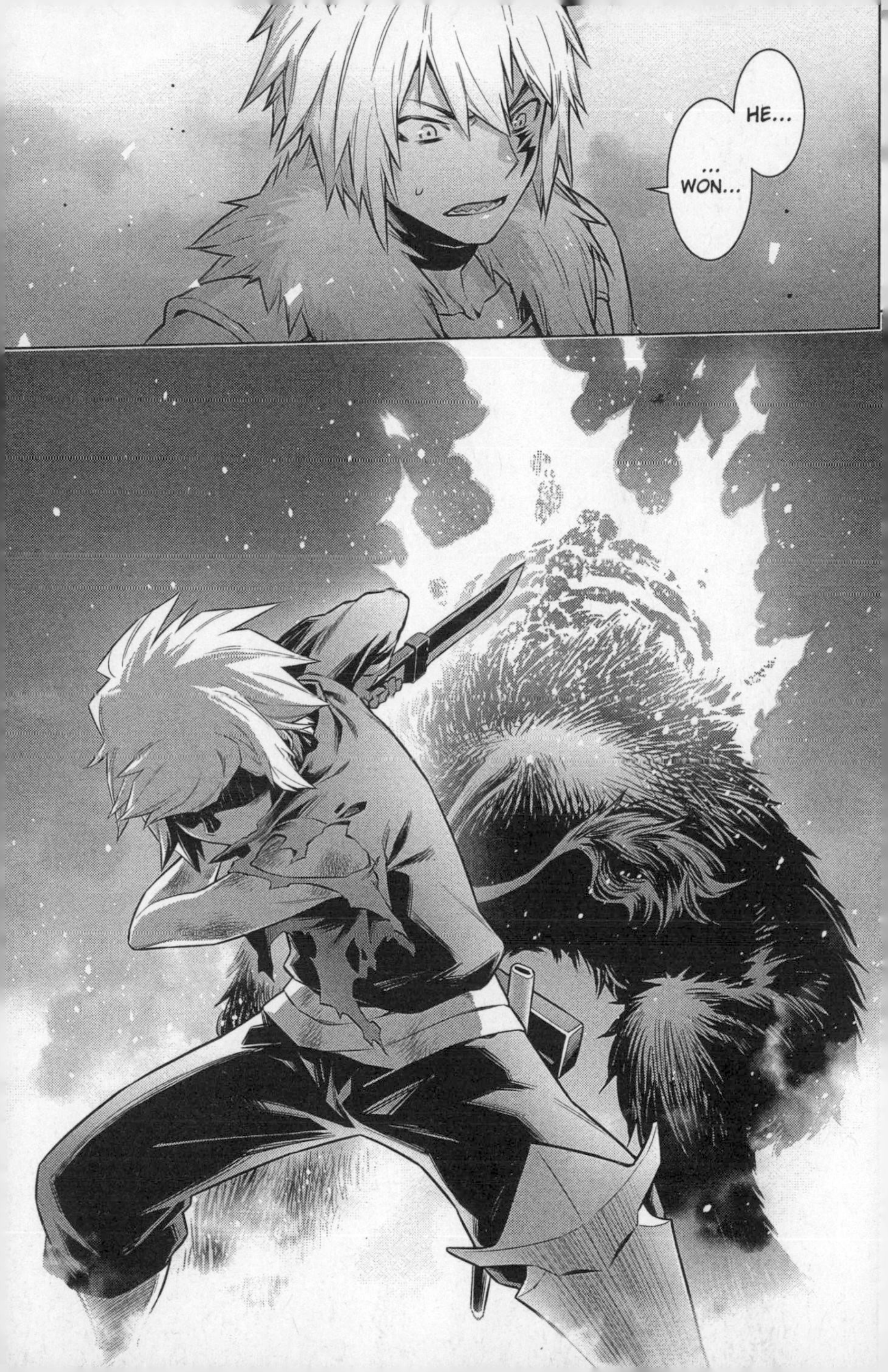
HE...
...WON...

IS IT WRONG TO TRY TO PICK UP GIRLS IN A DUNGEON?

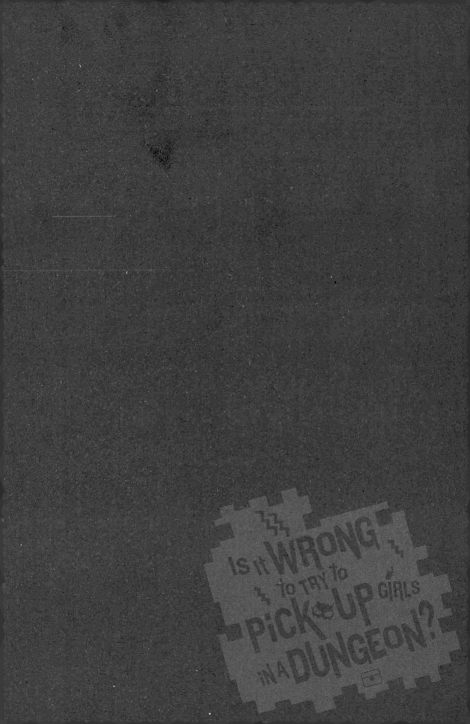

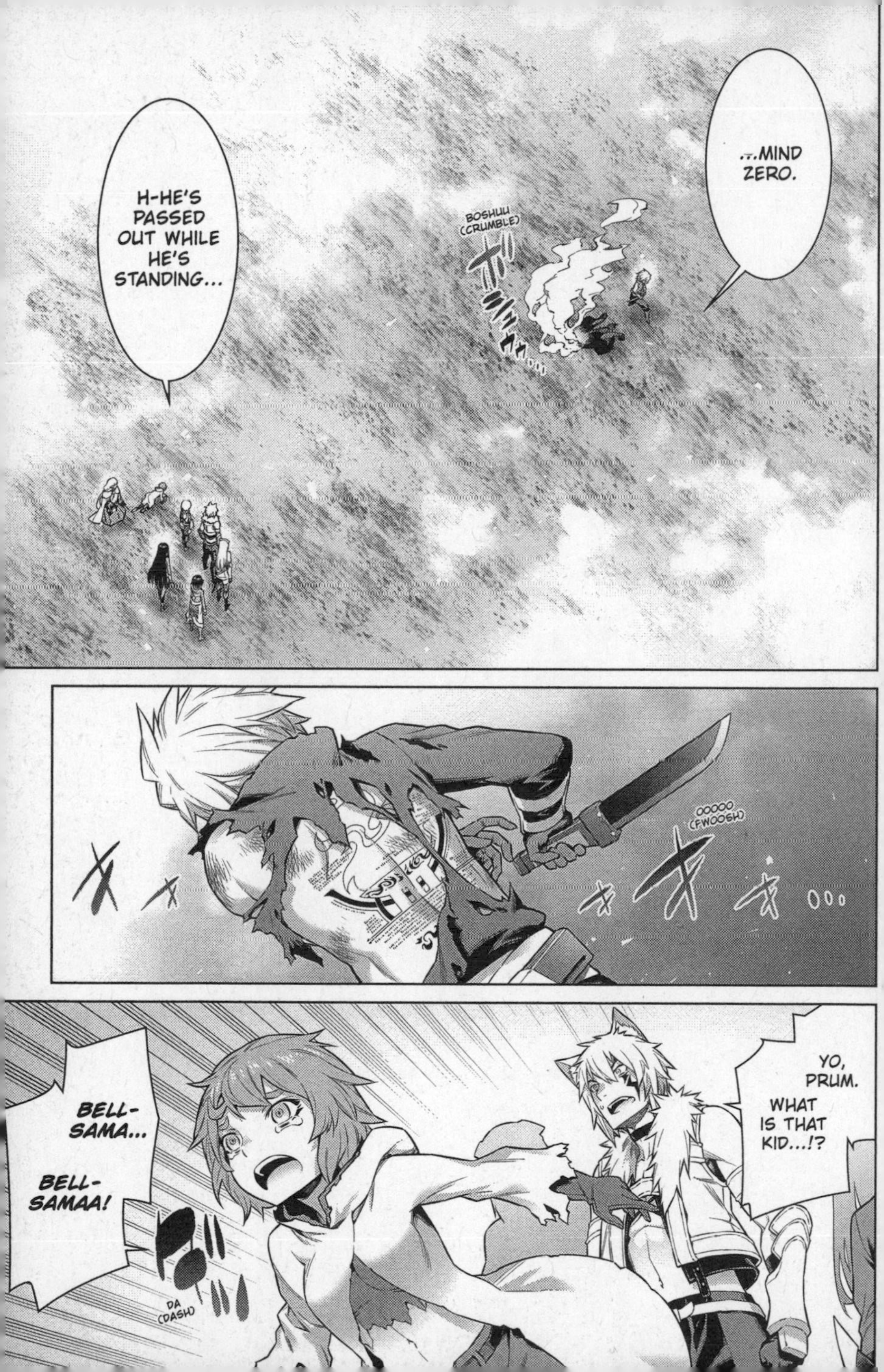
...MIND ZERO.
BOSHUU (CRUMBLE)
H-HE'S PASSED OUT WHILE HE'S STANDING...
OOOOO (FWOOSH)
YO, PRUM.
WHAT IS THAT KID...!?
BELL-SAMA...
BELL-SAMAA!
DA (DASH)

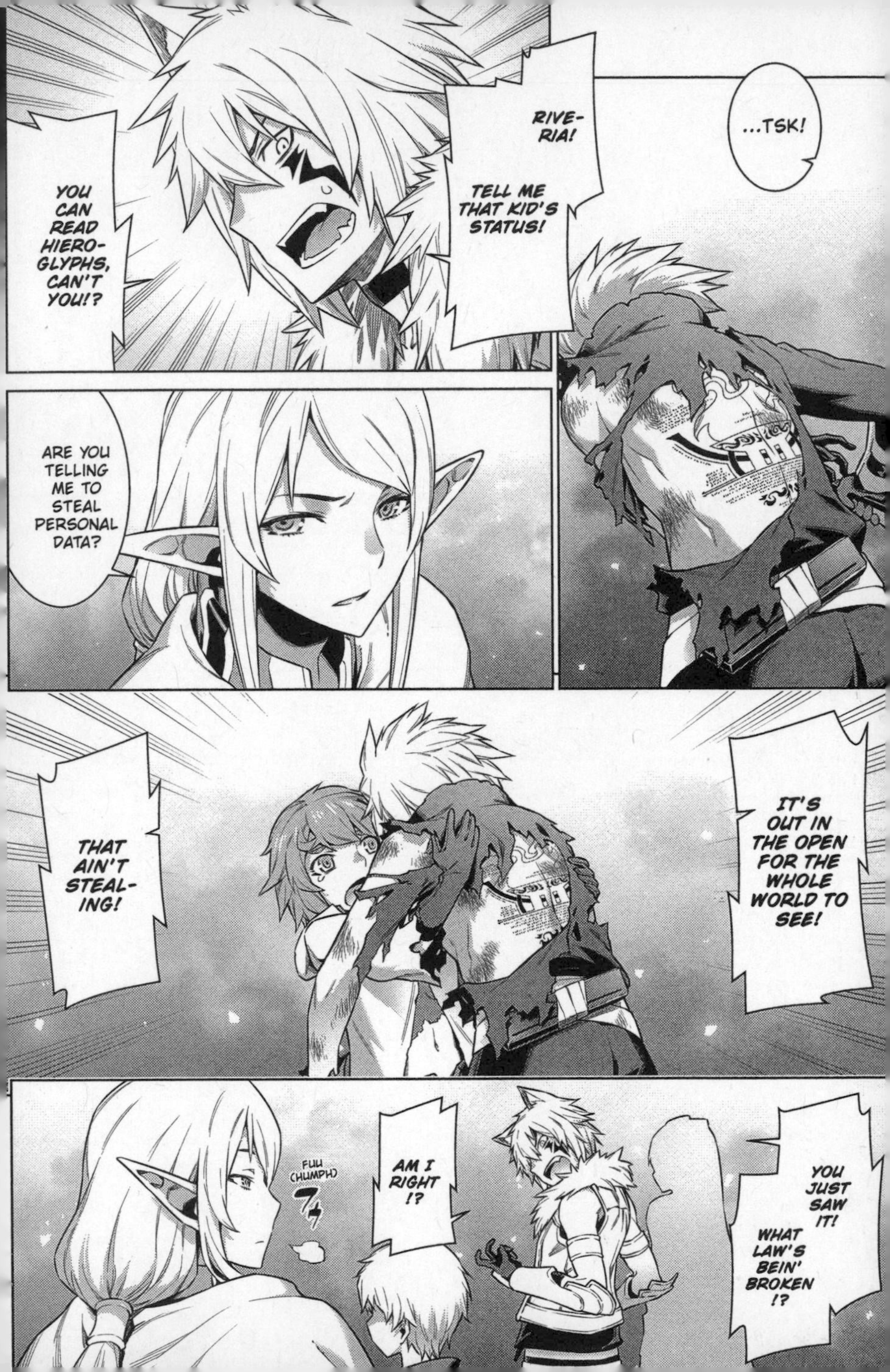
RIVE-RIA!
TELL ME THAT KID'S STATUS!
YOU CAN READ HIERO-GLYPHS, CAN'T YOU!?
...TSK!
ARE YOU TELLING ME TO STEAL PERSONAL DATA?
IT'S OUT IN THE OPEN FOR THE WHOLE WORLD TO SEE!
THAT AIN'T STEAL-ING!
YOU JUST SAW IT!
WHAT LAW'S BEIN' BROKEN!?
AM I RIGHT!?
FUU (HUMPH)

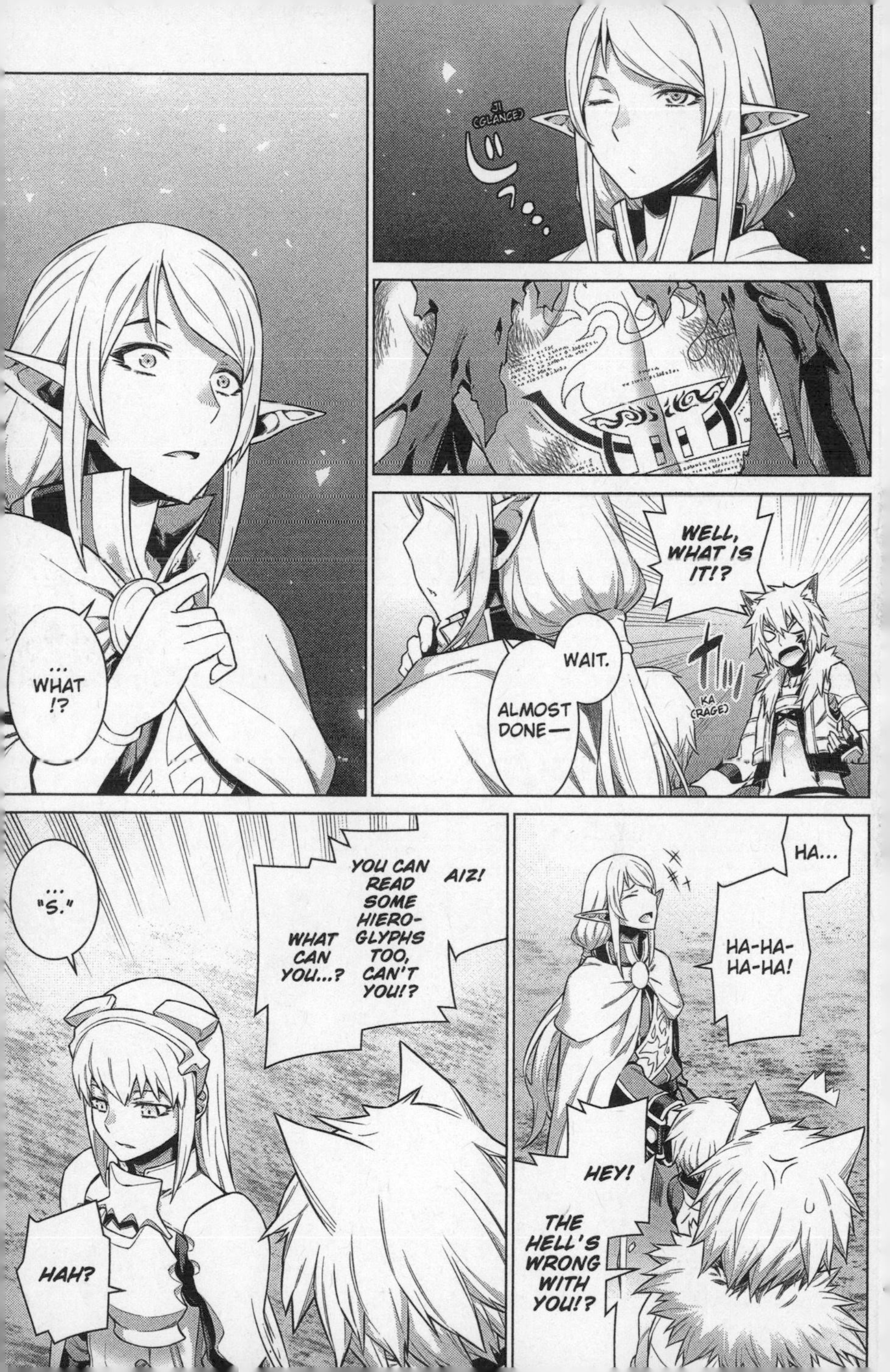
JI (GLANCE)
WELL, WHAT IS IT!?
KA (RAGE)
WAIT.
ALMOST DONE—
... WHAT !?
HA...
HA-HA-HA-HA!
HEY!
THE HELL'S WRONG WITH YOU!?
AIZ!
YOU CAN READ SOME HIEROGLYPHS TOO, CAN'T YOU!?
WHAT CAN YOU...?
... "S."
HAH?

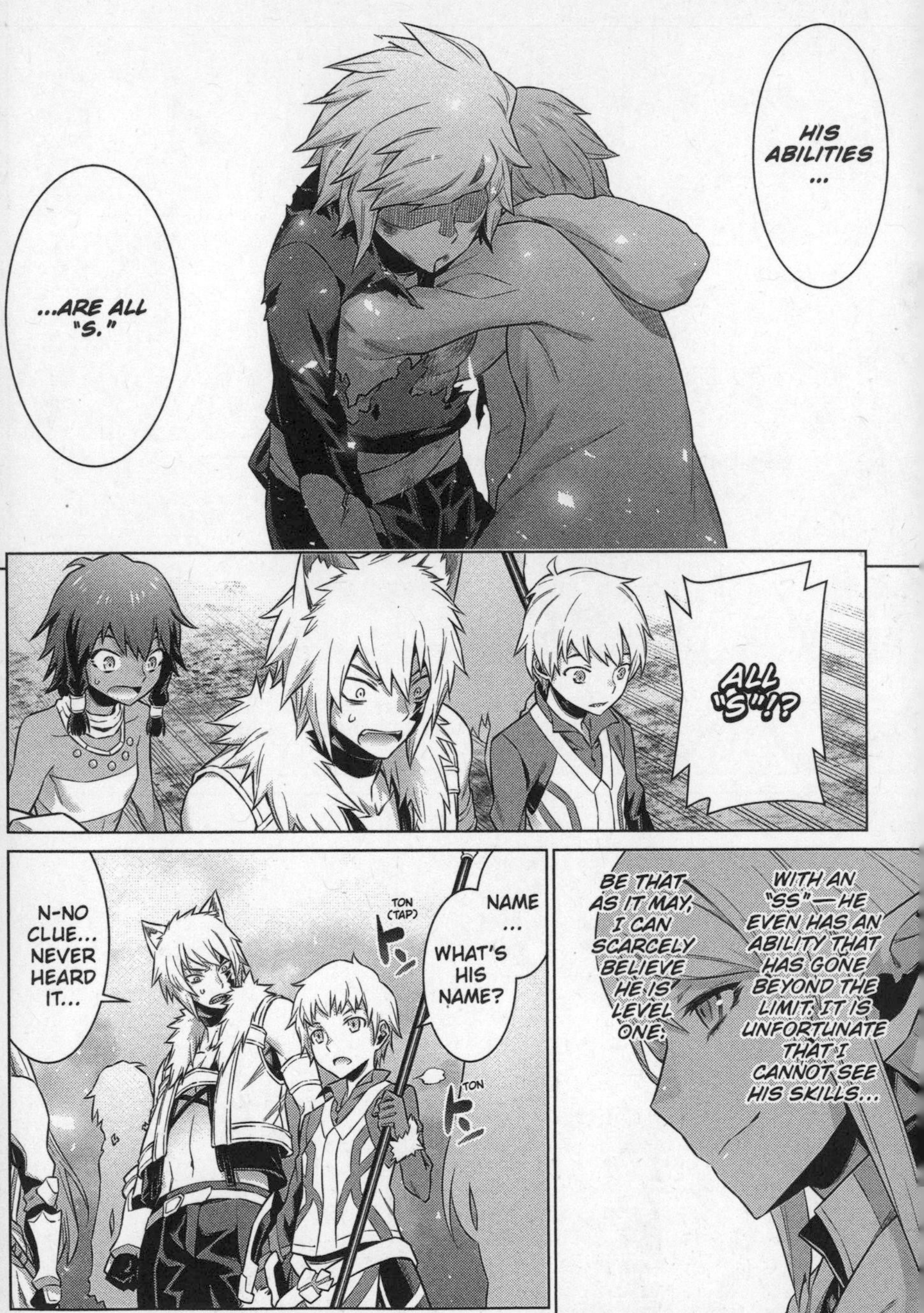
HIS ABILITIES ...
...ARE ALL "S."
ALL "S"!?
WITH AN "SS"—HE EVEN HAS AN ABILITY THAT HAS GONE BEYOND THE LIMIT. IT IS UNFORTUNATE THAT I CANNOT SEE HIS SKILLS...
BE THAT AS IT MAY, I CAN SCARCELY BELIEVE HE IS LEVEL ONE.
TON (TAP)
NAME ...
WHAT'S HIS NAME?
TON
N-NO CLUE... NEVER HEARD IT...

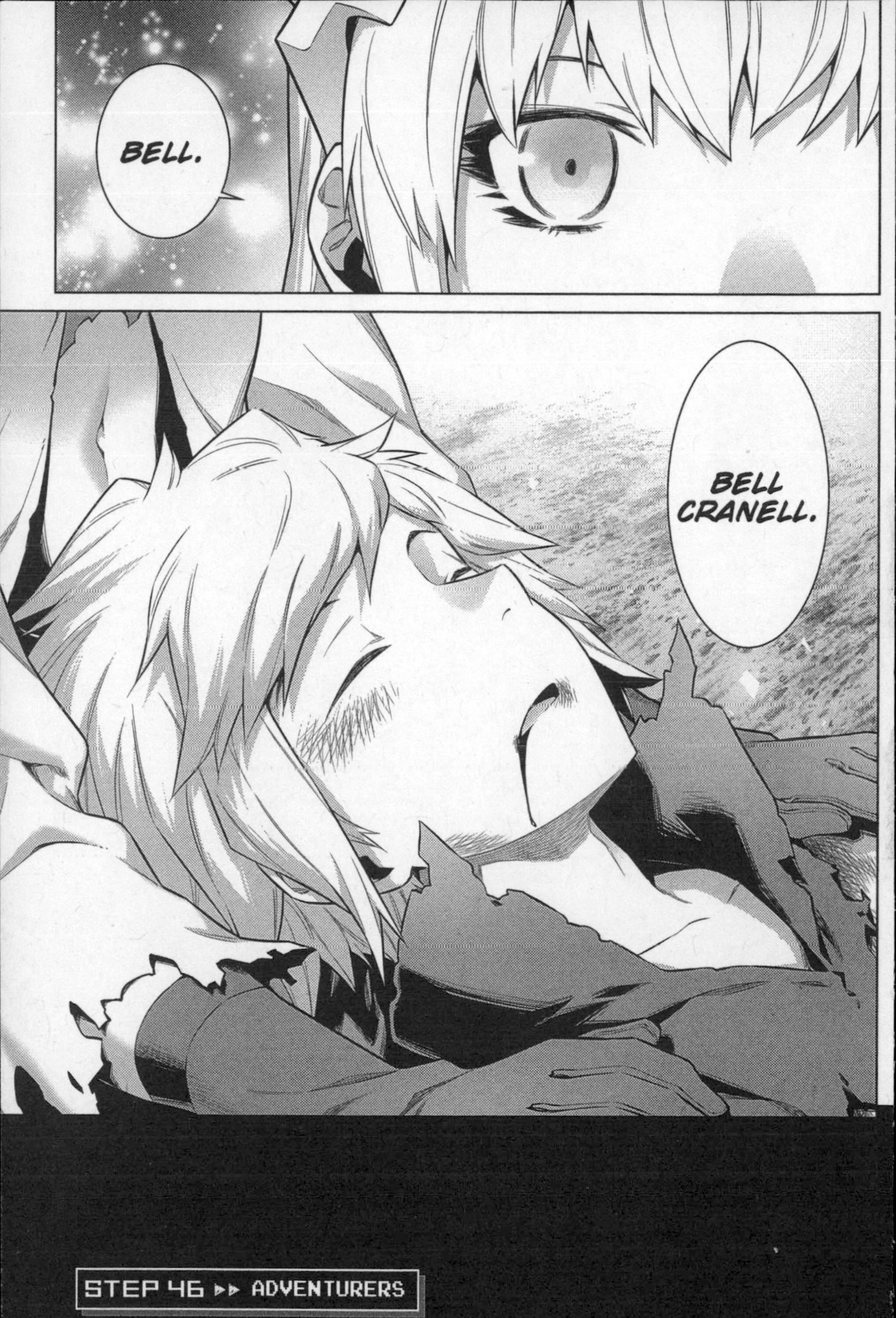
BELL.
BELL CRANELL.

STEP 46 ▸▸ ADVENTURERS

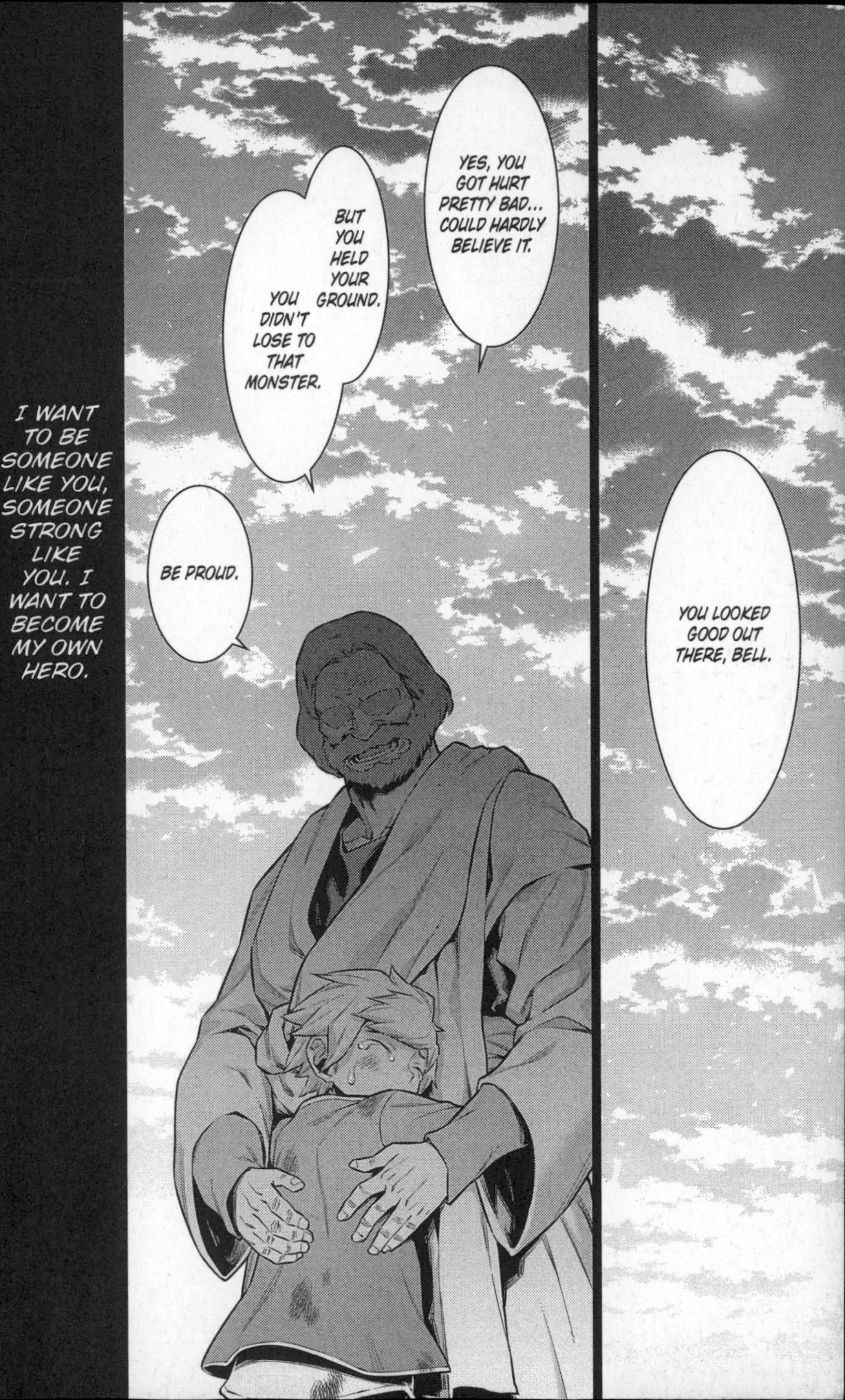
YOU LOOKED GOOD OUT THERE, BELL.
YES, YOU GOT HURT PRETTY BAD... COULD HARDLY BELIEVE IT.
BUT YOU HELD YOUR GROUND. YOU DIDN'T LOSE TO THAT MONSTER.
BE PROUD.
I WANT TO BE SOMEONE LIKE YOU, SOMEONE STRONG LIKE YOU. I WANT TO BECOME MY OWN HERO.

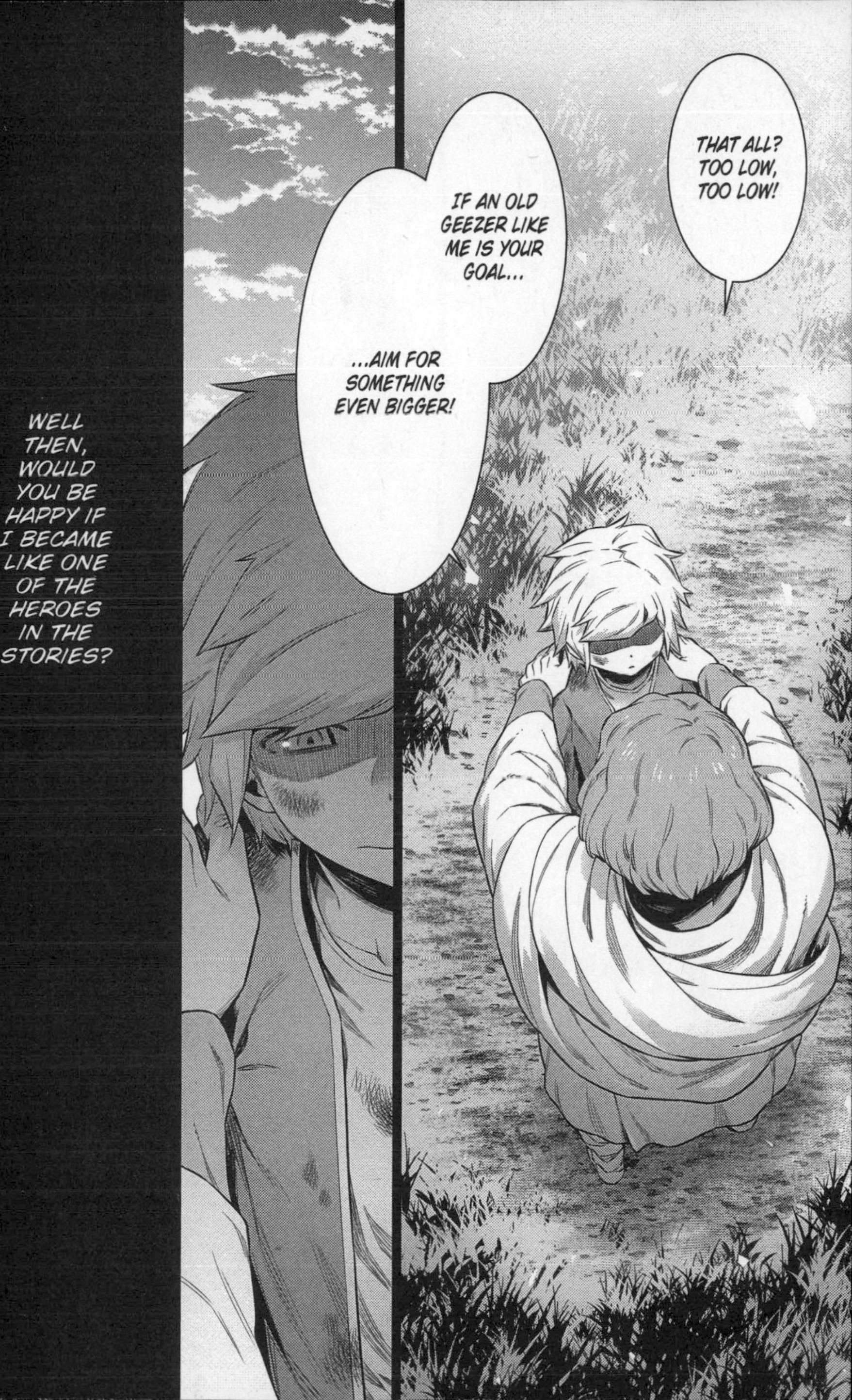
THAT ALL? TOO LOW, TOO LOW!
IF AN OLD GEEZER LIKE ME IS YOUR GOAL...
...AIM FOR SOMETHING EVEN BIGGER!
WELL THEN, WOULD YOU BE HAPPY IF I BECAME LIKE ONE OF THE HEROES IN THE STORIES?

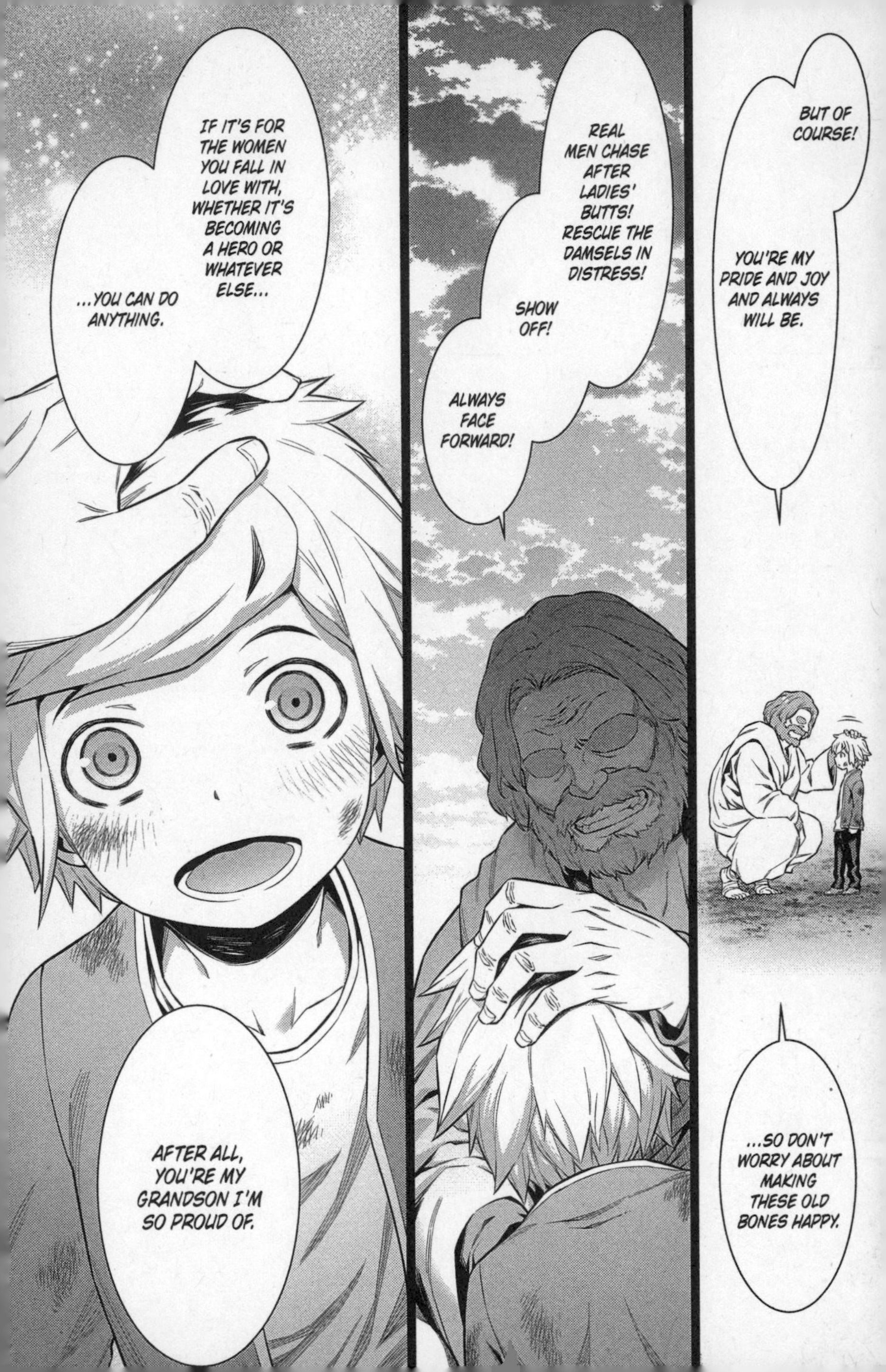
BUT OF COURSE!
YOU'RE MY PRIDE AND JOY AND ALWAYS WILL BE.
...SO DON'T WORRY ABOUT MAKING THESE OLD BONES HAPPY.
REAL MEN CHASE AFTER LADIES' BUTTS! RESCUE THE DAMSELS IN DISTRESS!
SHOW OFF!
ALWAYS FACE FORWARD!
IF IT'S FOR THE WOMEN YOU FALL IN LOVE WITH, WHETHER IT'S BECOMING A HERO OR WHATEVER ELSE...
...YOU CAN DO ANYTHING.
AFTER ALL, YOU'RE MY GRANDSON I'M SO PROUD OF.

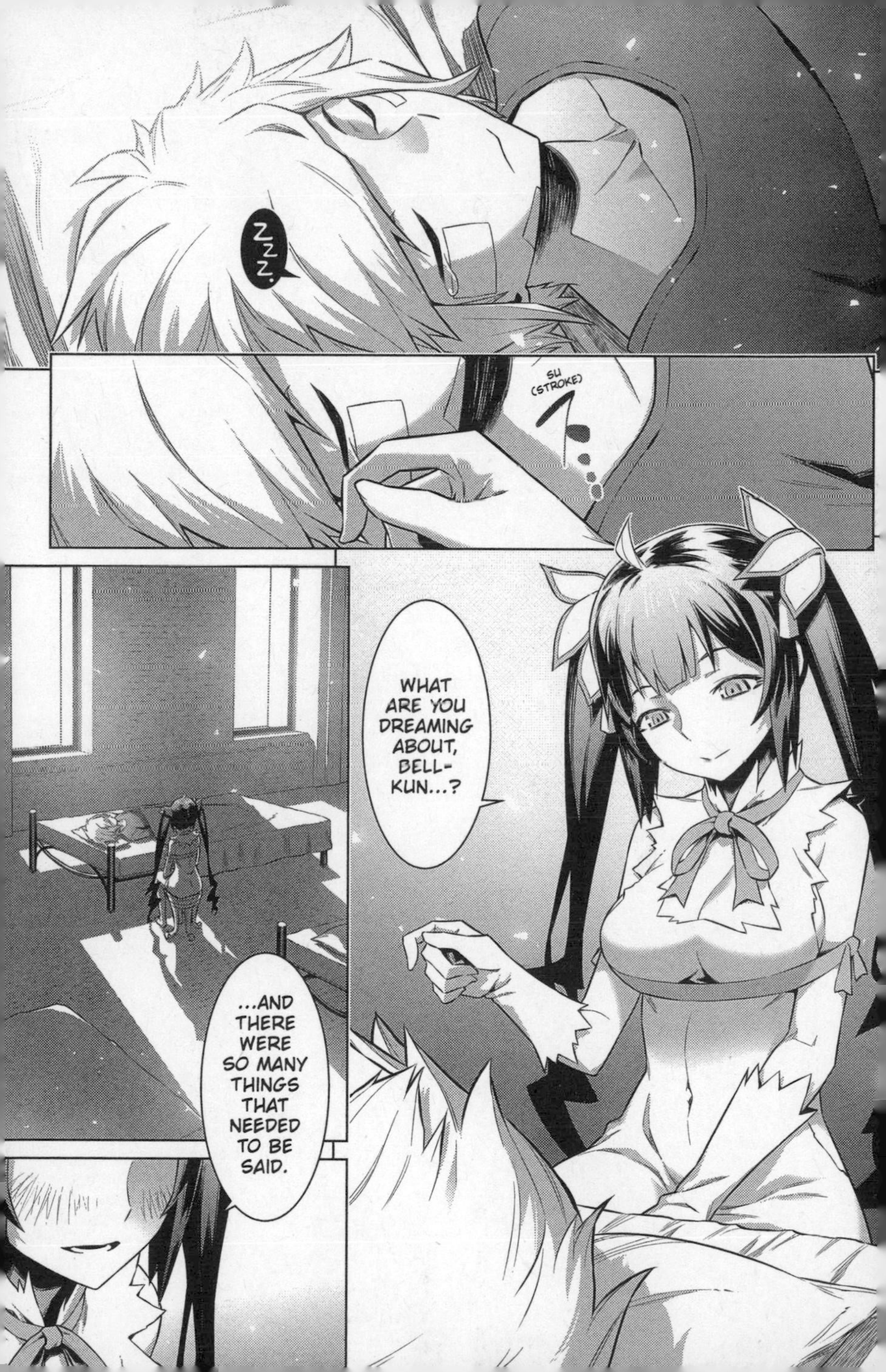
Z Z Z.
SU (STROKE)
WHAT ARE YOU DREAMING ABOUT, BELL-KUN...?
...AND THERE WERE SO MANY THINGS THAT NEEDED TO BE SAID.

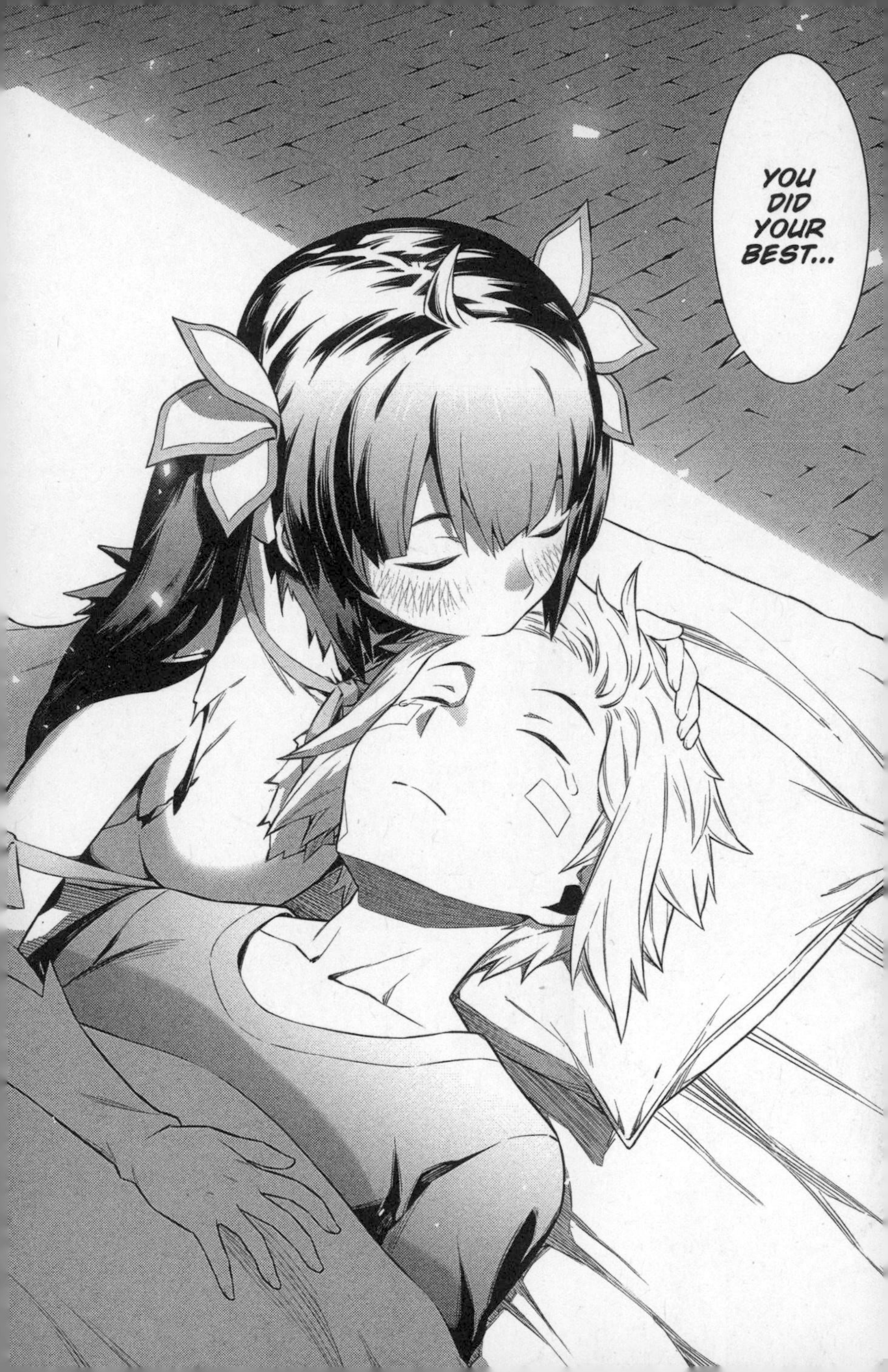
YOU DID YOUR BEST...

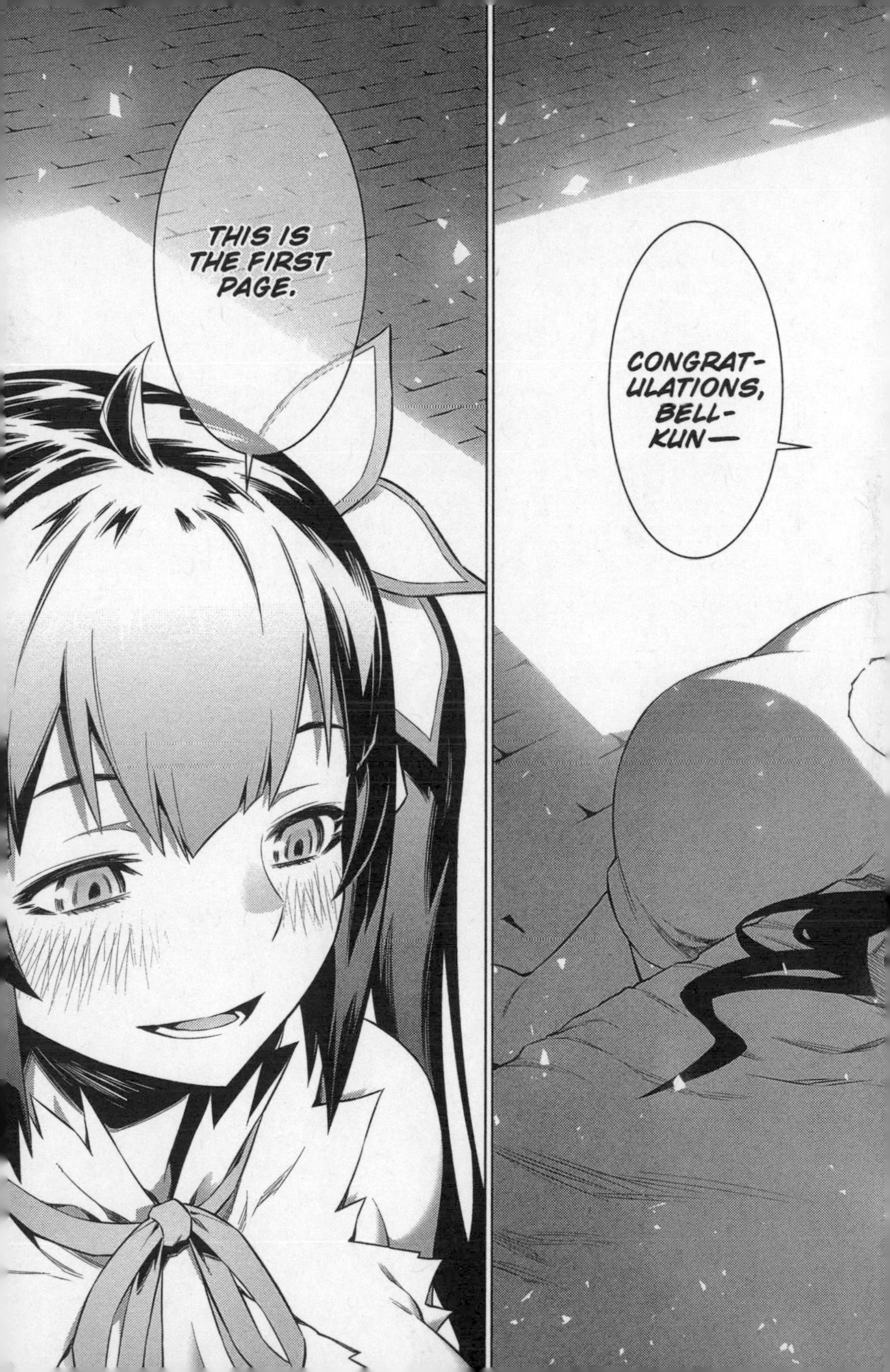
CONGRAT-ULATIONS, BELL-KUN—
THIS IS THE FIRST PAGE.

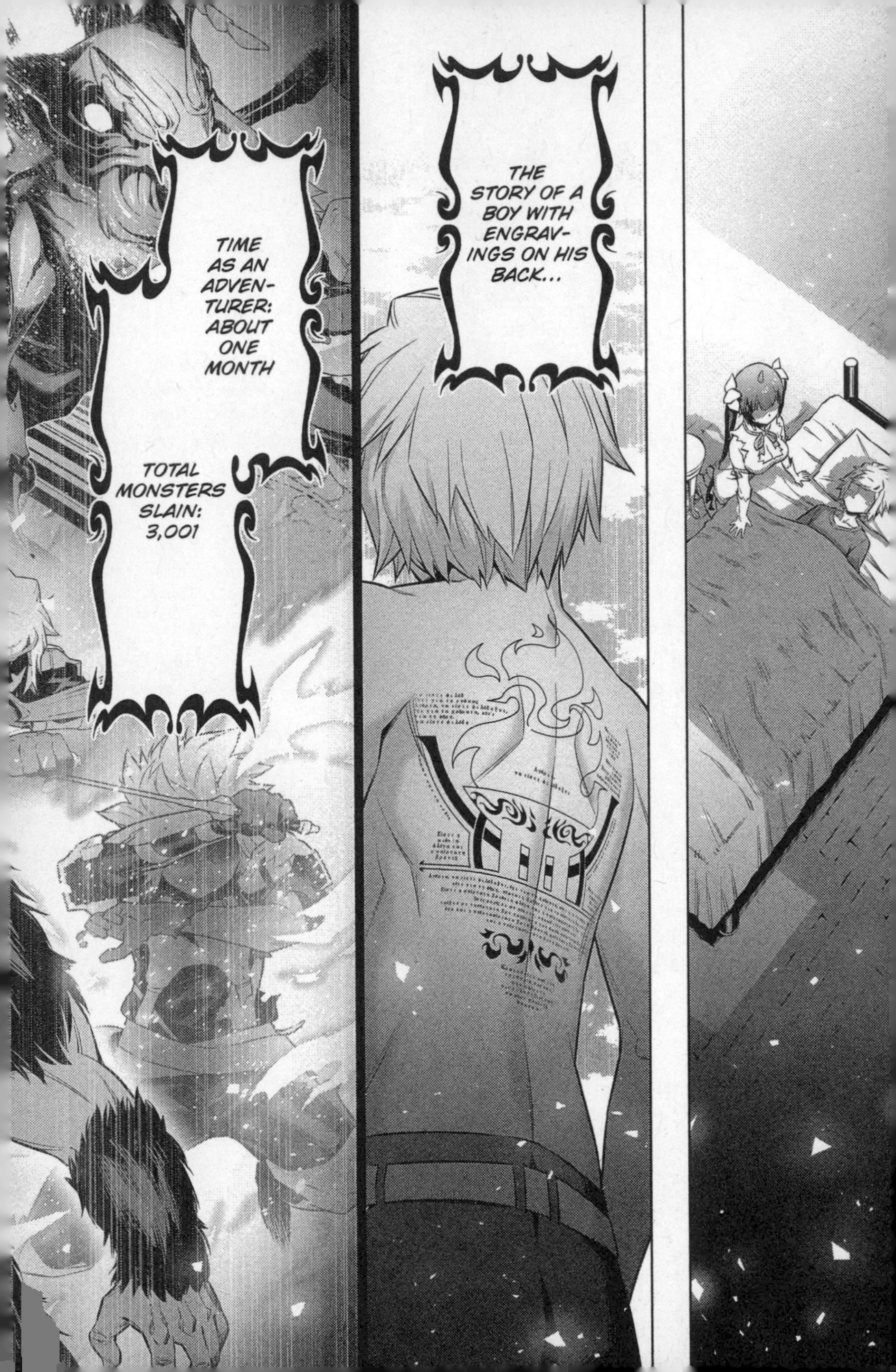
THE STORY OF A BOY WITH ENGRAV-INGS ON HIS BACK...
TIME AS AN ADVEN-TURER: ABOUT ONE MONTH
TOTAL MONSTERS SLAIN: 3,001

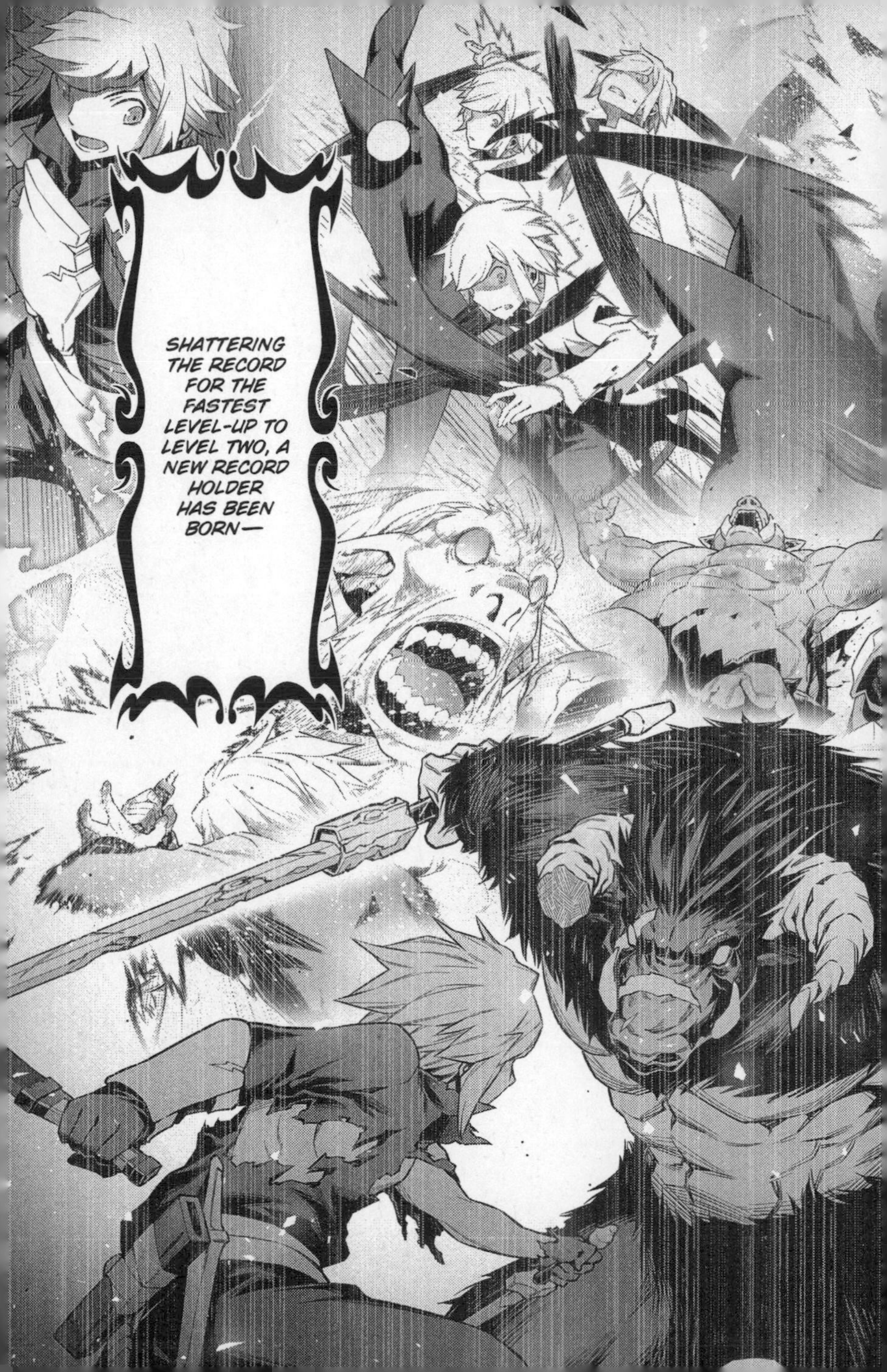
SHATTERING THE RECORD FOR THE FASTEST LEVEL-UP TO LEVEL TWO, A NEW RECORD HOLDER HAS BEEN BORN—

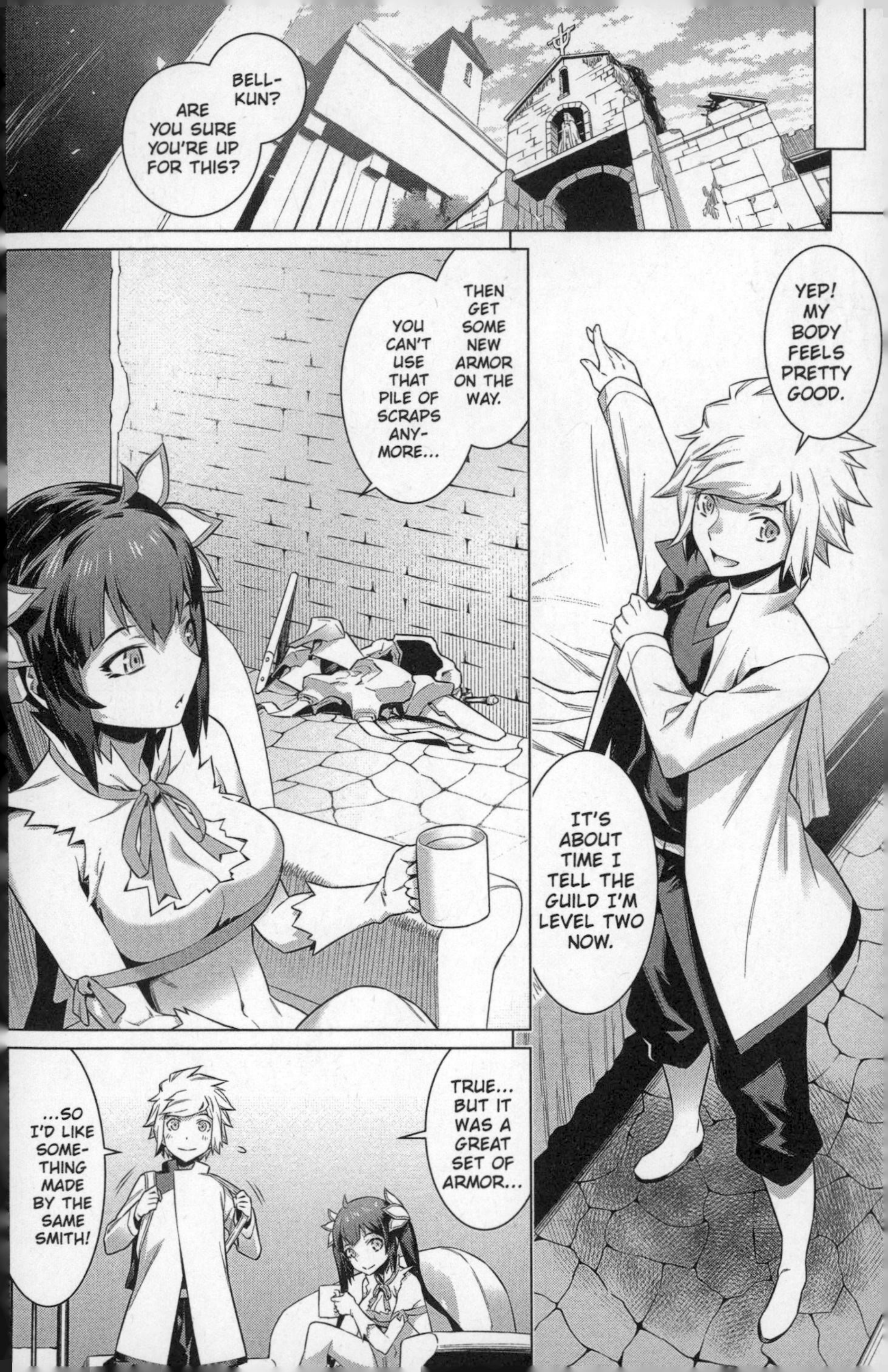
BELL-KUN? ARE YOU SURE YOU'RE UP FOR THIS?
YEP! MY BODY FEELS PRETTY GOOD.
IT'S ABOUT TIME I TELL THE GUILD I'M LEVEL TWO NOW.
THEN GET SOME NEW ARMOR ON THE WAY.
YOU CAN'T USE THAT PILE OF SCRAPS ANY-MORE...
TRUE... BUT IT WAS A GREAT SET OF ARMOR...
...SO I'D LIKE SOME-THING MADE BY THE SAME SMITH!

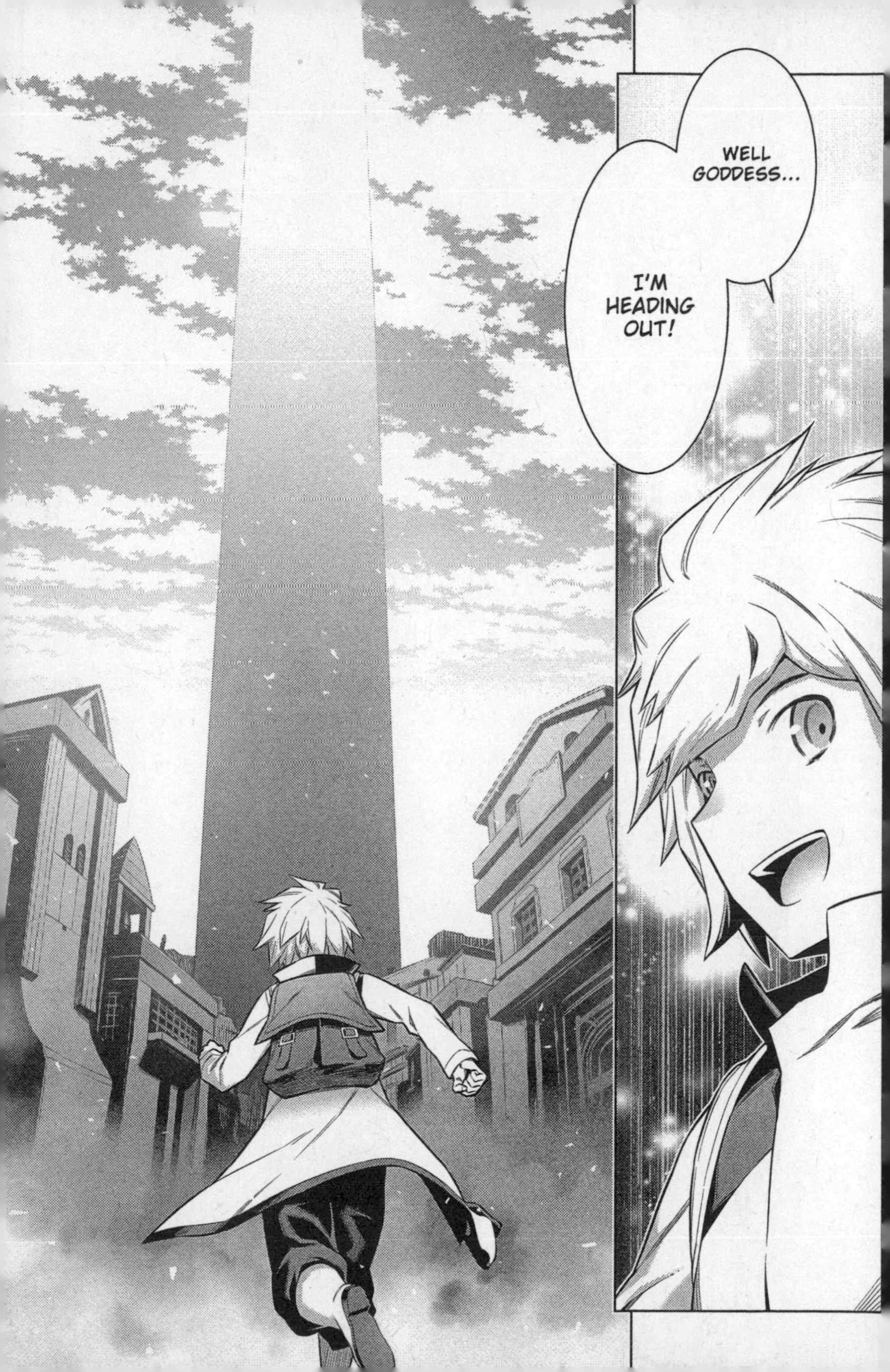
WELL GODDESS...
I'M HEADING OUT!

Is it WRONG to TRY to PICK UP GIRLS IN A DUNGEON?

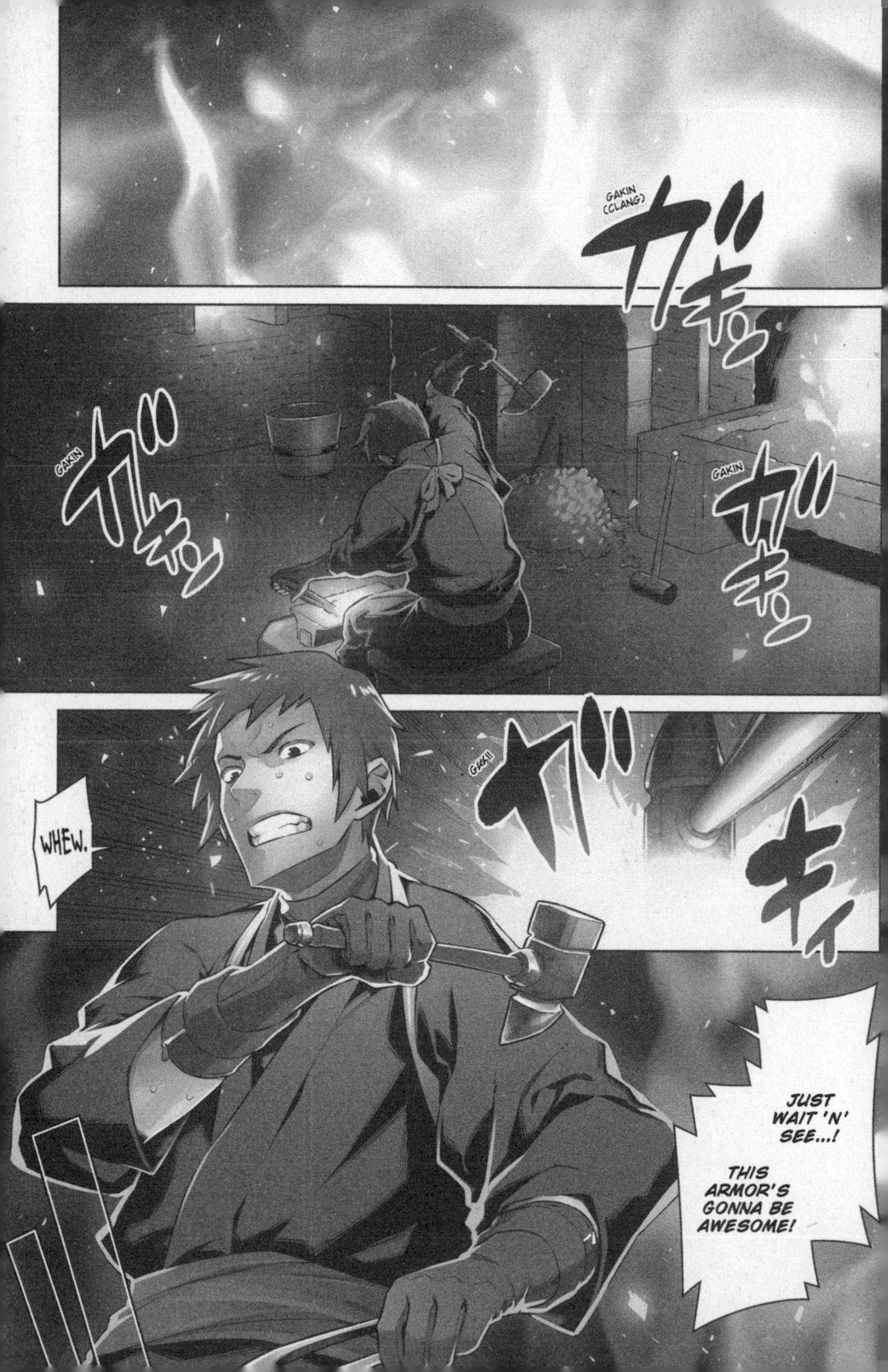
GAKIN (CLANG)
GAKIN
GAKIN
GAKII
WHEW.
JUST WAIT 'N' SEE...!
THIS ARMOR'S GONNA BE AWESOME!

STEP 47 ▸▸ THE SECRET CONNECTION BETWEEN LEVELING UP AND A CONFERENCE OF DEITIES

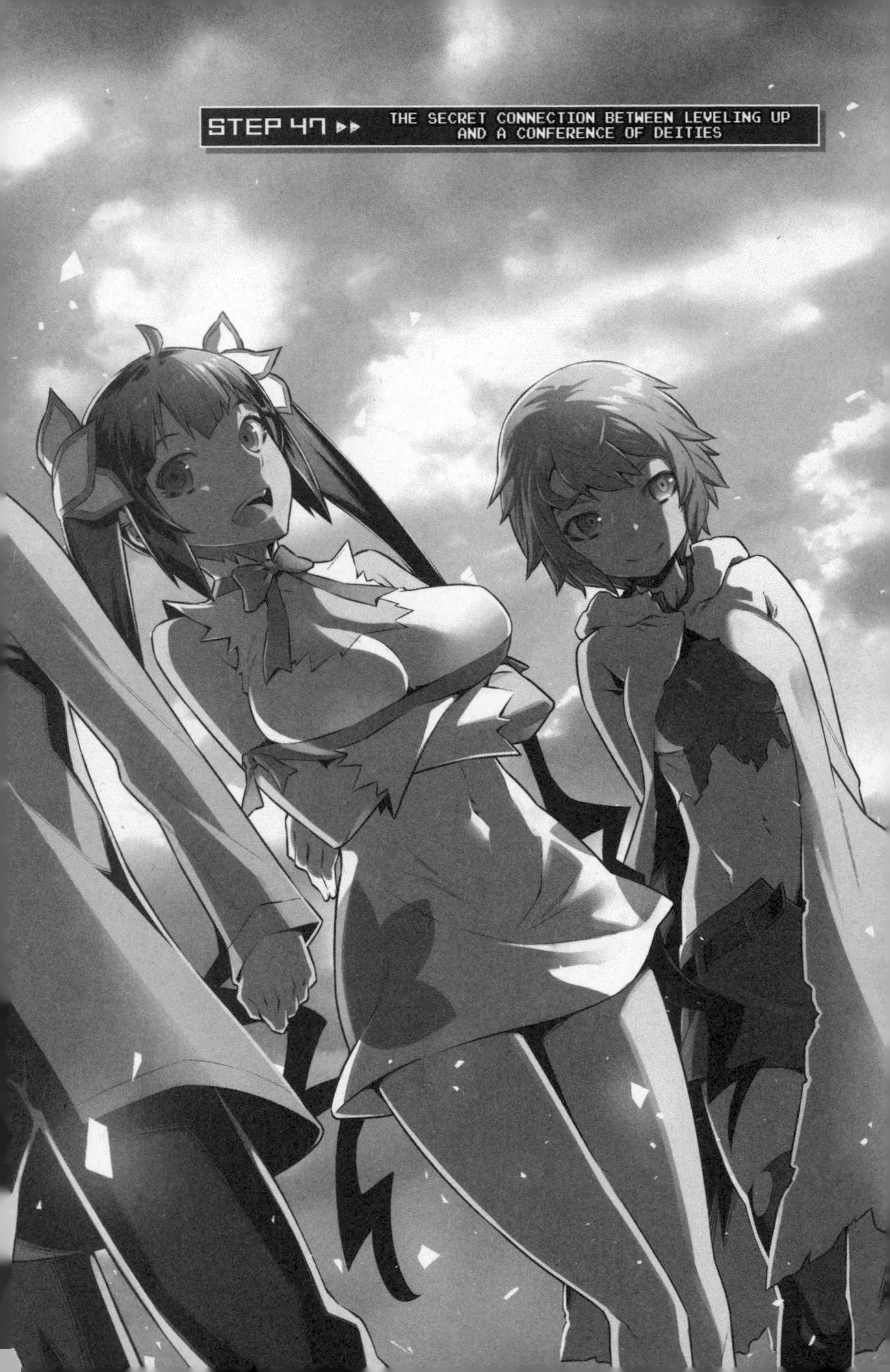

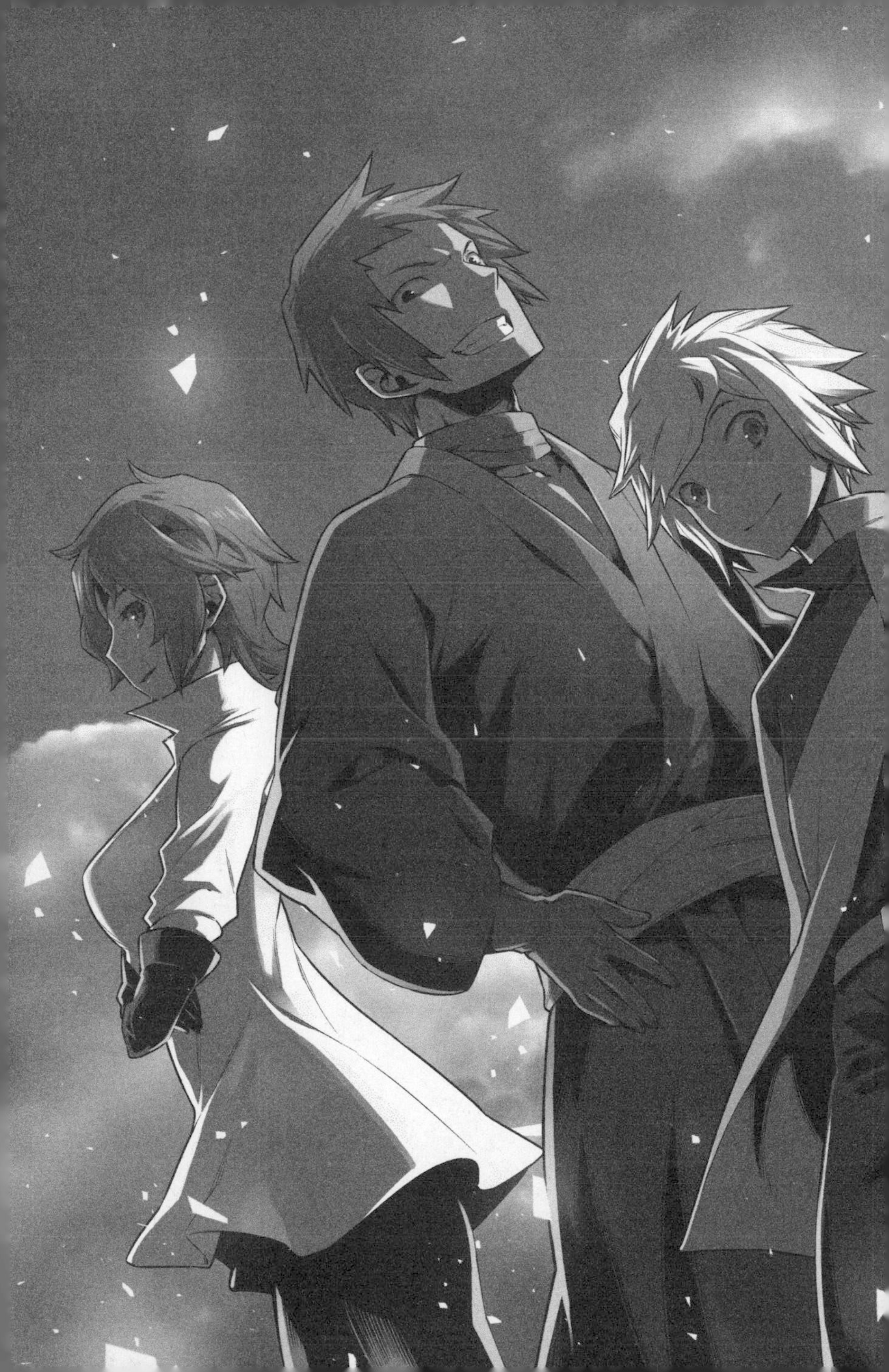

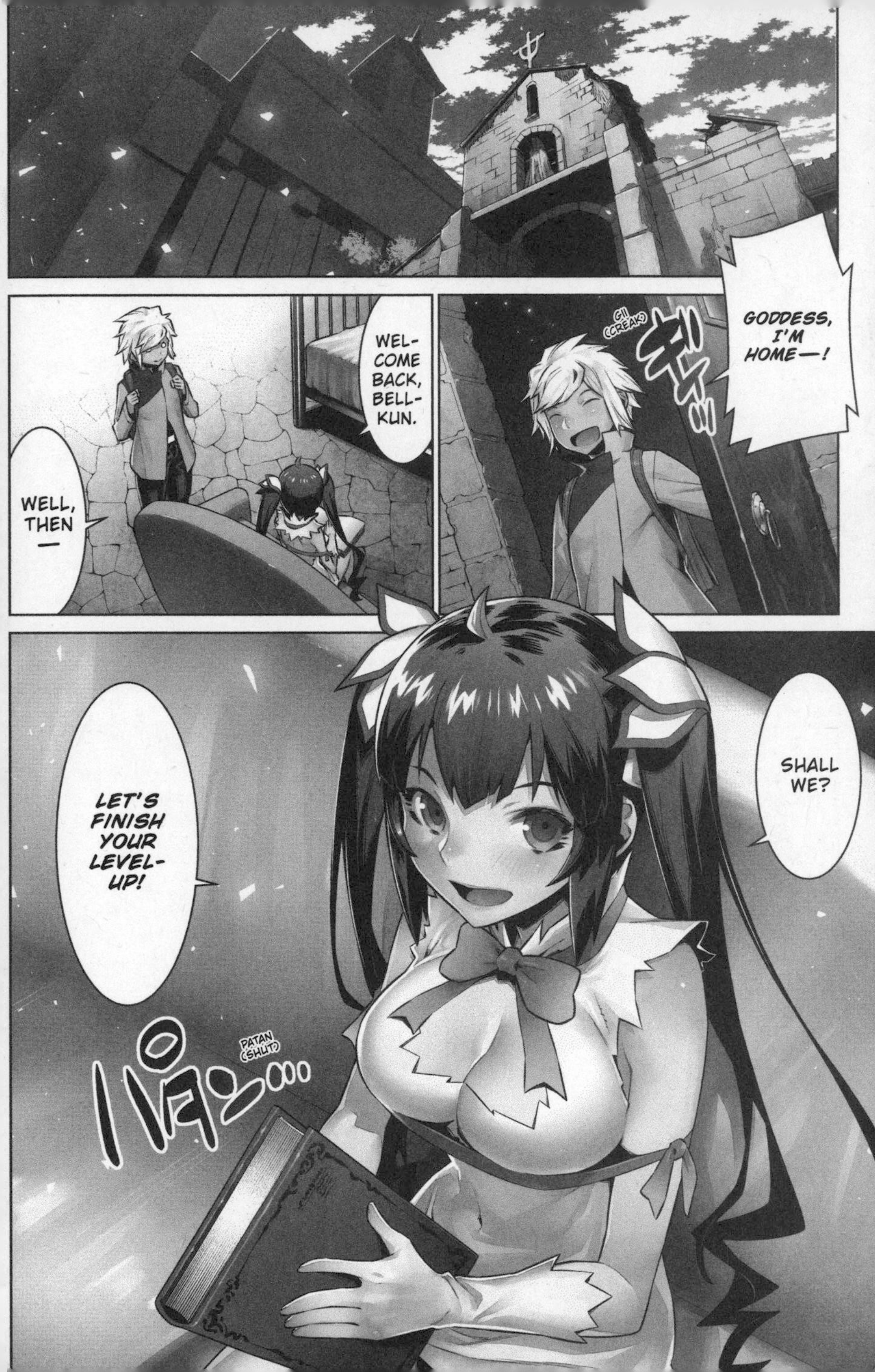
GOODDESS, I'M HOME—!
GII (CREAK)
WEL-COME BACK, BELL-KUN.
WELL, THEN—
SHALL WE?
LET'S FINISH YOUR LEVEL-UP!
PATAN (SHUT)

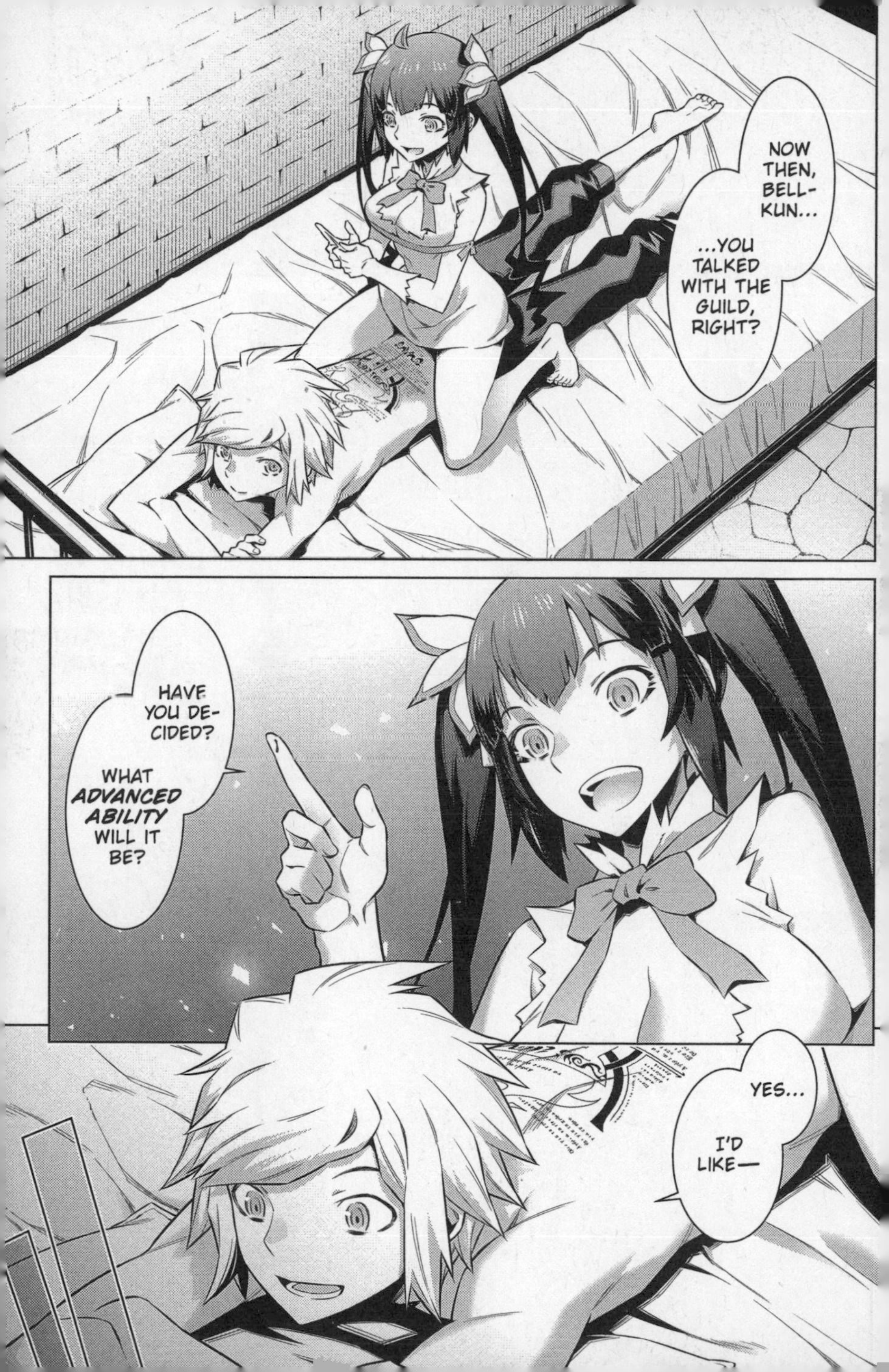
NOW THEN, BELL-KUN...
...YOU TALKED WITH THE GUILD, RIGHT?
HAVE YOU DE-CIDED?
WHAT ***ADVANCED ABILITY*** WILL IT BE?
YES...
I'D LIKE—

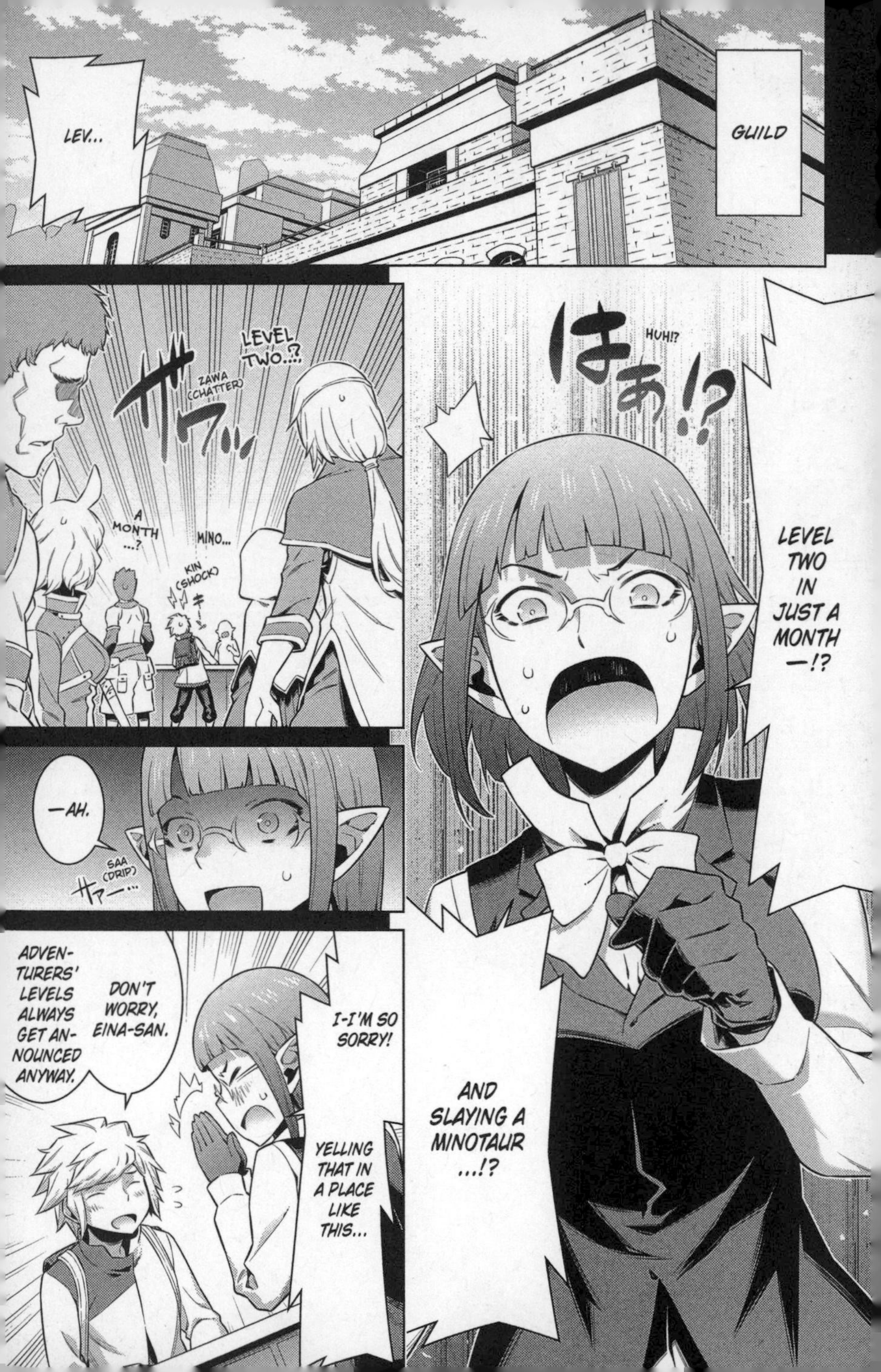
GUILD
LEV...
HUH!?
はぁ!?
LEVEL TWO IN JUST A MONTH—!?
AND SLAYING A MINOTAUR ...!?
LEVEL TWO...?
ザワッ
ZAWA (CHATTER)
MINO...
A MONTH ...?
KIN (SHOCK)
—AH.
SAA (DRIP)
サァー…
I-I'M SO SORRY!
YELLING THAT IN A PLACE LIKE THIS...
DON'T WORRY, EINA-SAN.
ADVENTURERS' LEVELS ALWAYS GET ANNOUNCED ANYWAY.

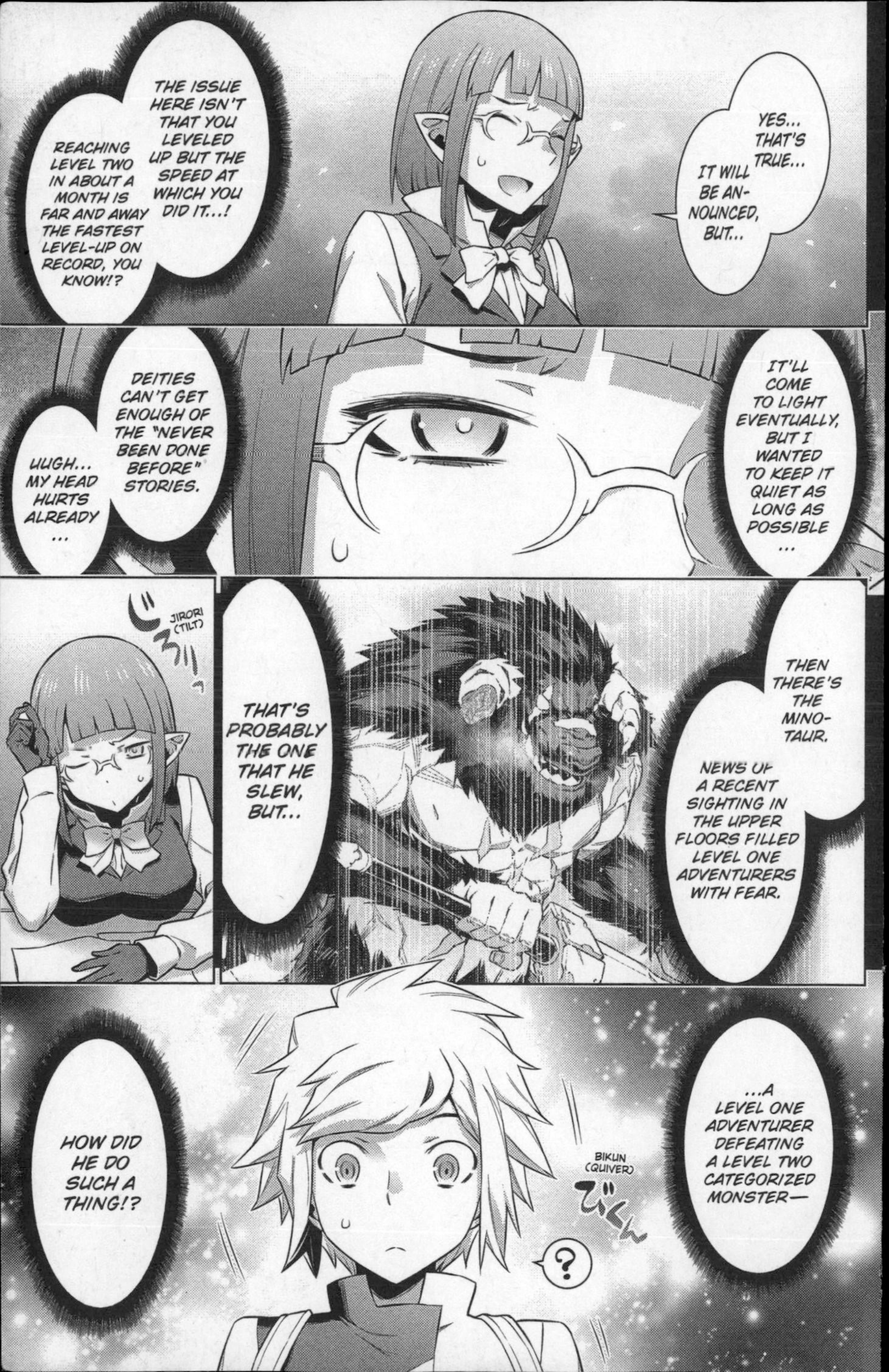
YES... THAT'S TRUE...
IT WILL BE AN-NOUNCED, BUT...
THE ISSUE HERE ISN'T THAT YOU LEVELED UP BUT THE SPEED AT WHICH YOU DID IT...!
REACHING LEVEL TWO IN ABOUT A MONTH IS FAR AND AWAY THE FASTEST LEVEL-UP ON RECORD, YOU KNOW!?
IT'LL COME TO LIGHT EVENTUALLY, BUT I WANTED TO KEEP IT QUIET AS LONG AS POSSIBLE...
DEITIES CAN'T GET ENOUGH OF THE "NEVER BEEN DONE BEFORE" STORIES.
UUGH... MY HEAD HURTS ALREADY...
THEN THERE'S THE MINO-TAUR.
NEWS OF A RECENT SIGHTING IN THE UPPER FLOORS FILLED LEVEL ONE ADVENTURERS WITH FEAR.
THAT'S PROBABLY THE ONE THAT HE SLEW, BUT...
JIRORI (TILT)
...A LEVEL ONE ADVENTURER DEFEATING A LEVEL TWO CATEGORIZED MONSTER—
BIKUN (QUIVER)
?
HOW DID HE DO SUCH A THING!?

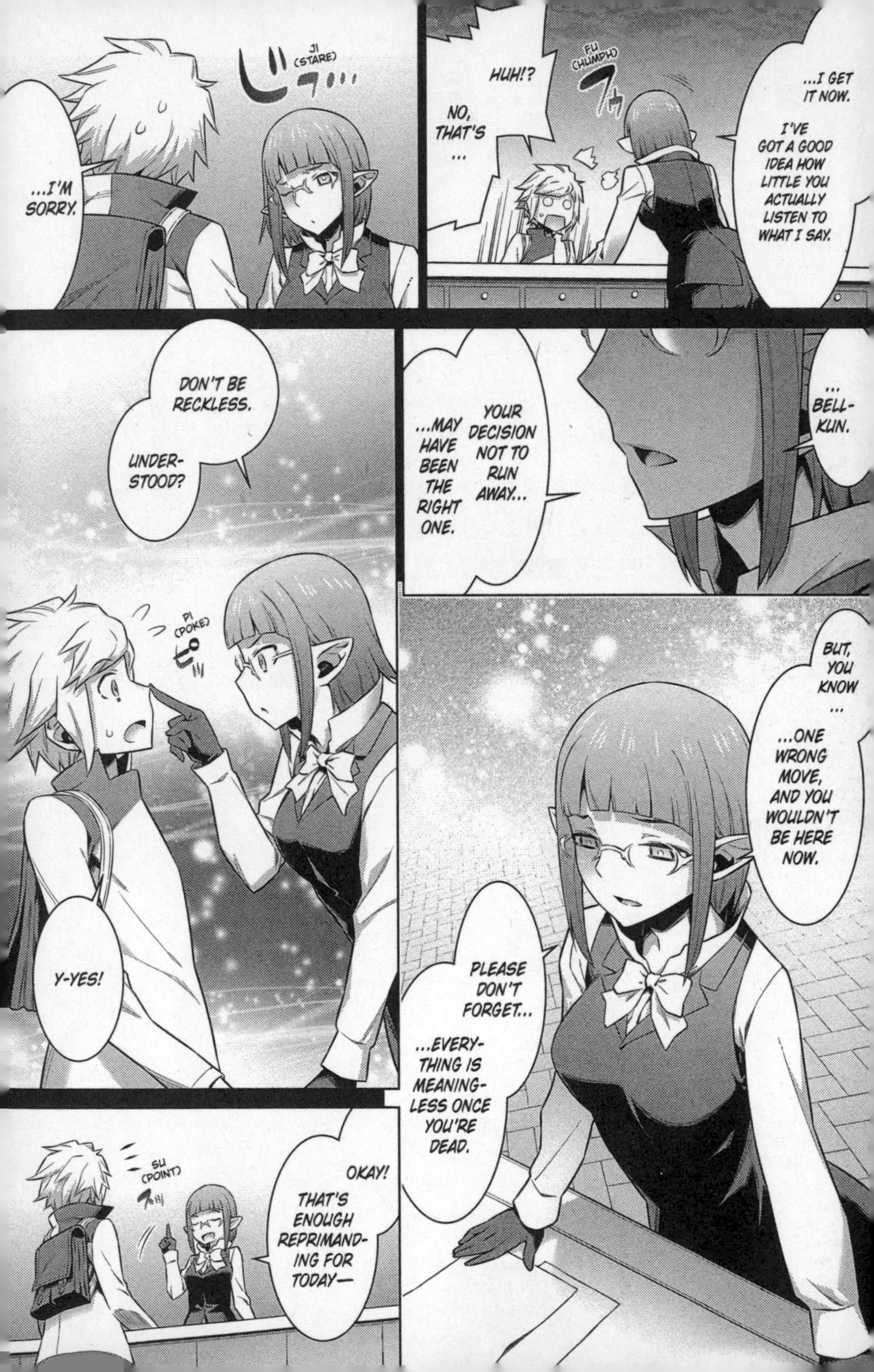
...I GET IT NOW.
I'VE GOT A GOOD IDEA HOW LITTLE YOU ACTUALLY LISTEN TO WHAT I SAY.
FU (HUMPH)
HUH!?
NO, THAT'S ...
JI (STARE)
...I'M SORRY.
... BELL-KUN.
YOUR DECISION NOT TO RUN AWAY...
...MAY HAVE BEEN THE RIGHT ONE.
BUT, YOU KNOW ...
...ONE WRONG MOVE, AND YOU WOULDN'T BE HERE NOW.
PLEASE DON'T FORGET...
...EVERY-THING IS MEANING-LESS ONCE YOU'RE DEAD.
DON'T BE RECKLESS.
UNDER-STOOD?
PI (POKE)
Y-YES!
SU (POINT)
OKAY!
THAT'S ENOUGH REPRIMAND-ING FOR TODAY—

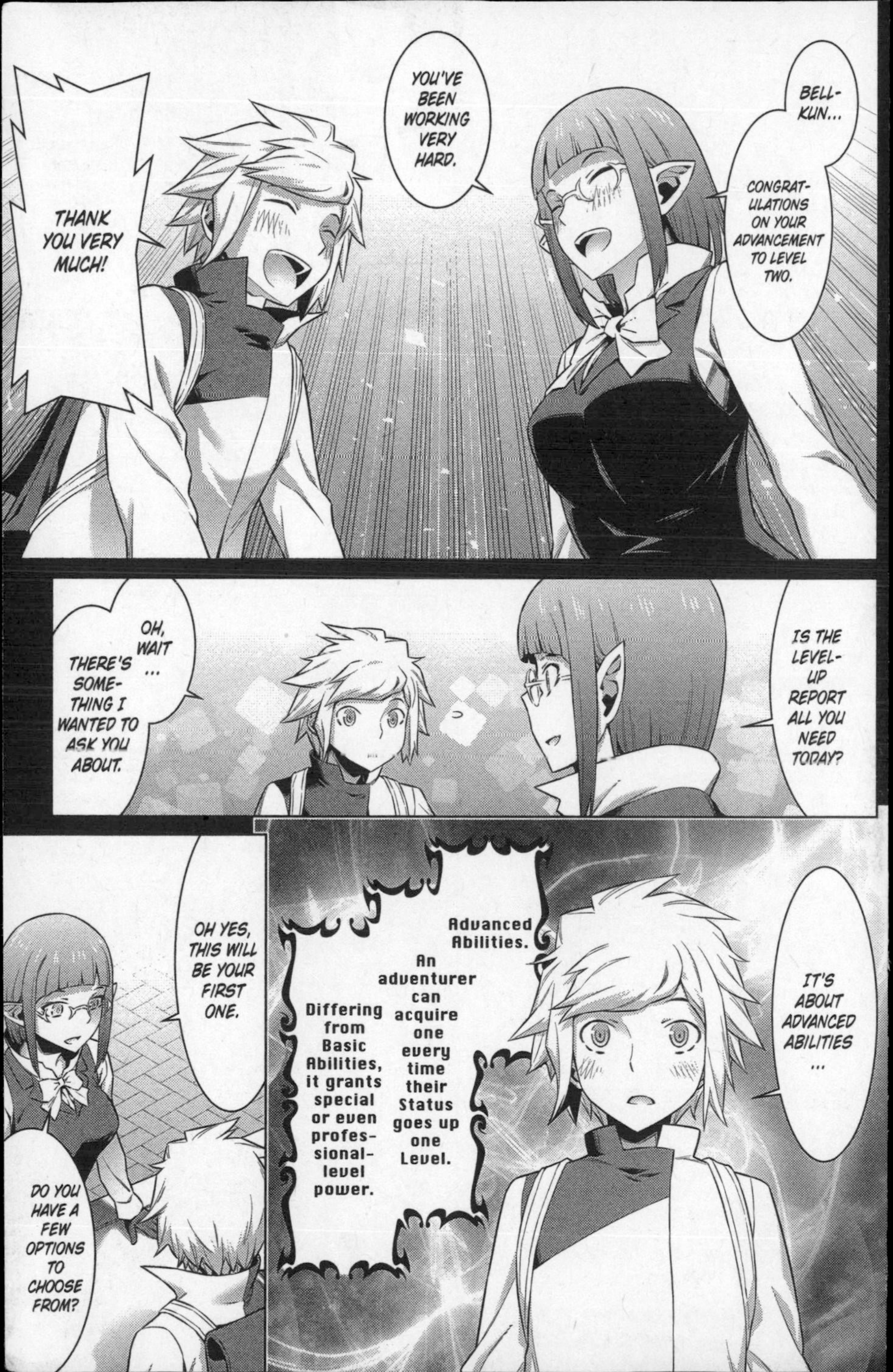
BELL-KUN...
CONGRATULATIONS ON YOUR ADVANCEMENT TO LEVEL TWO.
YOU'VE BEEN WORKING VERY HARD.
THANK YOU VERY MUCH!
IS THE LEVEL-UP REPORT ALL YOU NEED TODAY?
OH, WAIT...
THERE'S SOMETHING I WANTED TO ASK YOU ABOUT.
IT'S ABOUT ADVANCED ABILITIES...
Advanced Abilities.
An adventurer can acquire one every time their Status goes up one Level.
Differing from Basic Abilities, it grants special or even professional-level power.
OH YES, THIS WILL BE YOUR FIRST ONE.
DO YOU HAVE A FEW OPTIONS TO CHOOSE FROM?

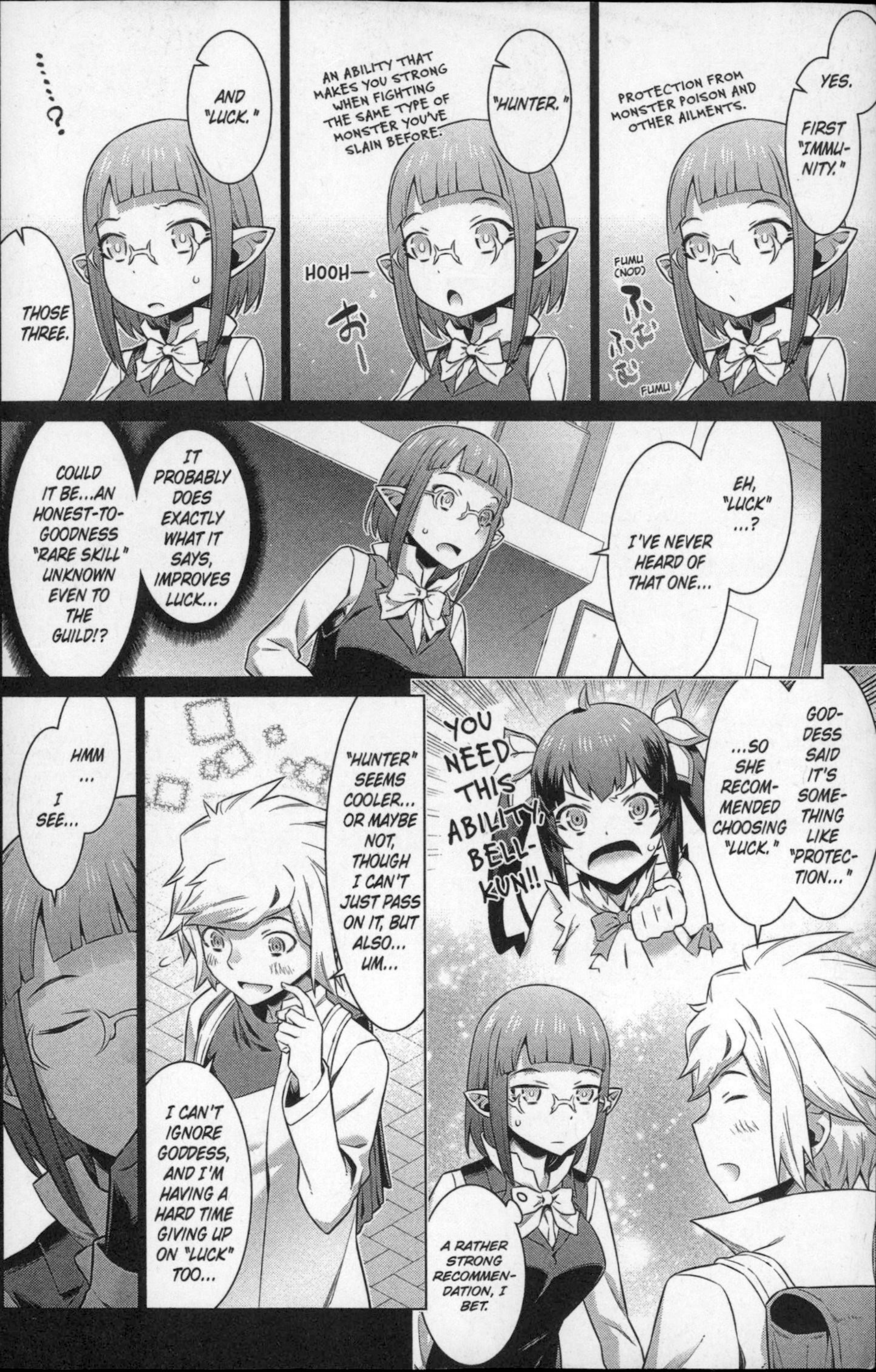
YES.
FIRST "IMMUNITY."
PROTECTION FROM MONSTER POISON AND OTHER AILMENTS.
FUMU (NOD)
FUMU
"HUNTER."
AN ABILITY THAT MAKES YOU STRONG WHEN FIGHTING THE SAME TYPE OF MONSTER YOU'VE SLAIN BEFORE.
HOOH—
AND "LUCK."
......?
THOSE THREE.
EH, "LUCK" ...?
I'VE NEVER HEARD OF THAT ONE...
IT PROBABLY DOES EXACTLY WHAT IT SAYS, IMPROVES LUCK...
COULD IT BE...AN HONEST-TO-GOODNESS "RARE SKILL" UNKNOWN EVEN TO THE GUILD!?
GODDESS SAID IT'S SOMETHING LIKE "PROTECTION..."
...SO SHE RECOMMENDED CHOOSING "LUCK."
YOU NEED THIS ABILITY, BELL-KUN!!
A RATHER STRONG RECOMMENDATION, I BET.
"HUNTER" SEEMS COOLER... OR MAYBE NOT, THOUGH I CAN'T JUST PASS ON IT, BUT ALSO... UM...
I CAN'T IGNORE GODDESS, AND I'M HAVING A HARD TIME GIVING UP ON "LUCK" TOO...
HMM ... I SEE...

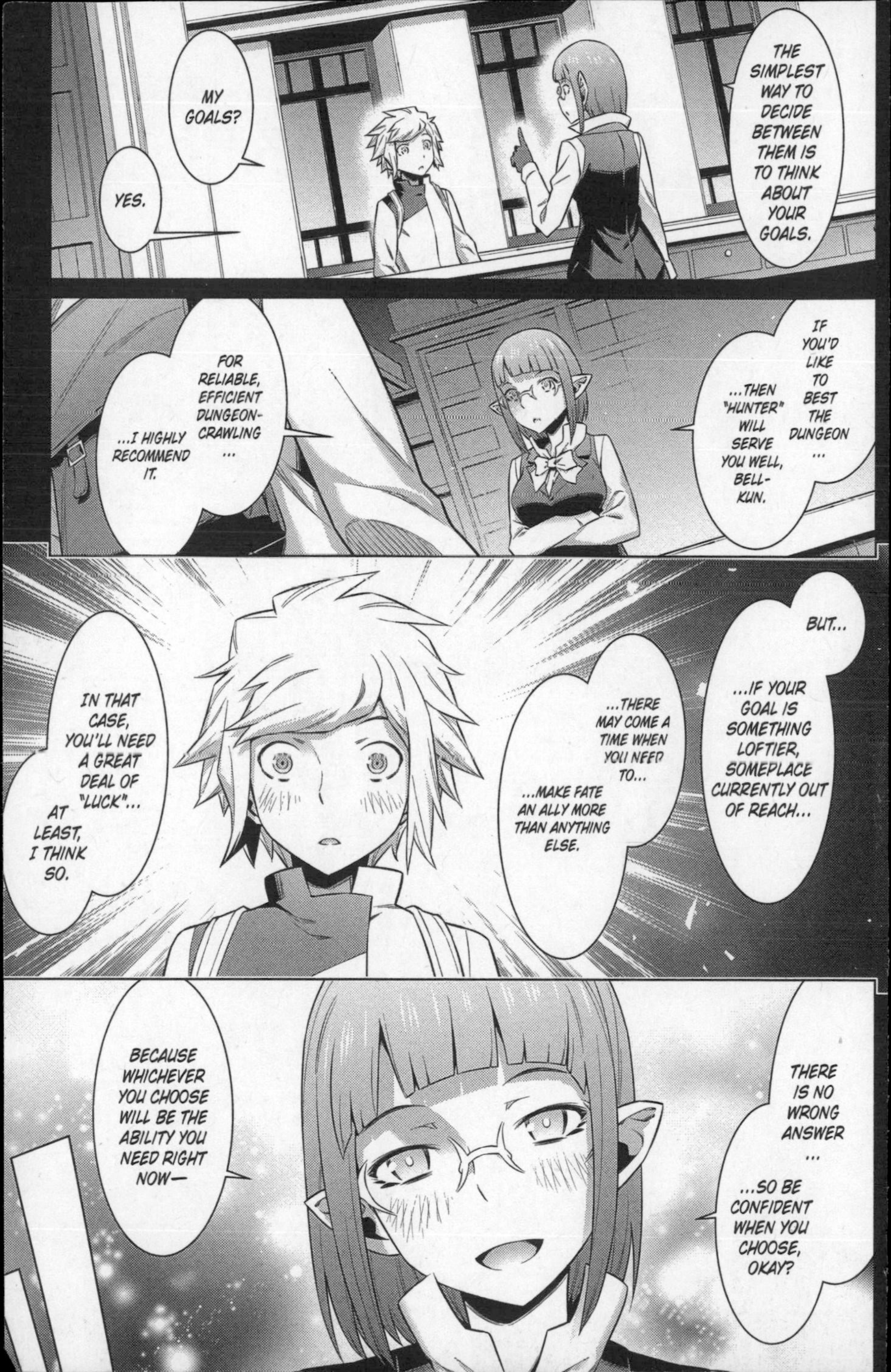
THE SIMPLEST WAY TO DECIDE BETWEEN THEM IS TO THINK ABOUT YOUR GOALS.
MY GOALS?
YES.
IF YOU'D LIKE TO BEST THE DUNGEON...
...THEN "HUNTER" WILL SERVE YOU WELL, BELL-KUN.
FOR RELIABLE, EFFICIENT DUNGEON-CRAWLING...
...I HIGHLY RECOMMEND IT.
BUT...
...IF YOUR GOAL IS SOMETHING LOFTIER, SOMEPLACE CURRENTLY OUT OF REACH...
...THERE MAY COME A TIME WHEN YOU NEED TO...
...MAKE FATE AN ALLY MORE THAN ANYTHING ELSE.
IN THAT CASE, YOU'LL NEED A GREAT DEAL OF "LUCK"...
AT LEAST, I THINK SO.
THERE IS NO WRONG ANSWER...
...SO BE CONFIDENT WHEN YOU CHOOSE, OKAY?
BECAUSE WHICHEVER YOU CHOOSE WILL BE THE ABILITY YOU NEED RIGHT NOW—

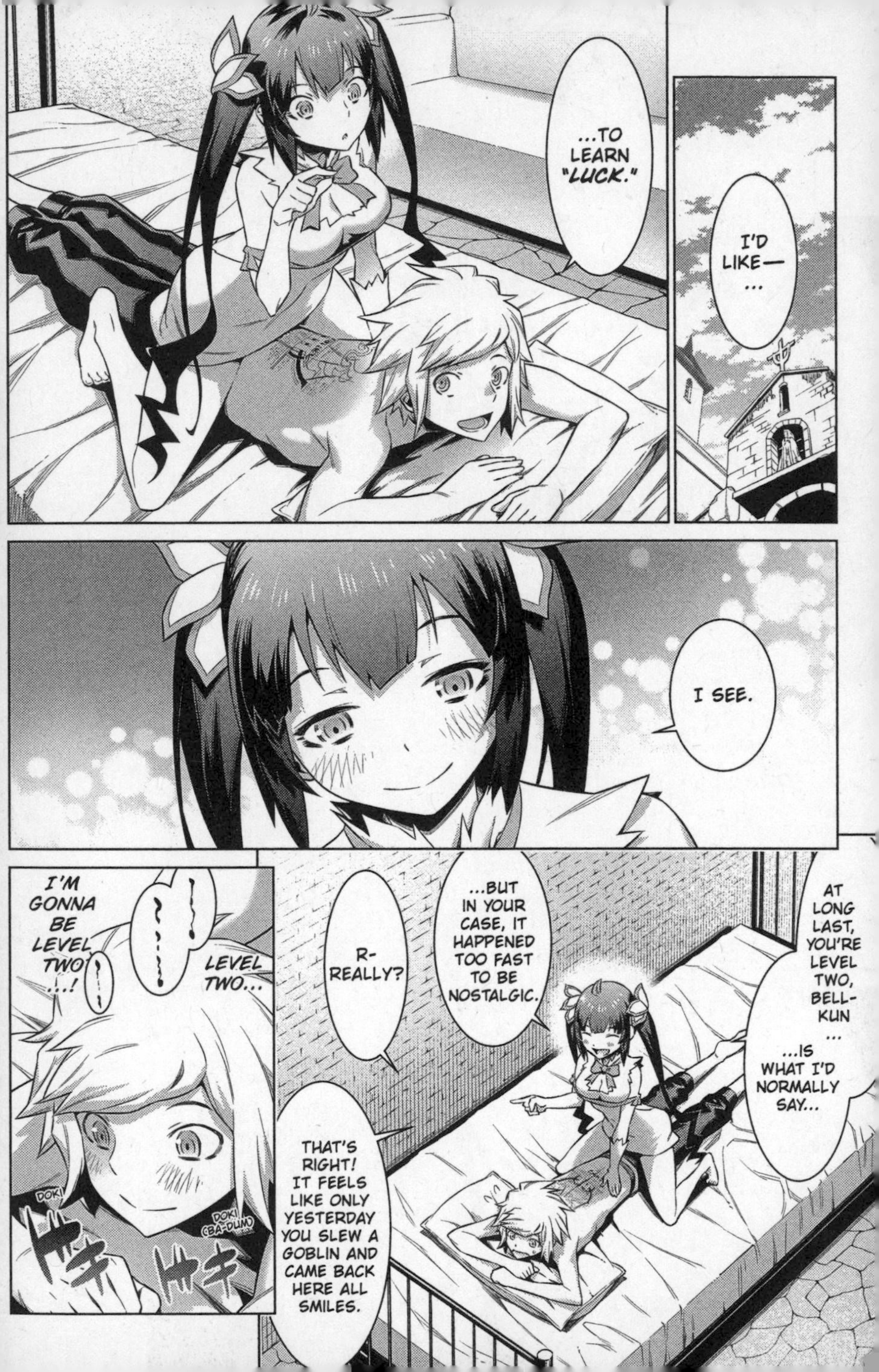

I'D LIKE— ...
...TO LEARN "LUCK."
I SEE.
AT LONG LAST, YOU'RE LEVEL TWO, BELL-KUN ...
...IS WHAT I'D NORMALLY SAY...
...BUT IN YOUR CASE, IT HAPPENED TOO FAST TO BE NOSTALGIC.
R-REALLY?
THAT'S RIGHT! IT FEELS LIKE ONLY YESTERDAY YOU SLEW A GOBLIN AND CAME BACK HERE ALL SMILES.
LEVEL TWO...
I'M GONNA BE LEVEL TWO ...!
DOKI
DOKI (BA-DUM)

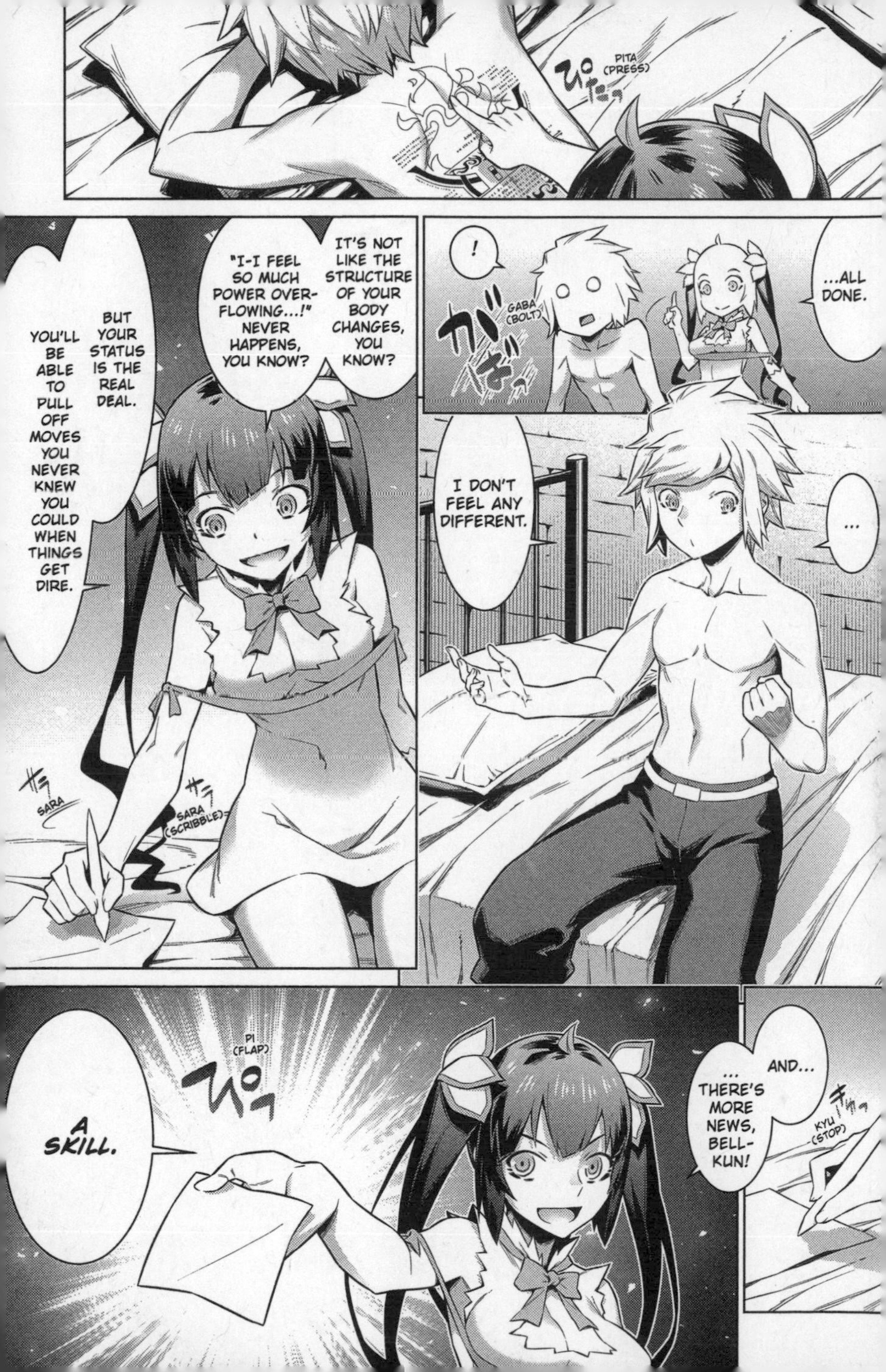
PITA (PRESS)
...ALL DONE.
!
GABA (BOLT)
...
I DON'T FEEL ANY DIFFERENT.
IT'S NOT LIKE THE STRUCTURE OF YOUR BODY CHANGES, YOU KNOW?
"I-I FEEL SO MUCH POWER OVER-FLOWING...!" NEVER HAPPENS, YOU KNOW?
BUT YOUR STATUS IS THE REAL DEAL.
YOU'LL BE ABLE TO PULL OFF MOVES YOU NEVER KNEW YOU COULD WHEN THINGS GET DIRE.
SARA (SCRIBBLE)
SARA
AND...
KYU (STOP)
...THERE'S MORE NEWS, BELL-KUN!
PI (FLAP)
A SKILL.

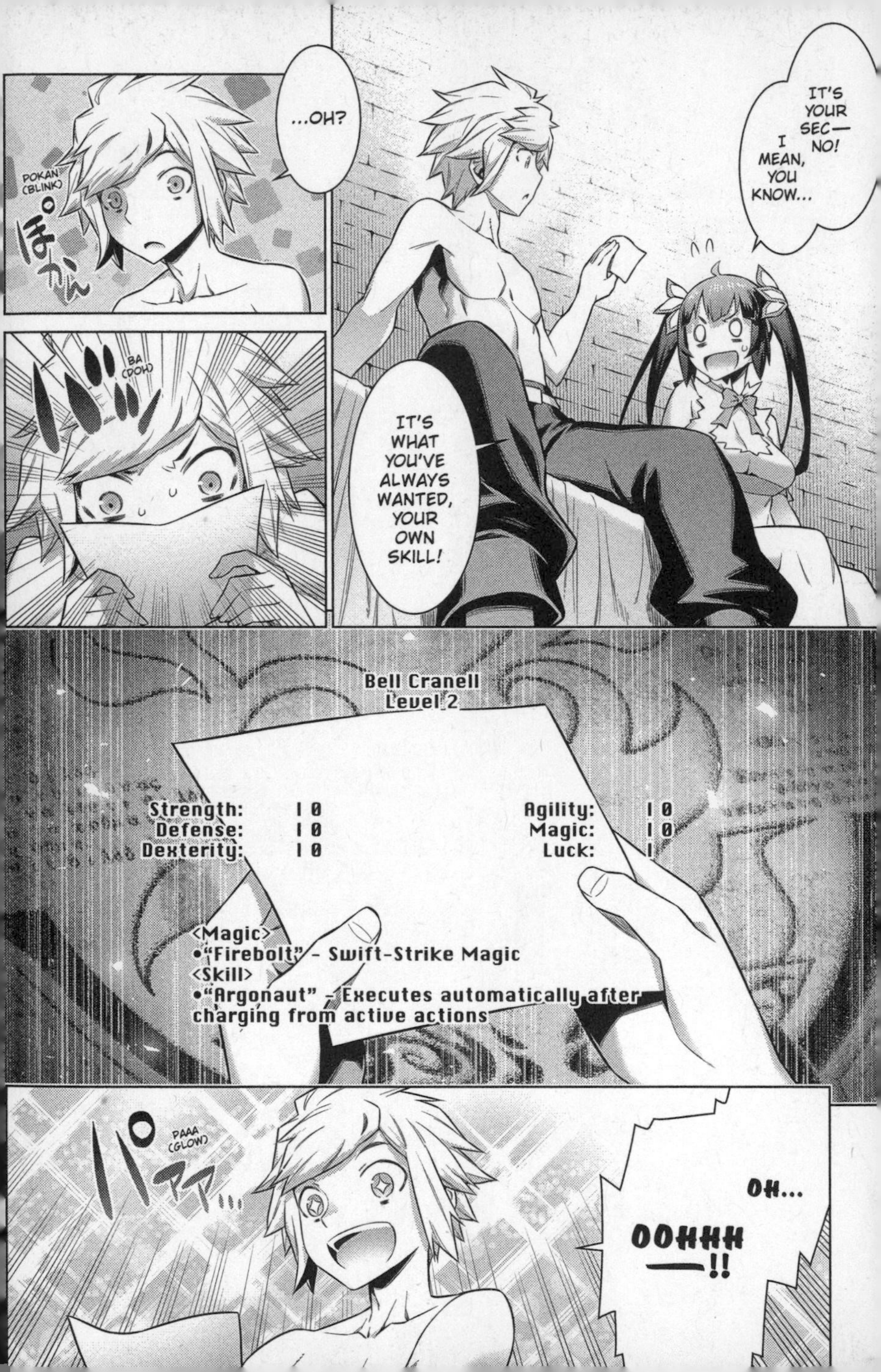

IT'S YOUR SEC— NO! I MEAN, YOU KNOW...
...OH?
IT'S WHAT YOU'VE ALWAYS WANTED, YOUR OWN SKILL!
POKAN (BLINK)
ぽかん
BA (DOH)
Bell Cranell
Level 2
Strength: I 0
Defense: I 0
Dexterity: I 0
Agility: I 0
Magic: I 0
Luck: I
<Magic>
•"Firebolt" - Swift-Strike Magic
<Skill>
•"Argonaut" - Executes automatically after charging from active actions
PAAA (GLOW)
パァァ
OH...
OOHHHH—!!

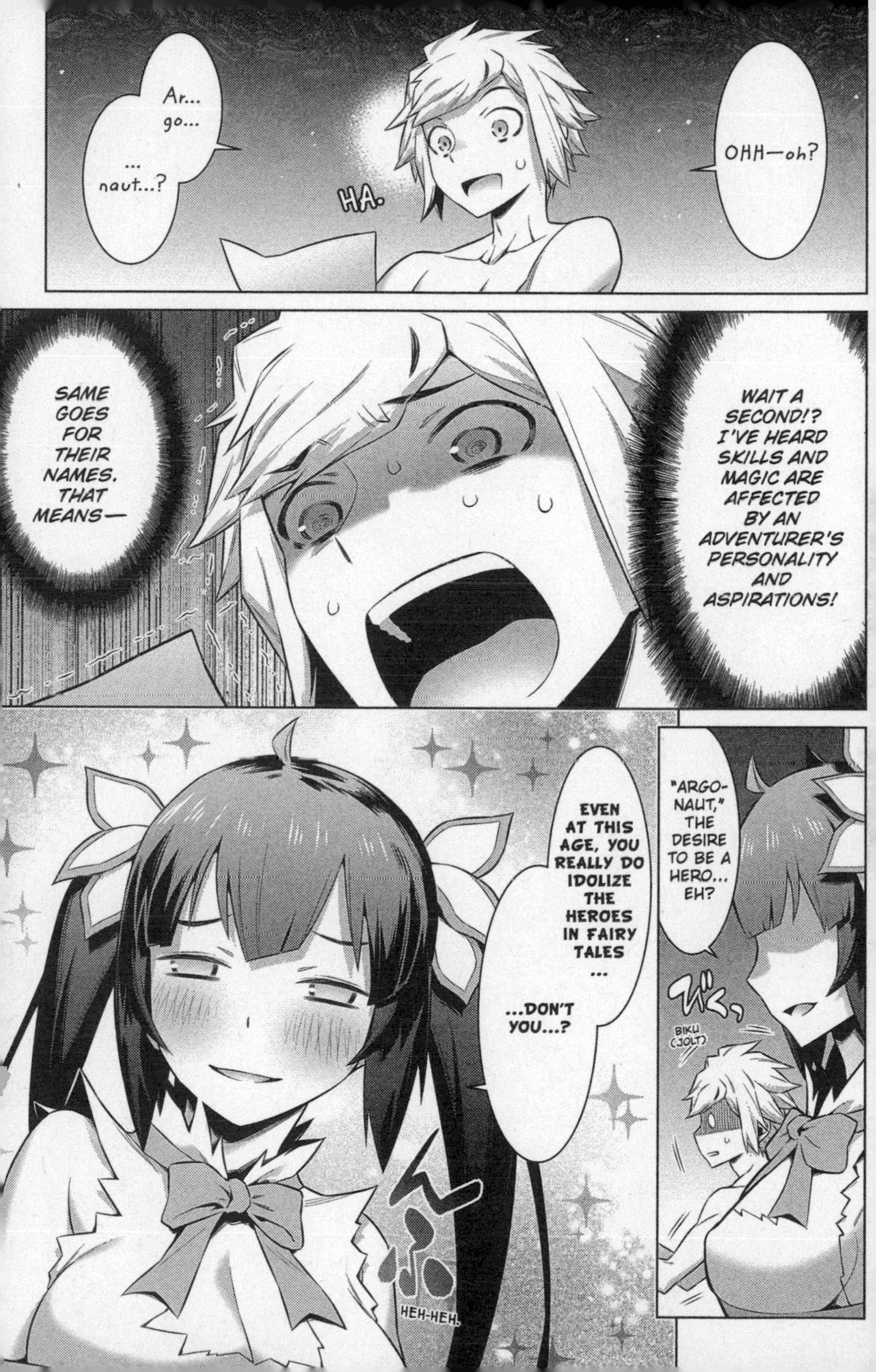
OHH—oh?
HA.
Ar... go... ... naut...?
WAIT A SECOND!? I'VE HEARD SKILLS AND MAGIC ARE AFFECTED BY AN ADVENTURER'S PERSONALITY AND ASPIRATIONS!
SAME GOES FOR THEIR NAMES. THAT MEANS—
"ARGO-NAUT," THE DESIRE TO BE A HERO... EH?
びく,
BIKU (JOLT)
EVEN AT THIS AGE, YOU REALLY DO IDOLIZE THE HEROES IN FAIRY TALES ...
...DON'T YOU...?
HEH-HEH.

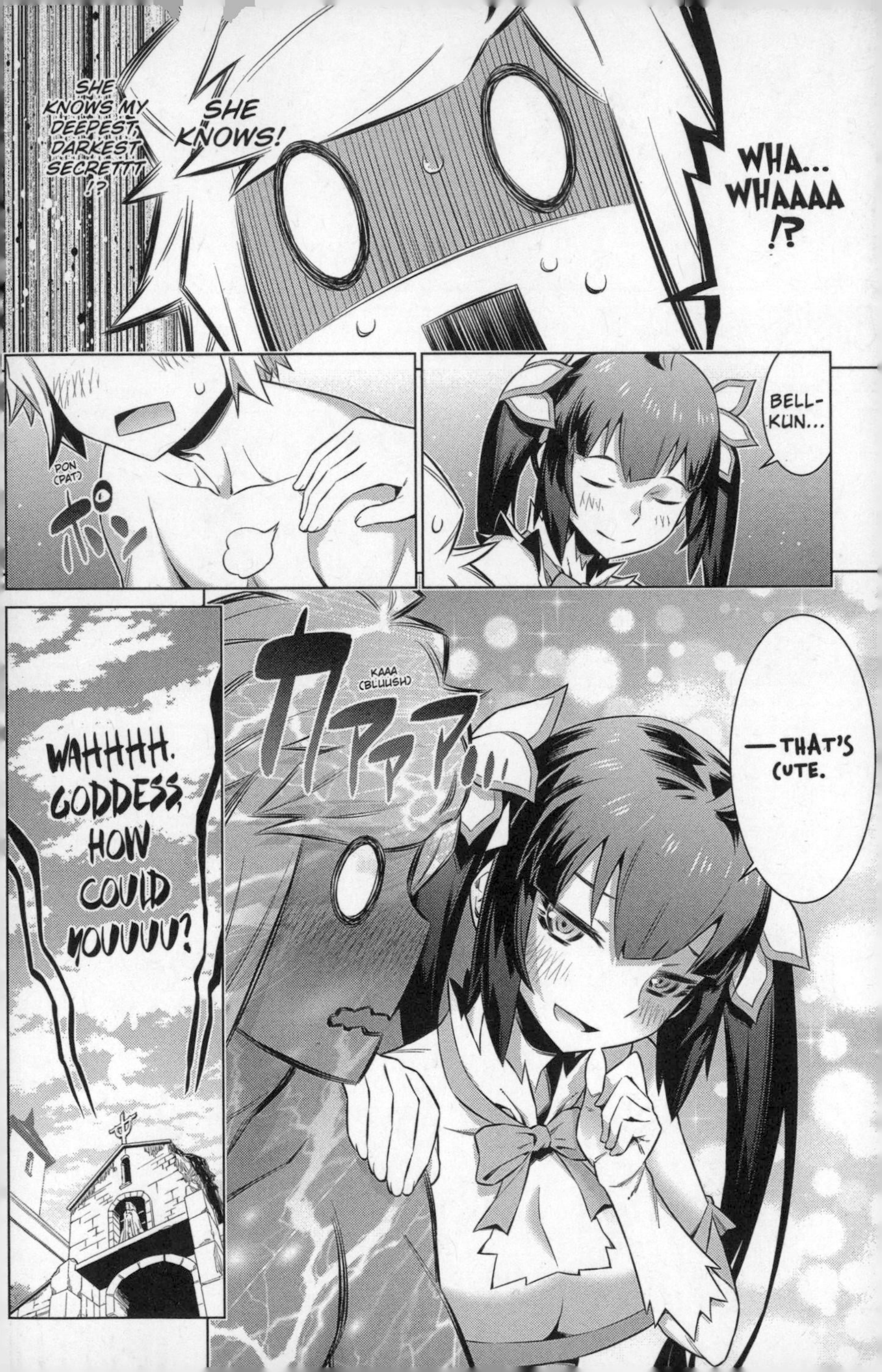
WHA... WHAAAA!?
SHE KNOWS!
SHE KNOWS MY DEEPEST, DARKEST SECRETTT!?
BELL-KUN...
PON (PAT)
—THAT'S CUTE.
KAAA (BLUUSH)
WAHHHH. GODDESS, HOW COULD YOUUUU?

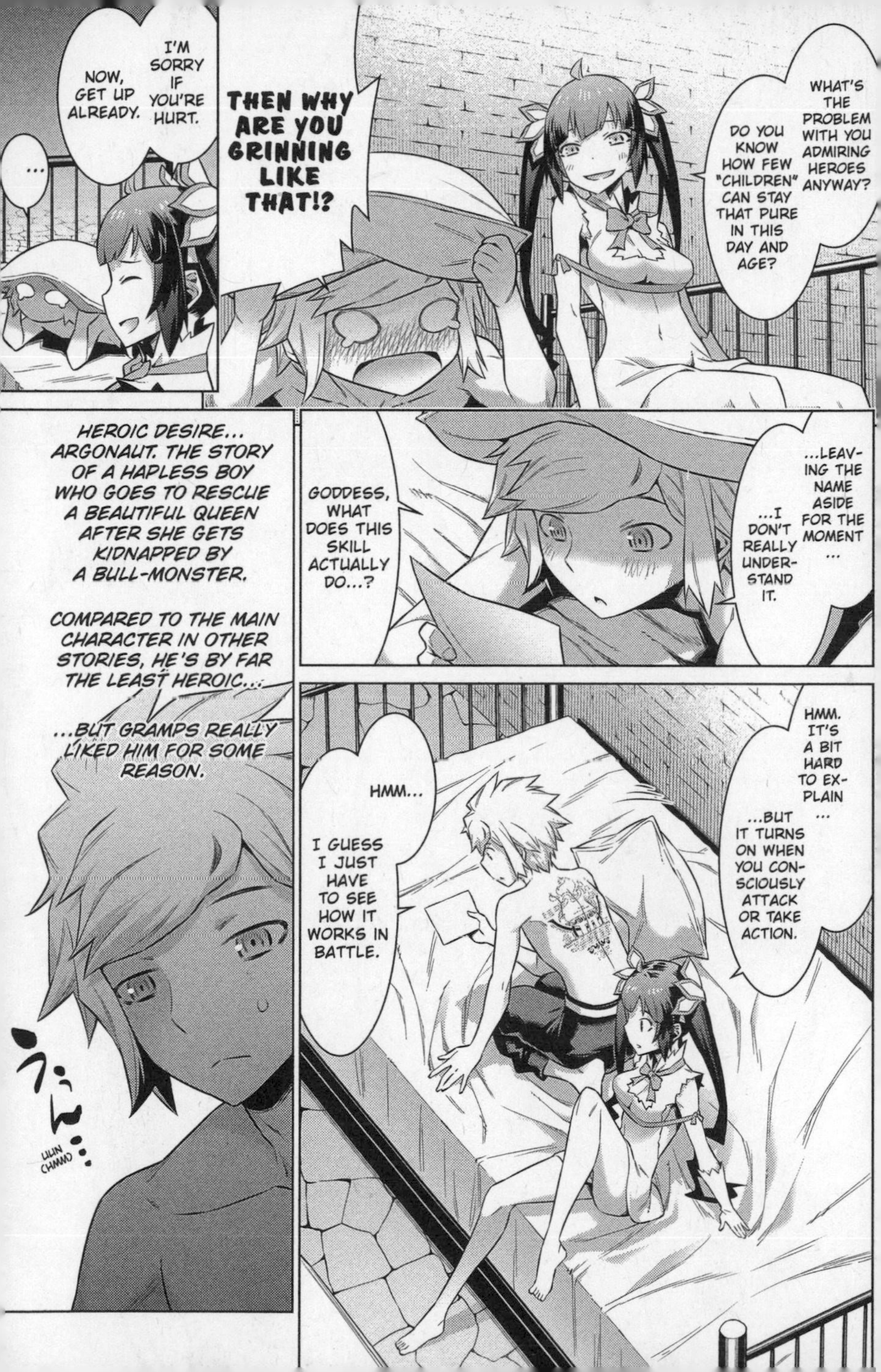
WHAT'S THE PROBLEM WITH YOU ADMIRING HEROES ANYWAY?
DO YOU KNOW HOW FEW "CHILDREN" CAN STAY THAT PURE IN THIS DAY AND AGE?
THEN WHY ARE YOU GRINNING LIKE THAT!?
I'M SORRY IF YOU'RE HURT.
NOW, GET UP ALREADY.
...
...LEAVING THE NAME ASIDE FOR THE MOMENT...
...I DON'T REALLY UNDERSTAND IT.
GODDESS, WHAT DOES THIS SKILL ACTUALLY DO...?
HMM. IT'S A BIT HARD TO EXPLAIN...
...BUT IT TURNS ON WHEN YOU CONSCIOUSLY ATTACK OR TAKE ACTION.
HMM...
I GUESS I JUST HAVE TO SEE HOW IT WORKS IN BATTLE.
HEROIC DESIRE... ARGONAUT. THE STORY OF A HAPLESS BOY WHO GOES TO RESCUE A BEAUTIFUL QUEEN AFTER SHE GETS KIDNAPPED BY A BULL-MONSTER.
COMPARED TO THE MAIN CHARACTER IN OTHER STORIES, HE'S BY FAR THE LEAST HEROIC...
...BUT GRAMPS REALLY LIKED HIM FOR SOME REASON.
うーん…
UUN CHMM

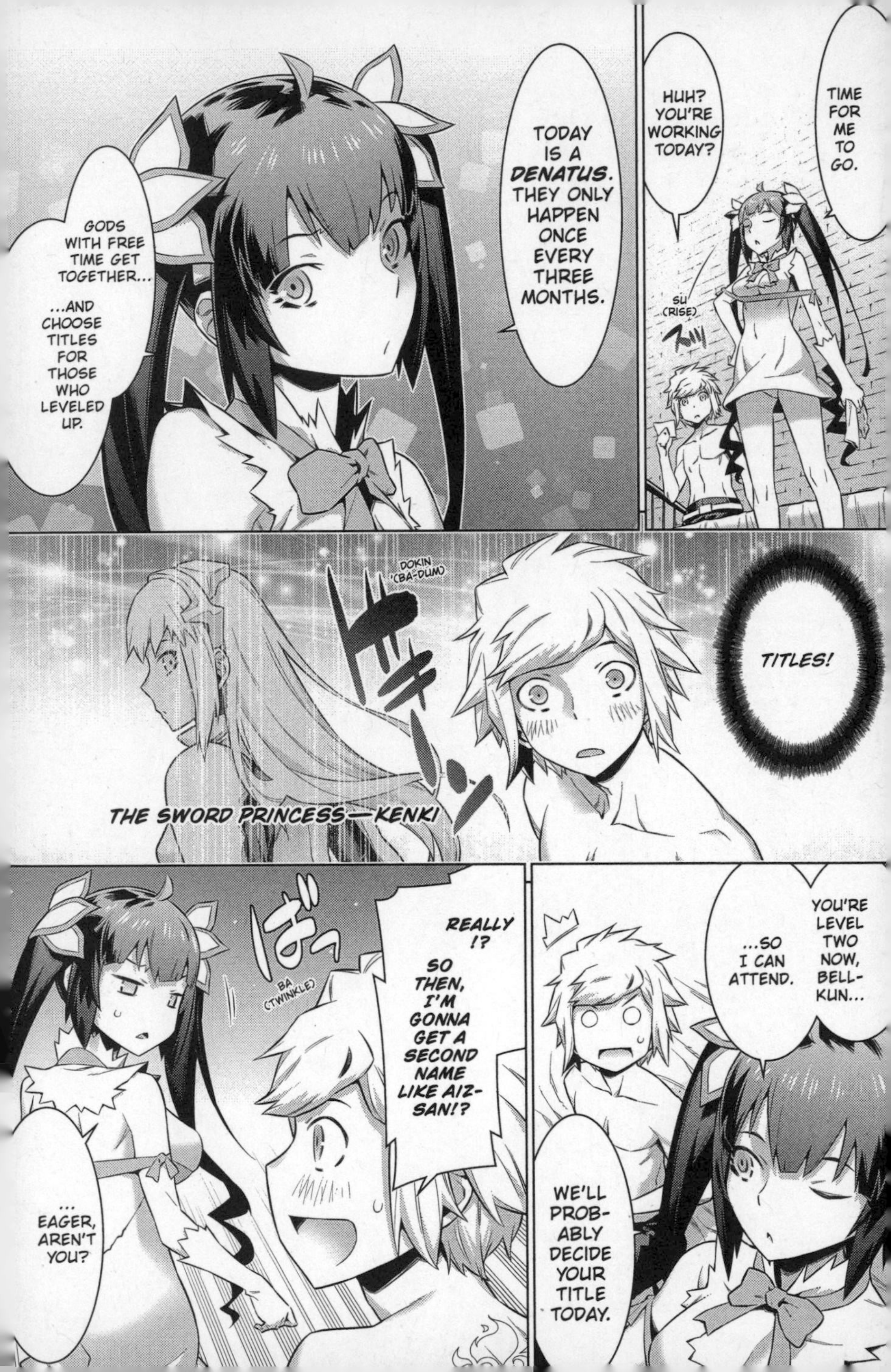
TIME FOR ME TO GO.
HUH? YOU'RE WORKING TODAY?
SU (RISE)
TODAY IS A DENATUS. THEY ONLY HAPPEN ONCE EVERY THREE MONTHS.
GODS WITH FREE TIME GET TOGETHER...
...AND CHOOSE TITLES FOR THOSE WHO LEVELED UP.
TITLES!
DOKIN (BA-DUM)
THE SWORD PRINCESS—KENKI
YOU'RE LEVEL TWO NOW, BELL-KUN...
...SO I CAN ATTEND.
WE'LL PROBABLY DECIDE YOUR TITLE TODAY.
REALLY!?
SO THEN, I'M GONNA GET A SECOND NAME LIKE AIZ-SAN!?
BA (TWINKLE)
...EAGER, AREN'T YOU?

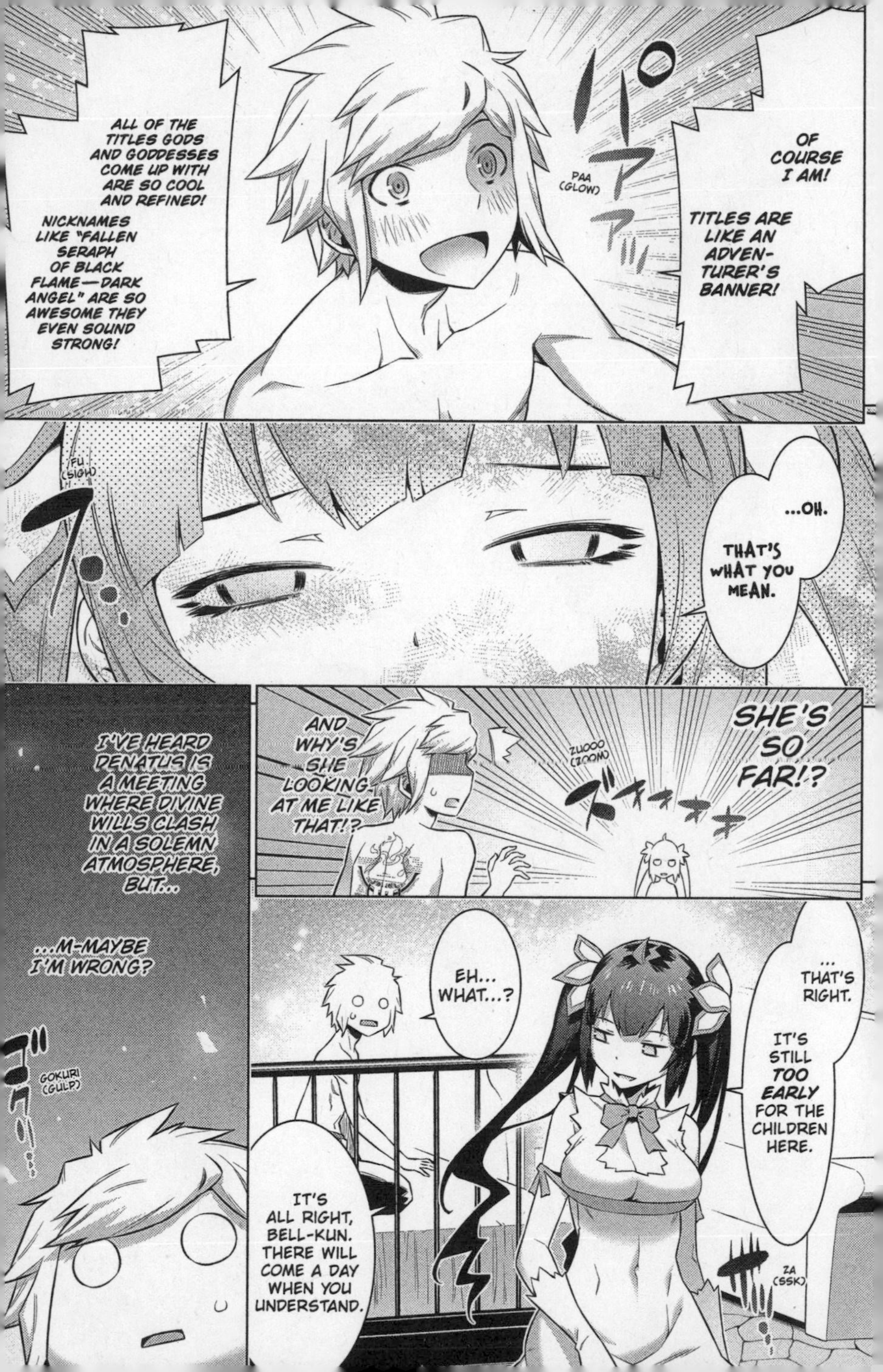

OF COURSE I AM!
TITLES ARE LIKE AN ADVENTURER'S BANNER!
PAA (GLOW)
ALL OF THE TITLES GODS AND GODDESSES COME UP WITH ARE SO COOL AND REFINED!
NICKNAMES LIKE "FALLEN SERAPH OF BLACK FLAME—DARK ANGEL" ARE SO AWESOME THEY EVEN SOUND STRONG!
...OH.
THAT'S WHAT YOU MEAN.
FU (SIGH)
SHE'S SO FAR!?
ZUOOO (ZOOM)
AND WHY'S SHE LOOKING AT ME LIKE THAT!?
... THAT'S RIGHT.
IT'S STILL TOO EARLY FOR THE CHILDREN HERE.
EH... WHAT...?
ZA (SSK)
IT'S ALL RIGHT, BELL-KUN. THERE WILL COME A DAY WHEN YOU UNDERSTAND.
I'VE HEARD DENATUS IS A MEETING WHERE DIVINE WILLS CLASH IN A SOLEMN ATMOSPHERE, BUT...
...M-MAYBE I'M WRONG?
GOKURI (GULP)

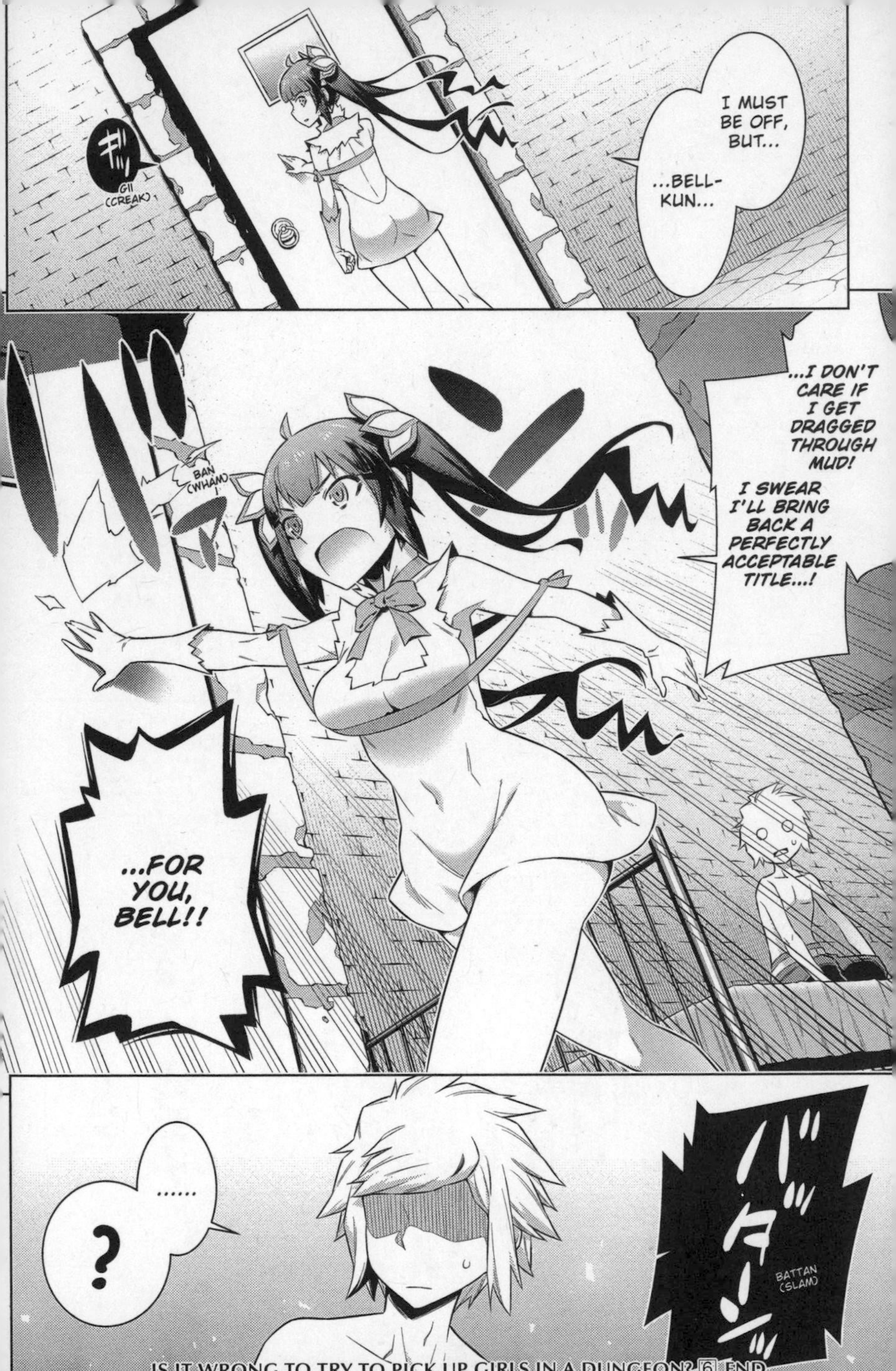
I MUST BE OFF, BUT...
...BELL-KUN...
GII (CREAK)
...I DON'T CARE IF I GET DRAGGED THROUGH MUD!
I SWEAR I'LL BRING BACK A PERFECTLY ACCEPTABLE TITLE...!
BAN (WHAM)
...FOR YOU, BELL!!
BATTAN (SLAM)
......
?

IS IT WRONG TO TRY TO PICK UP GIRLS IN A DUNGEON? 6 END

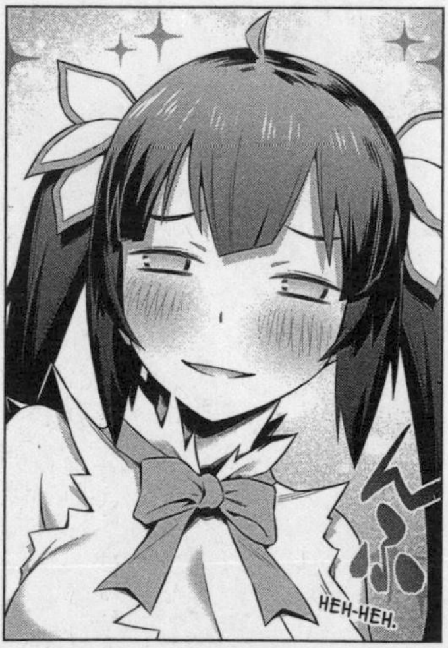
HEH-HEH.

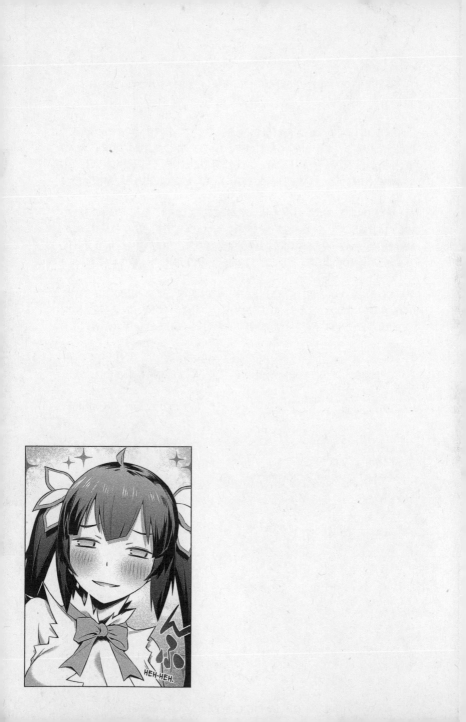

THANK YOU FOR PICKING UP THE SIXTH VOLUME IN THE
SERIES.

FIRST OF ALL, CONGRATULATIONS ON "SWORD ORATORIA'S"
TELEVISION DEBUT! I'M SO HAPPY THAT THE SIDE STORY ALSO
GETS TO BECOME AN ANIME ALONGSIDE THE ORIGINAL. AT THE
SAME TIME, IT MAKES ME WANT TO WORK EVEN HARDER!

MY FAVORITE PART OF THE ORIGINAL STORY, THE "MINOTAUR
ARC," CAME TO A CLOSE IN THIS VOLUME. IT WAS AN HONOR
TO DRAW MY WAY THROUGH IT. I HOPE THAT THE INTENSITY
OF THE ORIGINAL NOVEL CAME THROUGH IN MY WORK.

ALSO, THIS VOLUME STRETCHED INTO THE BEGINNING OF THE
ORIGINAL'S BOOK FOUR. IT'S FINALLY TIME FOR WELF TO JOIN
THE STORY. I'M RATHER FOND OF THIS GUY, SO I WANT TO
DO HIM JUSTICE.

PLEASE LOOK FORWARD TO THE NEXT INSTALLMENT.

KUNIEDA
九二枝

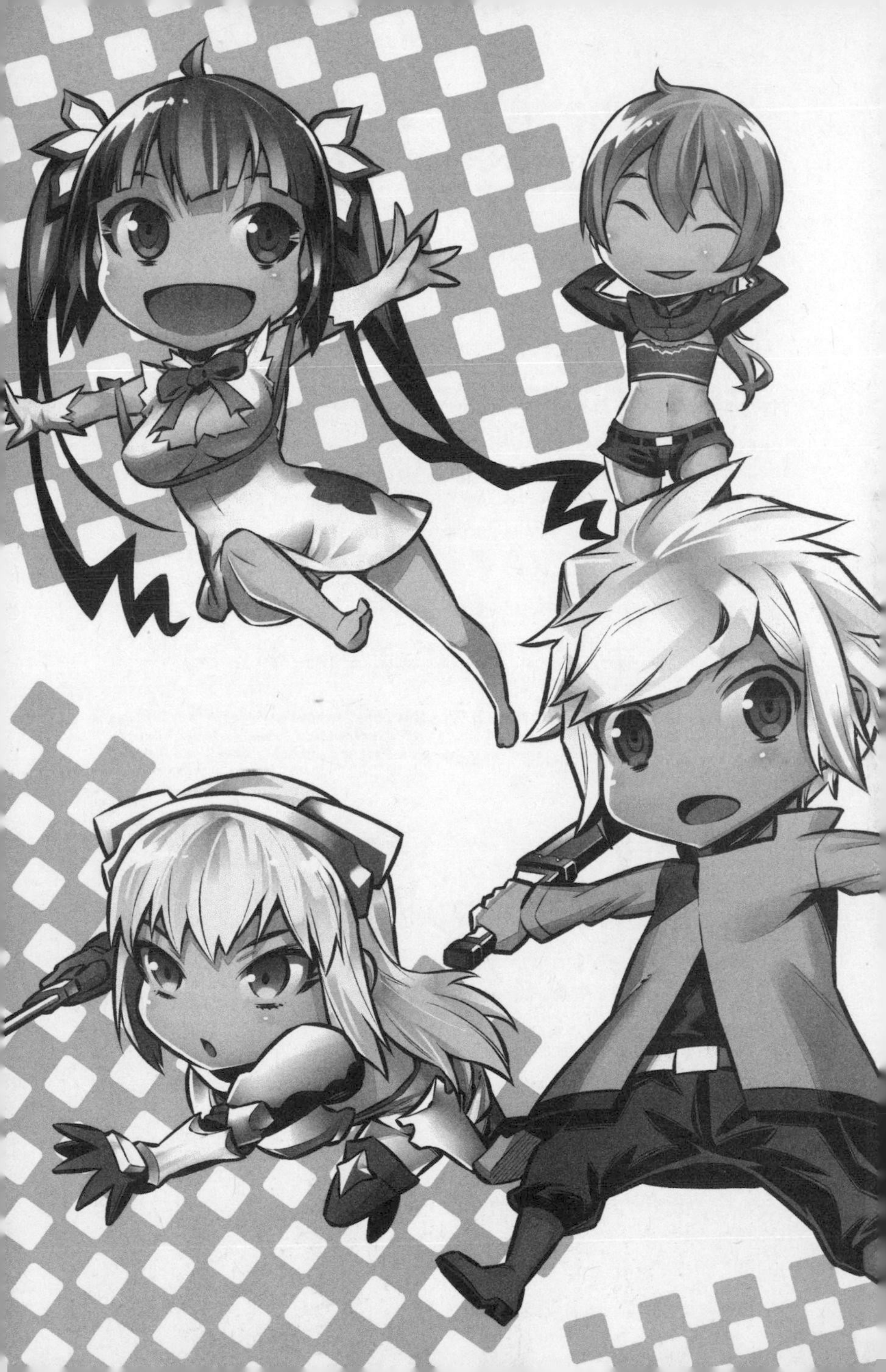

IS IT WRONG TO TRY TO PICK UP GIRLS IN A DUNGEON? ⑥

Fujino Omori
Kunieda
Yasuda Suzuhito

Translation: Andrew Gaippe • Lettering: Brndn Blakeslee

DUNGEON NI DEAI WO MOTOMERU NO WA MACHIGATTEIRUDAROUKA vol. 6
© 2016 Fujino Omori / SB Creative Corp. Character Design: Yasuda Suzuhito
© 2016 Kunieda / SQUARE ENIX CO., LTD.
First published in Japan in 2016 by SQUARE ENIX CO., LTD.
English translation rights arranged with SQUARE ENIX CO., LTD. and Yen Press, LLC through Tuttle Mori Agency, Inc.

English translation © 2016 SQUARE ENIX CO., LTD.

Yen Press
1290 Avenue of the Americas
New York, NY 10104

Visit us at yenpress.com
facebook.com/yenpress
twitter.com/yenpress
yenpress.tumblr.com
instagram.com/yenpress

First Yen Press Edition: November 2016

Yen Press is an imprint of Yen Press, LLC.
The Yen Press name and logo are trademarks of Yen Press, LLC.

Library of Congress Control Number: 2015288171

ISBNs: 978-0-316-55260-8 (paperback)
978-0-316-50674-8 (ebook)

10 9 8 7 6 5 4 3 2 1

BVG

Printed in the United States of America

HEY! FLIP THE BOOK TO
READ A SPECIAL, PREVIOUSLY
UNPUBLISHED STORY STRAIGHT
FROM FUJINO OMORI!

"Today, you did well...so, here, this is your reward."

Bell, full of expectations, watched as the girl presented him with...a reddish–orange root.

A carrot rested in her outstretched hand.

"..."

"..."

"..."

"...Eh?"

Several moments passed. The young boy's eyes became little more than dots on his face. Meanwhile, Aiz was overcome with flustered confusion.

"Um, do you...not like them?"

"Eh, ah, no!!......I'm...happy."

Bell managed to squeeze the words through his constricted throat. A wave of relief washed over Aiz's face.

The boy took the carrot from her, cold sweat running down his back. "I'm glad," beamed the girl, hands pressed against her chest.

A-a carrot? Why a carrot...?

It would be a long time and take much more interaction before the boy understood the reason for her naive misstep...

Aiz had asked Tiona and Finn for advice three days earlier.

"...!"

Then...

Her finger stopped on top of a particular line in a book she had been flipping through.

She stood like a statue in front of the bookshelf; her breathtaking golden eyes were wide open, staring. It was as if her pupils were nailed to the spot.

"Reward the ones who try their best. This will strengthen your bonds and increase the likelihood they will live up to your expectations."

It was a passage of just two sentences.

Aiz had found the book that would revolutionize her teaching style.

Its title: *You Can Become the Rabbit ☆ Master!*

The next morning, in a place with a perfect view of the brightening eastern sky, the city wall...

Bell was much more restless than usual this day after their training concluded. His blood was pumping with excitement.

It was all because of his instructor's promise:

"If you try very hard today, I'll give you a reward..."

That was what she'd said right before starting the day's practice.

A reward...? What kind of reward? I-I don't think it'll be anything too odd, but...!

All sorts of images ran like wildfire through Bell's mind. It was only natural; the person he admired more than anyone else had said that she would "reward" him. His cheeks blushed in spite of himself, slack jaw tightening to keep his mouth closed.

Aiz paused for a moment before returning her saber to its sheath. Then, she approached him.

instructor. With no knowledge or lesson plan, teaching the boy combat techniques was a real challenge. Even so, somehow, the boy picked things up very quickly—he listened to Aiz's teachings and accepted them in an honest and straightforward manner. He was the perfect student from a teacher's point of view. Therefore, she sought the wisdom of those who came before her and spent hours combing the archive for the books containing their insight.

Aiz read comprehensive treatises on strategy, encyclopedias of weaponry, and even books with such shady titles as *Adventurers! Aim for the Top Class!* from cover to cover. Her eyes passed over every page of any book dealing with martial arts and any style of combat.

So, sleepy, but...I can do, just a little more.

In fact, Aiz was involved with training members of her own familia, not just Bell. She would wake up in the dead of night to work with the white-haired boy until sunrise before returning home and sparring with her lower-ranking allies, all the while preparing for *Loki Familia*'s next expedition. She had very little time to rest. Aiz may have been one of Orario's top-class adventurers, but even she would fall asleep the moment she let her guard down.

The moon was already shining in the sky by the time she finished bathing.

Aiz, dressed in her sleep clothes as she continued reading, didn't really understand why she was putting forth so much effort. Of course, she was the one who suggested the training in the first place and would feel guilty for wasting his time. She swore not to let that happen.

It was still too early for Aiz to identify these strange feelings bubbling up within her.

"...Not, quite."

Aiz closed the book in her hands and placed it gently back on the shelf.

The smell of old books and parchment filled the air of an archive deep inside *Loki Familia*'s home. Every member of the familia was free to browse through the vast collection of Dungeon-related material and rather random books their goddess had collected as a hobby. The bookshelves were filled with used grimoires, tales of heroes, and other miscellaneous literature. With the tall shelves lined up in neat rows, the wide chamber seemed to impart the feeling of a library.

Aiz made her way through the small maze of shared resources, only stopping when her eyes spotted the title of an interesting book. She'd take it off the shelf, read it, and put it back before repeating the process over and over again.

She had been training a member of a different familia, Bell Cranell, for the past few days.

Be that as it may, she had very little experience as an

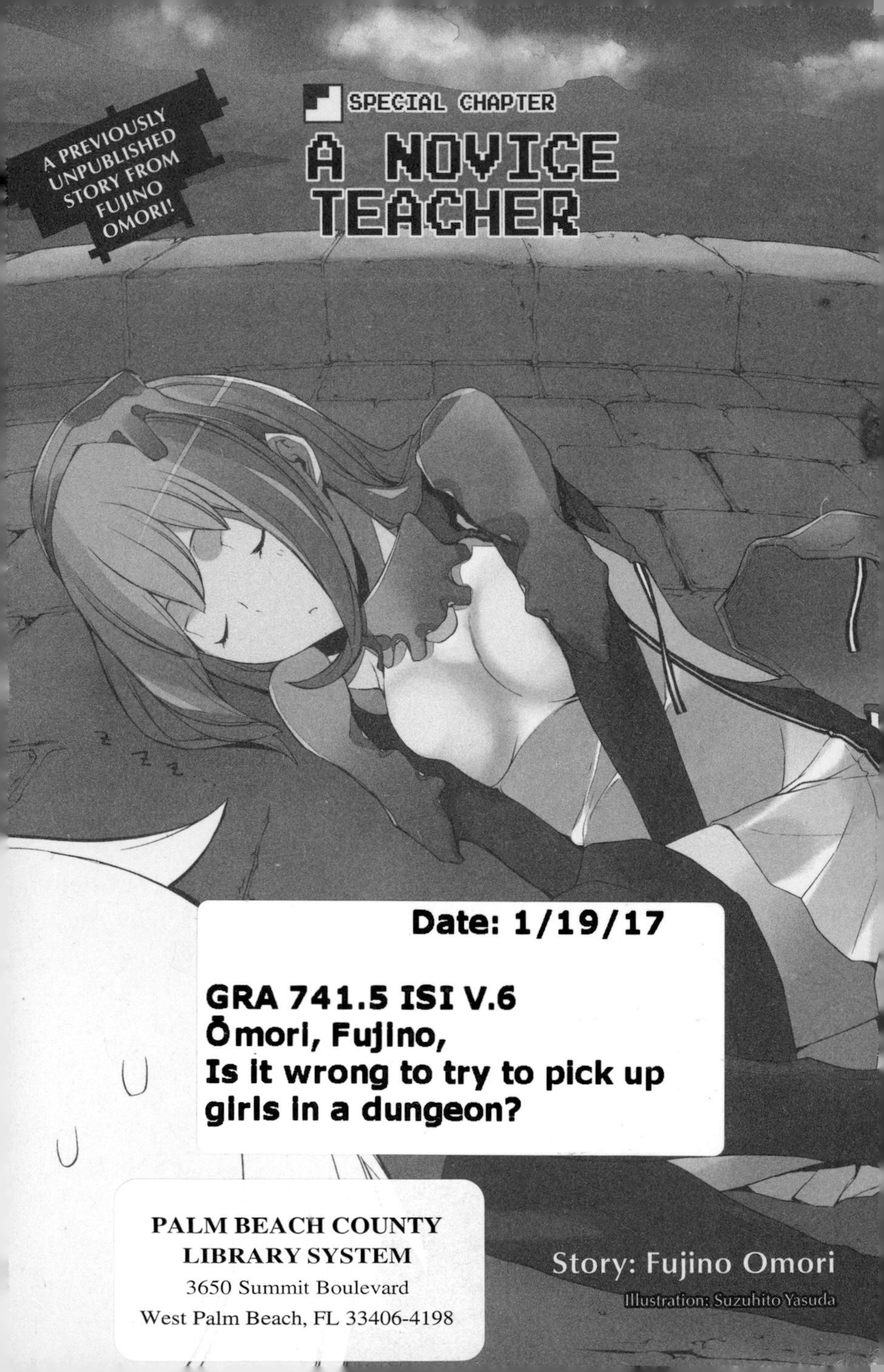
A PREVIOUSLY UNPUBLISHED STORY FROM FUJINO OMORI!
SPECIAL CHAPTER
A NOVICE TEACHER
Story: Fujino Omori
Illustration: Suzuhito Yasuda